THREE MILE ISLAND

THREE MILE ISLAND

A Nuclear Crisis in Historical Perspective

J. Samuel Walker

UNIVERSITY OF CALIFORNIA PRESS
Berkeley · Los Angeles · London

Published 2004 by The University of California Press
Berkeley and Los Angeles, California

University of California Press, Ltd.
London, England

Library of Congress Cataloging-in-Publication Data

Walker, J. Samuel.
    Three Mile Island : a nuclear crisis in historical
perspective / J. Samuel Walker.
        p.   cm.
Includes bibliographical references and index.
        ISBN 0-520-23940-7 (alk. paper).
        [1. Three Mile Island Nuclear Power Plant.
    2. Nuclear power plants—Accidents.]   I. Title.
TK1345.H37 W35   2004
363.17'99'0974818—dc21   2003010137

Manufactured in the United States of America

13   12   11   10   09   08   07   06   05   04
10   9   8   7   6   5   4   3   2

The paper used in this publication meets the minimum
requirements of ANSI/NISO Z39.48–1992 (R 1997)
(*Permanence of Paper*).

Contents

Illustrations

Preface

This book is the fourth in a series of volumes on the history of nuclear regulation sponsored by the United States Nuclear Regulatory Commission (NRC). I am the coauthor, with George T. Mazuzan, of the first volume, *Controlling the Atom: The Beginnings of Nuclear Regulation, 1946–1962* (1984), and the author of the other previous volumes, *Containing the Atom: Nuclear Regulation in a Changing Environment, 1963–1971* (1992) and *Permissible Dose: A History of Radiation Protection in the Twentieth Century* (2000), all published by the University of California Press. My original plan for this book was to write a comprehensive history of nuclear regulation during the 1970s, a time when many complex, critical, and controversial policy issues were weighed and debated. The culmination of that book, I thought, would be a chapter or two on the Three Mile Island accident.

Once I began to conduct research on the accident, however, I realized that it required a book of its own. The issues it raised were so important and the drama it created so absorbing that I wanted to provide a full account of the crisis in 1979 as well as its historical background and long-term consequences. The drawback to this approach was that other major issues of the 1970s were necessarily shortchanged. I have covered some of those questions in my book *Permissible Dose* and in two scholarly articles that draw on my research on nuclear regulation during the 1970s: "Regulating against Nuclear Terrorism: The Domestic Safeguards Issue, 1970–1979" (*Technology and Culture* 42 [January 2001]: 107–32), and "Nuclear Power and Nonproliferation: The Controversy over Nuclear Exports, 1974–1980" (*Diplomatic History* 25 [Spring 2001]: 215–49). But the topics I discussed in those publications and some other significant regulatory issues receive little or no attention in this volume. I regard this as a reasonable trade-off for focusing on Three Mile Island, which remains the single most important event in the fifty-year history of nuclear power regulation in the United States.

This book does not represent in any way an official position of the Nuclear Regulatory Commission. It is a product of my own professional training, experience, and judgment, and I bear full responsibility for its contents. The NRC placed no restrictions on me in writing the book, and I had complete independence in deciding on its structure, approach, and conclusions. The findings that I report and the conclusions I reach should be viewed as my own and not as a policy statement of the NRC.

I do not claim that I am unbiased, only that my biases are self-imposed. One important influence on my account of the accident is that I grew up in the town of Millersville, Pennsylvania, located in Lancaster County, six miles from the Susquehanna River and twenty miles or so from Three Mile Island. As a college student who held summer jobs with the state of Pennsylvania, I made frequent drives on Route 441 past still-undeveloped Three Mile Island, through Middletown, and on to Harrisburg. Although I had moved away from the area by the time of the Three Mile Island accident, members of my family, friends, and acquaintances were still living nearby, potentially in harm's way. I hope my Pennsylvania roots inform my understanding of the response of local residents and enhance my empathy for their plight during and after the accident. The NRC was not held in especially high regard by the population of my hometown in the aftermath of the crisis. During a visit to Millersville shortly after I joined the NRC in June 1979, I was asked by an acquaintance in a none-too-friendly tone, "What does the NRC expect you to do for them?" I replied that the NRC expected me to do my job according to the best standards and methods of historical scholarship. I hope this book meets that objective, which has not changed over a period of a quarter of a century.

I am grateful to the many people who helped make this book possible. Several friends read the entire manuscript in draft form and provided both informed commentary and unfailing encouragement. Collectively, they saved me from a series of logical, mathematical, terminological, technical, typographical, and stylistic lapses. I extend my thanks to Andy Bates, Phil Cantelon, Steve Crockett, Bill Lanouette, George Mazuzan, Jack Sorensen, and Allan Winkler. I would like to attribute any remaining shortcomings to that all-encompassing explanation—"computer error." But I'm afraid the responsibility is mine alone.

I benefited greatly from the research assistance of John Kinzie, at that time a historian with History Associates Incorporated. He conducted much of the research on the first three chapters of the book with skill, dedication, and vision. Without his efforts, I might still be looking for the text of a *60 Minutes* program that aired in 1976. I appreciated his work even more when I carried out my own research in the voluminous records relating to the Three Mile Island accident.

Archivists in a number of institutions offered me invaluable assistance. Nancy Watson, the archivist extraordinaire of the papers of Richard Thornburgh at the University of Pittsburgh, was very knowledgeable and enormously helpful. She made examining the documents in the Thornburgh collection a welcome relief from watching the Pirates play at the now-demolished Three Rivers Stadium. Martin Elzy of the Jimmy Carter Library was always prompt and gracious in responding to my numerous requests, and his colleagues David Stanhope and Jim Yancey were equally accommodating. Many members of the library staff went out of their way to be helpful when I showed up at their doorstep, somewhat to their surprise, on the morning of September 12, 2001. Marjorie Ciarlante and Tab Lewis of the National Archives in College Park, Maryland, delivered expert guidance on the records of the Kemeny Commission and other materials in their custody. Linda Ries and other staff members provided the same services for my research at the Pennsylvania State Archives in Harrisburg. Robert Hill furnished much appreciated assistance in my review of the Dauphin County Historical Society's excellent collection of Three Mile Island photographs. Elena Danielson and the staff of the Hoover Institution Archives at Stanford University did much to make a trip to Palo Alto enjoyable and productive despite outside temperatures in the upper nineties. The staff of the NRC's Public Document Room, in Rockville, Maryland, as always, went beyond the call of duty in assisting me to find, copy, and, in some cases, make public the NRC documents cited in this book. Special kudos go to Linda Kilgore for checking a long list of documents to determine their status.

I remain deeply appreciative for the support and assistance I receive from my friends and colleagues in the Office of the Secretary of the NRC and, for that matter, in every office of the NRC. Stan Holwitz and his colleagues at the University of California Press have made the publication of four books on the subject of nuclear regulation over a period of twenty years a source of enduring pleasure and pride.

J. Samuel Walker
Rockville, Maryland
March 2003

Chapter 1

The Nuclear Power Debate

Kimberly Wells, a reporter for a Los Angeles television station, was an unlikely source for a major story on the hazards of nuclear power. She specialized in lightweight human interest pieces, such as a feature on singing telegrams, rather than issues as controversial and complex as nuclear power during the 1970s. But after inadvertently witnessing a near accident at the Ventana nuclear power station in California, she learned about the dangers of a core meltdown. Greg Minor, a nuclear engineer, told her that not only was she "lucky to be alive" but that "we might say the same for the rest of southern California." Elliot Lowell, a physics professor who opposed nuclear power, affirmed this frightening assessment. He claimed that if the fuel rods in the core of a nuclear reactor overheated, they would melt through the floor of the plant in a matter of minutes and release enough radioactivity to "render an area the size of Pennsylvania permanently uninhabitable."

Spurred by her new knowledge, Wells, at considerable risk to her own career, joined forces with a television cameraman, Richard Adams, to find out what happened at Ventana the day she had visited. Eventually, she gained the confidence of Jack Goodell, a nuclear engineer and control room supervisor, who had discovered shoddy construction practices that imperiled the plant. After officials of California Gas and Electric, the utility that owned the plant, refused to heed Goodell's warnings and publicly dismissed the near accident as a routine malfunction, he decided that drastic measures were necessary. He took over the control room by grabbing a guard's pistol and then threatened to "flood containment with radiation." Utility executives were informed that this action would destroy the plant. While Goodell enlisted Wells to broadcast the dangerous conditions at the plant and a throng of reporters descended on the site, the utility sent an armed police squad to force its way into the locked control room. As the tension escalated, the police team rushed into the control room and killed Goodell in a burst of gunfire. Wells inherited the responsibility of revealing the causes of the showdown at the Ventana reactor.

This was the plot of the motion picture *The China Syndrome,* which opened in more than six hundred theaters across the United States on March 16, 1979.[1] The title referred to a tongue-in-cheek term that nuclear experts had coined during the 1960s to describe an accident in which an overheated core would melt through the bottom of a plant and presumably through the earth's core toward China. The film starred Jane Fonda as Kimberly Wells, Jack Lemmon as Jack Goodell, and Michael Douglas as Richard Adams. It received many favorable reviews as a suspenseful and entertaining thriller. Within two weeks, Columbia Pictures reported that *The China Syndrome* had produced the highest income of any film it had ever released in a "nonholiday period."[2]

Although *The China Syndrome* commanded attention because of its entertainment value, it also received wide notice because of its unflattering depiction of nuclear power. It was the latest salvo in a bitter national debate that had intensified throughout the 1970s. The filmmakers denied that they had set out to present a strongly antinuclear message. Fonda claimed that the movie was "intended as an attack on greed, not on nuclear energy." Nevertheless, the director, James Bridges, conceded that it was "not impartial," and Mike Gray, who conceived the project and coauthored the screenplay, wrote privately that it explained "the fundamental horrors of nuclear technology." A reviewer in *The Progressive* predicted that the film's treatment of nuclear power would have a major influence on public opinion: "Simply put, *The China Syndrome* is an incendiary piece of work that promises to cripple if not destroy whatever effect two decades of Nice Mr. Nuclear ads have had in making the public receptive to nuclear power."[3]

While nuclear critics hailed the movie as a way to alert the public to the hazards of the technology, nuclear proponents complained that it greatly exaggerated the risks. Supporters of nuclear power agreed that a major reactor accident could, in the worst case, release large amounts of radiation to the environment. But they took issue with the film's suggestion that the China syndrome would inevitably result if the core of a plant overheated. Although such an accident was possible, they insisted that it was highly unlikely. Pronuclear groups sent information packets to news organizations to counter the manner in which the technology was presented in *The China Syndrome.* An executive for a nuclear utility, perhaps with Jack Goodell's nonsensical threat to "flood containment with radiation" in mind, charged that the movie had "no scientific credibility."[4]

The impact of *The China Syndrome* was magnified when, less than two weeks after its release, the worst accident in the history of commercial nuclear power in the United States occurred at the Three Mile Island (TMI) Nuclear Generating Station in Pennsylvania. "Like certain other functional structures on the modern American landscape—the bridge at Selma, Alabama; the Watergate complex; the Texas Schoolbook Depository in Dallas—the towers at 'TMI' have slipped into an unprojected half-life as reminders of steep depressions in our national lifeline," a report on the accident observed in 1980. "Three Mile Island is a big deal; something important happened here."[5] Few would question this assertion; judging the response to and evaluating the effects of the "something important" that happened are matters of greater ambiguity.

Three Mile Island was a severe crisis that resulted from mistakes, oversights, and misjudgments. It worried and confounded responsible officials in federal, state, and local government agencies. With good cause, it alarmed the residents of the surrounding area, who were whipsawed by conflicting information from authorities and sometimes exaggerated reports from the news media. The accident generated anger, anxiety, and uncertainty that continued to plague the local population long after the emergency ended. But it did not produce a catastrophe by releasing large amounts of radiation to the environment that could have seriously threatened the health of people in neighboring communities. A full accounting of the causes and consequences of the Three Mile Island accident must begin with a look at its historical setting. The most prominent feature of the political and technological context of the crisis, as the response to *The China Syndrome* strikingly demonstrated, was the acrimonious national controversy over nuclear power.

THE GROWTH OF COMMERCIAL NUCLEAR POWER

The competing positions and spirited debate over nuclear power during the 1970s contrasted sharply with the widespread support for the technology that prevailed when it was introduced commercially during the 1950s. In 1954, Congress passed the Atomic Energy Act, a law that made the development of nuclear power possible by allowing for the first time the dissemination of basic information about atomic energy for civilian applications. It hoped to encourage the rapid growth of a nuclear industry that would provide a new source of electrical power. But privately owned utilities, though interested in exploring the use of nuclear technology to meet future energy needs, did not, for the most part, rush to build nuclear plants. Their response was lukewarm for several reasons. First, supplies of conventional fuel for the production of electricity, especially coal and oil, were plentiful and cheap. There was no pressing need for nuclear power to meet energy requirements for the near future. Further, many technical and economic questions about the technology remained to be answered. Although experiments with government reactors had established the technical feasibility of using nuclear energy to generate electricity, those tests did not prove that the technology could meet the demands of commercial power production. And finally, utilities were cautious because of nuclear power's potential hazards. Experts regarded the chances of a disastrous nuclear accident as remote, but they did not dismiss them entirely.[6]

Burdened by those drawbacks, the nuclear power industry did not grow as quickly as its advocates had hoped. Nevertheless, the electrical power industry viewed nuclear technology as an important long-term source of energy, and many utilities took steps to investigate its potential. By 1962, six relatively small, privately owned nuclear plants were generating power on the commercial grid, and several more reactors were under construction or on order. Although those plants were far from being technologically proven or commercially competitive, they signaled substantial progress since passage of the Atomic Energy Act. Despite some lingering uncertainty about the prospects for the industry, the omens were good. The public strongly favored nuclear power. A February 1956 public opinion poll showed that 69 percent of those questioned had "no fear" of having a nuclear plant located in their community, while only 20 percent expressed concern. In the spring of 1960, among responses to a national telephone survey on the proposition that "atomic power should be used to produce electricity," 64 percent were positive and only 6 percent were negative. In October 1963, *Nucleonics,* a monthly trade journal, suggested that "public acceptance of nuclear power would not be a significant problem."[7]

The first few years of the nuclear industry's existence were generally tranquil; the growth of nuclear power occurred at a measured pace in a stable and supportive political environment. In the mid-1960s the trend suddenly and unexpectedly changed. The industry experienced a surge in reactor orders, which Philip Sporn, past president of the American Electric Power Service Corporation, described in 1967 as the "great bandwagon market." The boom in the nuclear industry was accompanied by increasingly visible and vocal opposition to nuclear power that soon created a major national controversy.[8]

The bandwagon market was an outgrowth of several developments that enhanced nuclear power's appeal to utilities in the mid- and late 1960s. One was the intense competition between the two leading builders of nuclear plants, the General Electric Company and the Westinghouse Electric Corporation. In 1963, General Electric made a daring move to increase its reactor sales and convince utilities that nuclear power had arrived as a safe, reliable, and cost-competitive alternative to fossil fuel. It offered a turnkey contract to Jersey Central Power and Light Company, a subsidiary of the General Public Utilities Corporation, to build a 515-megawatt nuclear plant near Toms River, New Jersey. For a fixed cost of $66 million, General Electric agreed to supply the entire Oyster Creek plant to the utility (the term *turnkey* suggested that the utility would merely have to turn a key to start operating the facility). The company's bid was successful, winning out over not only Westinghouse but also manufacturers of coal-fired units. General Electric expected to lose money on the Oyster Creek contract but hoped that the plant would help stimulate the market for nuclear power.

The Oyster Creek contract opened the "turnkey era" of commercial nuclear power and came to symbolize the competitive debut of the technology. Westinghouse followed General Electric's lead by offering turnkey contracts for nuclear plants, setting off a fierce corporate battle. The turnkey plants were a financial drain for both companies; their losses ran into the hundreds of millions of dollars before they stopped making turnkey arrangements. One General Electric official commented, "It's going to take a long time to restore to the treasury the demands we put on it to establish ourselves in the nuclear business." But the turnkey contracts fulfilled General Electric's hopes of stirring interest among utilities and played a major role in triggering the bandwagon market.[9]

Other important considerations helped convince a growing number of utilities to buy nuclear plants during the latter part of the 1960s. One was the spread of power-pooling arrangements among utilities, which encouraged the construction of larger generating stations by easing fears of excess capacity and overexpansion. A utility with extra or reserve power could sell it to other companies through a widening network of interconnections. The desirability and feasibility of using larger individual plants benefited nuclear vendors, who emphasized that bigger plants would produce "economies of scale" by cutting capital costs per unit of power and improving efficiency. This helped to overcome a major disadvantage of nuclear power reactors relative to fossil fuel: the significantly heavier capital requirements for building them. During the late 1960s, designs for nuclear facilities jumped from the 500- to 800- to 1,100-megawatt range, even though operating experience was still limited to units generating 200 megawatts or less. The practice of design by extrapolation, or scaling up the size of plants based on experience with smaller facilities, had been employed for fossil-fuel units since the 1950s. It appeared to work well, and therefore it was natural for vendors to apply the same procedures to nuclear power plants.

In addition to turnkey contracts, system interconnections, and increasing unit size, growing national concern about air pollution made nuclear power more attractive to utilities. During the 1960s, the deteriorating quality of the environment, including visible evidence of foul air, took on increasing urgency as a public policy issue. Plants that burned fossil fuels provided more than 85 percent of the nation's electricity and contributed heavily to air pollution. Coal, by far the most commonly used fuel for producing power, placed a much greater burden on the environment than other fossil fuels, releasing millions of tons of noxious chemicals into the atmosphere annually. But the demand for electricity was steadily rising, and experts predicted it would continue to grow at a high rate of 7 percent or more per year. An article in *Fortune* magazine vividly explained the predicament: "Americans do not seem willing to let the utilities continue devouring . . . ever increasing quantities of water, air, and land. And yet clearly they also are not willing to contemplate doing without all the electricity they want. These two wishes are incompatible. That is the dilemma faced by utilities." After the mid-1960s, utilities increasingly viewed nuclear power as the answer to that dilemma. Because nuclear plants did not burn fossil fuels, they did not contribute to air pollution. The trade publication *Nucleonics Week* commented in 1965 that, in comparison with coal, "the one issue on which nuclear power can make an invincible case is the air pollution issue."[10]

A combination of technological, economic, and environmental developments launched the bandwagon market for nuclear power plants. Between 1966 and 1968, utilities committed to purchasing sixty-eight nuclear units, in contrast with the twenty-two they had ordered between 1955 and 1965. After a modest slowdown, the boom in orders resumed in the early 1970s. Utilities bought twenty-three nuclear stations in 1971, thirty-nine in 1972, and a record forty-four in 1973. By the end of 1973, thirty-seven nuclear plants were producing commercial power or had recently received operating licenses, and this number was dwarfed by projections of future requirements. In early 1973, the U.S. Atomic Energy Commission (AEC), the government agency mandated by the 1954 Atomic Energy Act to encourage the growth of the nuclear industry and regulate its safety, estimated that, by the year 2000, nuclear units in the United States would increase their capacity to 1.2 million megawatts. This would mean that the total number of plants would grow to more than 1,000. The future looked so bright for nuclear proponents that the trade magazine *Nuclear Industry* suggested the industry had witnessed the "virtual collapse of competition from fossil fuels." *Nucleonics Week* reported in December 1972 that the prevalent attitude among utility officials was "one of enthusiastic optimism." It added, "Utility executive after executive repeats the theme that nuclear power is the only way to go for future generation needs."[11]

THE NUCLEAR POWER SLUMP

The soaring optimism of the nuclear industry proved to be short-lived. The immediate cause of the downturn in the industry's fortunes, ironically, was an energy crisis that emerged as a prominent national issue in the fall of 1973. As early as 1971, President Richard M. Nixon publicly expressed concern about the long-range energy needs of the United States, and in June 1973 he issued a statement on energy in which he declared, "America faces a serious energy problem." A short time later, a war between Israel and its Arab neighbors led to an oil embargo by the Organization of Petroleum Exporting Countries, which gave much greater urgency to Nixon's efforts to increase the nation's energy supplies. In a televised speech on November 7, 1973, he called for a program he named Project Independence, so that "by the end of this decade we will have developed the potential to meet our own energy needs without depending on any foreign energy sources." A key component of Project Independence was a major expansion in nuclear power. After succeeding Nixon as president, Gerald R. Ford placed the same emphasis on boosting nuclear power production to keep up with national energy requirements. In his State of the Union address on January 15, 1975, he set a goal of having "200 major nuclear power plants" in operation within ten years, an ambitious objective even if less lofty than the AEC's projections two years earlier.[12]

The energy crisis initially seemed likely to spur further growth in nuclear power. Industry executives expressed confidence in early 1974 that "the energy crisis will result in a net increase in utility commitment to nuclear power." But this prediction turned out to be woefully inaccurate. The energy crisis severely damaged the electric power industry and, by extension, the nuclear industry in two ways. It quickly and sharply drove up the price of oil and other fuels that utilities purchased to run their plants, which drained their financial resources. It also exacerbated the already serious problem of inflation, which greatly increased the cost of borrowing money for plant construction. At the same time, an economic slump and increasing unemployment curtailed demand for electricity, which grew at a substantially slower rate than experts had anticipated. As expenses skyrocketed and markets diminished, utilities postponed or canceled plans to build many new plants. Although utilities cut back on both coal and nuclear projects, the blow fell disproportionately on builders of nuclear units because of higher capital costs. By September 1974, 57 of 191 nuclear plants under construction, under licensing review, on order, or announced by utilities had been delayed, generally by a year or two but sometimes by several years, and a few had been canceled altogether. Fourteen months later, 122 of the 191 nuclear projects had been deferred and 9 canceled. Sales of new plants declined sharply from the peak levels of the early 1970s; between 1975 and 1978, U.S. utilities ordered only 11 nuclear units.[13]

The nuclear industry's suddenly worsening prospects shook its confidence and, within a short time, threatened its financial well-being. *Nucleonics Week* informed its readers in January 1975 that the industry was in a state of "utter chaos," and that utilities had "no idea how to finance nuclear plants." A few months later, *Nuclear Industry* found a "scene of almost unrelieved gloom and anger" at a meeting sponsored by the Atomic Industrial Forum, an organization that promoted industrial applications of nuclear energy. The mood had not improved by December 1977, when the same magazine reported that the "collective frame of mind" of delegates at the Atomic Industrial Forum's annual conference was "as appropriate for wringing hands as for shaking hands." Nuclear industry officials were deeply troubled by evidence that a growing number of utilities, especially those in precarious financial condition, were turning away from the nuclear option in favor of building coal-fired plants. The forecasts for the expansion of nuclear power were much less promising than those of the early 1970s. Whereas in 1973 the AEC had predicted that more than 1,000 nuclear plants would be operating by the year 2000, just five years later the recently created U.S. Department of Energy reduced the estimate to 500 at most and perhaps only about 200.

In March 1978, *Business Week* suggested that the outlook for the nuclear industry was so bleak that within ten years it was "apt to contract dramatically and it may collapse altogether."[14]

EXPANDING OPPOSITION TO NUCLEAR POWER

The rising costs and slowing demand that plagued the nuclear industry on the financial front were compounded by increasing controversy on the political front. To industry officials, the emerging antinuclear movement—described by one executive as populated with "latter-day Luddites"—was the "root of the political problem." Eroding support for and growing protests against nuclear power were closely tied to increasing public fear of exposure to radiation. This, in turn, was a direct result of a major scientific debate during the late 1950s and early 1960s over the effects of radioactive fallout from aboveground nuclear bomb tests by the United States, the Soviet Union, and Great Britain. The tests spread fallout to populated areas far from the test sites and ignited a highly publicized controversy over the hazards of low levels of radiation. Although it was clear that exposure to heavy doses of radiation was harmful, the risk of exposure to low doses was a source of uncertainty and sometimes sharp disagreement among scientists. The fallout debate moved the issue of low-level radiation hazards from the realms of scientific and medical discourse to the popular realm of newspaper reports, magazine stories, and political campaigns. For the first time, it became a matter of sustained public concern.[15]

The Limited Test Ban Treaty of 1963, which prohibited nuclear atmospheric testing by its signatories, effectively ended the fallout debate as a prominent public issue. But it did not dispel public concern about low-level radiation that the fallout controversy had fostered. This was evident in public protests against the construction of several nuclear power plants in the early 1960s. Critics of the proposed Ravenswood plant in New York City and the proposed Bodega Bay and Malibu plants in California cited the dangers of radiological contamination that might result if the reactors were built. Citizen objections to those projects played an important role in their eventual termination. Organized opposition to nuclear power remained sporadic and localized; it focused on conditions that applied to a particular area, such as the density of the population in New York and the threat of earthquakes at the California sites. Nevertheless, it was disquieting for nuclear power proponents. In June 1963, *Nucleonics Week* advised the nuclear industry and the government to deal "fully and forthrightly" with public concern about the technology. "If the public does not accept nuclear power," it warned, "there will be no nuclear power."

As the nuclear power industry expanded during the late 1960s, so too did challenges to the construction of new plants. The growing objections focused not only on plans for specific sites but also on concerns over the implications of building a large number of reactors. The increase in antinuclear activism went hand in hand with the expansion of the industry. Most of the plants built during the bandwagon market years met with little or no opposition, but several triggered strong dissent. Although there was no organized, broad-based movement against nuclear power, the cumulative effect of antinuclear activities called attention to reservations about nuclear technology in general.[16]

The growth of the nuclear industry occurred simultaneously, if coincidentally, with the rise of the environmental movement in the United States. Environmentalists recognized the advantages of nuclear power in reducing air pollution, but they became increasingly critical of the technology on other grounds. The view of nuclear power as better for the environment than conventional fuels was undermined in the late 1960s by a major controversy over the effects of waste heat from nuclear plants on water quality, widely known as thermal pollution. The nuclear industry gradually and reluctantly took action to combat thermal pollution by building cooling towers or cooling ponds for plants that lay on inland waterways, but not before it sustained a barrage of attacks that aroused public doubts about the environmental effects of nuclear power. As the thermal pollution question generated criticism, an even more bitter debate over radiation emissions from nuclear plants gained prominence across the nation. Several scientists challenged the prevailing view that the small amounts of radiation released by nuclear plants during normal operation were not a serious problem. They charged that the routine releases were a severe threat to public health that could cause tens of thousands of deaths from cancer every year. The exchange of views over radiation risks stirred further uneasiness about nuclear power, especially among those unable to evaluate the conflicting claims.

Within a short time, the concern about radiation exposure from routine emissions was intensified by even more potent apprehensions about reactor safety. The larger size of individual plants ordered during the late 1960s raised new safety questions and provoked fears of a severe reactor accident that would spew large quantities of radiation into the environment. In the early 1970s, a highly contentious controversy over the performance of emergency core cooling systems in nuclear plants, designed to prevent a core meltdown that could lead to the "China syndrome," received coverage in the popular media as well as in technical journals. By highlighting the uncertainties about the technology that its supporters acknowledged, sometimes involuntarily, the controversy enhanced the stature of critics who questioned the safety of nuclear power.[17]

Those problems, along with a series of other environmental, technical, and public health questions, emerged within a short period of a few years and made nuclear power the source of acute controversy. Public support, which had seemed so strong in the early 1960s, was shaken. As the combination of key issues that arose in rapid sequence fed public misgivings, the arguments of nuclear critics substantially affected the fortunes of the industry. "The antinuclear coalition has been remarkably successful," commented *Forbes* in September 1975. "It has certainly slowed the expansion of nuclear power."[18]

The individuals and groups who opposed nuclear power, or at least objected to specific nuclear projects, did not constitute a monolithic front in their tactics or motivation. By the mid-1970s, antinuclear activism had moved beyond localized protests and politics to gain wider appeal and influence. Although it lacked a single coordinating organization and uniform goals, it emerged as a movement sharply focused on fighting nuclear power. Its efforts attracted a great deal of national attention. According to one estimate, coverage of nuclear power issues in the print media grew by 400 percent between 1972 and 1976. Antinuclear activism was spearheaded by a number of leaders who, as even their opponents conceded, were well informed, articulate, and increasingly media-savvy. They were frequently brash and sometimes belligerent in taking on nuclear proponents, whom they regarded with attitudes ranging from skepticism to contempt. Few nuclear critics were nuclear physicists or engineers, but many were scientifically literate. Even those not trained in science often were skillful at learning the fundamentals of nuclear technology and challenging the positions of its supporters. Myron M. Cherry, an attorney who argued against the licensing of several nuclear plants, commented in 1977, "There are some things I'm not so good at, but I'm absolutely *fantastic* at asking questions." None of his adversaries in the hearings in which he participated would have disagreed. The nuclear industry discovered that the antinuclear movement was too tenacious to be dismissed and too influential to be ignored.[19]

Some prominent critics of nuclear power first became involved in opposing local projects and then branched out to gain recognition as national antinuclear leaders. As a young attorney in a large Chicago law firm, Cherry had received an assignment from a senior partner in 1969 to give the utility constructing the Palisades nuclear station in Michigan a "hard time." Although at first he knew little about nuclear power, he participated in licensing proceedings on the plant and raised questions about the environmental and health effects of nuclear power. After playing the same role in a variety of other hearings, he commented privately in 1976 that he had become so "seriously afraid of nuclear accidents" that he wanted to "put people in jail," presumably people from the nuclear industry.[20]

Cherry's opposition to specific nuclear projects often received support from David Dinsmore Comey, whom *Nuclear Industry* described in early 1973 as "probably the most formidable . . . foe of nuclear power." As a faculty member in Soviet studies at Cornell University, Comey organized a successful campaign in 1968 to halt plans to build a nuclear plant on nearby Lake Cayuga, largely because of concerns about thermal pollution. He was then hired by a Chicago-based nonprofit group called Business and Professional People for the Public Interest to carry out extensive antinuclear activities. Although Comey was regarded by industry officials as less confrontational and doctrinaire than many other environmentalists, he was relentless in citing objections to the design and performance of nuclear plants. Another well-known critic, Anthony Z. Roisman, was a lawyer who had made a name for himself by representing environmental groups petitioning the AEC to greatly expand its consideration of the environmental impact of two plants under construction on the Chesapeake Bay in Maryland. When the issue went to court, Roisman won a milestone victory in 1971 that applied not only to the twin Calvert Cliffs facilities but to all nuclear plants under construction or under licensing review. The Calvert Cliffs decision established Roisman as a leading voice among the antinuclear forces.[21]

The efforts of individuals such as Cherry, Comey, Roisman, and a dedicated but disparate cadre of other nuclear critics were often combined with and enhanced by a growing number of antinuclear organizations. Although many of those groups pursued issues unrelated to nuclear power, they formed a crucial component of the antinuclear coalition. The Sierra Club, for example, was an organization of 140,000 members that addressed a wide range of environmental questions. Despite the appeals of some of its leaders and a serious internal rift, it had refused to take a stand against nuclear power in general during the 1960s and early 1970s. In 1974, however, its board of directors voted in favor of a nuclear moratorium. Other organizations were less ambivalent in their opposition to nuclear power. The Natural Resources Defense Council (NRDC) was founded in 1969 as a "public interest law firm" to take legal action on environmental issues. Its goal was to advance environmental protection through "responsible militancy." By 1976, it had enlisted about 15,000 members and litigated on matters ranging from administration of antipollution legislation to cleanup of industrial sites. It also "invested a steadily increasing portion of its resources in the nuclear energy issue" because, the group concluded, "for too long, we let the glimmering promise of nuclear energy blind us to the fact that we may have opted for an unforgiving and potentially unmanageable technology."[22]

The smallest of the national organizations that contested nuclear power was perhaps the most influential. The Union of Concerned Scientists (UCS) was formed at the Massachusetts Institute of Technology in late 1968. It began largely as a faculty organization that published an appeal in March 1969 to use science and technology for addressing social and environmental problems rather than for building nuclear, chemical, and biological weapons. It soon turned its attention to environmental issues and increasingly became involved in the debate over nuclear power. Key leaders of the UCS were Henry W. Kendall, a high-energy physicist at the Massachusetts Institute of Technology who later won a Nobel Prize in physics, and Daniel F. Ford, a graduate student in economics at Harvard University before devoting his efforts to the nuclear controversy. The organization had only two hundred to three hundred members, but Kendall and Ford together provided it with energy, commitment, and credibility. *Science* magazine reported in 1975 that Kendall and Ford "in large part, *are* the UCS." The UCS first joined the nuclear debate when it intervened in a licensing hearing for the Pilgrim plant near Plymouth, Massachusetts, and it won increased recognition after it challenged the AEC and the industry on the performance of emergency core cooling systems in 1971.[23]

The UCS was disappointed, however, that its warnings about the risks of a core meltdown during the emergency-cooling debate did not receive more media coverage. Therefore, in November 1972 Kendall and Ford approached the consumer advocate and corporate watchdog Ralph Nader to ask that he join their campaign to resolve the "number one public safety problem in the country today." Nader had earned enormous public respect for his well-publicized efforts to improve automobile safety and to lobby for other regulatory, environmental, and tax reforms. Kendall and Ford concluded that, with Nader's assistance, "the reactor safety issue that the UCS has been pursuing can finally achieve widespread public attention[,] and that important remedial changes can result." Nader accepted the invitation of the UCS and, within a short time, emerged as the leading, or at least the best-known, critic of nuclear power. In a speech on November 21, 1972, he called nuclear power "a terrible hazard" that could cause "the greatest destruction that this country has ever known." A short time later, he told approximately 3 million viewers of the nationally televised *Dick Cavett Show* that "the risks of something going wrong with these nuclear power plants are so catastrophic that they are not worth the benefit."[24]

On January 3, 1973, Nader held a press conference with Kendall and Ford that was attended by about forty reporters from the print media and television. He told them he wanted to raise the debate over the role of nuclear power "to the moral level that is so important." He further suggested that the issue was more urgent than the "so-called energy crisis" because, "if we don't deal with it now, we'll have perhaps a radioactive crisis 10 years hence." The alliance with Nader went a long way toward accomplishing the goals that Kendall and Ford had sought when they recruited him. A consultant for the nuclear industry thought "Nader's entry into the antinuclear business" was "ample cause for concern," and *Nuclear Industry* commented that "the support of a public figure such as Nader gives [UCS] demands public exposure to a degree that Kendall and Ford could not achieve on their own." Nader's activities clearly boosted the visibility, credibility, and morale of the antinuclear movement. In November 1974 he organized a three-day conference called "Critical Mass '74" that attracted 750 enthusiastic participants and about 80 press representatives. "The tone of the meeting, in sharp contrast to the nuclear industry meetings a month earlier, was one of buoyant optimism," observed *Nucleonics Week*. "The lasting impression of the affair was that the antinuclear movement is growing in size and dedication."[25]

Nuclear power critics did not fully agree on their objectives, which ranged along a spectrum from appealing for an immediate shutdown of plants to demanding major improvements. Although Nader had not actively opposed the technology until Kendall and Ford approached him, he gradually took a more hard-nosed position than that of the UCS. In their joint press conference of January 3, 1973, he supported the UCS's call for a moratorium on the completion of nuclear plants already in the early stages of construction until safety issues were resolved and for "derating," or reducing the power output of, facilities in operation or nearing completion, by as much as 50 percent. By the time the "Critical Mass

'74" conference took place, Nader had toughened his stance. "There has to be a moratorium on all construction of nuclear power plants and the most expeditious shutdown of existing plants," he declared. "I don't think that a position as to the hazards of nuclear power is consistent with any other position than a moratorium and a shutdown." Nader's hard-line position was echoed by other nuclear opponents. Cherry made clear that he was "firmly committed to stopping nuclear power in the U.S.," and a staff member of the national environmental organization Friends of the Earth announced, "We oppose nuclear power completely. Something that produces radioactivity cannot be made safe any more than war can be made safe."

Other nuclear critics took a more moderate position while continuing to emphasize their deep reservations about nuclear power. The UCS did not support an immediate moratorium on nuclear plants. It suggested that nuclear power could be made acceptable, at least on a temporary basis, if its "grave weaknesses" were corrected. When Kendall told the "Critical Mass '74" meeting that he opposed an immediate moratorium and favored "sharp restrictions" on nuclear plants and a gradual phase-out instead, the audience groaned audibly. David Comey remarked in 1977 that "nuclear energy can probably be made safe," though he added that it was "nowhere near that point now," and that the costs of improving its safety would make it economically uncompetitive. Anthony Roisman, an effective adversary of the industry in several licensing and rule-making hearings, told a group of staff members from utilities and the AEC that publicists for both sides in the nuclear debate had misrepresented their opponents. He urged his listeners to take the views of nuclear critics seriously, but also advised them, "Don't treat us as your enemies. We both have the same goals." Frank von Hippel, a physicist at Princeton University who had expressed serious misgivings about the performance of the nuclear industry and the AEC, regretted that the controversy focused on the question of whether nuclear power should be abandoned completely or pushed "full steam ahead." He hoped that the debate would be couched in less categorical terms and would deal responsibly with the issue of improving existing safety programs.[26]

THE ANTINUCLEAR POSITION

Despite differences in goals and priorities, leading critics marshaled similar complaints against nuclear power, which were, in turn, echoed by local citizens and organizations that took an antinuclear position or objected to plans for specific sites. Grassroots opposition reflected concerns ranging from aesthetics to scientific uncertainties, but by the mid-1970s the antinuclear movement highlighted several major arguments in its indictments of the technology. Convinced that the risks of nuclear power far outweighed the benefits, it placed its greatest emphasis on the issue of nuclear safety. Nuclear opponents asserted that, despite the efforts of the industry and the AEC to ensure the safe operation of nuclear plants, a core meltdown was possible, if not probable. They pointed out that nuclear plants contained as much radioactivity as thousands of Hiroshima-type atomic bombs and estimated that the large amount of radiation, if released to the environment in an accident, would cause tens of thousands of deaths. Nuclear critics argued that a system as large and complex as a nuclear power plant was vulnerable to human errors. They claimed that even if plants were well designed and well built, which they regarded as unlikely, nuclear safety depended on flawless operating performance.

Moreover, from the perspective of nuclear opponents, the routine operation of plants was a dire threat to public health even if severe accidents were avoided. Drawing on the views of several scientists who dissented from the prevailing consensus, one writer alleged in 1977, for example, that the death toll from normal releases of low levels of radiation from nuclear units "may now be in the thousands" and would "in time climb into the hundreds of thousands." In addition, nuclear critics pointed out that the nuclear industry and the government had not found a satisfactory method of disposing of the radioactive wastes produced by nuclear fission, which they claimed would pose a grave danger to the public for generations. Concerns about the safety of nuclear plant operation and the risks of population exposure to radiation were intensified by the hazards that the projected use of plutonium for reactors seemed to present. Although the slightly enriched uranium employed in existing nuclear power plants was not suitable for nuclear weapons, most experts believed that plutonium would be widely used in the future to fuel reactors. Many nuclear opponents cited the potential catastrophe that could occur if terrorists acquired enough plutonium to build an atomic bomb. They further suggested that protecting plants from terrorist activities would require measures so extensive and intrusive that it would undermine American civil liberties. One antinuclear group, the Citizens Energy Project, contended in 1978 that "nuclear power and civil liberties cannot co-exist; to the extent that nuclear power is expanded, civil liberties must be restricted."[27]

In the calculus of antinuclear activists, the risks of nuclear power generation were unacceptably large while the benefits were slight. They argued that nuclear power was unnecessary to meet the energy requirements of the United States. Nader, for example, told a congressional committee in January 1974 that by 1985 geothermal energy could produce "the equivalent of one half of the electric energy which is now produced in our economy." The idea that nuclear power could be replaced by more benign sources of energy was a staple of antinuclear literature. The foremost champion of this view, Amory B. Lovins, attracted a great deal of notice for an article he published in the journal *Foreign Affairs* in October 1976. Lovins was a twenty-eight-year-old "consultant physicist" who worked for the Friends of the Earth in London. He urged the adoption of a "soft path" to energy sufficiency rather than continuing along the "hard path" of dependence on fossil fuels and nuclear power. He called for the immediate abandonment of nuclear power and a more gradual retreat from fossil fuels in favor of conservation and development of alternative sources of power from solar, wind, and geothermal energy. "Enterprises like nuclear power are not only unnecessary but a positive encumbrance," he wrote, "for they prevent us . . . from pursuing the tasks of a soft path at a high enough priority to make them work."[28]

In addition to submitting that nuclear power was unsafe and unnecessary, nuclear critics maintained that it was unreliable. They pointed to AEC statistics showing that nuclear plants fell short of targets for generating power. Their average capacity factor, which was the ratio of the actual power a plant produced compared to its capacity if it operated all the time, usually ran in the 50–60 percent range during the mid-1970s because of a variety of equipment and operating problems. Most of the problems were minor, but many required shutdowns in order to be corrected or repaired.[29]

THE PRONUCLEAR POSITION

Supporters of nuclear power took strong exception to the arguments of its opponents. They acknowledged that developing the technology imposed risks on the population, but they insisted that the benefits far exceeded those risks. While they admitted that a serious accident was conceivable and that the loss of life and property could be severe if one occurred, they contended that the chances of an accident releasing large amounts of radiation to the environment were remote. Alvin M. Weinberg, director of Oak Ridge National Laboratory in Tennessee, who was widely regarded as one of the most thoughtful nuclear power advocates, wrote in 1972, "Nuclear people have made a Faustian bargain with society." He suggested that advanced reactor designs could provide a cheap, clean, and virtually inexhaustible source of energy but required "a vigilance and a longevity of our social institutions that we are quite unaccustomed to." Weinberg concluded that the advantages of nuclear power made the bargain "well worth the price." Another prominent defender of nuclear power, Hans A. Bethe, a professor of theoretical physics at Cornell University, made the same point about nuclear safety. He had been a pioneer in the field of nuclear physics during the 1930s, a leading scientist on the Manhattan Project during World War II, and a recipient of the Nobel Prize for physics in 1967. The physicist Frank von Hippel thought that "a large fraction of the scientific community" saw Bethe as a "model of independence, incisive analysis, and public responsibility." In a series of articles and interviews, Bethe asserted that, even in the "extremely unlikely" event of a core meltdown in a nuclear plant, the probability of a major release of radiation was "extremely small."

Nuclear proponents countered the critics' argument that a nuclear plant contained more radiation than an atomic bomb by emphasizing that a reactor could not explode like a bomb. Nearly all the nuclear power reactors in operation or on order used uranium fuel enriched to a level of about 3 percent of the fissionable isotope uranium-235. A nuclear bomb, by contrast, needed fuel enriched to 80 percent or more of uranium-235 (as in the atomic bomb dropped on Hiroshima) or fissionable plutonium (as in the atomic bomb dropped on Nagasaki and in U.S. nuclear weapons tested after World War II). "Comparing a reactor to an A-bomb is a popular scare tactic," declared A. David Rossin, an official with the Commonwealth Edison Company of Chicago. He pointed out that, whereas radiation from a bomb was released when it exploded, nuclear plants were designed to keep the radioactivity "isolated and sealed." Supporters of nuclear power also denied the charge that plants were safe only if their design, construction, and operation were infallible. They insisted that the redundant safety systems and multiple barriers to a large release of radiation provided ample protection from the consequences of equipment failures and human errors.[30]

Nuclear advocates sharply disputed the claim that even routine operation of plants would cause large numbers of cancer deaths annually. This issue, which won headline treatment in the late 1960s and early 1970s, centered on the effects of exposure to low levels of radiation, and the scientific evidence did not provide definitive guidance. But most radiation protection professionals, while cautioning against unnecessary exposure to any amount of radiation, believed the available data strongly indicated that the risks of low-level exposure were slight. They maintained that the charge that normal emissions of radiation from nuclear plants would greatly increase the incidence of cancer were exaggerated beyond evidence or reason. Nuclear supporters dismissed other health and safety concerns raised by critics as overstated or alarmist. They admitted that the disposal of nuclear waste was a problem, but they expressed confidence that satisfactory solutions would be found. They acknowledged that the future use of plutonium, which experts believed would largely replace uranium as reactor fuel by the end of the century, would require adequate safeguards against terrorist threats. But nuclear proponents argued that power reactors were a poor target for terrorists, and that newly strengthened regulations offered sufficient protection against them. They denied that measures taken to guard nuclear plants against terrorist activities would undermine American civil liberties.[31]

In the minds of its supporters, nuclear power was essential to meet the energy requirements of the United States. They dismissed the conclusion of Lovins, Nader, and other critics that alternative sources of energy along with conservation could replace nuclear power. Ralph E. Lapp, a nuclear physicist and freelance writer, played a prominent role in attacking this point of view. Lapp was a veteran of the Manhattan Project who had challenged the AEC's assurances during the 1950s that radioactive fallout from nuclear weapons testing did not present a significant threat to public health. He had later criticized the AEC and the nuclear industry on reactor safety issues, but by the mid-1970s he concluded that nuclear opponents, especially Nader, had overestimated the risks of nuclear power and undervalued its benefits. He commented in 1975 on Nader's views on energy supplies: "It is extremely difficult to critique Mr. Nader's proposals for alternative energy sources because he has never put them together in anything approaching a coherent framework. His emotional attachment to the sun seems profound, but on questioning about its value, he usually concedes it is a future source."

Nuclear supporters agreed on the need for conservation and new energy sources, but they discounted the "soft" path to energy sufficiency that Lovins recommended. Bethe responded skeptically to Lovins's article in *Foreign Affairs:* "The energy problem of the United States and other industrial countries is extremely serious. We need to combine many different techniques to solve it. But it cannot be solved by combining 'soft' arithmetic with wishful thinking." Although Bethe and other nuclear proponents favored the development of solar, wind, and geothermal energy, they denied that those alternatives to nuclear power could satisfy either the short-term or long-term energy requirements of the United States. Advocates contended that nuclear power was reasonably reliable and predicted that it would improve with more operating experience. They presented data showing that the industry-wide capacity factor for nuclear units was comparable to that of large coal facilities, and that for some nuclear plants it was better.[32]

THE NUCLEAR POWER CONTROVERSY

The issues surrounding the safety, necessity, and reliability of nuclear power had erupted into a full-fledged national controversy by the mid-1970s. The debate was intense, dogmatic, and highly polarized; representatives of both sides described it as a "religious war." With the fervor of holy warriors, partisans used emotional appeals to win public support. "The result has been a flood of advertising and pamphlets," observed the reporter Joanne Omang in the *Washington Post,* "either scaring us about the horrors of [a] nuclear holocaust or scaring us about the horrors of inadequate electricity." Howard K. Smith, a commentator for the *ABC Evening News,* repeated a favorite theme of nuclear proponents when he told viewers in 1975 that, without an expansion of nuclear power, "the day will come, probably in the early 1980s, when the home will grow cold, auto traffic [will turn] to a trickle, and industries [will] go on two days a week, with lots of unemployment, for lack of fuel." Although supporters of the technology seldom drew the issue in terms as stark and alarming as Smith's commentary, they insisted that nuclear power development was necessary to avoid a serious energy shortage.

While nuclear advocates used emotional appeals in advancing their arguments, critics were even more inclined to make their case by evoking strong sentiments. Perhaps the most arresting example was a poster that antinuclear protesters often carried at rallies. It asked the question "What Do You Do in Case of a Nuclear Accident?" and provided a hauntingly apocalyptic answer: "Kiss Your Children Goodbye." Students from Archbishop Carroll High School in Washington, D.C., made a similar argument in a letter to President Jimmy Carter. "People often say, 'I don't want my kids to sit around in the cold twenty years from now,'" they wrote. "But the proliferation of nuclear power raises the more important question of whether there will be anyone alive twenty years from now." Hans Bethe complained that trying to explain the advantages of nuclear power to opponents was like "carving a cubic foot out of a lake." He related an incident that occurred when he spoke to a largely antinuclear audience at a meeting in Berkeley, California. After he had presented his position on the need for nuclear power, a woman in the audience stood up, turned her back on him, and shouted, "Save the Earth!" The crowd reacted, he said, with "thunderous applause."[33]

In keeping with its heavy emotional content, the contest over nuclear power featured a strong element of gamesmanship. This was evident in competing petitions that each side publicized to show authoritative scientific support for its position. In January 1975, a group of thirty-four eminent American scientists, including eleven Nobel laureates, released a statement on energy policy that had been drafted primarily by Bethe and Lapp. Contending that the energy crisis confronted the United States with "the most serious situation since World War II," it maintained that there was "no reasonable alternative to an increased use of nuclear power to satisfy our energy needs." The petition faulted nuclear critics for a lack of "perspective as to the feasibility of non-nuclear power sources and the gravity of the fuel crisis." When Bethe and Lapp issued the statement at a press conference attended by about a hundred reporters, Ralph Nader countered by attending the event and handing out an appeal of his own. It was a letter to President Ford signed by eight prominent scientists, including five Nobel laureates, that opposed a "massive speedup of nuclear power plant construction." *Science* magazine scored this exchange as "Nuclear Advocates 34, Opponents 8."

A short time later, the Union of Concerned Scientists circulated yet another petition that urged a "drastic reduction" in new construction of reactors. Of the approximately sixteen thousand people who received the statement from the UCS, about twenty-three hundred signed. The UCS then delivered the petition to the White House and Congress on August 6, 1975, the thirtieth anniversary of the atomic bombing of Hiroshima. This initiative, in turn, prompted the American Nuclear Society, an organization of nuclear professionals in industry, government, and academic institutions, to launch its own drive. Eventually it secured more than thirty-two thousand signatures on a statement that underlined the need for both coal and nuclear power and asserted that there were "no technical problems incapable of being solved" in the use of either technology.[34]

As the adversaries in the nuclear debate attempted to win public favor by citing the numbers and professional qualifications of their supporters,

each also acclaimed defectors from the competing side. Nuclear proponents pointed to the views expressed by Ian A. Forbes, a former member of the UCS who had coauthored a stinging reproach of the AEC's
treatment of the emergency core cooling question in 1971. By 1974, he
had concluded that the issue had been satisfactorily resolved, and he became a vocal backer of nuclear power. He rebuked Nader and the UCS
for polarizing discussion in a way that "made reasoned debate almost
impossible." The effect of Forbes's changeover from a critic to a defender
of nuclear power was modest, however, compared to the highly publicized resignation of three midlevel engineers from their positions with
General Electric's nuclear power division in 1976. The three men, Greg-
ory C. Minor, Richard B. Hubbard, and Dale C. Bridenbaugh, had a total
of fifty-four years' experience with General Electric, families to support,
and no immediate job prospects. They resigned with a flourish by announcing that "nuclear power is a technological monster that threatens
all future generations." General Electric sought to deflate the effect of
their action by pointing out that they were a small portion of the hundreds of nuclear engineers that it employed. Nevertheless, as *Time* reported, the "trio's defection seemed like a major victory for the antinuke
forces in the great nuclear debate."[35]

Although the battle over nuclear power was usually fought in press
conferences, hearings, meetings, petitions, articles, and television appearances, it occasionally was joined in more direct confrontations. In May
1977, a demonstration against two proposed nuclear plants in Seabrook,
New Hampshire, attracted about two thousand poster-carrying, slogan-
chanting, nonviolent protesters. "We feel Seabrook in particular and nuclear power in general are life and death issues," explained one of their
leaders. After the demonstrators occupied the construction site, police
arrested more than fourteen hundred of them for trespassing. The conflict
over Seabrook commanded a great deal of attention and suggested that
citizen protests against nuclear plants would grow. Nader predicted that
direct action "will spread all over the country as needed . . . if there is
no more formal way to protest." Opponents of nuclear plants in Indi-
ana, Oklahoma, Missouri, Alabama, California, and elsewhere adopted
similar nonviolent tactics in efforts to halt or slow construction, promote their views, and win sympathy for their cause. The result was to
amplify the emotional and uncompromising quality of the nuclear
power debate. "Increasingly, the debate is constituted less of reason and
logic and more of emotion," lamented Jon Payne, editor of *Nuclear News,*
the monthly publication of the American Nuclear Society. "And its out-

Figure 1. Demonstrator at an antinuclear rally in Harrisburg, Pennsylvania, 1979 (National Archives 220-TMI-DE9040041-5).

come is based less on the accuracy of the arguments than on the number of voices behind them."[36]

The influence of the nuclear controversy on public attitudes toward the technology was difficult to assess. Public opinion surveys showed strong support for nuclear power. A poll conducted by Louis Harris and Associates in August 1975 indicated that 63 percent of the public favored the expansion of nuclear power in the United States, while 19 percent opposed and 18 percent were not sure. Later polls yielded similar results. Nevertheless, the polls were not unequivocally favorable to nuclear power. The 1975 Harris survey, for example, found that support for construction of individual plants was substantially weaker if Ralph Nader opposed it. A Gallup poll conducted in June 1976 showed that 71 percent of those interviewed thought it was "extremely important" or "somewhat important" to build more nuclear power plants, but it also showed that 40 percent of the respondents believed that operations of existing plants should be cut back until stricter safety regulations were imposed.[37]

The outcome of antinuclear initiatives that appeared on ballots in seven states in 1976 were similarly ambiguous. The campaign with the broadest potential consequences occurred in California, where nuclear opponents collected four hundred thousand signatures to place a proposition on the ballot for elections held in June. The initiative, known as Proposition 15, was intended to stop construction of new plants, reduce operation of existing ones, and eventually close down nuclear power in the state. The battle over the initiative underscored the bitter and emotional nature of the nuclear debate. Foes of Proposition 15 claimed it would cause the economy to collapse. Supporters of the measure asserted that nuclear power was a severe public health threat; one flyer proclaimed, "We are irreversibly committed to one million deaths from nuclear radiation." The nuclear industry spent heavily to defeat Proposition 15, and California voters rejected it by a margin of two to one. Even so, the message of the outcome was mixed. As David Pesonen, the leader of the initiative drive, commented, "A million and a half people were willing to vote to shut down nuclear power. Those people are firm and will not go away."[38]

Five months later, voters in six other states turned down proposals to place restrictions on nuclear power by decisive margins. Nuclear supporters welcomed the election results but recognized that they did not represent final victories. Antinuclear opposition and reservations about nuclear technology among a substantial segment of the public had become a permanent part of the political landscape. "It's a funny situation, where we're losing all the battles but winning the war," said one nuclear opponent. "Even when these proposals go down to defeat, we've educated more millions of people about the problems we see." In 1978, 63 percent of the voters in Montana provided support for that view when they approved a referendum imposing sharp restrictions on nuclear power, even though the state had no nuclear plants. Other samplings of public opinion also produced some ominous indications for nuclear advocates. A poll of college students and members of the League of Women Voters in Oregon in 1978, for example, offered startling information about the public's fear of nuclear power. Asked to rank thirty sources of risk "according to the present risk of death from each," both groups rated nuclear power as number one, ahead of smoking, motor vehicles, motorcycles, handguns, and alcoholic beverages.[39]

There were several reasons for the intensity and polarization of the nuclear power controversy; it was not simply a debate over energy sufficiency. Like a religious controversy, the nuclear power issue was so emotional in part because it could not be resolved with available information. All the key questions surrounding the technology—the probability of a severe accident, the consequences of a severe accident, the effects of low-level radiation, the dangers of radioactive waste disposal, the level of threat from terrorist attacks on nuclear facilities, and the costs and reliability of nuclear power—were subjects of dispute among experts. Operating experience and scientific evidence were still too limited to provide conclusive answers. When Hans Bethe acknowledged at a public hearing that he could not say for certain that safety systems in reactors would work as designed, a woman in the audience audibly murmured, "My God!—they really don't have the answers, do they?" Further, many political and social questions regarding the risks and benefits of nuclear power compared to other energy sources remained to be addressed. John P. Holdren, a physicist at the University of California, Berkeley, suggested in 1976 that "the disagreement among experts on major aspects of nuclear power is not a temporary condition."[40]

In addition to the lack of definitive evidence in crucial matters, longstanding public attitudes toward nuclear energy in general and cultural trends in the United States during the 1970s contributed in critical ways to the temper of the nuclear power debate. Perhaps the key issue was the connection between nuclear power and nuclear bombs. Despite the efforts of nuclear proponents to dispel popular misconceptions, a significant percentage of the public continued to believe that a nuclear plant could explode like an atomic bomb. A Harris poll conducted in 1975, for example, showed that 39 percent of those surveyed believed that a failure in a nuclear power plant could produce a "massive nuclear explosion" (24 percent thought this could not occur, and 37 percent were not sure). Nuclear critics claimed that nuclear power could not be separated from nuclear weapons because they used the same materials for fuel and posed the same threat of radioactive contamination. "If you're against nuclear warfare, you're also against nuclear power," declared one environmentalist. This argument played a vital role in shaping public attitudes toward nuclear power. Three scholars who studied growing public concern about the technology during the 1970s concluded that "distrust of nuclear power is . . . rooted in the fear of nuclear weapons."[41]

Public misgivings that arose from the stigma of nuclear weapons were reinforced by deep-seated fear of radiation. Although public apprehension about radiation predated World War II, it was greatly increased by the development and use of atomic weapons. Within a short time after the atomic bombings of Hiroshima and Nagasaki, accounts of the effects of radiation, embellished in science fiction books and articles, comics, and films, combined to heighten existing anxieties. During the 1950s and 1960s, debates over radioactive fallout and the effects of radioactive emissions from nuclear plants made radiation safety a bitterly contested issue. The allegation that routine radiation releases from nuclear plants would cause thousands of cases of cancer every year among the population was a staple of nuclear opponents. In 1973, E. F. Schumacher, an economist and technology critic, wrote in his influential book, *Small Is Beautiful,* that radiation from nuclear power was perhaps a greater menace to humanity than the atomic bomb. It was, he argued, "the most serious agent of pollution of the environment and the greatest threat to man's survival on earth." The hazards of low-level radiation were a source of sustained publicity during the postwar period and, as a result, of uniquely intense public fears that played an important part in setting the tone of the debate over nuclear power.[42]

The controversy was further inflamed by suggestions that whether to use the technology was not only a technical question but also a serious moral issue. Some national church organizations were prominent in opposing nuclear power on moral grounds. The General Conference of the United Methodist Church passed a resolution in May 1976, for example, that stated, "In our opinion, no generation has a right to assume risks in its decision making which bear heavily upon the potential destruction of the earth as a habitable place for future generations." At about the same time, the National Council of Churches, an ecumenical organization of thirty Protestant and Orthodox denominations, considered an even sharper condemnation of nuclear power. Drafted by a committee chaired by Margaret Mead, the eminent anthropologist, and Rene Dubos, a professor emeritus of pathology at Rockefeller University, it focused on the dangers of using plutonium for nuclear fuel, a prospect it called "morally indefensible and technically objectionable." To the council leaders' surprise, the report stirred many protests from, as one staff member put it, "good church people working in the industry who said, 'How dare you say that what I'm doing is immoral.'" After nuclear industry representatives and some theologians vigorously complained that nuclear power should not be "prejudged as intrinsically evil," the council softened the draft statement. Its deliberations called attention to differing moral assessments that greatly reduced the likelihood of compromise on technical, economic, and political issues.[43]

In addition to continuing disagreements among experts, fears of atomic explosions and radiation, and conflicting moral positions, the impassioned tone of the nuclear power debate was a result of cultural and philosophical trends in America during the 1970s. A growing chorus of social critics claimed that technological development and economic growth threatened to undermine democratic freedoms, moral values, environmental resources, public health, and eventually economic well-being. E. F. Schumacher, a leading advocate of this view, warned, "In the excitement over the unfolding of his scientific and technical powers, modern man has built a system of production that ravishes nature and a type of society that mutilates man." Condemning bigness and centralization in industry and government, Schumacher and other critics urged alternative systems that were modest in scale and decentralized in authority. Adherents to a "small is beautiful" outlook identified nuclear power as a powerful threat to their vision, and although they did not represent a large percentage of the population, they provided leadership, commitment, energy, and often money to antinuclear campaigns. A group called the Creative Initiative Foundation, whose numbers included the three engineers who created a stir by resigning from General Electric, was instrumental in placing the antinuclear initiative on the ballot in California in 1976. Opposition to nuclear power on the basis of its violation of the principles of smallness and decentralization added another dimension to the nuclear power debate that made accommodations between the competing sides unlikely.[44]

Many observers complained about the prevalence of emotional, moral, and philosophical appeals that polarized the nuclear controversy. Representatives of both sides of the debate called for a calm, reasoned discussion of the topic, and each expressed confidence that its arguments would prevail if the American people were well informed about the issues. Nader claimed in 1973, "If the country knew what the facts were and if they had to choose between nuclear reactors and candles, they would choose candles." Bethe affirmed that he welcomed "a factual public discussion on a broad basis," but he wanted it "conducted with rational arguments, not vast exaggerations." The nature of the nuclear power debate, however, made a dispassionate exchange of views difficult, if not impossible. The arguments used by both sides contained an ample measure of theoretical projections and unprovable assertions, and nuclear critics added a liberal portion of frightening associations. The adversaries in the debate contended that the stakes were very high, ranging from the economic welfare of the nation to the survival of the human race. *Fortune* commented on March 12, 1979, that the nuclear controversy, "the bitterest environmental confrontation of the Seventies," was "complex, confusing, and muddied by overstatements from both sides."[45]

The contention showed no signs of abating as the end of the 1970s neared. The issues were divisive, emotions were high, and opportunities for compromise were meager. In that atmosphere, *The China Syndrome* was more than simply an exciting motion picture. A screenplay in which utility executives were willing to gun down an honorable man for trying to correct unsafe conditions seemed disturbingly plausible to the growing number of Americans who believed that the benefits nuclear power provided were a poor trade-off for the risks it imposed.

Chapter 2

The Regulation of Nuclear Power

At the center of the nuclear power controversy stood the federal agencies primarily responsible for regulating the safety of the technology: the Atomic Energy Commission and subsequently the Nuclear Regulatory Commission (NRC). In the 1954 Atomic Energy Act, Congress had assigned the AEC the dual responsibilities of promoting atomic energy for peaceful purposes and protecting public health and safety from its hazards. Those functions were in many respects inseparable yet incompatible. The AEC's statutory conflict of interest became a prominent issue as the nuclear debate gathered momentum during the late 1960s and early 1970s. Both sides in the growing controversy over nuclear safety complained about the agency's regulatory policies and procedures. Opponents argued that the AEC failed to provide sufficient protection against radiation hazards, environmental abuse, and severe reactor accidents. They showed little confidence in the AEC's ability or willingness to regulate the nuclear industry adequately, particularly in light of the agency's statutory obligation to promote the use of nuclear power. The nuclear industry, by contrast, grumbled that the AEC was overzealous in its regulatory approach, imposing unnecessary and sometimes unreasonable demands.

The assertions of both critics and supporters of nuclear power were frequently exaggerated and self-serving, but they contained important elements of truth. Industry representatives were correct in pointing out that the AEC's regulatory decisions and requirements often conflicted with the views of nuclear vendors and utilities. The agency always weighed the effect of regulatory changes on nuclear development, but it did not always follow the recommendations, or bow to the pressure, of the industry. Nevertheless, critics justifiably emphasized that the inherent conflict of interest in the AEC's dual responsibilities predisposed it to treat industry concerns sympathetically. The AEC was vitally concerned with encouraging the growth of nuclear power partly because of the enormous and relentless pressure applied by its congressional oversight committee, the Joint Committee on Atomic Energy, and partly because of its own commitment to expanding use of the technology.[1]

By the early 1970s, the AEC was an embattled agency. "Public confidence in the safety of nuclear power plants and in the determination of the AEC to enforce adequate safety standards is at a low ebb," observed a *Washington Post* editorial in October 1971. The chairman of the AEC, James R. Schlesinger, recognized that the regulatory program needed reform. Shortly after joining the agency in August 1971, he took action to repair the agency's image and improve its regulatory performance. Schlesinger had earned a Ph.D. in economics at Harvard University, taught at the University of Virginia for several years, and worked as director of strategic studies at the RAND Corporation, a think tank in California. He was appointed assistant director of President Nixon's Bureau of the Budget in 1969, where he acquired a reputation as a skillful budget-cutter and no-nonsense administrator. On October 20, 1971, at a combined meeting of the Atomic Industrial Forum and the American Nuclear Society in Bal Harbour, Florida, Schlesinger outlined his views on the AEC's regulatory role in a speech that sent shock waves through the industry. He told his listeners that, although it "should be difficult to be other than bullish" about the long-term prospects for nuclear power, the pace of development would depend on two variables: "first, the provision of a safe, reliable product; second, achievement of public confidence in that product." To achieve those ends, he announced, the AEC would "perform as a referee serving the public interest" and would not "fight the industry's political, social, and commercial battles."[2]

Schlesinger made the same point in a meeting with members of the AEC's regulatory staff; he told them, "We are not here to solve industry's problems." He also emphasized that the AEC should avoid undue delays in making decisions on license applications, favorable or not. To perform those duties, he and his colleagues on the commission substantially increased the size and budget of the regulatory staff—a move that was essential to keep pace with the flood of bandwagon-market license applications. Schlesinger's initiatives won plaudits from many observers with varying opinions on nuclear power, but they did not restore confidence in the AEC or silence criticism. The anthropologist Margaret Mead, for example, contended in 1974 that the AEC had failed as a "watchdog who guards us from the demonic capabilities of nuclear fission" because it had "become a killer dog with tremendous power for harm." The AEC under Schlesinger and his successor as chairman, Dixy Lee Ray, continued to insist that nuclear power was safe, though not risk-free, and necessary. This put them at odds with doctrinaire critics who wanted to shut down nuclear power and who were not placated by regulatory reforms. Antinuclear partisans assailed the AEC as arrogant, secretive, and more concerned about the health of the nuclear industry than that of the public.[3]

THE ENERGY REORGANIZATION ACT OF 1974

Despite the AEC's efforts under Schlesinger and Ray to elevate the size and status of the regulatory staff and to rebut charges that the agency was inattentive to public health, proposals to separate its regulatory responsibilities from its promotional functions gained strength. Although the AEC continued to deny that its promotional obligations compromised its commitment to safety, it recognized that its dual roles undermined public confidence in its decisions. Most observers assumed that at some point its regulatory duties would be assigned to another agency. But for years the AEC, the Joint Committee on Atomic Energy, and the nuclear industry had agreed that such a step was premature. They worried that an independent regulatory body would impede the growth of nuclear power by imposing overly strict requirements. However, in the early 1970s, as the nuclear industry expanded and the nuclear debate intensified, the idea of detaching the AEC's safety programs won growing support from nuclear proponents and reform-minded critics.[4]

President Nixon submitted the first legislative proposal to dissociate the AEC's regulatory responsibilities in June 1973 as a part of a sweeping reorganization of federal energy agencies. Nixon's primary objective was to consolidate government programs to deal with the energy crisis. He called for creation of the Energy Research and Development Administration (ERDA), which would take over virtually all the AEC's non-regulatory duties, and the independent Nuclear Energy Commission (NEC), which would carry out the AEC's licensing and regulatory functions. The Nixon administration devoted little attention to questions surrounding establishment of the NEC; it focused on ways to expand energy supplies through the creation of ERDA and other actions. It did not recommend substantial changes in existing regulatory policies, and it initially contemplated, without making any commitments, placing the sitting AEC commissioners in the same positions as commissioners of the NEC.[5]

The proposal to assign the AEC's programs to separate agencies won wide support. Although the precise allocation of responsibilities remained an open question, *Nucleonics Week* reported "almost unanimous agreement in favor of splitting off the regulatory staff and creating an independent agency." *Business Week* commented in June 1973, "The breakup of the AEC is long overdue. Nuclear power is under attack as never before, and even nuclear proponents contend that the AEC is largely to blame." Representatives of the nuclear industry expressed hope that an independent NEC would not only increase public confidence in regulatory decisions but also expedite the licensing process for new plants. Perhaps more surprisingly, AEC officials endorsed the dissolution of their organization. The AEC chairman, Dixy Lee Ray, told the House Government Operations Committee in November 1973 that creation of the NEC would "eliminate the appearance of regulatory and developmental conflicts" and "maximize regulatory objectivity and impartiality." Ray, who held a Ph.D. in marine biology from Stanford University, had become the second woman to serve as an AEC commissioner when she was appointed in 1972, and the following year, the first to become chairman (she preferred the title of "chairman" to "chairwoman" or "chairperson"). Although she lacked a background in nuclear affairs, she soon emerged as an articulate, combative, and controversial defender of nuclear power. Despite some initial reservations about the demise of the AEC, she eventually concluded that it was necessary and desirable. Her colleagues on the commission took the same position.[6]

The Nixon administration enlisted powerful allies to steer its energy reorganization plans through Congress. In the House of Representatives, it received critical support from Chet Holifield, a Democrat from California, who helped draft the legislation. Holifield was chairman of the Government Operations Committee, which held hearings on the measure and reported to the House. He was also a charter member and former chairman of the Joint Committee on Atomic Energy, which was in a position to heavily influence the outcome of the bill. Holifield's efforts won the House's prompt approval of the legislation by a vote of 355 to 24. The progress of the legislation was considerably less certain and expeditious in the Senate, where Senator Abraham Ribicoff, chairman of the Government Operations Committee's Subcommittee on Reorganization, Research, and International Organizations, held hearings that for the first time closely examined the functions of the proposed NEC. Ribi-coff was a frequent critic of the AEC, and his hearings featured a series of complaints about nuclear safety and regulatory procedures. Daniel Ford of the Union of Concerned Scientists, for example, commented that establishing the NEC would not resolve the "tremendous safety prob-lems" in nuclear plants. It would, he said, take "the same people who have, in our judgment, performed quite badly and simply [say] to them that you're going to have continuing powers in this area."[7]

Eventually, the Senate passed a bill to separate the responsibilities of the AEC. But the measure included several provisions that many House supporters strongly opposed, especially an amendment that would offer technical assistance and financial aid to interveners in reactor licensing cases. Anthony Roisman, representing the environmental organization Friends of the Earth, had told Ribicoff's subcommittee of the financial disadvantages imposed on interveners who challenged utilities and the AEC in licensing proceedings, and the amendment was intended to ad-dress the problem. The Senate's bill angered Holifield, who said he was "appalled" by its "anti-nuclear bias." As a result, for more than a month he refused to appoint House conferees to negotiate with the Senate over the differences in the bills. When the conference took place, the partici-pants agreed easily on a new name for the regulatory agency they planned to create: the Nuclear Regulatory Commission. But other issues were more difficult. In the end, Holifield succeeded in eliminating the public funding of interveners and significantly modifying other provisions that he found objectionable. "Holifield gave inches to the senators," observed *Nucleonics Week*, "but he won by a mile on the . . . most controversial issues." One of the lesser questions on which the Senate version of the legislation prevailed was the formal abolition of the AEC; the House ver-sion had envisioned merely renaming it. This meant that AEC commis-sioners appointed to the NRC would have to undergo confirmation hear-ings. After Congress overwhelmingly approved the final version of the bill, President Ford signed the Energy Reorganization Act into law on October 11, 1974.[8]

THE NRC AND THE NUCLEAR POWER DEBATE

The demise of the AEC, at least from a regulatory perspective, went largely unmourned. Nuclear industry representatives optimistically spec-ulated that the NRC would prove to be a more efficient and predictable regulator than its predecessor. "I may be a Pollyanna on this one," a util-

ity lawyer remarked, "but I really look forward to the new commission."
Although some industry officials worried that the NRC would impose
more stringent rules, others thought this unlikely. "Quite frankly, I don't
see how they can get any more conservative than they have been in recent years," one observer said of the regulatory staff. Nuclear critics, by
contrast, hoped that the NRC would be tougher than the AEC. An attorney for interveners anticipated a "substantial strengthening" in the
new agency's policies because "there is no doubt that to some extent the
[AEC regulatory] staff has been inhibited in its ability to do the job it
should do."[9]

The continuing controversy over nuclear power and the uncertainties
about the new agency's approach to regulatory issues generated considerable interest in the appointment of the five commissioners. The White
House began to consider candidates in earnest soon after the president
signed the Energy Reorganization Act, which specified that no more than
three commissioners could come from one political party. The terms of
the first appointees would be staggered, so that one commissioner would
serve for one year, one for two years, and so on for the first five years of
the NRC's existence. The fact that the NRC was an independent regulatory agency meant that once appointees were confirmed by the Senate
they could not be removed simply at the pleasure of the president. On
October 29, President Ford announced that he would nominate William
A. Anders as NRC chairman. Anders was a retired Air Force lieutenant
colonel and an astronaut on the Apollo 8 mission in 1968, the first
manned flight to orbit the moon. He held a master's degree in nuclear
engineering and had served as an AEC commissioner since 1973. He was
the only AEC commissioner appointed to the NRC. Although Dixy Lee
Ray had expressed interest in heading ERDA or perhaps the NRC, the
White House did not offer her a position in either agency, apparently because of the ill will her leadership style had created among the commissioners. She often did not consult with her colleagues on matters they
considered to be appropriate for review by the full commission.[10]

After his nomination, Anders was highly influential in advising the
White House about other appointments to the commission. One obvious possibility was L. Manning Muntzing, who had earned wide respect
as director of the AEC's regulatory staff since 1971. But he had clashed
with Anders on regulatory issues and, according to the White House staff,
Anders doubted that he "could work successfully with Muntzing." After
interviewing more than a dozen candidates, the White House decided on
four other nominees it hoped would provide a good balance of engi-

Figure 2. Members of the Nuclear Regulatory Commission at a swearing-in ceremony at the U.S. Capitol, January 23, 1975. Left to right: Richard T. Kennedy, Edward A. Mason, Victor Gilinsky, Marcus A. Rowden, William A. Anders, Vice President Nelson A. Rockefeller, Mrs. Valerie Anders, and Supreme Court Justice Harry A. Blackmun (NRC).

neering, legal, environmental, and nuclear expertise. Marcus A. Rowden, general counsel of the AEC, had risen through the ranks as a career civil servant and was regarded by Anders and others as an able lawyer with "in-depth technical expertise in the nuclear field." He was nominated for the two-year term on the commission. Edward A. Mason, who received the three-year term, was chairman of the nuclear engineering department at MIT, where he had gained "broad practical experience as well as recognized academic stature." Victor Gilinsky, who held a Ph.D. in physics from the California Institute of Technology, was head of the physical sciences department at the RAND Corporation and, during the early 1970s, had served as a special assistant to Muntzing on the AEC's regulatory staff. James Schlesinger, who had known Gilinsky when they both worked at RAND during the 1960s and who had recruited him for the AEC, described him as "low-key and quiet"; the White House staff was impressed with his "excellent reputation for objective analysis." He was offered the four-year term on the commission.

The final nominee was Richard T. Kennedy, whom the White House staff had not initially supported because, although he seemed to be a person of "considerable ability," he was not "a well-qualified candidate" for the NRC. Kennedy was a retired U.S. Army colonel who had served on the National Security Council staff under Henry A. Kissinger. Despite Kennedy's lack of nuclear experience, Kissinger pushed hard and successfully for his appointment to the five-year term on the NRC. By design, the designated commissioners varied in background and experience, although candidates with the strongest environmental credentials had not been offered appointments. The nominees were not particularly well known within the nuclear community and were not closely identified with any faction in the nuclear debate. Some industry representatives complained that the commission would not include a strong pronuclear voice, but neither nuclear supporters nor opponents objected strenuously to any of the individual nominees. When the White House announced their names in December 1974, the general reaction was, in the view of *Nucleonics Week,* "no enthusiasm but little hostility."[11]

After the Senate confirmed the nominees, the NRC officially began operations on January 19, 1975. Although the commissioners were the heads of the new agency, the Energy Reorganization Act did not spell out the specific role they would play in managing its affairs or the precise boundaries of their domain. In general terms, they exercised final authority over policy formulation, rule making, and other broad regulatory issues, and in those areas they exercised equal authority and responsibility. They made decisions by a majority vote. The NRC had a full-time staff of about two thousand, nearly all of whom came from the regulatory organization of the AEC. The top staff official was the executive director for operations, who was responsible for the day-to-day functions of the agency and for liaison between the staff and the commission. The commissioners and the staff were physically separated; the commissioners' offices were located in downtown Washington, while the staff occupied several different buildings in suburban Maryland. Travel between the Washington and Maryland sites normally took at least half an hour.

The Energy Reorganization Act established three statutory offices within the NRC: the Office of Nuclear Reactor Regulation, which licensed and monitored nuclear power plants; the Office of Nuclear Material Safety and Safeguards, which regulated the large number of industrial, medical, and academic users of nuclear materials as well as the protection of nuclear plants from sabotage and nuclear fuel from theft; and the Office of Nuclear Regulatory Research, which sponsored confirmatory research on nuclear safety issues. Congress mandated creation of the latter two offices in large part because of its concern that the AEC had not done enough to protect nuclear plants and materials from terrorist attacks and because the agency had delayed vital research on nuclear safety in favor of other projects. The directors of the three statutory offices reported to the executive director for operations but could, if necessary, take issues straight to the commissioners. Thus the reorganization act left the lines of authority between the commissioners and staff poorly defined. Although the NRC had a clear mandate to protect public health from the hazards of nuclear power and nuclear materials, the ways in which it would administer its duties remained uncertain.[12]

The NRC soon confronted a series of complex and controversial issues relating to organizing the agency, improving reactor safety, reporting "abnormal occurrences" at nuclear plants, revising radiation standards, protecting nuclear plants from sabotage, safeguarding nuclear materials from theft, licensing the export of nuclear equipment and fuel, authorizing steps to use plutonium as fuel for nuclear power, and other matters. In dealing with those issues, agency officials sought to replace the perception of the AEC as a lax regulator with public confidence in the NRC as a fair, credible, and objective regulator. Anders pledged to listen to both nuclear proponents and critics with an open mind, but only if they addressed issues in straightforward and unemotional terms. "Demagoguery from either side cannot be a substitute for rationality and fact," he said. He announced that the NRC would take the role of umpire or referee, which he contrasted with the AEC's reputation as a cheerleader for the nuclear industry. "There'll be no pompons in our hands," he declared. Anders outlined the NRC's position in a speech to the annual meeting of the National Wildlife Federation on March 15, 1975: "I hope you will view me not as a proponent of either side of the nuclear power debate but as one who has the possibility to be an objective regulator, judge, or umpire concerned with the public safety and environmental compatibility of the nuclear uses that we regulate."[13]

As *Newsweek* pointed out in a cover story on the nuclear debate in April 1976, the "universal fate of referees" was to suffer "abuse from both sides." This observation clearly applied to the NRC, which gradually became the target of criticism from both nuclear supporters and opponents. Nuclear industry representatives were wary of the agency because they feared it would seek to prove itself a tough regulator by taking actions unfavorable to their interests. During the NRC's first few months of operation, they cited several decisions, or nondecisions, that seemed to vindicate their concerns, including the agency's failure to approve pending construction permits or operating licenses for plants and its slug-

gish pace on some rule-making proceedings. Industry officials were particularly indignant when the NRC postponed a ruling on the issue of reprocessing spent fuel from nuclear plants to extract plutonium for reactor fuel. The industry regarded reprocessing as vital to the future of
nuclear power because of the prevailing view that uranium reserves were
insufficient for long-term needs. When the NRC made a tentative decision in April 1975 to defer action on reprocessing until more studies had
been conducted, it "set the industry in a tizzy," according to *Nuclear Industry*. Further, some nuclear supporters claimed that the NRC commissioners avoided meeting with them but talked frequently with nuclear
critics. One attorney who represented industry clients commented, "No
one in the industry that I know of seriously would offer the view that
NRC is the enemy, or that it has become the conscious agent of opposition groups. But virtually everyone shares the view that something is seriously wrong with NRC."[14]

Nuclear critics were pleased by NRC actions that incensed the industry,
and they generally withheld judgment on the agency's performance for
several months. As the debate over nuclear power continued to escalate,
however, they gradually reached the conclusion that the NRC, like the
AEC before it, was strongly biased in favor of the industry. The turning
point in their attitude came after the NRC modified its decision on fuel
reprocessing in November 1975. In response to the industry's vocal complaints, it pledged to expedite its review of the safety questions raised by
the prospects for increased availability and use of plutonium. Gus Speth,
an attorney with the Natural Resources Defense Council, charged that
the NRC "has said in effect that it is more interested in reassuring the
nuclear industry than in reassuring the public. In so doing, the new agency
has shown that it has no more stomach for opposing the industry than
did the AEC." Other nuclear opponents expressed the same view. One
unnamed critic commented, "NRC is exactly the same as the old AEC
only a lot cleverer." Another partially dissented, "I am not sure they are
cleverer."[15]

Nuclear foes' increasingly negative opinion of the NRC was reinforced
when an agency staff member resigned from his job with much fanfare
in January 1976. Robert D. Pollard was an electrical engineer who joined
the AEC in 1969 and became a project manager coordinating technical
reviews of plant applications in late 1974. He acted in this capacity during reviews of several license applications, including the nearly completed
Indian Point-3 plant, located in Buchanan, New York, about twenty-four
miles north of downtown Manhattan. Over several months, Pollard con-

cluded that the NRC was failing to meet its responsibility to protect the public from the dangers of a nuclear accident. He also was convinced that his supervisors had brushed off concerns that he had raised about the safety of Indian Point-3 and another reactor at the site, Indian Point-2, which had begun operating in 1974. For those reasons, he decided to resign from the NRC and to do it in a way that would command public attention.

On January 13, 1976, Pollard submitted his resignation to his NRC supervisor. A few minutes later, he filmed an interview with the CBS reporter Mike Wallace for *60 Minutes,* a popular program that attracted about 23 million viewers every week. He told Wallace that, in his opinion, "it will be just a matter of luck if Indian Point doesn't sometime during its life have a major accident." Immediately after interviewing Pollard, Wallace confronted Anders in his office as the *60 Minutes* camera rolled. Anders, who had not known of Pollard's resignation or the causes for it, was caught completely off guard. Told by Wallace that Pollard resigned because he was "not sure about the safety of your program," Anders responded, "Bob Pollard has never tried to contact me or any of the members of the Commission. I've never heard of Bob Pollard before."

On January 20, the NRC announced it would conduct an investigation of Pollard's allegations that the agency was ignoring reactor safety issues and that top staff managers had dismissed his concerns. The NRC's Office of Inspector and Auditor interviewed Pollard at length and talked with other agency employees in comparable positions. It concluded that the issues that Pollard cited had been thoroughly considered by the NRC staff, which did not agree that the operating Indian Point-2 plant should be closed down. The report also suggested that the problem that led to Pollard's resignation was not that his views had been ignored but that he refused to accept the differing, prevailing judgment of his colleagues and supervisors. Although some agency experts complained about the difficulty of resolving technical issues, the NRC investigation found that the "views of the professional staff are not being ignored or suppressed."[16]

While the NRC was conducting its internal investigation, Pollard's charges were receiving a great deal of public notice. On February 8, 1976, *60 Minutes* ran its interview with Pollard. "At each turn I'm told I shouldn't rock the boat," he said on camera. "I shouldn't keep raising these concerns." The following day, he held a press conference to air his charges. He also announced that he had accepted a position as the Washington, D.C., representative of the Union of Concerned Scientists.

Pollard's complaints about the NRC and reservations about nuclear safety would have won considerable attention under any circumstances, but the timing of his *60 Minutes* appearance and his press conference increased their impact. He made his allegations public just a few days after the three General Electric engineers quit their jobs with the company. The resignation of four professional engineers who cited strong concerns about nuclear safety was a major story that supported the arguments and enhanced the credibility of nuclear opponents. When the *New York Times* ran its first story on Pollard, on January 21, 1976, it placed the article on page 62. After the *60 Minutes* segment and his press conference, the *Times* ran front-page stories on two consecutive days that detailed his charges and the responses of the NRC and Consolidated Edison, which owned the Indian Point-2 unit. A few days later, the *Times* published an editorial in which it called for suspending operation of Indian Point-2 until Pollard's concerns were addressed, and suggested that coal rather than nuclear power "offers the best hope for providing this country with electric power." It also sharply criticized the NRC, commenting that "the year-old Nuclear Regulatory Commission has not yet fully lived down the fears that—like its predecessor agency, the Atomic Energy Commission—it may sometimes understate potential danger spots in reactor design because of eagerness to promote the expansion of nuclear power."

Anders defended the NRC by telling the *Times* that it took "whatever steps are necessary to protect the public," and added that "there is no responsible basis" for closing Indian Point-2. Although the NRC was relieved that press coverage of the objections cited by Pollard and the General Electric engineers was "more restrained" than expected, the resignations were a setback for nuclear supporters. "For an industry already smarting from reduced electrical demand, uncertain licensing proceedings, difficulties in raising capital and regulatory delays," commented *Nuclear Industry,* "the resignations . . . were further psychological blows." They contributed substantially to the bitterness of the nuclear debate and to perceptions that the NRC was committed to protecting the well-being of the nuclear power industry.[17]

THE NUCLEAR LICENSING PROCESS

The publicity over Pollard's resignation called attention to a key source of contention in the debate over nuclear power: the NRC's licensing process for nuclear plants. Procedures for obtaining a license to build and operate a nuclear plant were complex, burdensome, and convoluted, and they evoked spirited protests from the nuclear industry. At the same time, for different reasons, they elicited strong criticism from nuclear opponents. Despite the ample time and effort that the Nixon, Ford, and Carter administrations, the Joint Committee on Atomic Energy and other congressional committees, and the AEC, the NRC, and other federal agencies devoted to reforming the licensing process, it remained a perpetually troublesome issue.

The 1954 Atomic Energy Act outlined a two-step licensing process. An applicant meeting the AEC's requirements would first receive a construction permit and, after the plant was built, an operating license. This arrangement allowed the construction of reactors to go forward before all the technical questions about their operation had been answered. The licensing process gradually became more complicated, and by the mid-1960s its complexity and redundancy prompted chronic complaints from the nuclear industry. To negotiate the process successfully, nuclear plant applicants faced a series of reviews by the staff of the AEC or, later, the NRC, which frequently found the technical and financial information insufficient or unsatisfactory. The application was also scrutinized by the Advisory Committee on Reactor Safeguards, an independent body of reactor experts from outside the AEC and NRC, and by other federal agencies with an interest in the effects of the proposed facility. Once the application cleared those hurdles, it was the subject of public hearings before an Atomic Safety and Licensing Board, composed of an administrative law expert and two technical experts. Licensing boards for individual proceedings were drawn from a larger panel of full-time hearing examiners and part-time members with strong technical qualifications. A favorable decision by the board authorized construction of the plant, unless the commissioners decided to review the proposal. Further comprehensive safety reviews and, often, additional public hearings were required before a utility could obtain an operating license for the plant. The goal of this process was to provide "reasonable assurance" that the facility would be operated safely and, during the AEC's existence, to insulate regulatory procedures from promotional functions.[18]

The flood of license applications in the late 1960s and early 1970s slowed the review process considerably. The AEC was unable to keep pace with the rapidly growing workload not only because of the large number of applications but also because of the dramatically increased size of the individual plants it evaluated. Applications for plants in the range of eight hundred to eleven hundred electrical megawatts raised many new and complex safety issues. Delays were compounded by the expanding controversy over nuclear power, which made intervention in the licensing process by plant opponents more common. The growing number of contested applications extended the licensing process by lengthening hearings in individual cases and by further stretching the resources of the regulatory staff. In 1967, the time required to plan, build, and begin operating a nuclear power plant was about seven years. By 1973, the lead time had become nine to ten years, and by the end of the decade ten to eleven years. The licensing process was only one of many causes of the long delays: others included labor strikes, difficulty with obtaining building materials, problems with securing financing, and management decisions to defer projects. The Congressional Budget Office concluded in 1979, "About 80 percent of the total amount of delay reported by reactors under construction occurred because of events or decisions in the private sector unrelated to the regulatory decisions of the NRC." Nevertheless, much of the effort to reduce lead times focused on licensing reforms.[19]

The energy crisis of the early 1970s made nuclear licensing delays an issue that received attention at the highest levels of government. President Nixon declared in November 1973 that he was "personally concerned about the excessive time now required for the planning and construction of nuclear power plants in the United States." The Nixon, Ford, and Carter administrations sent proposals to Congress for streamlining the process through such measures as encouraging the standardization of plant designs, developing a one-step licensing process, improving cooperation among state and federal agencies involved in evaluating applications, and providing assistance to interveners. All the bills that Congress considered stirred sharply conflicting opinions, and none were enacted.[20]

As a result, the licensing process remained largely intact and continued to generate strong protests from both sides of the debate. The nuclear industry and its allies complained that the licensing "morass" of the AEC and then the NRC was arbitrary, unpredictable, and sometimes unreasonable. Leonard J. Koch, manager of nuclear projects for the Illinois Power Company, asserted in 1975 that the "present regulatory process will strangle the nuclear power industry . . . unless some significant revisions are made." Nuclear proponents charged that the regulatory process allowed interveners to raise trivial or barely relevant issues for the sole purpose of delaying the operation of plants. A staff member of the Joint Committee on Atomic Energy accused the AEC in 1972 of "leaning over backwards to accommodate intervention." Nuclear critics responded by pointing out that government and industry studies showed that objections from interveners were not the primary source of delays. They also cited regulatory authorities and licensing board decisions to demonstrate that their actions had raised important safety issues that deserved careful review.[21]

Nuclear power opponents also found much to fault in licensing procedures. They claimed that the AEC and NRC's commitment to licensing plants made the regulatory process a charade intended to give the appearance but not the substance of public participation. Two scholars who studied the licensing process in the early 1970s concluded that the AEC had established "clearer and more orderly procedures . . . to accommodate interventions by citizen groups than have other Federal agencies with major environmental responsibilities." Nevertheless, critics were convinced that licensing proceedings were designed to "assure the AEC's desired goal: the licensing and construction of nuclear power plants as expeditiously as possible." The creation of the NRC did not change nuclear opponents' views on this question.[22]

THE LICENSING OF TMI-2

In a highly polarized atmosphere of intense controversy over nuclear power, one of the plants that made its way through the licensing process was unit 2 of the Three Mile Island Nuclear Generating Station. It shared a narrow island on the Susquehanna River near Middletown, Pennsylvania, with an adjacent nuclear plant; even before the accident that made Three Mile Island a household name, the two units were commonly referred to as TMI-1 and TMI-2. The Three Mile Island facilities were a part of the assets of the General Public Utilities Corporation (GPU), a holding company based in Parsippanny, New Jersey, that was the fourteenth-largest publicly owned electric utility in the United States. GPU owned three operating subsidiaries that in turn owned the TMI plants; the principal owner and operator was the Metropolitan Edison Company, headquartered in Reading, Pennsylvania. Met Ed, as the company was known, provided power to about 350,000 customers in southern and eastern Pennsylvania, though its service area did not include residents who lived closest to Three Mile Island.[23]

TMI-1 was an eight-hundred-megawatt facility that had received a construction permit from the AEC in 1968 and gone into commercial operation in September 1974. The plant that became TMI-2 was originally planned to share the site of the Oyster Creek reactor in New Jersey, owned by Jersey Central Power and Light, another GPU subsidiary. In December 1968, however, GPU decided to move the location of the plant to Three Mile Island, largely because of the threat of labor problems, described by one executive as union "extortion." Although the plant was in an advanced stage of design, GPU concluded that the favorable labor conditions in central Pennsylvania outweighed the disadvantages of changing sites. The move required Burns and Roe, the company chosen as the architect-engineer for the New Jersey site, to make some substantial alterations in the plant's design. The final design of TMI-2 was somewhat different from that of TMI-1, which had employed a different architect-engineer. However, since both units used the same company, Babcock and Wilcox, to manufacture the reactors, associated safety equipment, and other parts of the nuclear steam supply system, the nuclear components of the two plants were virtually identical. Babcock and Wilcox was the smallest of the four American firms that built nuclear steam supply systems. Long a leading producer of equipment for fossil-fuel power plants, it had entered the market for commercial nuclear facilities in the 1950s. A year after TMI-1 went on-line, it advertised its nuclear prowess in *Nuclear News* by quoting John G. (Jack) Herbein, Met Ed's manager of nuclear generation operations: "You could classify GPU and Met-Ed as tough customers. But when it came right down to it, B&W could deliver." The advertisement cited Herbein's hope that, when unit 2 was completed, it would surpass the "excellent start-up and performance record" of TMI-1.[24]

Three Mile Island—the name refers to its length—sits in the Susquehanna River just west of State Highway 441, about ten miles south of Harrisburg, the state capital of Pennsylvania. The Susquehanna, the longest nonnavigable river in North America, has two branches that join in central Pennsylvania. From there the river flows more than one hundred miles to deliver an average of 25 billion gallons of water a day to the Chesapeake Bay. Three Mile Island's 814 acres make it the largest island in the river. Although it had been owned by Met Ed and a predecessor utility company since the early twentieth century, the island remained undeveloped until the 1960s. Area residents had farmed, fished, picnicked, and collected Indian artifacts there.[25]

The economy of the surrounding region was a mix of agriculture and industry. The areas closest to the island were largely rural and dotted with small towns. Three Mile Island was located in Dauphin County, which also included Harrisburg, a city of about 53,000. The county had some heavy industry, notably the large Bethlehem Steel mills in Steelton, along the river between TMI and Harrisburg. It also contained the famous chocolate factories and tourist attractions of the town of Hershey. Lancaster County, which lay to the south and east of Three Mile Island, was the home of some of the richest farmland in the world and was often called the "Garden Spot of America." It hosted a prosperous tourist industry centered in the Pennsylvania Dutch country in its eastern portion. The city of Lancaster, approximately twenty-five miles from the TMI plants, had a population of about 55,000. York County, across the river to the south and west of Three Mile Island, had a similar combination of agriculture and mostly light industry, although, unlike its neighbors, it was not a tourist destination. The city of York, with a population of about 45,000, lay approximately fifteen miles from the TMI facilities.

The towns nearest to the TMI plants were small. Goldsboro, about one mile due west across the river in York County, had fewer than 600 residents. Royalton, two miles north of the plants in Dauphin County, had a population of about 1,100. One mile farther north lay Middletown, home to about 10,000 people, the closest sizeable town to Three Mile Island. The population within a five-mile radius of the site was about 38,000, within a ten-mile radius about 165,000, and within a twenty-mile radius about 636,000.[26]

The culture of the Susquehanna Valley distinguished it from other areas of Pennsylvania, and particularly from the urban and suburban populations that lived near the state's two largest cities, Philadelphia and Pittsburgh. Although informed commentators recognized the pitfalls of generalizing about the values and priorities of hundreds of thousands of people, they discerned distinct qualities in the population of central Pennsylvania. It was, most obviously, politically and socially conservative. Paul B. Beers, a columnist for the *Harrisburg Evening News* and a keen observer of the affairs of the Susquehanna Valley, described the prevailing principles of the area in 1973: "common decency within orthodox morality, unoppressive and good-natured hometown leadership, the sanctity of contract and property, and, in general, the doctrines of the Puritan Ethic." Politically, the most conservative part of the region was Lancaster County; it had not sent a Democrat to Congress since 1828, when it elected James Buchanan, a future president of the United States (and even he was a lapsed Federalist). The rest of the tri-county region was of a similar political persuasion. In addition, many of the people of central Pennsylvania were deeply religious. Shortly after the Three Mile Island accident, a telephone survey of area residents found that, in households

in which no family members evacuated, 65 percent cited their conviction that "whatever happens is in God's hands" as a reason for not leaving their homes.

According to the same survey, 71 percent of the respondents said they
did not evacuate because they were "waiting for [an] evacuation order."
This was consistent with another much-noticed characteristic of the
people of central Pennsylvania—their respect for authority. They tended
to be stoic, unflappable, and deferential to their leaders, especially at the
state and local level. Officeholders and other authorities generally enjoyed
a reservoir of goodwill that could be squandered, but they had to earn
the disrespect of their constituents. In keeping with their conservatism,
residents of central Pennsylvania were proudly patriotic. They loved their
country intensely, though they generally did not care much for its government. They were not inclined to extend their innate respect for authority to the federal government, especially its bureaucracy, unless they
had reason to do so. Their reservations perhaps reflected a perception
that the federal government was too big, too distant, and too unsympa-
thetic to their values. Two months after the Three Mile Island accident,
a resident of Middletown demonstrated this attitude when he advised his
neighbors: "Don't listen to the big national government that can't, that
doesn't touch you anymore. . . . This is our town. This is our land."[27]

The nuclear power controversy did not elicit much interest among the
citizens of central Pennsylvania, even though, by the mid-1970s, several
plants were operating or under construction in the general area. In addition to the Three Mile Island reactors, two plants at Peach Bottom in
southern York County began operation in 1974, two others were under
construction near Berwick, about a hundred miles northeast of Harrisburg, and another two received construction permits for a site near Lim-
erick, about seventy-five miles east of Harrisburg, in 1974. The population around TMI-2 was receptive to the plant, and its licensing proceeded
with little opposition. In 1974, Met Ed conducted a survey of 1,178 residents of various locations in eastern and central Pennsylvania, including York, and found that 55 percent approved of siting a nuclear facility in their area. The citizens of Middletown and its vicinity welcomed
the jobs and lower taxes that the new plant would offer, and their favorable attitudes toward both TMI plants were reinforced by Met Ed's
aggressive public relations programs. The antinuclear movement had
little influence among the people of the Susquehanna Valley; opposition
groups were small and their meetings sparsely attended. One local jour-

nalist commented that "most people around the [Harrisburg] area considered them a bunch of radicals." Anything regarded as radical did not attract much support in central Pennsylvania.[28]

Metropolitan Edison and its sister GPU subsidiary, Jersey Central Power and Light, first submitted an application for a construction permit for the plant that became TMI-2 to the AEC on April 29, 1968. When GPU decided to move the prospective site for the plant from New Jersey, the operating companies filed an amendment to the application in March 1969 that proposed the Three Mile Island location. After a series of meetings and requests for further information on safety issues, the AEC's regulatory staff and the Advisory Committee on Reactor Safeguards found the application acceptable. When the Atomic Safety and Licensing Board conducted a public hearing in Middletown in October 1969, no interveners expressed opposition to the plant. On December 11, 1969, the AEC issued a construction permit for TMI-2, which allowed construction to go forward while some safety issues remained unresolved.[29]

On February 15, 1974, Met Ed submitted an application for an operating license. Once again the AEC's regulatory staff and the Advisory Committee on Reactor Safeguards conducted detailed reviews; they required much more information at this stage of the process. The AEC also provided an opportunity for the public to participate in a hearing for an operating license, and this time, two antinuclear groups, Citizens for a Safe Environment and the York Committee for a Safe Environment, raised a series of safety questions. Among other complaints, they alleged that emergency evacuation plans for the plant were "inadequate and unworkable." The NRC staff responded that the population of a quadrant containing a plume of radiation released by an accident could be evacuated to a distance of five miles in three to six hours without receiving heavy exposures. State and county civil defense authorities supported this position. The Atomic Safety and Licensing Board that conducted public hearings rejected the interveners' contentions, and on February 8, 1978, the NRC issued an operating license for TMI-2. The license included conditions that required Met Ed to carry out a series of tests successfully before the NRC authorized full power operation of the plant.

While Met Ed was working to fulfill the NRC's requirements, plant opponents appealed the approval of the operating license. The issue that received the greatest attention, partly because it had not been raised earlier, was the possibility that an airplane could crash into the plant on its way to Harrisburg International Airport, about three miles up the river on the edge of Middletown. The plant was built to withstand collision by a large airplane, but interveners contended that some planes using the Harrisburg airport could present a serious threat to public health and safety. The Atomic Safety and Licensing Appeal Board, which reviewed decisions of the licensing boards, concluded that the probability of a crash that would compromise the safety of the plant was exceedingly low. It further suggested that if more planes surpassing the design basis for the plant flew into the Harrisburg airport in the future, corrective measures, such as restrictions on air space or hardening plant structures, could be taken. The appeal board agreed to hold further hearings on the issue but, in a sharply divided opinion, denied the interveners' request that operation of the plant be suspended. On September 15, 1978, the commissioners unanimously upheld the ruling of the appeal board but ordered it to gather, during its hearings, additional information about the likelihood of a crash beyond the design basis of TMI-2.[30]

As the appeals were considered, Met Ed ran into difficulties during the start-up activities for TMI-2. On March 28, 1978, even before the reactor first sustained a chain reaction to produce energy, one of its reactor coolant pumps failed. Other problems occurred with major valves, feedwater pumps, and emergency core cooling systems. In the year after it received its operating license, TMI-2 experienced at least twenty reactor trips. A trip, also called a scram, is an immediate shutdown of a reactor, either automatically or manually by an operator, in response to a malfunction. The problems at TMI-2 were not unusual; all reactors demonstrated kinks and deficiencies during their start-up and testing periods. The plant was off-line about 71 percent of the time during its testing phase, which ranked it below average in the "efficiency of its start-up." In the cases of safety equipment failures, the backup systems worked according to design, and the NRC found TMI-2's performance to be satisfactory. The plant produced power for distribution on the grid for the first time in September 1978 and began commercial operation on December 30, 1978, at which time it reached 80 percent of its capacity. The declaration of commercial operation was an essential step for entering the plant into the company's rate base as a part of the financial oversight of the Pennsylvania Public Utility Commission. Achieving commercial operation before the end of the calendar year enabled Met Ed to secure certain rate and tax benefits, but the process was completely separate from the NRC's safety evaluation.[31]

The TMI-2 plant had a capacity of nine hundred electrical megawatts. It contained 190,000 cubic yards of concrete, 24,000 tons of steel, and 740 miles of electrical wiring. It cost about $700 million to build. Together,

Figure 3. Three Mile Island, looking northeast. The reactor buildings are the concrete structures with domes. TMI-1 is at the left center of the photo between its two cooling towers. TMI-2 is in the center of the photo (NRC).

the two TMI units required an investment of more than $1 billion, about $350 million of which went for construction payrolls. During normal operation, the plants employed about five hundred people. Visually, the most striking features of the two plants were their four cooling towers, which rose 350 feet above the gently rolling hills of the Susquehanna Valley. The towers cooled the water that was used to condense the steam that drove the plants' turbines, and that became heated in the process. The cooling was done to avoid the thermal pollution caused by discharging heated condensate water into the river. The cooling towers were not a part of the nuclear steam supply system and, contrary to popular misconceptions, did not release clouds of radioactive vapor into the atmosphere.[32]

There was nothing particularly prominent or noteworthy about TMI-2 when it went into operation. It was one of dozens of plants licensed after the bandwagon-market boom of the late 1960s and early 1970s. It did not incite large demonstrations, prompt lengthy legal proceedings, or generate a great deal of interest even in central Pennsylvania. Other plants were larger, more controversial, and a much more visible part of the debate over nuclear power. One of the few critical reports appeared in the *York Daily Record,* which ran a series of articles suggesting that Three Mile Island posed a grave threat to the citizens of the area. Walter Creitz, president of Met Ed, responded in a op-ed article on March 26, 1979, insisting that the plants were "operated in a way that places top priority on safety." He chided the newspaper for misleading "its readers toward a conclusion that TMI threatens not only their lives but also those of generations to come."[33] Two days later, the credibility of Creitz's assurances was profoundly impaired when TMI-2 involuntarily emerged from relative obscurity to become the most famous and most reviled nuclear power plant in the world.

Chapter 3

Defense in Depth

An operating nuclear power reactor performs the same basic functions as a teakettle—it heats water and produces steam. The steam, in turn, drives turbines to generate electrical power. This process, however simple in principle, requires an enormously complex, carefully fabricated, and finely tuned system of pipes, valves, pumps, cables, instruments, electrical circuits, vents, and other components that make the technology bewildering to untrained observers. The heat in a reactor comes from fission of the nuclei of uranium atoms contained in fuel pellets in the core of the reactor. When uranium atoms undergo fission in a controlled chain reaction, they give off vast amounts of energy, which is used to boil water and produce steam. The process of fission also creates a huge inventory of radioactive elements known as fission products. The possibility of an accident that releases massive quantities of fission products to the environment is the chief danger of nuclear power.

Nuclear plants were built to generate sufficient heat for the maximum output of power within their design capabilities but to guard against the production of excessive heat that could cause an accident and endanger the public. Nearly all the commercial reactors in the United States were cooled by the circulation of water through the core. In the event of a major loss of coolant from the core, the reactor could conceivably generate enough heat to overwhelm safety systems and structures and spew hazardous levels of radiation into the surrounding area. Therefore, ensuring an adequate supply of water for cooling purposes was the key to avoiding a severe accident. Nuclear facilities included safety systems that served two purposes: first, to prevent an accident, and second, to limit the consequences if an accident occurred. When utilities ordered dramatically larger plants in the mid- and late 1960s, some experts became concerned that in a worst-case accident safety equipment might fail. The uncertainties they expressed about the performance of safety systems not only provided the basis for much of the controversy over nuclear power during the 1970s but also spawned many of the fears about the potential consequences of the accident at Three Mile Island in 1979.

REACTOR SAFETY

From the earliest days of commercial nuclear power, reactor vendors and the AEC had relied on a concept known as defense-in-depth to promote reactor safety. As a result of the many unresolved technical questions about reactor performance and the risks of nuclear power, they used conservative assumptions, redundant safety systems, and multiple barriers to protect against a large release of radiation to the environment. Neither the industry nor the AEC dismissed the possibility of a serious reactor accident, and they sought to make certain that if one occurred, it did not turn into a catastrophe. Clifford K. Beck, the AEC's deputy director of regulation, summarized this approach in a statement presented to the Joint Committee on Atomic Energy in 1967: "In overall perspective, the purpose of the combined elements in this system of protection is to insure that reactor facilities are designed, built, and operated to high standards, with specific emphasis placed on reducing to the lowest feasible level the likelihood of [a] serious accident, and with provisions made to confine or minimize the escape of radioactivity to the environment if a serious accident should occur."[1]

Although the designs and safety features in nuclear plants varied substantially, they all used a system of control rods to operate the reactor, manipulate the level of power, and prevent accidents. Control rods provided the first means of defense against the effects of an excursion, a term that safety experts often applied to an unplanned increase in the rate of nuclear fission and, as a consequence, in the level of heat in the core. The control rods contained elements, such as boron or cadmium, that absorbed neutrons, the particles that cause fission by colliding with atomic nuclei. When the rods were inserted into the core, they stopped the fission process. They automatically tripped (or "scrammed") the reactor if, for example, the power level rose above the designated settings or excessive heat or pressure was detected in the core. The reactor could also be scrammed manually by plant operators. The rapid insertion of the control rods in response to an indication of an operational problem was the primary, but not the only, means of preventing accidents. Other systems critical to avoiding accidents included sensitive and redundant instrumentation, emergency electrical power to run the essential plant equipment if the normal supply was interrupted, and backup equipment in the event of a failure in a basic system.

If, despite all precautions, a reactor accident took place, nuclear plants were designed so that the consequences, both to the facility and to the population beyond its boundaries, would be limited. During the 1960s and 1970s, reactor experts' primary concern was an accident in which the supply of coolant to the core would be lost because of a rupture in a large pipe or other major breakdown. Under the worst-case circumstances, the core could overheat in a matter of seconds. Even the rapid insertion of control rods would not end the emergency. Control rods would shut down the major source of heat by halting the fission process, but they would not stop the creation of decay heat, which resulted from the spontaneous radioactive decay of fission products already in the core. At its highest point at the time of the shutdown, decay heat would amount to only about 7 percent of the level before the reactor tripped. But without adequate cooling, this would still be enough to cause serious damage to, and perhaps to melt, the core. If the core melted, it could set off a series of events that could allow radioactivity to escape into the environment. A core meltdown was the most dangerous potential consequence of a reactor accident.

In the event of a serious accident, an inherent feature common to all reactors would reduce the release of radioactive materials. The reactor fuel pellets and the metal tubes in which they were encased, called cladding, would trap significant amounts of the fission products created in the core. The extent of the protection provided by the fuel and cladding was uncertain, but it was an important first barrier to the release of radioactivity. The next barrier was the pressure vessel, a huge container made of steel three to ten inches thick, which held the core of the reactor, including the fuel assemblies, control rods, and related equipment, as well as the coolant. To protect further against the effects of an accident, reactor builders added a series of engineered safety features. Although the safety systems varied in design and operation among different types of reactors, they served the same basic functions. They included emergency core cooling systems (ECCS) placed in reactors to remove heat and reduce excessive pressure. These systems were designed to flood the core with water in the case of loss of coolant. Another system of filters, vents, scrubbers, and air circulators would collect and retain radioactive gases and particles released by an accident before they escaped from the plant.

The final line of defense was the massive containment building, often a dome-shaped structure made of steel and concrete that rose as high as twenty stories. In some designs, it consisted of double steel walls covered with concrete designed to keep fission products inside. The containment building surrounded the reactor, the associated steam-producing equipment, and the safety systems.[2]

THE ECCS CONTROVERSY

In the early years of commercial nuclear power, reactor designers were confident that in an unlikely worst-case accident—one in which a loss of coolant caused the core to melt and the molten core, in turn, penetrated the pressure vessel—the containment structure would prevent a massive release of radiation to the environment. Even if the plant were destroyed, public health would not be jeopardized. As proposed plants increased significantly in size after the mid-1960s, however, experts began to worry that under some improbable but still plausible conditions, a core melt could lead to a breach of containment. They postulated that, in the event of a loss-of-coolant accident, the decay heat in newer, larger plants could cause the containment structure to fail. The greatest worry was that fuel would melt not only through the pressure vessel but also through the thick layer of concrete at the foundation of the containment building. As the intensely radioactive fuel continued on a downward path into the ground, it could spew radiation into the environment with disastrous consequences. This was the scenario that reactor experts called the China syndrome. Other possible dangers of a core meltdown were that the molten fuel would breach containment by reacting with water to cause a steam explosion or by releasing elements that could combine to cause a chemical explosion.

At the prodding of its Advisory Committee on Reactor Safeguards, which first sounded the alarm about the China syndrome, the AEC established a special task force in 1966 to look into the problem of core melting. The committee, chaired by William K. Ergen, a reactor safety expert at Oak Ridge National Laboratory, submitted its findings to the AEC in October 1967. The report offered assurances that a core meltdown was highly improbable, but it also acknowledged that a loss-of-coolant accident could lead to a breach of containment if the emergency core cooling systems did not perform as designed. Therefore, containment could not be regarded as a virtually inviolable barrier to the escape of radioactivity, one that could be breached only by calamitous happenstance, such as a door inadvertently left open. This conclusion represented a milestone in the evolution of reactor regulation and imposed a modified approach to reactor safety. If under some circumstances the containment structure might not hold, the key to protecting the public from a large release of radiation was to prevent accidents severe enough to cause it to fail. And this depended heavily on a properly designed and functioning ECCS.

The problem that faced the AEC's regulatory staff when it reviewed applications for plants was that experimental work on and experience with emergency cooling was very limited. Older plants had, at best, only primitive emergency core cooling systems. The AEC lacked conclusive evidence to show that ECCS would perform as designed, and finding a way to test the reliability of emergency cooling became the primary concern of the agency's safety research program. Plans had been under way since the early 1960s to build an experimental reactor that would provide data about the effects of a loss-of-coolant accident. For a variety of reasons, including weak management of the test program, a change of design, and reduced funding, progress on the tests was chronically delayed. Despite the objections of the regulatory staff, the AEC diverted money from safety research projects to work on the development of fast-breeder reactors, an advanced technology that could create a larger amount of fissile material for reactor fuel than the amount of fuel they consumed. AEC policy makers viewed research on fast breeders as, in the words of Chairman Glenn T. Seaborg, a "priority national goal" that could assure "an essentially unlimited energy supply, free from problems of fuel resources and atmospheric contamination."

To the consternation of the AEC, experiments that were finally run at its reactor testing station in Idaho in late 1970 and early 1971 suggested that ECCS might not work as designed. Researchers ran a series of scaled-down tests, referred to as "semiscale" tests, on a core that was only 9 inches long (compared to 144 inches in a power reactor). The experiments were conducted by heating a simulated core electrically, allowing the cooling water to escape, and then injecting the emergency coolant. To the surprise of the investigators, the high steam pressure created in the vessel by the loss of coolant blocked the flow of water from the ECCS. Without ever reaching the core, about 90 percent of the emergency coolant flowed out of the same break that had caused the loss of coolant in the first place.

In many ways, the semiscale experiments were not accurate simulations of designs or conditions in power reactors. Not only the size, scale, and design but also the channels that directed the flow of coolant in the test model were markedly different from those in an actual reactor. Nevertheless, the results of the tests were disquieting. They introduced new uncertainty into assessing the performance of ECCS. The outcome of the tests had not been anticipated, and it called into question the analytical methods used to predict what would happen in a loss-of-coolant accident.

The semiscale tests caught the AEC unprepared and uncertain how to respond. It established an internal task force to review the problem of emergency cooling and, while waiting for the findings of the investigation, it tried to keep information about the tests from getting out to the public. The results came at an awkward time for the AEC. It was under intense pressure from the Joint Committee on Atomic Energy to streamline the licensing process and eliminate excessive delays. At the same time, Seaborg was appealing—successfully—to President Nixon for support of the breeder reactor as a means to ensure adequate energy supplies in the future. Controversy over the semiscale tests could slow the licensing process and undermine White House support for the breeder program. In addition, by the spring of 1971, nuclear critics opposed the licensing of several proposed reactors, and news of the semiscale experiments undoubtedly would spur their efforts.

For those reasons, the AEC sought to resolve the ECCS issue as quickly and quietly as possible. It wanted to settle the uncertainties about safety without arousing a sustained public debate. Even before the task force assigned to study the ECCS problem completed its work, the commissioners decided to publish interim acceptance criteria for emergency core cooling systems that licensees would have to meet. They approved a series of requirements they believed would ensure that ECCS would prevent a core melt in a plant that suffered a loss-of-coolant accident. The AEC did not prescribe methods of conforming with the interim criteria, but in effect, it mandated that manufacturers and utilities set an upper limit on the amount of heat generated in reactors. In some cases, this would force utilities to reduce the peak operating temperatures (and hence the power) of their plants. Harold L. Price, the AEC's director of regulation, told a press conference on June 19, 1971, that, even though it was impossible to "guarantee absolute safety," he was "confident that these criteria will assure that the emergency core cooling systems will perform adequately to protect the temperature of the core from getting out of hand."

The interim ECCS criteria failed to achieve the AEC's objectives. News about the semiscale experiments inevitably leaked to outsiders, which triggered complaints even from friendly observers about the agency's handling of the issue. It also prompted calls from nuclear critics for a licensing moratorium and a shutdown of the eleven plants then operating. The Union of Concerned Scientists, which was still a new and largely unknown organization, issued a report on the ECCS issue that took sharp exception to the AEC's position. It concluded that emergency core cooling systems were "likely to fail" in the event of a loss-of-coolant accident, producing a "peace-time catastrophe whose scale . . . might well exceed anything the nation has ever known."

The AEC insisted that its critics exaggerated the severity of the ECCS problem. The regulatory staff viewed the results of the failed semiscale tests as serious but believed that the technical issues raised by the experiments would be resolved within a short time. Although the mock-up ECCS had not performed according to expectations in some tests, the outcome in others had turned out as predicted. The AEC did not regard the unsuccessful tests as indications that existing designs were fundamentally flawed. But its approach to the ECCS controversy played into the hands of critics. Instead of frankly acknowledging the potential significance of the problem and taking time to fully evaluate its technical uncertainties, the agency hastily issued the interim criteria in a futile effort to keep the issue from undermining public confidence in reactor safety or causing licensing delays.[3]

To help resolve the technical issues, the AEC scheduled public hearings to collect information about the ECCS question. It hoped the results would provide the basis for a final regulation to replace the interim criteria and thus prevent the need to deal with the issue repeatedly during individual licensing proceedings for the more than fifty plant applications under review. The ECCS hearings began on January 27, 1972, before a three-member panel. The style of the hearings was legislative rather than judicial, but the AEC also allowed parties in the proceedings to question witnesses, who presented their testimony under oath. Nuclear critics, who combined their resources to form a coalition called the National Intervenors, announced that they would participate in the hearings because the AEC was "needlessly jeopardizing the lives of hundreds of thousands of Americans." The interveners' most prominent participants were Daniel Ford of the Union of Concerned Scientists, who served as their technical expert despite his lack of training in fields related to nuclear technology, and Myron Cherry, who, in his capacity as counsel for the National Intervenors, displayed an aggressive and often belligerent approach to interrogating witnesses. Even before the hearings got under way, informed observers predicted that they would "drag on for months."[4]

The hearings quickly produced a great deal of acrimony. The interveners probed for weaknesses and inconsistencies in the AEC's position that the interim criteria and the defense-in-depth principle provided adequate protection from the effects of a major accident. Cherry grilled AEC regulatory staff witnesses with a barrage of pointed questions and frequently caustic remarks. Early in the proceedings, he directed his questions and comments at Stephen H. Hanauer, technical adviser to the AEC's director of regulation and chair of the task force appointed to investigate ECCS issues. He complained that Hanauer had not volunteered information that Cherry regarded as important about record-keeping procedures. "Dr. Hanauer . . . is *not* contributing to an honest dissertation in this hearing," he said, and then added, "All I am suggesting is that that kind of attitude prompts me to begin thinking about perjury and every other thing. . . . I will use everything that is within the law to make sure that a witness who is shading testimony will be properly and appropriately penalized for it." AEC attorneys took sharp issue with Cherry's allegations, and the barbed exchanges over this and other disputed matters set the tone for the hearings.

The contending sides in the hearings consumed much time jockeying over procedures, access to AEC documents, and the qualifications of participants. Industry representatives and members of the hearing board cited strong reservations about Ford's qualifications to act as the technical adviser for the interveners, but, after spending almost a full day on the issue, the board allowed Ford to question witnesses. He soon proved that, although he was not a nuclear scientist or engineer, he had learned enough about the subject to ask informed questions. On April 6, 1972, he quizzed Milton Shaw, the director of the AEC's Office of Reactor Technology and Development, who was responsible for the agency's research programs. Shaw, a confident and articulate proponent of the fast-breeder reactor, often viewed the AEC's regulatory staff as an obstacle to his goals, even to the point of forbidding researchers on ECCS experiments to discuss their work with regulatory officials. During the ECCS hearings, Shaw forcefully defended the interim criteria and the AEC's reactor safety programs. He apparently did not prepare thoroughly for his appearance in the hearings, however, and Ford posed a series of questions about technical matters that he could not answer. "Mr. Shaw, what, if any, experiments demonstrate the conservatism of applying steady state heat transfer correlations to blowdown analysis?" Ford asked at one point. "I cannot recall which experiments or analytical work were used in arriving at that conclusion," Shaw replied, in a refrain to which he returned often. *Nucleonics Week* reported that Shaw was "verbally floored" for "several embarrassing hours during which he resembled a witness who has just been undermined by [famed fictional lawyer] Perry Mason."[5]

In addition to challenging the integrity and technical knowledge of AEC staff members, the interveners pursued a number of substantive issues regarding the performance of emergency core cooling systems. One was the problem raised by the semiscale tests of whether sufficient cooling water from ECCS would reach the core in the event of an accident. Another was the possibility of fuel rod failure that would prevent core cooling. Tests conducted at Oak Ridge National Laboratory indicated that in a loss-of-coolant accident the fuel cladding might swell enough to block the circulation of cooling water. Or, as a result of elevated temperatures in the core, the cladding could become brittle and shatter. If the cladding fractured and the core collapsed, water from the ECCS would not circulate through the molten mass that this loss of "core geometry" created. The temperature at which fuel cladding might become brittle was uncertain, though the industry claimed it would not occur below twenty-seven hundred degrees Fahrenheit. A third major question was the reliability of computer programs and calculational techniques used to predict the performance of the ECCS, which drew on a limited base of experimental evidence.

The AEC acknowledged that important issues regarding ECCS remained to be resolved, especially with verifying computer analyses, but it insisted that its interim criteria provided an ample margin of safety. It applied what it regarded as conservative assumptions to the requirements that licensees had to meet. For example, it stipulated that in a loss-of-coolant accident the temperature of the fuel cladding must not exceed twenty-three hundred degrees. Further, the criteria specified that plant designers assume that, during the "blowdown" phase of an accident, when the reactor underwent a rapid loss of coolant, water from the ECCS would bypass the core. This would mean that one-fourth to one-third of the total ECCS coolant would be lost (the remainder would enter the vessel after the blowdown ended and pressure fell). The AEC did not prescribe methods for complying with the ECCS criteria, which necessarily depended on projections and computer analyses. But it emphasized that its "conservative view of present knowledge" and the defense-in-depth

approach to designing and building nuclear plants offered a "high degree of assurance" that the public would not be exposed to hazardous
levels of radiation even in the improbable event of an accident.[6]

Nuclear critics expressed strong reservations about the soundness of
the AEC's strategy. Even before the ECCS hearings began, the Union of
Concerned Scientists published a critique of the agency's requirements,
in which it charged that allowing a potential maximum cladding temperature of twenty-three hundred degrees was excessive, that the computer programs used to predict ECCS performance were "highly inadequate," and that the interim criteria were "operationally vague and
meaningless." It denied the AEC's claim that the criteria reflected conservative engineering judgment. The major revelation of the ECCS hearings was that a number of reactor experts held similar views on some
safety issues. Several members of the AEC's regulatory staff and researchers from Oak Ridge and the National Reactor Testing Station in
Idaho voiced doubts that the interim criteria provided sufficient protection from the consequences of a severe reactor accident.

The principal, though not the only, causes of uncertainty were the
computer programs used to design and evaluate the performance of emergency core cooling systems in accident situations. Alvin Weinberg, director of Oak Ridge National Laboratory, summarized those concerns
in a letter to AEC chairman Schlesinger on February 9, 1972: "As an old
timer who grew up in this business before the computing machine dom-
inated it so completely, I have a basic distrust of very elaborate calculations of complex situations, especially when the calculations have not
been checked by full-scale experiments. . . . It seems to me—when the
consequences of failure are serious—then the ability of codes to arrive
at a conservative prediction must be verified." Most experts who agreed
with Weinberg's position did not endorse the interveners' argument that
the interim criteria were necessarily invalid or indefensible, but they did
suggest that existing computer analyses were too ambiguous or unproven
to reliably judge the extent of conservatism in the designs and regulation
of ECCS.[7]

The reservations about the interim criteria, and the lack of definitive
information about the performance of vital safety systems that the ECCS
hearings highlighted, prompted both the nuclear industry and the AEC
to reexamine their assumptions and step up their efforts to resolve outstanding issues. When witnesses who had expressed misgivings about the
reliability of emergency core cooling systems were cross-examined by attorneys for the nuclear industry, they acknowledged errors in some of

their calculations, which placed the interim criteria in a more favorable light. Nevertheless, industry representatives recognized that weaknesses in and doubts about ECCS required corrective action. One Westinghouse official told Ford privately that the hearings were having a "good effect" on his company because they were "bringing to everyone's attention a lot of concerns and problems." As a result, Westinghouse and other nuclear vendors developed new experiments to test ECCS and sought to make major improvements in computer evaluation models. In addition, Westinghouse redesigned its fuel assemblies to reduce the potential maximum cladding temperature in the event of a loss-of-coolant accident.[8]

The AEC conducted a careful reassessment of the bases for its interim criteria. Schlesinger was troubled by the questions that the interveners raised and the reservations that AEC staff members and other experts aired during the ECCS hearings. After receiving Weinberg's letter about potential flaws in computer calculations used to evaluate ECCS performance, he asked for an explanation of the ways in which the interim criteria did and did not reflect conservative assumptions. The regulatory staff listed more than twenty worst-case assumptions or conservative estimates used to project the consequences of a severe loss-of-coolant accident and the operation of ECCS. It also cited "a few nonconservative aspects" of the interim criteria and calculations, including the important issues of core collapse and clad swelling. The staff focused on those matters as it undertook a thorough review of the interim criteria in light of the information presented in the ECCS hearings.

In April 1973, the regulatory staff issued its final recommendations for criteria that took a more conservative approach to cladding temperatures, core geometry, and other potential threats to core cooling. It reduced the maximum allowable cladding temperature from twenty-three hundred to twenty-two hundred degrees; the peak temperature applied to the cladding of the hottest fuel rod, so that about 80 percent of the fuel rods would not exceed nineteen hundred degrees. The staff also specified that the core must be designed so that swelling, rupture, or other losses of geometry would not prevent cooling. And it added new requirements to address weaknesses and uncertainties in computer analyses of ECCS performance. The regulatory staff estimated that, if the commissioners accepted its recommendations, some plants would be forced to reduce their power output by as much as 20 percent. When the industry complained about the prospect of such large power deratings, director of regulation Manning Muntzing commented, "We find the added conservatism to be dictated by safety."[9]

The ECCS hearings finally ended on July 25, 1973. They consumed 125 days in sessions before the hearing panel, accumulated 22,380 pages of transcripts, and according to *Nuclear Industry*, created "enough bitterness and ill-will to launch a small war." After listening to oral arguments from the participants in the proceedings, the commissioners unanimously approved the recommendations of the regulatory staff virtually intact. The AEC issued the final version of its rule on December 28, 1973. The new ECCS regulations drew strong complaints from both interveners and nuclear industry representatives. Henry Kendall of the Union of Concerned Scientists suggested that the revisions in the interim criteria were "merely cosmetic changes." He insisted that power deratings of 50 percent or more were necessary to provide an adequate margin of safety for the operation of nuclear plants. Industry officials, by contrast, contended that the regulations "would have significant and possibly prohibitive economic impacts" while adding little to reactor safety.[10]

The ECCS controversy, which continued despite the AEC's efforts to evaluate competing arguments and make appropriate revisions in its regulations, reflected the emotional and partisan nature of the nuclear power debate. It also seriously undermined the credibility of the AEC as an effective regulator. The hearings did not attract extensive media attention, but the coverage they received in popular newspapers and magazines and scientific journals was generally unfavorable to the AEC. The stories published about the issue often questioned the AEC's commitment to safety by emphasizing the doubts about the interim criteria expressed by some reactor experts and highlighted by the interveners during the hearings. Although it is impossible to measure the impact of the debate on Congress, the scientific community, or the public with any precision, it clearly contributed significantly, if not decisively, to the demise of the AEC. The ECCS hearings, Ralph Lapp commented in April 1973, were "the AEC's technological Vietnam."[11]

REACTOR SAFETY PROBLEMS

The performance of ECCS was the most visible and contentious reactor safety question of the 1970s, but not the only one. A series of other issues commanded the attention of reactor safety experts and fueled the nuclear power controversy. In some cases, growing operating experience with commercial reactors revealed unanticipated problems. In May 1972, the Rochester Gas and Electric Corporation discovered serious damage to the fuel cladding in its Robert E. Ginna Nuclear Power Plant in upstate New York. Within a short time, the same signs of partially collapsed or crushed fuel rods showed up in a few other plants. Investigation revealed that the densification, or shrinking, of some fuel pellets in the affected plants had caused them to slip down in their cladding. The implications for reactor safety were unclear, but the fuel densification problem raised the possibility of radiation leaking from the fuel or, worse, of impaired core cooling in the event of an accident. As a result, the AEC required derating of the power output at several plants until the flawed fuel rods were replaced with an improved design.[12]

In addition, new evidence that important pipes in reactors had developed cracks generated considerable concern. In September 1974, as the AEC's existence was drawing to a close, the Commonwealth Edison Company reported a leak of cooling water in its Dresden-2 plant near Morris, Illinois. The source of the leak was found to be small cracks in piping with a four-inch diameter, and the AEC ordered twenty-one other plants of similar design to shut down within sixty days to inspect for defective pipes or welds. While the extent and cause of the problem were still being investigated, Commonwealth Edison detected cracks in ten-inch diameter pipes in Dresden-2's emergency core cooling system. This discovery increased the potential gravity of the issue, and it fell to the NRC, which had begun operating just a few days earlier, to respond. It ordered the immediate shutdown of twenty-three reactors for new inspections. Chairman Anders told his former AEC colleague Dixy Lee Ray that the NRC's action was "severe," and the White House staff viewed it as important enough to inform President Ford.

The NRC established a Pipe Crack Study Group, and in October 1975 it reported that the probability of pipes cracking to an extent where they created a major safety hazard was very low. As long as cracks were located and faulty pipes replaced, they did not constitute a significant safety issue. It recommended a series of steps that licensees could take to prevent pipe cracks from posing serious safety problems, including augmented inspections and use of materials less likely to crack. The NRC affirmed that existing means of inspecting pipes and finding leaks had proved reliable, and it suggested that even if a large crack developed and went undetected, the public would be adequately protected by ECCS, containment, and other defense-in-depth mechanisms. Nuclear critics were not convinced. David Comey charged in October 1978 that the NRC was "not acting fast enough to avert a pipe rupture that would result in a catastrophic reactor meltdown and major casualties."[13]

In other cases, safety issues arose not directly from operating experience, but, like the question of ECCS performance, from hypothetical projections about causes and effects of severe accidents. One problem was the potential for a series of failures that would disable control-rod mechanisms and prevent a reactor scram in the event of a malfunction (or "transient"), such as a loss of power to feed-water pumps. This scenario, which reactor experts called "anticipated transient without scram," could lead to a rapid increase in power and pressure in the core and conceivably to a core meltdown. An anticipated transient was expected to occur one or more times during the life of a nuclear plant, and, as with many other safety issues, the Advisory Committee on Reactor Safeguards first raised alarms about whether a reactor might fail to scram under such conditions. The AEC, after conducting an investigation and instructing nuclear vendors to evaluate their designs, weighed requirements to upgrade the reliability of scram mechanisms in plants operating or under construction and to improve designs to cope with the problem in future applications. One AEC staff member commented that the "great bulk" of a "great long list of possible anticipated transients" did not amount to a "hill of beans," but he added that a few could be serious. The nuclear industry complained that the position of the AEC and later the NRC was "excessively conservative," and that the chances of a failure in reactor shutdown systems were so low that costs of fully carrying out all proposed regulatory requirements were unjustified. The NRC's approach continued to generate sharp criticism as it considered a final regulation in the late 1970s.[14]

While the AEC's regulatory staff and the NRC were working on questions concerning ECCS, fuel densification, pipe cracks, and failures to scram, they were also reviewing a growing list of unresolved safety issues. In December 1972, the Advisory Committee on Reactor Safeguards compiled a list of generic items that applied to all reactors or at least to groups of reactors. It cited 25 safety issues it considered to be satisfactorily resolved and another 22 unresolved ones. The AEC responded that it would give high priority to the "resolution pending" list and try to complete action on most of them within several months. By early 1974 it had resolved five of those items, but it had also added 11 new items to the same list. When the NRC began operations, it inherited from the AEC a total of 34 "diverse, difficult technical issues" that remained unresolved. In early 1979, the NRC identified 133 "generic tasks" that it was considering. It assigned priorities to those items for the first time and specified 20 as "potentially risk significant issues that apply to operating or near operating plants." By focusing on those items, it sought to finish its evaluation of unresolved safety issues in a "timely fashion."[15]

The fact that the NRC did not halt the licensing or operation of nuclear power facilities while it addressed unresolved safety issues triggered attacks from nuclear critics, who argued that the NRC was endangering public health. John Abbotts, who collaborated with Ralph Nader on a 1977 book titled *The Menace of Atomic Energy,* charged that "on generic issues, the NRC's program can be categorized as incomplete and in a state of disrepair." It indicated, he declared, "that the agency is more interested in allowing continued plant operation than upholding its own safety regulations." The NRC denied the allegation by explaining that it assessed outstanding safety issues within a framework of "maintaining adequate safety margins through the overall philosophy of defense-in-depth." In some cases, the agency had quickly imposed derating or taken other steps to maintain safety margins. But in most cases, it concluded that immediate action was not necessary. As always, the NRC maintained that defense-in-depth more than compensated for uncertainties in reactor design and operation.[16]

THE BROWNS FERRY FIRE

Unresolved safety issues were just part of a running argument between nuclear proponents, who claimed that the principle of defense-in-depth provided an ample margin of safety, and nuclear critics, who insisted that the AEC and NRC's approach was unproven and unsatisfactory. Two months after the NRC began operating, a fire with potentially severe consequences at the Browns Ferry nuclear station near Decatur, Alabama, provided new fuel for the debate. The Browns Ferry site included three large reactors owned and operated by the Tennessee Valley Authority; each had a generating capacity of 1,067 megawatts. Unit 1 had gone into commercial operation in August 1974, unit 2 had done so six months later, and unit 3 was still under construction. On March 22, 1975, the completed plants were operating at full power as several employees checked for air leaks between the unit 1 reactor building and a cable-spreading room one floor beneath the control room shared by both reactors.

The cable-spreading room housed hundreds of electrical wires and cables that provided power to monitor and operate the reactors. In openings where cables, wires, and pipes penetrated the walls between the containment structure and the cable-spreading room, polyurethane foam was used as a sealant to prevent air leaks. The common practice at Browns Ferry was to hold a lighted candle near the openings to see if the flame moved, indicating a leak. Although small fires had occurred previously when checking for air leaks with a candle, they had always been easily extinguished. On this occasion, a rush of air sucked the open flame into the polyurethane foam, which was a highly combustible grade of material that did not conform to design standards, and the fire spread quickly. Despite the efforts of plant workers to extinguish the flames, the fire destroyed some electrical wiring in the cable-spreading room and caused even more damage in the unit 1 reactor building on the other side of the wall. About seven hours after the fire began, it was finally doused with water from a fire hose. Water had not been used earlier for fear of causing short circuits that would impair the operation of safety systems.

The Browns Ferry fire consumed about two thousand electrical cables, and the loss of electrical power, in turn, incapacitated valves, pumps, and other equipment. It also disabled the emergency core cooling systems in unit 1 completely and in unit 2 partially. Nevertheless, both plants were scrammed successfully (one automatically and one manually), the cores were adequately cooled, no radiation was released to the environment, and no injuries to plant personnel or the public occurred. A Special Review Group headed by Stephen Hanauer that the NRC established to study the causes and effects of the fire posed the fundamental question, "How can a serious fire that involved inoperability of so many important systems result in no adverse effect on the public health and safety?" Its answer was that the principle of defense-in-depth offered a "high degree of safety assurance by echelons of safety features." The Hanauer group pointed out that, even without a functioning ECCS, other systems provided sufficient water to the core to avoid a loss-of-coolant accident. It identified "significant inadequacies" in design, procedures, and performance, however, and urged a series of regulatory reforms to prevent a repetition of the events at Browns Ferry. The NRC promptly began work on new guidelines and regulations on fire prevention and protection.[17]

Nuclear critics cited the Browns Ferry fire as compelling evidence that power reactors were unsafe. Daniel Ford commented that "one electrician with a candle may have refuted in an instant the industry's fundamental and long-standing claim about the reliability of reactor safety systems." *Newsweek* reported, "Government investigations of the fire have revealed a series of errors and omissions by both men and machines, so great as to shake confidence in the adequacy of safety arrangements in the nation's nuclear power plants." Industry officials echoed the NRC's argument that multiple layers of safety features had effectively prevented a serious accident, but they also recognized that the events at Browns Ferry made clear that safety improvements were necessary. Asked how close the unit 1 plant came to a meltdown, a General Electric official replied, "We really weren't very close, but I'd just as soon not be that close again."[18]

The steps that the NRC took to correct the deficiencies exposed by the fire focused largely, though not exclusively, on plant design, building materials, and equipment. This was consistent with the prevailing approach to reactor safety taken by the AEC's regulatory staff and the NRC. They concentrated primarily on the integrity of the core and the operation of the safety systems designed to keep it properly cooled. The nature and quality of the materials used in nuclear plant construction received secondary, but still prominent, emphasis. Other safety questions, especially those that did not involve plant hardware, were given much lower priority. The Browns Ferry fire revealed substantial problems in areas beyond reactor design and engineering that were critical, at least potentially, to protecting public health. The most obvious was the performance of plant workers; in this case the dangerous if not foolhardy practice of searching for air leaks with a lighted candle had gravely threatened plant safety. Further, the operating staff had been poorly prepared for dealing with the fire once it started. The NRC's Special Review Group concluded that the actions taken during the fire did not indicate "a high state of training of plant personnel in fire fighting operations."

The Browns Ferry accident had caused other problems that greatly complicated the task of responding to the fire. Communications were difficult, partly because the control room was sometimes filled with smoke and crowded with dozens of people. The control room telephones and the public address system within the plants went dead. The computer used to monitor the functions of plant systems failed. Emergency planning procedures in areas surrounding the Browns Ferry site were, at best, ill defined. Neither the sheriff nor civil defense officials in Limestone County, where the plant was located, learned about the fire until after the emergency ended. Authorities in other jurisdictions received notification but were uncertain of what, if any, actions they should take. Some Alabama state agencies did not have a copy of the state's emergency plan for Browns Ferry, and others had received "very little information concerning their defined responsibilities relating to an emergency at the plant." Although the NRC was well aware of the shortcomings in the training and performance of plant workers, the lack of dependable means of communication during the accident, and the lapses in emergency preparedness, it did not focus on those issues as generic problems that needed careful attention and correction.[19]

A PRECURSOR AT DAVIS-BESSE

During the first few years of its existence, the NRC placed top priority on timely licensing of plants and the resolution of safety questions relating to core integrity. Although the number of applications for construction permits had declined drastically from a peak in the early 1970s, many licensing reviews were still in process. Despite the growing number of plants on line—sixty-five in early 1979—the NRC dedicated relatively few resources to systematically collecting and evaluating information from operating reactors. Agency officials were aware of the need to assess the performance of operating plants for safety purposes, but they were uncertain about how to design a program that would achieve their objectives without an inordinate commitment of staff and money. In cases in which information from on-line plants clearly revealed important safety concerns, such as fuel densification, pipe cracking, and the fire at Browns Ferry, the NRC acted to correct what it identified as problems with broad safety implications. Less dramatic occurrences had a limited effect beyond the boundaries of the affected plant and, consequently, exerted little influence on the general direction or content of the NRC's safety programs.[20]

The aftermath of a potentially serious incident at the Davis-Besse Nuclear Power Station near Toledo, Ohio, demonstrated shortcomings in the NRC's approach that inhibited an effective response to information about the safety performance of operating reactors. On September 24, 1977, the reactor was running at 9 percent of full power when it tripped because of a disruption in the feed-water system. A few seconds later, a relief valve stuck open, which allowed reactor coolant to escape. As many alarms activated, plant operators tried to figure out, amid a series of perplexing signs, what had occurred. At one point they turned off emergency cooling pumps because of erroneous analyses of conditions in the core. Finally, after twenty-two minutes of uncertainty and confusion, one operator recognized that the open valve was the source of the problem. After he shut a backup valve known as a block valve to stop the escape of coolant, the plant returned to a stable state and the emergency ended. Although the Davis-Besse event did not cause a release of radiation or

damage to the plant, its consequences could have been much more severe if the operator had not closed the block valve or if the plant had
been running at a higher power level.

The owner of the Davis-Besse plant, the Toledo Edison Company, conducted an investigation of the incident but apparently failed to recognize
its significance. The utility took no action to address the difficulties that
confronted the operators when they received unclear signals about what
caused the problem and what to do about it. Safety experts for the de-
signer of the plant, Babcock and Wilcox, realized that improper operator response to a situation such as occurred at Davis-Besse could cause
a serious accident. They drafted a memorandum for distribution to owners of all Babcock and Wilcox nuclear plants, cautioning against termination of emergency core cooling systems. They suggested that under different conditions, it was "quite possible, perhaps probable" that the
decision of plant operators to turn off emergency cooling pumps would
have led to a loss-of-coolant accident. The memorandum failed to make
a strong impression within various divisions at Babcock and Wilcox, however, and the guidance it contained was never sent to plant owners.

Inspectors from the NRC's regional office in Chicago conducted an
extensive investigation of the Davis-Besse events, and two other offices
looked into the incident's causes and plant operators' response to it. They
concluded that it did not reveal safety problems that applied to other
plants or required generic corrective measures. The issue surfaced again,
however, because of the efforts of James Creswell, another NRC regional
inspector, who regarded the incident—especially the difficulty that plant
operators encountered in understanding conditions in the plant and their
ill-advised decision to cut off the emergency cooling pumps—as part of
a pattern of deficient management and operation by Toledo Edison.
Creswell spoke to authorities at various levels within the NRC and, in
early March 1979, met with two of the commissioners, Peter A. Bradford and John F. Ahearne, to recommend that the plant be shut down.
On March 29, 1979, Ahearne requested a report from the staff on the
issues Creswell raised. By that time, the agency's attention was focused
on the accident at Three Mile Island, which had occurred the previous
day, and which, it turned out, was in important ways strikingly similar
to the 1977 incident at Davis-Besse.[21]

In the face of existing uncertainties about reactor safety that nuclear
critics emphasized during the public debate over nuclear power, the AEC
and the NRC relied on the concept of defense-in-depth as the bulwark
against an accident that would jeopardize the public. They acknowledged

that outstanding questions about reactor safety and performance remained to be answered, and they sought, not always successfully, to address those issues in a reasonably timely manner. But they were confident that defense-in-depth provided substantial if not inviolable margins of safety in the event of any imaginable occurrence. The accident at Three Mile Island challenged their judgment, undermined their confidence, and subjected defense-in-depth to an extraordinarily harrowing trial.

Chapter 4

Wednesday, March 28

"This Is the Biggie"

The first five hours of the graveyard shift that began at 11:00 P.M. on March 27, 1979, at the TMI-2 reactor were uneventful. The plant ran at 97 percent of full power while a staff of six employees monitored its operation and performed routine duties. The generator produced nearly nine hundred megawatts of electricity as clouds of steam billowed out of the plant's two cooling towers. TMI-1 was not operating because it had been shut down for routine refueling.

Like all power reactors built by Babcock and Wilcox and about two-thirds of the nuclear plants in operation in early 1979, both units at Three Mile Island were pressurized water reactors (PWRs). Three nuclear plant manufacturers used the principles of PWR design: Westinghouse, Combustion Engineering, and Babcock and Wilcox. A fourth vendor, General Electric, employed a different design called a boiling water reactor. In PWRs, the water pumped through the pressure vessel (at a rate of some ninety thousand gallons per minute) is kept under high pressure. As the water passes through the core, it is heated to about six hundred degrees Fahrenheit under normal operating conditions, but the high pressure of about twenty-two hundred pounds per square inch (150 times greater than atmospheric pressure) prevents it from boiling. In the TMI-2 plant, the core contained about a hundred tons of uranium encased in 36,816 thin, twelve-foot-long fuel rods. The pressure vessel that housed the core was thirty-six feet high and had steel walls nine inches thick.

Water circulates through the core in a PWR in what is known as the primary loop. After the heated water exits the core, it proceeds to one or more large containers called steam generators; the two steam generators at the TMI-2 plant were each seventy-three feet high. In the steam generators, the heat from the water passing through the core is transferred to the secondary loop, a separate system for circulating water. The

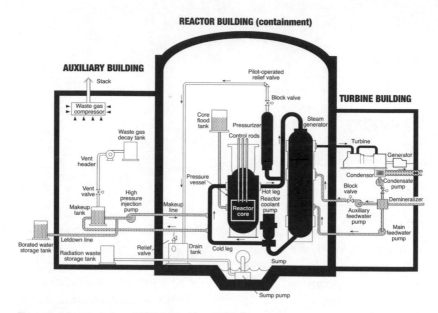

Figure 4. Schematic diagram of TMI-2 (adapted from *IEEE Spectrum* 16 [November 1979]: 43–45. © 1979 by the Institute of Electrical and Electronics Engineers, Inc.).

water in the secondary loop is allowed to boil, creating the highly forceful steam that runs the turbine. The water from the primary loop becomes mildly radioactive from its contact with the core, but it is isolated from the water in the secondary loop. After transferring its heat in the steam generators, the water in the primary loop returns to the core. The steam in the secondary loop that drives the turbine is condensed back into liquid form and recirculated.[1]

THE CAUSES OF THE ACCIDENT

The chain of events that set off the severe accident at TMI-2 and melted a substantial portion of its core began innocently enough at 4:00 A.M. on March 28. The initial problem occurred when pumps in the condensate polishing system tripped. After steam that drives the turbine is condensed back to a liquid state, it passes through the condensate polishers, which remove impurities in the water. This process is a part of the secondary loop. Operators at TMI-2 had been working for several hours to clear a blockage in one of the eight polishers when the system's pumps unexpectedly shut down for reasons that have never been determined. A polisher bypass valve that would have allowed the water to continue flowing failed to open. One second after the pumps quit, the main feed-water pumps that sent water to the steam generators automatically tripped in response to the cutoff of water from the condensate polishers. Immediately, according to design, the turbine tripped, shutting down the plant. As soon as the turbine tripped, auxiliary feed-water pumps came on. But the flow of water from the auxiliary pumps to the steam generators was blocked by two valves that had inadvertently been left in a closed position. At this point the secondary system was unable to provide water to the steam generators.

The closing of the secondary system caused heat and pressure to rise rapidly in the primary system, largely because the steam generators could no longer remove heat from the water that had come from the core. As a result, eight seconds after the polisher pumps tripped, the reactor scrammed automatically. The control rods entered the core and terminated the production of heat from nuclear fission. But the problem of dealing with decay heat remained, and it was greatly complicated when a critical valve, called a pilot-operated relief valve (PORV), stuck open. This permitted large volumes of cooling water from the primary system to escape. The earlier events in the accident were serious but not unprecedented, irreparable, or particularly alarming. The failure of the relief valve was the principal mechanical cause of what soon became a grave crisis at Three Mile Island.

The PORV sat on top of a large container called the pressurizer, which at TMI-2 was forty-two feet high. The pressurizer performs a vital function in PWRs: using electric heaters and water sprays, it regulates the pressure in the primary system. Maintaining proper pressure is essential not only for operating efficiency but also for safety. A sudden increase can damage pipes and other equipment in the primary system, including the pressure vessel that holds the core (the pressurizer should not be confused with the reactor pressure vessel). If the pressure in a reactor rises so rapidly that the normal operation of the pressurizer cannot handle it, the PORV opens automatically to reduce system pressure. At TMI-2, the PORV opened three seconds after the condensate pumps tripped, exactly as designed. Unfortunately, ten seconds later, after the temperature and pressure in the primary system had diminished, it failed to close as designed. The open relief valve allowed growing quantities of reactor coolant to escape. This was not the first time that the PORV had stuck open at TMI-2, and it was a chronic problem at Babcock and Wilcox plants. The same sequence of events had occurred at Davis-Besse in 1977.

In that case, an operator recognized that the valve was open and immediately blocked it.[2]

The operators at TMI-2, however, did not realize what had happened and did not promptly shut off the PORV. Within a few seconds after the accident began, the plant's alarm systems, including a loud horn and more than a hundred flashing lights on the control panels, announced the loss of feed-water in the secondary loop, the turbine trip, the reactor trip, and other abnormal events. But they offered little guidance about the causes of those occurrences and did not differentiate between trivial and vital problems. One of the operators, Craig Faust, later commented, "I would have liked to have thrown away the alarm panel. It wasn't giving us any useful information." To make matters worse, there was no clear signal to show the position of the PORV. A signal light that had been installed during start-up testing a year earlier showed only that electrical current was sent to the valve to open it; by inference the valve was closed when the current (and the signal) were off. The operators checked the signal on the morning of the accident, saw that it was not lighted, and assumed, therefore, that the valve had closed properly. The operators might have determined that the valve was open by looking at a pressure indicator for the reactor-coolant drain tank, which was where the water that poured out of the open PORV wound up. But that signal was situated behind the seven-foot-high instrument panels that were the dominant feature of the control room. The operators had to walk around the tall panels to look at the drain-tank indicator, and did not do so frequently enough to identify the problem as they attempted to cope with the flurry of confusing signals they were receiving.[3]

The operators saw no definite signs that the plant was suffering a loss-of-coolant accident and was in danger of core "uncovery," in which the core is not fully covered with water. Their training programs had not prepared them for the conditions they confronted on the morning of March 28. The operators and supervisors on duty were well-qualified professionals, but they were baffled by the information they received. The two operators in the control room, Faust and Edward Frederick, were veterans of the navy's nuclear submarine program, had joined Met Ed in 1973, and had completed operator qualifying programs. The shift foreman, Fred Scheimann, who was in the turbine building trying to unclog a condensate polisher when the accident began, had also served in the nuclear navy. He had acquired fifteen years of nuclear experience and had worked at TMI for six years. Like his colleagues, the shift supervisor, William Zewe, had received his initial nuclear training in the navy.

Figure 5. The control room of TMI-2 as it appeared on April 3, 1979 (National Archives 220-TMI-DE9040061-13).

He had a total of thirteen years of nuclear experience and had been employed at TMI for seven years.

The navy provided the foremost talent pool for operators in the commercial nuclear industry, and it gave them solid training in the principles and procedures involved in running reactors. In addition, TMI-2 operators received training from Met Ed and from Babcock and Wilcox, which provided extensive experience on a reactor simulator. They were required to pass examinations administered by the NRC to qualify for operator licenses and to renew the licenses every two years. As a group, operators at TMI scored above the national average on NRC qualifying exams. Nevertheless, the experience and training of the operators on duty at TMI-2 when the accident occurred, and of the reinforcements that they soon called in, did not prepare them to cope with the deteriorating conditions in the plant. Their training courses and testing procedures placed much more emphasis on carrying out routine operating tasks, responding to minor malfunctions, and memorizing course materials than on developing the analytical skills needed to deal effectively with unanticipated problems. Operator training was not a high priority for the NRC or the nuclear industry, and the deficiencies in existing programs exacted a heavy price during the TMI-2 accident.[4]

The fundamental source of confusion for the operators on the morning of March 28 was that the water level in the pressurizer was high but the pressure in the primary system was low. This condition occurred because water was leaving the core and escaping out of the primary system through the open PORV. The water level in the pressurizer rose as coolant flowed through it. There was no instrument in the control room that acted like a gasoline gauge in an automobile to show the amount of coolant in the core. Operators judged the level of water in the core by the level in the pressurizer, and since that was high, they assumed that the core was covered with coolant. They were confused by the seemingly contradictory signals that the water level indicator for the pressurizer kept climbing while the pressure in the core was low.

The operators' primary concern was not the possibility that the plant was experiencing a loss-of-coolant accident but the possibility that the pressurizer was "going solid." Under normal conditions, the pressurizer contains both water and a steam cushion that are used to maintain proper pressure in the primary loop. If the pressurizer goes solid, it fills with water, which eliminates the steam and severely impairs the means of controlling pressure in the system. The operators at TMI-2 had been trained by both Babcock and Wilcox and Met Ed to avoid letting the pressurizer go solid, and they were keenly aware that filling it with water was undesirable and perhaps disastrous. Zewe, the shift supervisor, later explained that "if you go solid, you worry about an overpressure condition; you also worry about an underpressure condition, too, and the uncontrolled aspect of it."[5]

While the TMI-2 staff struggled to sort out conflicting signs and decide on appropriate actions, the plant's emergency core cooling system began to operate as designed. About two minutes into the accident, the high-pressure injection pumps, a part of the ECCS, automatically activated in response to the loss of coolant from the core. The two pumps fed water into the primary system at a rate of about a thousand gallons per minute, which was sufficient to make up for the coolant escaping through the open PORV. The high-pressure injection system, triggered by the low pressure and rising temperatures in the core, performed flawlessly. Despite the fact that the ECCS came on, the operators remained focused on their concern about the pressurizer going solid. In that context, the addition of a large volume of water to the primary loop was not a welcome development because it seemed to increase the chances that the pressurizer would fill with water. Therefore, about four and a half minutes into the accident, Scheimann, the shift foreman, ordered that one of the high-pressure injection pumps be shut down and the other sharply throttled back. He did so, he later recalled, because "pressurizer [water] level at that point was indicating that it was coming up at a rapid rate, and was rapidly approaching your solid indication." As a result, the plant lost much of a vital component of its defense against a loss-of-coolant accident.[6]

The effects of the ill-advised decision to scale back on the flow of water from the ECCS were compounded when the operators also shut off the four reactor coolant pumps. The pumps were huge pieces of equipment, described in one report as each the "size of a small truck." They were a part of the reactor's primary system; their function during normal operation of the plant was to force coolant through the core. A little more than an hour into the accident, the pumps began to shake so furiously that the operators could feel the vibrations in the control room. This was a result of the rising heat in the core and the growing presence of steam in the coolant. The operators still did not recognize that they were dealing with a loss-of-coolant accident, and in accordance with their training, at 5:14 A.M. they shut down two of the pumps to prevent damage to them. At 5:41 A.M. they turned off the other two.

As long as the reactor coolant pumps were operating, they circulated enough water and steam through the core to keep it covered. After the pumps were closed down, however, the steam in the pressure vessel (which provided some core cooling) separated from the water and rose to the top of the vessel, the level of cooling water fell even further, and the fuel assemblies in the core soon became uncovered. At that point the plant was suffering the kind of loss-of-coolant accident that reactor experts had long feared and tried to prevent. As a consequence of mechanical failures and operator errors, what began as a series of minor malfunctions escalated into a major crisis.[7]

In the first one hundred minutes or so of the accident, any one of a number of actions would have maintained adequate core cooling. If the operators had closed the PORV, allowed the ECCS to perform as designed, or kept the reactor coolant pumps running, the core would have remained covered and the emergency would have ended with minimal effects. As it was, water continued to pour out of the open PORV, the throttled high-pressure injection pumps could not provide more than a fraction of the coolant that was lost, and the shut-off reactor coolant pumps could not circulate coolant through the core. The plant operators failed to recognize indications of an increasingly serious loss-of-coolant accident. Although they did not panic, they grew progressively more troubled by the conflicting signals they received from the control panels. The plant's alarms contributed to a general atmosphere of confusion by continually reactivating. Finally, Brian Mehler, a shift supervisor who had just arrived at the plant to relieve Zewe, concluded from the pressure and temperature readings in the primary loop that the PORV was at least partially open. He was not certain of what was happening in the core, but he reasoned that no harm and perhaps some benefit could be achieved by shutting the offending relief valve. At 6:22 A.M., he ordered that a backup for the PORV, called a block valve, be closed. By that time, about thirty-two thousand gallons of coolant, more than one-third of the volume in the primary system, had flowed out of the stuck-open PORV. None of the staff in the control room took action to determine how long the PORV had been open or to replace the coolant that had escaped. Closing the block valve was a sound decision but insufficient in itself to prevent the severe damage to the core that leaving the PORV open for about two hours and twenty minutes had caused.

Within a short time after the reactor coolant pumps were shut down, the core began to slump. Without adequate cooling, the water that remained in the primary loop began turning to steam. As the fuel rods were exposed, the metal in the cladding reacted chemically with the steam, which not only ruptured the cladding but also released large amounts of hydrogen. The core suffered a severe loss of core geometry as its upper sections crumbled into a molten mass; researchers later discovered that about half the core had melted during the early stages of the accident. The uncovering of the core at TMI-2 produced a meltdown that was unprecedented and, at that point, undetected, although officials from Met Ed and the NRC gradually realized that they faced a serious challenge in finding a way to cool the heated core. Later investigations estimated that in some parts of the core, the temperature reached four thousand degrees Fahrenheit or more.[8]

GENERAL EMERGENCY

Around 6:30 A.M. on March 28, two and a half hours after the accident began, radiation alarms sounded in the control room. As the cladding on a growing number of fuel rods ruptured, levels of radiation far above normal were measured in the containment building and in the coolant in the primary loop. In addition, at about the same time, increasing levels of radiation were detected in the plant's auxiliary building. The auxiliary building was adjacent to the containment building and housed cooling and waste storage equipment. During the accident, the coolant that escaped through the PORV went to a drain tank in the containment building. As more and more coolant accumulated, the drain tank overflowed and spilled water onto the floor of the containment building. It was then pumped into waste storage tanks in the auxiliary building, which also eventually overflowed and caused radiation levels in the auxiliary building to rise. The major source of increasing radiation in the atmosphere of the auxiliary building and of releases to the environment was the flow of coolant between the core and the auxiliary building in the "letdown" and "makeup" systems. Those systems, which under normal conditions served to filter and remove impurities from the water that cooled the core, were not designed to prevent the escape of radiation from highly contaminated water. Leakage from the letdown and makeup systems produced high levels of radiation in the auxiliary building, some of which was released outside the plant through a ventilation stack.

The indications of higher-than-normal radiation in containment and in the auxiliary building made clear to the operators that they were dealing with an emergency. George Kunder, the TMI-2 superintendent for technical support, who had arrived at the plant at about 4:50 A.M. to assist the operators on duty, exclaimed after hearing the radiation readings, "Oh my God, we're failing fuel." Kunder and his colleagues did not know that the core was uncovered, but they realized that the situation was far more critical than they had previously believed. At 6:56 A.M., one of the plant supervisors—accounts vary on which one—declared a site emergency. The emergency plan for TMI-2 directed that this action be taken if radiation alarms sounded in more than one area. A site emergency meant that there was a possibility of an "uncontrolled release of radioactivity" within the plant's boundaries. It required evacuation of the affected buildings, closure of the gates leading to the plant, and notification of the NRC and the state of Pennsylvania. Less than half an hour later, Gary Miller, the Three Mile Island station manager, declared a general emergency. Miller, who had been talking with plant operators by telephone since early in the accident, arrived at the site at 7:05 and assumed authority as emergency director. New and alarmingly high radiation readings in the containment building persuaded him to announce a general emergency, which was defined as having the "potential for serious radiological consequences to the health and safety of the general public." Met Ed promptly began to measure radiation on and beyond the plant site. It found no detectable radiation directly across the river in Goldsboro and found levels on the island to be only slightly above normal.[9]

Once the site emergency and then the general emergency were declared, the response to the accident at Three Mile Island moved beyond the exclusive domain of Metropolitan Edison. It soon commanded an expanding mobilization of resources and expertise from local, state, and federal government agencies. Because of the uncertainty that prevailed at the plant, the information that the utility provided to government agencies on March 28 was usually fragmentary and sometimes contradictory or ambiguous. The reports it issued to the press and the public understated the severity of the accident. In turn, state government and NRC officials all too frequently circulated confusing or erroneous information about the accident.

THE STATE'S RESPONSE

At 7:02 A.M., six minutes after the Met Ed operating crew declared a site emergency, Zewe called the Pennsylvania Emergency Management Agency (PEMA). He told the duty officer, Clarence Deller, that the plant had been shut down and that there was a "high level of radiation" in the reactor building. Deller immediately notified emergency offices in Dauphin, Lancaster, and York Counties and also promptly contacted William E. Dornsife, who was a staff member of the Bureau of Radiation Protection, a part of the Department of Environmental Resources. Dornsife, the only nuclear engineer employed by the state, passed the information he received to superiors and colleagues in his agency and called the TMI-2 control room for further details. He learned that Met Ed thought the reactor had suffered a small loss-of-coolant accident, but that it had detected no radiation outside the plant. As Dornsife was talking with the control room, he heard in the background an announcement that plant employees should evacuate the fuel-handling building adjacent to containment. "It didn't hit me until I heard that," he later recalled. "And I said to myself, 'This is the biggie.'"

At 7:36 A.M., PEMA received word from TMI that the utility had declared a general emergency. It immediately advised several state and county agencies that an evacuation of the area surrounding the plant might be necessary. The director of PEMA, Oran K. Henderson, called Governor Richard L. Thornburgh at his home in Harrisburg to inform him that an accident had occurred at Three Mile Island. Thornburgh, who had been inaugurated just a few weeks earlier, was on his way to a budget meeting with state legislators. In their brief conversation, he told Henderson to keep him informed and to call the lieutenant gover-

Figure 6. Richard L. Thornburgh (left) and William W. Scranton III (The Historical Society of Dauphin County).

nor, William W. Scranton III, who was chairman of the state's emergency management council. Even at that point, Thornburgh was concerned about the possible consequences of the problem at Three Mile Island, in part because he instinctively felt that any accident at a nuclear facility could not be regarded as a trivial matter. "I really didn't want to frame any response of the State Government until I had more facts," he later commented, "but I think the question of evacuation crossed my mind immediately."[10]

Thornburgh assigned responsibility for collecting and reporting information about the accident to Scranton because of his confidence in the ability and integrity of the lieutenant governor. "We are compatible," he explained. "We don't have a situation which some other states have, where Lieutenant Governors do nasty things when the Governor is out of the state." After graduating from Yale University in 1969, Scranton had worked as publisher of three family-owned weekly newspapers in the area of Scranton, Pennsylvania, a city named for his ancestors. In that capacity he had criticized nuclear power, but had not taken a doctrinaire position. Scranton's father had served as a popular governor of

Pennsylvania during the 1960s and mounted a reluctant and belated challenge to Senator Barry Goldwater for the Republican presidential nomination in 1964. The younger Scranton's campaign in the Republican primary for lieutenant governor in 1978 was the first time he had entered elective politics. His views did not always conform with party orthodoxy. In 1972, he had editorially endorsed the Democratic candidate for president, George S. McGovern, because of his dismay with the "moral tone of the Nixon administration." He was an admirer of the Democratic governor of California, Jerry Brown, and, like Brown, practiced transcendental meditation.[11]

Scranton was informed about the accident at TMI by Henderson at 8:20 A.M. He had previously scheduled a press conference for 10:00 that morning to discuss energy problems. In the short time available, he sought to gather as much information as possible about the situation at the plant. Stories about the accident were already being reported by the news media, and Scranton knew he would be quizzed about it at the press conference. The media first received sketchy information about the accident when "Captain Dave," a traffic reporter for a Harrisburg Top 40 radio station, picked up a state police notice on his citizens band radio. He alerted the news director at his station, Mike Pintek, who promptly placed a call to the plant. An apparently frazzled switchboard operator mistakenly transferred him to the TMI-2 control room. The person who answered told him to call Met Ed headquarters in Reading because "I can't talk now, we've got a problem." Pintek contacted Met Ed and was told that the shutdown at the plant did not endanger the public. He aired a brief story on his station's 8:25 news program. About half an hour later, after receiving vague reports of a general emergency at TMI, the Associated Press issued a bulletin on its national wire announcing that an accident had occurred at Three Mile Island. It added that few details were available but that no radiation had been released from the plant.[12]

Meanwhile, Met Ed was scrambling to prepare a response to the increasing volume of inquiries it was receiving. Its public affairs staff members in Reading knew little about the situation at the plant and were unable to provide reliable or up-to-date information. Instead they offered bland affirmations about the safety of the plant that became increasingly less credible. The first statement from Met Ed declared that a malfunction had occurred at the plant and that it would be "out of service for about a week." The next statement, drafted at about 8:30 A.M., disclosed that TMI-2 had been "shut down due to a mechanical malfunction," but that "there have been no recordings of significant levels of radiation and none are expected outside the plant." The meaning of the phrase "significant levels of radiation" was ambiguous and, since extremely high levels had been detected in the containment building, misleading. An executive from Met Ed's parent company, GPU, complained the following day that Met Ed's press release "substantially" downplayed "the seriousness of the incident at that time." Later in the morning, GPU issued a press release that was more candid. It announced that a "low level release of radioactive gas beyond the site boundary" had occurred, but that it did "not believe that the level constitutes a danger to the health and safety of the public."[13]

By that time, reporters who attended Scranton's press conference had already been told about an off-site release of radiation. After gathering as much information as he could and receiving a briefing from Dornsife, Scranton prepared a statement on the TMI accident to present to reporters. Those activities made him almost an hour late in meeting with an increasingly impatient press corps. Scranton's opening statement was reassuring but confusing about the threat of radioactive releases. He declared that "everything is under control" and that "there is and was no danger to public health and safety." He went on to say that, although "there was a small release of radiation to the environment, . . . no increase in normal radiation levels has been detected." Scranton did not make clear whether the "small release" had occurred within or beyond the plant boundaries or why it could not be detected. Reporters, after expressing resentment about having to wait so long for the lieutenant governor's appearance, raised questions about radiation hazards. As Scranton attempted to answer, Dornsife stepped in and announced that Met Ed had detected a small amount of radioactive iodine in Goldsboro. Dornsife had received this information just before the press conference began and had not had a chance to inform Scranton.

After Dornsife's statement, reporters addressed a series of pointed questions about radiation to him. They wanted to know what the measurements of radiation meant, how the radiation had escaped from the plant, and whether the state depended on Met Ed for information about the levels of radiation in the environment. The atmosphere of the press briefing was tense, and as a Pennsylvania official later commented, the exchange did not provide a "neat, orderly transfer of information." To make matters worse, Scranton learned shortly after the news conference that Met Ed in Reading was still claiming that no radiation had been detected off the Three Mile Island site, which contradicted what Dornsife had just told the press. It later turned out that Dornsife's report was incorrect; at that point, radiation had not been detected in Goldsboro. But the erroneous information that Dornsife received was made moot by radiation surveys that the state conducted in the late morning and early afternoon. Thomas Gerusky, the director of the Bureau of Radiation Protection, advised Scranton that slightly above-normal levels of radiation released from the plant had been detected as far away as Harrisburg. He attributed the radiation that showed up in the state's measurements to a steam venting that Met Ed had carried out without consulting state officials. An angry Scranton demanded that Met Ed immediately send a representative to brief him about the situation at the plant and the releases of radiation.[14]

RADIATION HAZARDS

The dearth of reliable and timely information was exacerbated by the difficulty that Scranton faced in evaluating the information he received. This remained a serious obstacle throughout the crisis for government officials, reporters, and members of the public who lacked a technical background; it was first graphically apparent when Dornsife tried, with limited success, during the lieutenant governor's press conference, to explain what measurements of radiation meant. The basic units for measuring radiation in 1979 were the *rad,* which indicated the amount of radiation delivered to human tissue, and the *rem,* which applied to chronic low-level exposures and indicated the effectiveness of different kinds of radiation in causing biological injury. For gamma radiation, which can penetrate far into the body from external sources, rads and rems are equivalent. The NRC and other regulatory agencies, drawing on the recommendations of leading scientists in the field, allowed those who worked in jobs where they were exposed to radiation a maximum of 5 rems per year "whole-body" exposure, which by definition included the most sensitive areas of the body. The permissible dose for individual members of the general population was one-tenth of the occupational level, or .5 rem per year. This was usually expressed as 500 millirems—a millirem is one one-thousandth of a rem. The average allowable exposure for large population groups, such as the population around TMI, was one-thirtieth of the occupational level, or 170 millirems per year. The NRC further required that nuclear plants restrict their emissions during normal operation so that a person who stood on the boundary of a plant twenty-four hours a day, 365 days a year, would not be exposed to more than about 5 millirems per year.

Neither scientific experts nor regulatory bodies guaranteed that a person who received less than a permissible dose of radiation would remain free of injury; they did not claim that a threshold existed below which exposure was harmless. But they were confident that the limits offered an ample, if not absolute, margin of safety from radiation hazards. Radiation protection professionals urged that exposure for radiation workers and the general public be reduced to a minimum without discontinuing the use of radiation sources that provided valuable benefits. They agreed that exposures to radiation in amounts of 50 rads or more within a short period were progressively more likely to cause serious health effects, and that acute doses of 600 to 1,000 rads would be lethal to nearly everyone receiving them. Although there was strong evidence that exposure to radiation increased the risk of cancer, there was no conclusive information about the level of exposure likely to produce cancer or other illnesses.

The levels measured outside TMI-2 on March 28 were, by any standard, very small and unlikely to threaten public health—as long as they did not occur continuously over an extended period. Met Ed had twenty instruments for measuring environmental radioactivity in locations surrounding the site. Although one stack monitor that was calibrated to measure very low levels of radiation went off-scale early in the accident, readings from other instruments provided reasonably reliable information about releases from the plant. The highest reading was 7 millirems per hour; most measurements were in the range of 1 millirem per hour or less. Those values were far below the amount of radiation normally present in the environment. Natural background radiation, which comes from cosmic rays, radioactive elements in rocks and soil, and other natural sources, caused an average exposure to the population around TMI of about 100 millirems per year. The measurements of radiation released from the plant in the early hours of the accident, therefore, were not terribly alarming to experts. But neither were they insignificant. If, for example, continuous measurements of 1 millirem per hour were recorded off-site for seven days, they would reach the regulatory limit for population groups. The even more disturbing possibility was that higher and more dangerous amounts of radiation might escape if the reactor was not brought under control and if containment was breached as a result.

By the time Met Ed declared a general emergency, it was clear that radiation levels in the containment building of the plant were extraordinarily high, estimated at 800 rads per hour or more. As fuel cladding ruptured, releasing fission products from the fuel rods and pellets, the water and steam in the core became increasingly and intensely radioactive. By 9:00 A.M., radiation levels in containment had risen to about 6,000 rads per hour. Therefore, measuring the amount of radiation that leaked from the plant was a vital function for protecting public health and for deciding whether to order an evacuation from the area surrounding the plant. The Met Ed and state radiation teams who began to take measurements on the morning of March 28 were soon joined by experts from federal agencies. They included experienced and well-equipped emergency units from the U.S. Department of Energy, which performed essential functions while maintaining a low profile. The combined efforts of utility, state, and federal scientists provided wide-ranging surveys of radiation levels in the soil, water, and atmosphere surrounding the plant.[15]

MET ED AND THE STATE

In response to Scranton's urgent request for information, Jack Herbein, Met Ed's vice president for generation, accompanied by George Kunder and Gary Miller from the plant, went to Harrisburg to brief the lieutenant governor and other state officials. Herbein, the senior Met Ed official most familiar with the TMI plants, had arrived at the site by helicopter in late morning. He was a capable and dedicated engineer whose ability and performance had lifted him to the top ranks of Met Ed. His training and experience, however, had not prepared him to deal in a crisis situation with public officials or reporters whose knowledge of nuclear power was, at best, limited. When their questions tried his patience, he could be abrupt and dismissive. His role as a spokesman for Met Ed during the early stages of the accident was made more difficult by the many uncertainties about what was happening inside the plant. By the time he appeared at the site on March 28, about thirty reporters were waiting, many from outside of the Harrisburg area. Herbein told them that the problem seemed to be "some minor fuel failure" and suggested that "only a few" of the fuel rods had suffered serious damage.[16]

Herbein then departed from the site to meet with state officials in Harrisburg. The briefing did not go well; Scranton later commented that it "was not the most cheery get-together." The source of contention was the venting of steam that operators had carried out in an effort to stabilize the plant. Since the steam came from the secondary loop, it would be radioactive only if there were a leak in the steam generators. Gerusky, director of the Bureau of Radiation Protection, had told Scranton that dumping steam into the atmosphere was the cause of the radiation measured off-site. At the meeting, Herbein reported that he had ordered a halt to the release of steam begun that morning, but he also remarked that the process was "normal ventilation" that might be required periodically. Scranton complained bitterly that Met Ed had not informed the state before venting the steam.

In fact, it turned out that the information Gerusky gave Scranton was incorrect. The source of the off-site radiation was not the steam from the secondary loop but rather radioactive gases leaking from the auxiliary building. Herbein either did not know that the dumped steam was clean or did not explain it well. If Dornsife had been present, he might have been able to draw on his knowledge of reactor systems to sort out what those at the meeting perceived about the situation. But he had not been invited to attend. Scranton and the other state officials at the meeting believed that Herbein took an unduly optimistic view of conditions at the plant, and that he played down the threat that the accident posed to public health. They were also convinced that Herbein pledged not to vent steam again without informing the state, an impression that Herbein did not share. The meeting ended amid a clutter of confusion. But the main conclusion that state officials took from the conference was clear—that Med Ed could not be regarded as a source of reliable information. "Right from that moment on," commented Paul Critchlow, Thornburgh's press secretary, "we had virtually nothing to do with Met Ed."[17]

Shortly after the meeting with Herbein, Scranton held his second news conference of the day. He announced his disillusionment with Met Ed by stating that the situation at TMI was "more complex than the company first led us to believe." He told reporters that the utility "has given you and us conflicting information," and that "detectable amounts of radiation" from the plant had been released to the atmosphere. He added, "At this point, we believe there is still no danger to public health." Scranton's statements left no doubt that the state had written off the utility as a partner in responding to the accident. The state hoped that it would realize greater benefits in its efforts to guard public health by collaborating with the NRC. As Critchlow recalled, "I think we just almost instinctively preferred to deal with NRC people."[18]

THE NRC'S RESPONSE

The NRC, like the state, tried throughout the day to find out what had happened at the plant but had limited success. Immediately after declaring a site emergency, Met Ed placed a call to the agency's Region I office in King of Prussia, Pennsylvania, a suburb of Philadelphia. It was one of five NRC regional offices primarily responsible for, among other things, inspection of reactors under construction and in operation, investigation of plant problems and accidents, and verification of environmental monitoring procedures. When Region I's answering service received the first call from TMI, it was unable to reach the duty officer or other emergency contacts, who had left their homes and were on their way to work. It was not until 7:45 A.M., shortly after Met Ed declared a general emergency, that the NRC learned about the accident. Region I officials immediately called the TMI-2 control room and obtained the information then available about the situation at the plant, which was still very sketchy. It was clear, however, that the accident was serious enough to warrant prompt action. The director of the regional office, Boyce H. Grier, called NRC headquarters with news about the accident and quickly activated a regional incident response center that maintained constant communications with the TMI-2 control room. Grier also sent a team of five staff members to the site. They departed at 8:39 A.M. for the plant, a trip of about two hours, after informing the state police that they would be traveling in an NRC emergency vehicle on the Pennsylvania Turnpike.[19]

By the time Grier made his call to NRC headquarters, John G. Davis, the acting director of the Office of Inspection and Enforcement, had already heard about the accident from Joseph J. Fouchard, director of the NRC's Office of Public Affairs, who had been informed by the Region I public affairs officer. Davis immediately opened the headquarters incident response center, located in Bethesda, Maryland, a suburb of Washington, to respond to the developing emergency. He and others at the incident response center called senior staff officials and the commissioners to tell them about the accident. The chairman of the NRC, Joseph M. Hendrie, was out of his office for the entire day of March 28 to accompany his daughter to a local hospital for wisdom tooth surgery. He talked periodically with members of his personal staff about the accident from the hospital. He viewed the situation as serious but "reasonably well in hand," and he was confident that the acting chairman, Victor Gilinsky, would take appropriate action to deal with the problem.[20]

Gilinsky, one of the two original members still serving on the commission, had stirred considerable controversy during his tenure. He had first been appointed to the commission because of his expertise in the field of nuclear safeguards, which focused on the dangers of nuclear plant sabotage or theft of nuclear fuel. But he took a strong interest in other regulatory issues as well. He complained to his colleagues in December 1976, "Despite the fact that we all regard our principal responsibility as assuring the safety of nuclear power plants, . . . we spend astonishingly little time on the substance of reactor safety." Gilinsky, who had worked as a member of the regulatory staff of the AEC from 1971 to 1973, insisted that the NRC must be a stronger and more effective regulator than its predecessor. He believed that the AEC commissioners had deprived the regulatory staff of the resources it required and too often had dismissed the legitimate safety concerns it raised. "The safety experts at the Atomic Energy Commission were the low men on the AEC totem pole," he once declared. "The conditioning and attitudes that went with that status and—just as important—the consequent low regard of the nuclear industry for the regulators were inherited by the NRC in 1975."

Gilinsky was determined to improve the NRC's performance and enhance its reputation with the industry, nuclear critics, Congress, and the general public. He relentlessly raised difficult and inconvenient questions on a variety of issues with both the nuclear industry and the NRC staff, which annoyed staff members and convinced some industry officials that he was opposed to nuclear power. In fact, he subjected antinuclear arguments to the same kind of probing skepticism. Gilinsky's views won him bipartisan support among key members of congressional committees to which the NRC was responsible. Representative Morris K. Udall, chairman of the House Committee on Interior and Insular Affairs, told President Carter in 1978, "Commissioner Gilinsky . . . has shown his grasp of the full spectrum of knotty problems confronting the development of nuclear power, not the least of these being the critical need to instill public confidence in the NRC."[21]

Although Hendrie and Gilinsky frequently took opposing positions on regulatory issues, they reached similar conclusions about the severity of the Three Mile Island accident on the morning of March 28. Like Hendrie, Gilinsky regarded it as cause for concern but not alarm. He tried to keep his previously scheduled appointments to avoid the appearance of a crisis and, in his capacity as acting chairman, he spent much of the day responding to telephone queries from members of Congress and reporters.[22]

Less than half an hour after learning about the accident, Gilinsky placed a call to Jessica Tuchman Mathews, a member of the National Security Council staff at the White House. Mathews, who held a Ph.D. in biochemistry and biophysics from the California Institute of Technology, headed the council's office of Global Issues. She and Gilinsky knew and respected one another from their involvement in controversies over nuclear proliferation and the export of nuclear fuel to India. He decided to advise the White House about the situation at Three Mile Island, even if very little information was available, and he called Mathews because, as she recalled, "we had often informed each other of things that we felt the other one would be interested in." She, in turn, notified the White House Office of Science and Technology Policy, only to find to her annoyance that it was not inclined to act as the presidential staff's point of contact for the accident. By default, Mathews assumed that role. She immediately drafted a memorandum to her boss, national security adviser Zbigniew Brzezinski. She told him that the "reactor has been shut down and appears to be stable," but she added that a release of radiation to the environment was possible. Brzezinski promptly informed President Carter. Mathews continued to collect information about the accident as the day wore on.[23]

At about 10:00 A.M., Gilinsky and two of the other NRC commissioners, Richard Kennedy and Peter Bradford, met to receive a preliminary report about the accident from the incident response center. The other member of the commission, John Ahearne, had gone to the response center, which was located about ten miles from the commissioners' offices in downtown Washington. John Davis, the acting director of inspection and enforcement, told the commissioners that although radiation levels in the containment building were "very high," off-site measurements had "detected nothing." Edson G. Case, deputy director of the Office of Nuclear Reactor Regulation, reported that the emergency core cooling systems had been working for "up to several hours" and stated that "right now we have the situation under control." Fouchard, the director of public affairs, who had gone to the incident response center to consult with senior technical officials about the content of information provided to the public, requested and received the approval of the commissioners for a press release he had drafted. It declared that measurements for off-site radiation were "still being made," but that there had been "no indication of release off the site." At midmorning, therefore, the information available to NRC headquarters gave an incomplete and unduly favorable picture of conditions at the plant. The ECCS had been throttled back early in the accident, and the reactor was far from "under control." About the same time that the NRC issued its press release, off-site radiation was detected.[24]

The lack of clear information about the situation at Three Mile Island was paralleled by a lack of clearly defined roles and lines of authority within the NRC. By tradition, structure, and statutory mandate, the agency was ill prepared and ill equipped to deal with an emergency at a nuclear plant. It was not an operational agency that ran plants or carried out emergency procedures but a deliberative agency that made rules, considered license applications, and conducted inspections. It had no authority to tell the utility what it should do to stabilize the reactor, no capability for operating the plant, and no power to order an evacuation of the surrounding area. Its role was largely limited to collecting information and making recommendations. The NRC lacked a command structure for dealing with a major accident. Each component of the agency— commissioners, staff, and regional office—acted to fulfill its traditional functions. The commissioners weighed broad policy issues raised by the accident, including the delivery of accurate information to the public and the advisability of evacuating the area near the plant. The headquarters staff sought to grasp the technical details about the causes of the accident, figure out the condition of the reactor from the uncertain evidence available, and make appropriate recommendations to the commission and the utility. The regional office sent inspectors to observe and report on what was happening at the plant. No unit within the NRC and no single person was in charge of the situation. The absence of unambiguous lines of authority within the NRC became a source of confusion and embarrassment during the Three Mile Island emergency when the functions of the commission, the headquarters staff, and the region overlapped or, worse, left voids of responsibility.

From the outset, the regional office and the headquarters staffs acted with little guidance from or consultation with the commissioners. When Davis learned of the accident from Region I, he first informed the executive director for operations, Lee V. Gossick, who was the NRC's chief staff official. He then called other staff office directors, and only then tried to contact the commissioners. Operation of the incident response center in Bethesda was a staff function. Although two of the commissioners, Ahearne and Bradford, spent much of the day there, they were strictly observers who had gone to see how the agency performed during an emergency. What they witnessed about the NRC's ability to respond effectively to a major nuclear accident was edifying but not encouraging.

Ahearne, the newest member of the commission, had gone to Bethesda a short time after the staff had notified him that "an event" had occurred at Three Mile Island that required activating the incident response center. He had joined the NRC on July 31, 1978, the third member of the commission to be appointed by President Carter. Before his nomination, a series of tie votes among the four incumbent commissioners had produced, in the opinion of the White House science adviser, Frank Press, a "weak, divided NRC," and the president had sought a "highly qualified, balanced person" to break the stalemate. He selected Ahearne, who held a Ph.D. in physics from Princeton University and had served in a number of high-level posts in the Department of Defense during the 1970s. At the time of his appointment to the NRC, he was a deputy assistant secretary in the recently created Department of Energy. Although his background did not include direct experience in nuclear power safety, Ahearne had worked on energy policy as a member of the White House staff in 1977–1978. In that capacity, he had earned the admiration of Congressman John D. Dingell, who had lobbied the White House to make him an NRC commissioner. Widely regarded as moderate and nondoctrinaire in his approach to policy issues, Ahearne received support from partisans on both sides of the nuclear power debate and easily won approval from the Senate.[25]

Ahearne had arrived at the incident response center around 9:30 A.M. on the morning of the TMI-2 accident and stayed until after midnight. He realized that the staff was responsible for handling an emergency and "felt at times a little awkward being there because . . . the system was not structured to have Commissioners involved." Ahearne, who was familiar with the Defense Department's state-of-the-art emergency facilities, found the NRC's response center to be "very poorly equipped," even though it had been substantially upgraded after the Browns Ferry fire. Communications links were especially weak and ineffective. "The amount of information, the information flow . . . and the quality of the communication link [were] very poor," he later recalled. For example, the office had no speakerphone for group telephone calls. When a call came in from the plant or the Region I office, the receiver was placed on a chair and staff members gathered around to try to hear what was being reported. Regular telephone lines, which were frequently busy, had to be used because the response center had no dedicated lines from the plant or a data transmission system to speed the flow of information.[26]

EFFORTS TO STABILIZE THE PLANT

The technical problems of communicating with the plant were a source of frustration for NRC officials, but the fundamental difficulty in dealing with the accident remained the uncertainties and contradictions in the information they received. Although it was apparent that TMI-2 had

experienced a serious accident, the proper means to cool the core, stabilize the plant, and prevent a major release of radiation were far from
clear. One of the NRC regional inspectors, Charles O. Gallina, remembered that, when he and his colleagues reached the site around 10:30
A.M., they found the reactor in a state that "we never . . . had seen." By
the time the NRC team arrived, radioactive gas had begun to leak into
the control room of unit 2. This forced the twenty to thirty Met Ed employees in the control room to wear respirators and greatly complicated
their ability to communicate with one another for the several hours that
the masks were necessary.[27]

The plant operators and supervisors in the control room tried a series
of procedures to gain control of the overheated and unstable reactor. Although some of the Met Ed staff believed that the core was uncovered,
they did not convey their opinions to emergency director Gary Miller,
who received conflicting signals about conditions in the core. Temperature measuring devices called thermocouples on many of the fuel assemblies, for example, gave some readings that were exceedingly high and
others that were extremely low. This persuaded Miller and other Met Ed
experts to disregard all the readings as unreliable, even though the high
temperature readings turned out to be accurate. Whether or not the core
was uncovered, it was clear that at least some of the fuel rods had been
damaged and that finding a way to cool the core was essential. The fundamental problem was that much of the water in the core had turned to
steam and therefore could not adequately cool the core. Around 9:00 A.M.,
Miller and his colleagues decided to repressurize the reactor in hopes that
increasing the pressure would condense the steam back into water. They
forced as much water as possible into the primary system from the makeup
system and injection pumps, which had the salutary effect of covering
the core. But it did not succeed in collapsing the steam, because the temperatures in the core were so high that the steam had reached a "superheated" state. As a result, the operators' efforts to restart the reactor
coolant pumps that they had turned off hours earlier were futile.

When this attempt to reestablish adequate cooling by repressurizing
the system failed, the Met Ed team decided to depressurize the system.
In this way, they sought to activate a core flood tank, a part of the ECCS,
that would dump water on the core if the pressure was low enough. The
operators cut back on the flow of water to reduce pressure in the reactor, and the flood tank discharged a small volume into the core before
shutting off automatically. The shutdown of the flood tank seemed to indicate that the core was covered, and the operators continued the process

of depressurizing the reactor. In this way they hoped to reach a point where they could use a heat removal system that operated at low pressures. But the operators misinterpreted the signs of what was happening in the core. The flood tank had closed down because the water it sent to the core flashed to steam. As the operators continued to depressurize the system, the core was uncovered again.[28]

Throughout the day, NRC officials in the incident response center followed developments at Three Mile Island with increasing concern. In a conversation from the incident response center at about 1:45 P.M., Edson Case told Commissioners Gilinsky and Kennedy that depressurizing the reactor appeared to be working well. Asked how he felt about the "fate of the reactor," he replied, "I feel good. Now I get the impression that it's stabilized, or directly approaching a stabilized situation." Case, a veteran regulatory staff member, was highly regarded within the NRC for his technical knowledge and his plainspoken manner of expressing his views. His opinion carried a great deal of weight with the commissioners; Gilinsky insisted on talking to Case when he called the response center. Case based his judgment on the sparse information he had received from the NRC inspectors at the site, and within a short time, his evaluation was superseded by more ominous indications.

By the middle of the afternoon, NRC staff members, still forced to piece tidbits of information together to analyze the condition of the core, had become increasingly worried that at least a part of the core was uncovered. Their reading of the temperatures in reactor piping strongly suggested the presence of superheated steam in the pressure vessel, and the only logical explanation was that sections of the core had been exposed. At about 4:00 P.M., Victor Stello Jr., director of the division of operating reactors in the Office of Nuclear Reactor Regulation, grabbed a phone to inform plant operators of this conclusion and to impress upon them the need to "put more water in the core." Stello, one of the NRC's leading reactor experts, was a big man who spoke with a booming voice, and he stated his opinion with unmistakable clarity to the Met Ed staff member on the other end of the line. But even Stello's animated appeal did not convince the plant operators at that point that they must consider the implications of superheated steam. Stello told Gilinsky that he feared Met Ed failed to recognize that the core might not be covered. But he realized his information was so sketchy that he could not be certain of his judgment.[29]

Stello was not alone in his fears that the core of the reactor was uncovered. Babcock and Wilcox engineers, gathering information in their

offices in Lynchburg, Virginia, reached the same conclusions and conveyed their analyses to Met Ed and GPU officials during the afternoon
of March 28. Robert Arnold, vice president for generation of the GPU
Service Corporation, also raised questions with plant operators about
whether the core might be exposed. The Service Corporation was a GPU
subsidiary that provided technical expertise to the three GPU operating
companies, including Met Ed. Arnold talked with plant operators from
his office in New Jersey around 2:00 P.M. and received assurances, based
on the automatic shut-off of the core flood tank, that the core had not
been uncovered. He remained uneasy, but like Stello in Bethesda and Babcock and Wilcox experts in Lynchburg, he deferred to those at the site
who presumably had more complete information. Around 4:30 P.M.,
Arnold expressed his concerns to Jack Herbein, who had returned to the
plant after his meeting with Scranton. Herbein agreed with Arnold's assessment and ordered the operators to stop depressurizing the reactor,
which had not achieved its purposes, and to repressurize it again. This
time, at about 7:50 P.M., the process of injecting more water into the
core enabled the operators to start one of the reactor coolant pumps,
which circulated water through the core and allowed the removal of heat
by the steam generator. For the first time in hours, the plant made welcome progress toward a stable condition.[30]

THE NRC AND THE PRESS

While technical experts from Babcock and Wilcox, GPU, Met Ed, and
the NRC tried to figure out the causes and consequences of the Three
Mile Island accident, the NRC fielded a deluge of telephone calls from
Congress, the news media, state officials, federal agencies, the Union of
Concerned Scientists, and others. It sought to furnish accurate and up-
to-date information that sorted out fact from rumor or speculation, but
under the rapidly changing and highly uncertain circumstances, this was
difficult. NRC staff members at the incident response center checked on
and discredited some rumors about the accident, including a false report
that the state of Virginia had ordered the evacuation of three of its counties. A more plausible, though equally erroneous, rumor was that Pennsylvania had decided to evacuate three counties. In other cases, the NRC
was unable to provide current and reliable information or even to respond to the calls that poured in. Frank L. Ingram, Fouchard's deputy
in the Office of Public Affairs, received so many queries that the message
slips piled up to a point where "there was no way to sort through them."

He could not return most of the calls he received. Reporters who managed to get through to Ingram in his Bethesda office or officials at the incident response center in a separate building about a mile away were often exasperated. One newsman, Walter S. Mossberg of the *Wall Street Journal,* grew so frustrated by the problem of reaching technical staff members at the response center that he refused to get off the line when switchboard operators instructed him to call Ingram. He apparently never achieved his goal of talking with John Davis.[31]

During the afternoon of March 28, the NRC drafted a press release to provide the latest information it had about the accident. Gilinsky wanted the statement to be distributed in time to inform television news programs that would air at 6:00 P.M. Fouchard and the Region I public affairs officer, Karl Abraham, both former newspaper reporters, discussed the wording of the press release at length. They prepared a statement announcing that small amounts of radiation had been detected off-site from the plant, but they were uncertain of how best to explain the significance of the readings. Abraham said that he had been "very, very cagey" in talking to the news media because of the uncertainties about the accuracy of the measurements and about the source of the off-site radiation. Fouchard had been told by NRC experts at the incident response center that the off-site readings probably came from "direct radiation" that had penetrated the four-foot-thick concrete walls of the containment building. A very small amount of gamma radiation always escapes through the walls in an operating reactor, and the greatly elevated levels of radiation in the top of the containment structure at TMI-2 increased the likelihood that higher than usual amounts had reached the outside by that route. The press release that Fouchard and Abraham drafted did not mention the levels of radiation in containment or comment on the severity of the accident. Although it obviously qualified as a serious accident, its precise dimensions and the magnitude of the threat it posed to the public were still unclear.[32]

When Fouchard consulted with the commissioners about the draft press release, they raised several questions. Kennedy was concerned that the statement used the word *accident* twice to describe the situation at Three Mile Island. He feared that this would imply that the plant was in danger of the China syndrome and asked, "Is this an accident? What is an accident?" Fouchard replied, "I believe it's an accident, Mr. Kennedy." Eventually, the commissioners agreed to remove the second mention of the word *accident*. Although they had no policy or intention of understating the seriousness of the accident, they were careful to avoid over-

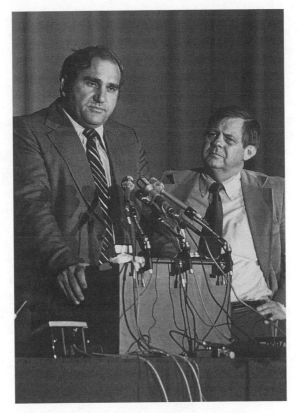

Figure 7. Victor Stello Jr. (left) and Joseph J. Fouchard (NRC).

stating it. Kennedy, who held a master's degree in business administration from Harvard University, worried that the press release would "scare everybody to death." Throughout his tenure on the commission, he had faulted the agency staff and his colleagues for bureaucratic delays and "interminable haggling" that impeded the licensing process and reflected poorly on the NRC's effectiveness. In his mind, it was the responsibility of Congress, not the NRC, to make "value judgments about the desirability of nuclear power." His job as commissioner, he once declared, was to make certain that the NRC did not cause "unwarranted delay" in the licensing process or "cast doubt upon the viability of the nuclear option." Kennedy's sensitivity to using the word *accident* was an extension of his outlook on the NRC's impact on the future of nuclear power.[33]

The press release that the NRC issued at about 5:00 P.M. announced that "low levels of radiation" had been detected off-site, and that the highest "confirmed" reading was about 3 millirems per hour at a point located one-third of a mile from the plant boundaries. This was presumably a ground-level measurement, though the statement was not clear on precisely where it was taken. The NRC reported that the off-site readings apparently were "principally direct radiation coming from radioactive material within the reactor containment building." In fact, the agency officials whom Fouchard consulted were mistaken; most of the off-site radiation came from releases from the auxiliary building.

The NRC's press release sought to outline clearly what the agency knew about the accident without indulging in speculation or unnecessarily alarming the public. But it fell short of its goals in important respects. It did not make clear that the NRC had reason to believe the accident was serious, and in that sense, it understated the severity of the crisis and the risk to public health. At the same time, by emphasizing that the radiation detected off-site probably had penetrated four feet of concrete, it made the radiation readings seem more ominous than the actual measurements suggested. Reporters were quick to interpret the releases through containment walls as a threat to public health. The *New York News,* for example, ran a headline in its March 29 editions that read, "Nuke Plant Spews Radiation in Pa., Goes thru 4-ft. Walls." NRC officials who talked with reporters were franker than the press release in assessing the accident. Fouchard told Stan Benjamin, a reporter for the Associated Press, in a widely quoted statement that, "they've got a hell of a lot of radioactivity in that containment building." Case was more specific; he told Benjamin that the radiation levels at the top of the containment dome were about 6,000 rads per hour.

In the absence of complete and unambiguous information, the NRC attempted to report accurately but also cautiously about conditions at the plant. Perhaps inevitably, the result was that in some ways it understated the severity of the accident and in other ways it provided the basis for disquieting stories about the hazards of off-site radiation releases.[34]

At the same time that the NRC deliberated over the release of information to the public, it conferred with Pennsylvania officials about the situation at the plant and the potential dangers to the public. After Herbein's meeting with Scranton, the state had lost confidence in Met Ed as a reliable source and looked to the NRC for expert advice. At about 6:00 P.M., following Scranton's second press conference, the lieutenant governor's executive assistant, Mark S. Knouse, called the plant and asked for a briefing from the NRC. In response, two members of the Region I contingent, James C. Higgins and Charles Gallina, traveled to Harrisburg; a third representative, Donald R. Neely, had planned to accompany them but had to stay behind because traces of radiation were detected on his trousers. Higgins, a reactor inspector, and Gallina, a Ph.D. and environmental radiation specialist, were well qualified to carry out their normal duties. Their training and experience did not extend to explaining reactor operations or radiation hazards to state government officials or the press, but they were forced into that role by default on the evening of March 28. There were no senior NRC officials at the site who could speak knowledgeably about conditions at the plant. In response to persistent questions from reporters and state leaders, Higgins and Gallina made statements on behalf of the NRC that soon turned out to have been ill advised.[35]

After arriving at the capitol, Higgins and Gallina met with Scranton and several other high state officials. They attempted to answer questions about the accident and radiation releases in terms that were accessible to nonexperts but had mixed success. Jay C. Waldman, Thornburgh's executive assistant, remembered asking them after listening for some time "to please explain in simple English terms what the hell happened here." The NRC representatives expressed confidence that the reactor was cooling and that radiation releases would soon be terminated. At 10:00 P.M., Scranton held his third press conference of the day. He provided a corrective to the NRC's earlier claim that the major source of emissions was direct radiation from containment. He declared more accurately that the radiation escaping from the plant came from ventilation of the auxiliary building. He added that measurements had not detected "any critical level" of radiation off-site. When reporters began to ask questions, Scranton turned the podium over to the NRC experts.

Higgins and Gallina provided a series of unsubstantiated assurances about the status of the plant that were not only speculative but also contradicted information coming out of NRC headquarters. They suggested that there was no "permanent damage" to the plant, that there had been "no significant core damage," and that the reactor would reach a "cold shutdown within a day." Although NRC experts at headquarters had told members of Congress and the press that they suspected operator error had contributed significantly to the accident, Gallina announced that he had seen no "indication of human error at this point." In Bethesda, one NRC staff member commented that if he learned the name of the "NRC spokesman in Harrisburg" who had claimed that the core of the plant had not been damaged, he would "strangle him."[36]

After the press conference, Higgins and Gallina went with Scranton and others to the governor's mansion to brief Thornburgh. While Mrs. Thornburgh offered sandwiches to a tired and hungry group of NRC, Department of Energy, and state officials, the governor sought to get a handle on "what the events of the day had been, and what the problem was, and what the prognosis was." Thornburgh was committed to collecting all the information he could before making decisions, an attribute that had served him well throughout his career. He had received a bachelor's degree in civil engineering from Yale University in 1954, but had decided that he was not a "very good engineering student" and turned to law instead. He attended law school in his hometown at the University of Pittsburgh and, after graduating in 1957, began practicing corporate law. When his first wife was killed in a car accident in 1960, however, he reassessed his career plans and decided to enter public service. He was appointed United States Attorney for Western Pennsylvania and won wide recognition for his efforts to crack down on corruption and organized crime. He won a stunning victory as the Republican candidate in the Pennsylvania gubernatorial election of 1978 by overcoming a huge early lead held by his Democratic opponent. Thornburgh's training as an engineer, and especially his experience as a prosecutor, taught him the importance of gathering reliable information before taking action on any problem. "When you don't have the facts, you don't have much of anything," he declared.[37]

Thornburgh applied his prosecutor's skills to seeking information about the Three Mile Island accident. He pressed Higgins and Gallina to "lower their jargon level to something that we could understand." They provided the same answers about the condition of the plant and the small likelihood of public health effects that they had given earlier, and the governor was satisfied that "there certainly was no sense of urgency about steps that had to be taken." But after the briefing ended, he became increasingly troubled by the fact that nobody had talked about the possibility that a meltdown might occur. Thornburgh's knowledge of nuclear power was largely limited to a book he had read a couple of years before called *We Almost Lost Detroit,* written by John G. Fuller. It was a gripping narrative about an accident at a small nuclear plant in Michigan in 1966 that provided a vivid description of nuclear hazards. Despite inaccuracies and exaggerations, the book became an antinuclear totem in the public debate over the technology. Thornburgh realized that the subject of severe core damage and a meltdown had probably been raised during other discussions of the TMI-2 accident, but the issue bothered him "a great deal" and he found it difficult to sleep that night.[38]

Thornburgh's uneasiness about the condition of the plant and the threat it might pose was shared by other officials responsible for protecting public health and safety. Some indications from the plant were encouraging; coolant was circulating, heat was being removed, and the reactor appeared to be relatively stable. This led some observers to believe that the emergency had ended. But officials in Harrisburg and in Bethesda remained wary. Despite the promising signs from Three Mile Island, information was still fragmentary, the causes of the accident and the damage it produced were unknown, the containment building was brimming with intensely radioactive gases, the auxiliary building was heavily contaminated, the ability of crucial equipment to operate was questionable, and the condition of the core was uncertain. Although there was reason for hope, there was less reason to be confident that the crisis had passed.

Chapter 5

Thursday, March 29

"The Danger Is Over for People Off Site"

A s a result of the uncertainties about the condition of the TMI-2 reactor, the principal parties who responded to the accident offered differing evaluations of the danger it posed, in a series of interviews, press
conferences, and briefings on Thursday, March 29. Through most of the
day, Met Ed executives were uniformly optimistic, offering assurances
that the plant was under control and did not endanger public health. State
leaders were less confident about the status of the plant as they weighed
the possible risks and benefits of ordering an evacuation of the surrounding area. Most NRC officials took a similar position, though their
caution was not reflected in some statements that Region I representatives made to the press. Both the state and the NRC, as they had done
on Wednesday, attempted to furnish accurate and current information
without giving credence to false rumors or exaggerated accounts that
could inflame public fears. This was a difficult balance to maintain in
light of the continuing shortage of reliable data, the changing perspectives on the plant's condition, and conflicting assessments of the meaning of available information. By Thursday evening, new findings about
the status of the reactor suggested to Met Ed, NRC, and state officials
that the accident had caused more damage and presented a greater threat
to the citizens of central Pennsylvania than they had previously realized.

MEDIA COVERAGE OF THE ACCIDENT

Media coverage of the first day of the accident was extensive and generally restrained. With the glaring exceptions of accounts in the New York
tabloids the *News* and the *Post,* most newspaper stories on the morning

Figure 8. Three Mile Island plants, looking east from Goldsboro, Pennsylvania (National Archives 220-TMI-DE9040064-34).

of March 29 avoided alarming or overstated headlines. Many accounts, while noting that radiation had "seeped" or "leaked" from the plant, also informed readers that the amounts released were small. Network television news programs, which devoted a great deal of time to the accident, presented a balanced perspective that neither accepted nor dismissed assurances that the plant did not threaten public health. The CBS anchor Walter Cronkite opened his newscast on the evening of March 28 by declaring that the TMI-2 accident was "the first step in a nuclear nightmare," but adding, "as far as we know at this hour, no worse than that." Radio stations in the Harrisburg vicinity, on which residents depended heavily for up-to-date reports, usually featured favorable appraisals of the danger to public health. The local population was obviously concerned about the accident without showing signs of panic. A woman who lived in Goldsboro said of the plant, "It's just something you live with, but this makes you think a little bit." She went on: "My husband and I built this house ourselves, so it would take a lot to make us leave."[1]

On the morning of March 29, Met Ed executives presented their views on national television programs about the status of the plant and the risks the accident created. Walter Creitz, president of the utility, appeared on NBC's *Today Show* and ABC's *Good Morning America,* and Jack Her-

bein was a guest on the CBS network news. Creitz told ABC's David Hart-
man that neither Met Ed employees nor members of the public had been
injured by the accident or "exposed to a radiation level which would be
considered dangerous." He conceded that the reactor was still releasing
small amounts of radiation but asserted that it was under control. Daniel
Ford of the Union of Concerned Scientists challenged Creitz's statements,
wondering how the utility, "without knowing what equipment has been
disabled," could be certain that the plant could be kept under control.
Creitz repeated his assurances on the *Today Show,* where he told a skeptical Tom Brokaw that he did not "have any doubt" that TMI-2 would
be returned to operation. Herbein offered an equally promising outlook
on the consequences of the accident. He expressed confidence that there
was "no danger" to the population of the area and predicted that the
plant would be "totally under control" within one or two days.[2]

Creitz and Herbein provided the same optimistic judgments to more
than a hundred media representatives who crowded a press conference
that Met Ed held in Hershey, Pennsylvania, about ten miles from Three
Mile Island, at 10:00 A.M. on March 29. By the second day of the accident, the size of the press corps had grown substantially. During the crisis, several major newspapers sent teams of reporters to Three Mile Island, led by the *Philadelphia Inquirer,* which assigned more than two
dozen staff writers to cover the story. In many cases, the reporters who
arrived on the scene knew little or nothing about nuclear power. Curtis
Wilkie of the *Boston Globe,* for example, recalled, "When people started
talking about the possibility of a meltdown, I didn't know what the hell
it was." Others covering TMI events were well acquainted with nuclear
technology and the controversies surrounding it. All the reporters who
attended the Met Ed press conference were anxious to learn about the
status of the plant and to clear up the ambiguities and contradictions in
the information they had received about the accident.[3]

Creitz and Herbein, who had not anticipated that so many reporters
would show up at the press conference, were ill prepared for the aggres-
siveness of their questions. Herbein estimated that, although the reactor
core had been uncovered during the accident, at most only 1 percent of
the fuel (or about 370 fuel rods) had been damaged. He maintained that
the level of radiation in the containment building did not exceed "80 rems
per hour" and suggested that, if the plant had suffered a "major fuel failure," releases of radiation would have been far greater. He explained the
accident and assessed its consequences in technical terms often inacces-
sible to much of his audience, especially those not familiar with nuclear

Figure 9. Jack Herbein (left) and Walter Creitz at a press conference in Hershey, Pennsylvania, March 29, 1979 (AP/Wide World Photos).

power. For his part, Herbein lost patience with questioners who refused to take his assurances about the plant at face value. At one point he was forced to state, "No, I don't think that this generator is a lemon." When reporters persisted in asking about the hazards of radiation that had escaped the plant, he replied irritably, "I can tell you that we didn't injure anybody through this accident, we didn't overexpose anybody, and we certainly didn't kill a single sole [sic] and as I've indicated, the levels of radiation we've had off-site have been absolutely minuscule." Many members of the press were dubious about Herbein's highly favorable assessment because it conflicted in important respects with information they had received from other sources, such as the amount of radiation in the containment building.[4]

Shortly after Creitz and Herbein spoke to the press, other commentators offered a sharply contrasting view about the potential public health consequences of the accident. Ernest J. Sternglass, a professor of radiological physics at the University of Pittsburgh School of Medicine, and George Wald, a Nobel Prize–winning biologist from Harvard University,

flew into Harrisburg on the afternoon of March 29 to speak at an antinuclear meeting. Sternglass told reporters that the portable radiation
monitor he carried with him showed readings fifteen times higher than
natural background radiation as his plane passed by the plant. He accused Met Ed and the federal government of covering up the true magnitude of radiation risks. "This government is going to take us over the
cliff if we let it," he declared. Sternglass advised that pregnant women
and young children should evacuate the area, a recommendation that
Wald supported. Wald also suggested that people who lived as far away
from TMI as Washington, Baltimore, or Philadelphia could be threatened by the accident "if contaminated milk, cheese, eggs and butter are
sent there."[5]

Sternglass had long been a central figure in a highly visible and fierce
controversy over the hazards of low-level radiation. Although radiation
protection professionals agreed that acute doses of radiation were harmful, they were much less certain about the effects of low-level exposure.
Most were confident that existing radiation standards for workers and
the public provided an ample margin of safety, but a few dissenters insisted that regulatory requirements were far from adequate. They contended that widespread public exposure to low levels of radiation would
cause thousands of cases of cancer and other diseases annually. In the
absence of conclusive evidence about the pathological or epidemiological effects of low-level radiation, the conflicting positions generated intense, sustained, and well-publicized controversy.[6]

Sternglass had made headlines in 1969 when he claimed that low-level
radioactive fallout from atmospheric nuclear weapons testing during the
1950s had caused an increased incidence in childhood leukemia, count-
less fetal deaths, and some 375,000 infant fatalities in the United States.
Those claims were sharply disputed by experts on both sides of the radiation debate who found his methodology to be deeply flawed and his
conclusions to be vastly overdrawn if not entirely fallacious. Within a
short time, Sternglass moved on to examine the effects of radiation releases from the routine operation of nuclear power plants. In 1973, he
charged that radiation emissions between 1958 and 1968 from the Shippingport nuclear station in western Pennsylvania had caused "horrify-
ing" increases in cancer, heart disease, and infant mortality in areas down
the Ohio River from the plant. Sternglass's findings created enough of
an uproar that the then-governor of Pennsylvania, Milton J. Shapp, established a special commission to investigate. The commission reported
in June 1974 that, although the monitoring of radiation emissions

around nuclear plants should be improved, Sternglass's allegations about increases in the incidence of serious diseases and in infant mortality from Shippingport releases were unfounded. One member of the governor's commission, Edward P. Radford of Johns Hopkins University, who was a frequent critic of existing radiation standards, commented that Sternglass's claims that nuclear power was killing fetuses and infants did "the scientific community a great disservice." Nevertheless, Sternglass continued to command attention and raise concerns by making similar charges about the effects of low-level emissions from nuclear plants in other locations.[7]

Sternglass's suggestion upon arriving in Harrisburg on March 29 that pregnant women and small children should leave the area caused the first signs of panic among local residents. The same radio station that had provided the initial news report about the accident carried a story on Sternglass's statement, followed by comments made by the station's disk jockey that sounded like an official order for pregnant women and preschool children to evacuate. The station's news director, Mike Pintek, recalled that, as a result, "people were calling [the station] in panic." An NRC staff member at the site reported that "they're going bananas around here," with calls pouring into the utility, the plant, the press, state agencies, and hospitals. The Region I administrator, Boyce Grier, told agency headquarters, "We have heard from every pregnant woman in the area." Pintek quickly sought to "balance the story" his station aired by running interviews with state officials who denied that an evacuation was necessary. But Sternglass's advisory clearly increased the edginess of the local population, to the frustration of state and federal officials who thought that his intervention was inappropriate and his recommendations unwarranted. Although the unborn and young children are especially susceptible to the effects of radiation, the levels released from TMI-2 had not reached proportions that prevailing expert opinion regarded as hazardous even to the most vulnerable members of society.[8]

STATE ASSESSMENTS OF THE ACCIDENT

Pennsylvania leaders continued to collect as much information as they could from state and federal experts to evaluate the condition of the plant and the danger to the public. There were some encouraging indications that the worst of the crisis had passed. The plant appeared to be stable and approaching a safe shutdown; William Dornsife, the state's nuclear engineer, concluded that the emergency was "essentially over." Although the plume of radiation from the plant had been measured as far away as sixteen miles, the off-site levels were low and the releases were not continuous. Nevertheless, the state remained on alert. The Pennsylvania Emergency Management Agency requested that its units in Dauphin, Lancaster, and York Counties review plans for an evacuation of the population within a five-mile radius of the plant. Governor Thornburgh, after a restless night, was still concerned about the possibility of severe core damage. His executive assistant, Jay Waldman, recalled that he "constantly weighed the potential risks from Three Mile Island against the hazards of an evacuation of an unprecedented nature."[9]

To gain a better understanding, or at least impression, of conditions at the plant, Lieutenant Governor Scranton decided to tour the auxiliary building, the source of most of the releases of radiation. He called Creitz, who offered to include him in a briefing for several members of Congress. Scranton declined because he did not wish to become involved in "a public thing or a media thing." Instead, he and two members of his staff went quietly to the site. Met Ed allowed only one person to enter the auxiliary building, so Scranton put on a protective plastic suit, rubber boots, and a respirator and proceeded into the contaminated structure. He measured radiation as high as 3,500 millirems per hour in the air and 80 millirems on his personal dosimeter. Scranton then returned to the capitol for a meeting with the governor, other state officials, and Charles Gallina and James Higgins of the NRC. He reported that the auxiliary building had some radioactive water on the floor, but that plant employees seemed to be calmly dealing with the problems at the plant.

After the meeting in his office, at 5:15 P.M. Thornburgh held his first press conference since the accident had occurred. In his opening statement, he assured the "people of Central Pennsylvania" that "there is no cause for alarm, nor any reason to disrupt your daily routine, nor any reason to feel that public health has been affected by the events on Three Mile Island." In a direct response to Sternglass, he continued: "This applies to pregnant women, this applies to small children and this applies to our food supplies." Thornburgh disclosed that he had "spent virtually the entire last 36 hours trying to separate fact from fiction about this situation," and that he had concluded that "the situation is under control at this time." He cautioned, however, "It is very important that all of us remain alert and informed."

Following Thornburgh's statement, Scranton briefed reporters on his trip to Three Mile Island. Then Higgins and Gallina responded to a number of questions relating to technical issues. Although they gave an upbeat assessment of conditions at the plant, they generally avoided the blanket assurances they had provided to reporters the previous day. In the most striking departure from that pattern, Gallina remarked, "Based on what we have been able to see so far the danger is over for people off site." This assertion surprised and disturbed Thornburgh and Scranton. "I remember a shudder kind of went up both Dick Thornburgh's and my spine," Scranton said later, "because neither of us really believed the danger was over." Thornburgh recalled that "to a man we were all very much concerned with Mr. Gallina's characterization . . . that the off-site problem was over," because "it just didn't sound right."[10]

The governor's concern was a visceral reaction that reflected his continuing misgivings about the status of the plant and the threat it presented. He was, on the one hand, committed to preventing general panic over phantom or exaggerated hazards. For that reason he had sharply taken issue with Sternglass's alarming and unsubstantiated assertions at his press conference. On the other hand, Thornburgh wanted to avoid lulling the citizens of the area into thinking the danger from the plant had passed, especially if an evacuation later became necessary. Gallina's statement, he feared, could undermine the objective of promoting a public attitude of calm, steady vigilance. Thornburgh realized that Gallina "had been thrust into a situation which he was not experienced in," but he still considered the statement that the off-site danger had ended to be inappropriate. His belief was reinforced when Gallina and Higgins returned to the plant and learned about recently taken measurements of radiation levels in the reactor coolant. The reading in the coolant sample was a very high 1,000 rads per hour, which suggested that damage to the core was more severe and the reactor less stable than had appeared to be the case earlier in the day. At about 10:00 P.M., Higgins relayed the new information to the governor's office. In the minds of Thornburgh and his advisers, this report underscored the need for continued caution. It also significantly impaired their confidence in the NRC.[11]

CHANGING NRC VIEWS OF THE ACCIDENT

NRC officials in Washington and Bethesda spent much of their time on March 29 collecting and analyzing the still fragmentary information that came in from Three Mile Island. Their goal of reaching solid conclusions about the condition of the plant remained elusive, and indications became more troubling as the day wore on. At 9:55 A.M., members of the technical staff provided a generally optimistic public briefing for the com-

Figure 10. Members of the Nuclear Regulatory Commission, shown here at a meeting held on April 4, 1979. Left to right: John F. Ahearne, Richard T. Kennedy, Joseph M. Hendrie, Victor Gilinsky, and Peter A. Bradford (NRC).

missioners. They summarized what the NRC staff knew at that point about the causes of the accident and the status of the plant and suggested, without saying so directly, that the worst phases of the accident had ended. Lee V. Gossick, executive director for operations, announced that a team of technical experts from headquarters was traveling to Three Mile Island to monitor "recovery operations" and make certain the plant was "kept in a safe condition."

The staff members who briefed the commissioners emphasized that their information was still "very preliminary," but said they saw a number of encouraging signs about the condition of the plant. Darrell G. Eisenhut, Victor Stello's deputy in the division of operating reactors of the Office of Nuclear Reactor Regulation, observed that the reactor had "somewhat stabilized" after the reactor coolant pump had been turned on the previous evening. The releases of radiation from the plant remained well below regulatory limits. Airborne radiation measured in the range of 20 millirems per hour at the site boundary, which meant that ground levels were much lower. The radiation that escaped the plant consisted "almost exclusively" of noble gases, which are chemically inert and do not bond with body tissues. They are, therefore, far less hazardous than other forms of radiation. One milk sample from a local cow had shown the presence of radioactive iodine, which is more dangerous because it lodges in the thyroid gland. It was "only slightly above the threshold of detection," however, and had come from "a cow on stored feed in a barn" rather than from a cow grazing in areas potentially contaminated by the accident. The staff briefers did not discuss the possibility that the core of the reactor had been uncovered, which had generated so much concern the previous afternoon, presumably because the situation had improved later in the day. Eisenhut informed the commissioners that, although "fuel failure" had occurred, the extent of it was unclear. He also reported that radiation levels in the containment dome were measuring 20,000 rads per hour, but submitted that this extraordinarily elevated reading probably was the result of "an instrument problem."[12]

A short time after the briefing for the commissioners, NRC chairman Hendrie, accompanied by several staff members, traveled to Capitol Hill to meet with members of the Subcommittee on Energy and the Environment of the House Committee on Interior and Insular Affairs. The chairman of the subcommittee (and the full committee), Morris K. Udall, who had requested that the NRC report on the accident, opened the session by expressing his skeptical view of nuclear power: "I think this is another of a series of events that lends credence to the contentions of those who think we have rushed headlong into a dangerous technology without sufficient understanding of the pitfalls." In a crowded hearing room, Eisenhut repeated the cautiously optimistic appraisal he had given to the commissioners a short time earlier. In response to questions, Hendrie took the same position. He told the subcommittee that the plant had not come close to a core meltdown or the China syndrome. He believed that the small emissions of radiation, primarily if not exclusively noble gases, indicated that the fuel had not melted. Hendrie estimated that "perhaps about one percent of the fuel in the core" had been damaged by cracks in the cladding. He described the accident as the most serious that had occurred at a commercial nuclear plant, and suggested that, although the levels of radiation released were low, they were not something "we ought to take casually." Hendrie offered what he regarded as a candid estimate of conditions at the plant based on the information available to him. But some members of the subcommittee viewed it as an uncritical whitewash. This led to an acrimonious exchange with Congressman James Weaver of Oregon, who snapped, "So, at the end you don't think there's any danger, any problem? . . . The whole thing is just fine, is that right?" Hendrie retorted, "I'm sorry, but you're not listening to me, and I certainly haven't said everything is all right."[13]

Hendrie's altercation with Weaver was symptomatic of the controversy that had dogged his tenure as chairman of the NRC, where he embodied the issues that galvanized the nuclear power debate. Hendrie had received his undergraduate degree from the Case Institute of Technology in 1950 and earned a Ph.D. in physics from Columbia University seven years later. Even before he finished at Columbia, he began working at Brookhaven National Laboratory, where he conducted research on the physics of nuclear reactors. Later, he headed design teams working on experimental reactors, which enhanced his knowledge of both reactor engineering and reactor safety issues. Hendrie's work at Brookhaven won wide respect and recognition in the field of nuclear engineering, and in 1966 he was offered an appointment on the AEC's Advisory Committee on Reactor Safeguards. A short time after his term on the committee ended, he accepted a position, or as he put it, "got snagged," as deputy director of licensing for technical review on the AEC's regulatory staff. This made him, in effect, the agency's chief safety engineer. Hendrie joined the AEC in 1972, just as the arrival of James Schlesinger as chairman, the ECCS hearings and other reactor safety controversies, and a heavy backlog of license applications were creating a great deal of turbulence. He viewed his position with the AEC as a temporary and in some ways a hardship assignment: he found it interesting but demanding and disruptive of family life. In July 1974 he left the agency because, he explained with a display of his wry sense of humor, he wished to "sit still and contemplate my navel."

Instead, Hendrie returned to Brookhaven, where he served as chairman of the laboratory's largest department. In 1977, as the result of strong advocacy by Schlesinger, who was serving as the White House energy adviser, President Carter named Hendrie chairman of the NRC. Although Hendrie won Senate confirmation without much trouble, he "had no illusions," he later commented, that he would "be greeted . . . with universal acclaim" in his new post. He told NRC staff members after becoming chairman that the agency performed the "terribly difficult role" of "trying to balance what is reasonable and prudent between, on the one hand, the outraged cries of the industrial people that we are choking the American economy . . . and, on the other hand, the cries from some that we are servants of the devil in having anything to do with this technology." Hendrie's professional background and pronuclear views invited sometimes harsh comments from critics. Daniel Ford called Hendrie "basically just one of the old Atomic Energy Commission hacks" who was not "fit to be the chief nuclear regulator of this country." Udall was only slightly more charitable. "Joe Hendrie is a very nice man," he once remarked, "but he is a true believer, a member of the original nuclear priesthood."

If Hendrie anticipated that his position on nuclear power would generate complaints, he was perhaps less prepared to find that his personal qualities also triggered attacks. In keeping with his scientific training, he was cool, analytical, and detached. In the polarized atmosphere of the nuclear power debate, some critics claimed that his demeanor was a sign of indifference or complacency. After interviewing Hendrie, reporter Stephen S. Rosenfeld charged in a *Washington Post* column in January 1978 that he was a "cold-blooded engineer" with "a mechanical and seemingly indifferent attitude" toward the NRC's role in curbing the proliferation of nuclear weapons. Hendrie responded immediately that Rosenfeld had badly misrepresented his position. "He seems to want a more emotional approach and is upset I did not talk that way," he wrote in a letter to the *Post*. "I am upset that he would think such a state of mind a fit one for dealing with my responsibilities." During the NRC's briefing of Udall's subcommittee on March 29, Hendrie's manner of presentation, more than the content of his statements, might have persuaded Weaver that he was insufficiently concerned about the effects of the Three Mile Island accident.[14]

By the time Hendrie and the other members of the NRC contingent returned to their offices, new information about the condition of TMI-2 cast doubts on the upbeat appraisal they had provided for Udall's subcommittee. The NRC staff in Bethesda had suspected for some time that the effects of the accident were more severe than Met Ed estimated, and as Roger J. Mattson, director of the division of systems safety in the Office of Nuclear Reactor Regulation, later put it, "The staff's view of severe got worse as it went along." By Thursday afternoon, strong indications of major fuel damage troubled agency officials at the incident response center. They were concerned about the possibility of "gross fuel failure," which, in Mattson's words, would include "swelling, ballooning, twisting, deformation of the fuel," and other consequences that went far beyond cracked cladding on a small percentage of the fuel rods. One ominous sign was that temperature readings from some thermocouples in the core remained extraordinarily high. The thermocouple readings had been largely disregarded the previous day because they were erratic, but by Thursday afternoon they seemed more consistent and more reliable. They suggested to Mattson, one of the NRC's leading technical experts, and several of his colleagues that "significant portions of the core" were not being adequately cooled.

The NRC staff's misgivings about the status of the core increased when Met Ed for the first time measured radiation in a sample of reactor coolant on Thursday afternoon. This procedure had not been performed earlier because of the high levels of radiation in the auxiliary building. The reading of 1,000 rads per hour indicated that the core had suffered serious damage and heavily contaminated the coolant. It also prompted James Higgins to inform the governor's office that the condition of the plant was more precarious than he and Gallina had reported at Thornburgh's press conference. Although the new measurements did not send up red flags of alarm for the NRC staff, they clearly caused greater uneasiness. Edson Case, who had spent long hours at the incident response center since Wednesday morning, recalled, "I think there was, at least on my part, a growing feeling on Thursday that things were getting worse, that we had a rather unusual change to a very unusual situation on our hands."[15]

The NRC's attempts to deal with the "unusual situation" continued to be greatly hindered by wretched communications between Bethesda and Three Mile Island—so much so that, early on Thursday morning, Stello decided to send a group of headquarters staff members to the site to try to obtain firsthand knowledge about the condition of the reactor. He asked Richard H. Vollmer, a senior member of his staff, to head a team of seven that included specialists in reactor systems, instrumentation, and radiological monitoring. When they arrived at the site, they found "a great deal of confusion."

As the day went on, Vollmer and his colleagues collected information they hoped would provide a more intelligible picture of the causes of the accident and the status of safety systems. They could not, however, come up with definite conclusions, and communications between the site and headquarters were "very bad." Vollmer encountered many difficulties when he tried to call Bethesda from the observation and visitors center across the highway from the plant, which he later described as a clamorous "free-for-all." The building was crowded with Met Ed employees and reporters, telephone lines were few, and circuits were often busy. When he managed to find a telephone and make connections with Bethesda, he had to crawl under a table to "get away from the noise and the people." The situation was so unsatisfactory that he went to his motel room several miles from the plant to use the phone.[16]

While Vollmer and his colleagues were attempting to improve the NRC's understanding of the accident, Met Ed and GPU officials were discovering that the condition of the plant was more uncertain and potentially more dangerous than they had realized. GPU sent Richard Wilson, one of its best technical experts, to investigate the status of the plant. After arriving at the site on Thursday afternoon, he concluded, based on the reactor's sluggish progress toward adequate cooling and on other troubling signs, that the plant was in far worse shape than he had anticipated. "I think it was clear," he later commented, "that the scope of the incident was . . . substantially greater than originally thought [and] that the reactor was not being and could not be shut down in a routine way." Wilson was so shaken by his findings that he looked "ashen" when he talked about them to Vollmer. His evaluation did not come as welcome news to company executives, especially after the sanguine assessments that Creitz and Herbein had given at their press conference in the morning, and that Herbein and Herman M. Dieckamp, the president of GPU, had provided to members of Congress later in the day. The problems they faced in bringing the plant under control now appeared more perplexing and more harrowing than they had previously believed.[17]

A FLARE-UP OVER WASTEWATER

By Thursday night, the new information from the plant gave the utility, the NRC, and the state ample reason for heightened concern. The focus of attention for NRC staff members at the incident response center and for state officials, however, was an unseemly fracas over a minor matter: the release of a large volume of slightly contaminated wastewater from the plant's toilets, drains, showers, and laundry facilities into the Susquehanna River. Under normal operating conditions, this water, which did not circulate through the plant's primary or secondary systems and contained little if any radioactivity, was diluted and discharged into the river. On the day the accident occurred, Met Ed, as a precautionary measure, had cut off its release, and by Thursday afternoon about four hundred thousand gallons of wastewater had accumulated in a holding tank. As a result of the accident, the water in the tank was slightly contaminated with radioactive xenon, a noble gas. The problem was that the tank was approaching its capacity, and if it overflowed, it would send undiluted wastewater through storm drains directly into the river. Met Ed, therefore, notified state officials in the Bureau of Radiation Protection

and NRC staff members in Region I (who in turn told colleagues in
Bethesda) that it planned to release the wastewater from the tank in a
controlled manner after dilution. Since the levels of radiation in the water
to be released were well within regulatory limits, neither the state nor
the NRC staff objected.

What began as a rather routine and seemingly uncomplicated matter soon created a great deal of confusion, anger, and ill will. Late in the
afternoon, when the NRC commissioners first heard about a release of
radioactive water into the river, they were "very upset." In a telephone
conversation with staff at the incident response center, Hendrie was un-
characteristically agitated. He believed that Met Ed had taken action
without consulting the NRC or the state and was greatly concerned that
"the impression everybody will have" was that the company was dumping contaminated water from the auxiliary building. Even if the levels
of radiation were "minimal" and it was "a perfectly acceptable release,"
he complained, Met Ed was "not quite running a plant [with a] normal
everyday configuration down there, for God's sake." Edson Case told
Hendrie that the information the staff in Bethesda received about the
water was "confused," and he did not know "where the hell it's coming from." He said that communications with the site were "just terrible." When the staff asked questions, "we just don't get any answers,"
and the incident response center could not talk to Vollmer except "by
pay phone." At Hendrie's suggestion, the staff ordered Met Ed to stop
dumping the wastewater into the river until further notice. By that time
about forty thousand gallons had been released, and the utility reluctantly discontinued the process.[18]

The same kind of confusion about the wastewater dump was evident
in Harrisburg, where Thornburgh and his staff tried to gather information about the source of the water, the level of contamination, and the
need for dumping. Eventually, after NRC and state executives learned
more about the situation, their concerns eased; Hendrie described it as
a "tempest in a teapot." Even after the technical uncertainties were
clarified, however, political issues caused tensions between the NRC and
the state. It seemed apparent that the releases were necessary and that
they posed little risk to public health. But the question of who should
authorize Med Ed to resume dumping led to considerable discord between state officials and Karl Abraham, the NRC's Region I public affairs officer. Abraham occupied temporary office space in the state capitol building that Paul Critchlow, the governor's press secretary, had
provided to facilitate liaison with the NRC. On Thursday evening, Abra-

ham told his boss, Joe Fouchard, that he and Critchlow "had very good relations." But those relations soured when Critchlow became convinced that Abraham was "trying to give the governor the stigma of having announced and approved the dumping of contaminated water into the river in order to remove it from the NRC, where it rightfully belonged." Abraham, who did not know at the time that the NRC had ordered Met Ed to stop the dumping, maintained that because the state provided the utility with a discharge permit for industrial wastewater, it had the responsibility for deciding whether to allow the dumping to resume.

Eventually, after a delay of several hours and some jockeying between Abraham and state officials, Clifford L. Jones, head of the Pennsylvania Department of Environmental Resources, issued a press release announcing the release of wastewater into the river. He declared that his agency "reluctantly agrees that the action must be taken," and that state and federal authorities concurred that the "discharge can be made without harmful radioactive pollution of the river." After Jones's statement settled the jurisdictional issue, Met Ed was allowed to proceed with the releases.

The wastewater affair reflected in part the growing stress and fatigue of the principals involved in dealing with the accident. One observer later remarked that employees of the Bureau of Radiation Protection "were just exhausted. . . . They were completely swamped with responding to requests from the Governor and their own state officials, and doing some interfacing with the public and the press." NRC officials faced the same difficulties. The wastewater issue also graphically demonstrated the acute communications problems that prevailed not only between Three Mile Island and Bethesda but also within the state government and the NRC. And, although the episode ended quietly, it left a residue of suspicion and disaffection between state and federal officials. The political issues that the dumping raised proved to be more delicate and obstinate than the technical questions, which were resolved easily once accurate information was available to decision makers. Thornburgh recalled the state's feeling that "we were getting nudged a little bit, that they were trying to hang this one on us." As a consequence, the state's confidence in the NRC, already undermined by Gallina's statement at Thornburgh's press conference and Higgins's troubling report on the condition of the plant, was further diminished.[19]

By the time Jones issued his press release on wastewater at midnight on Thursday, the optimism that had prevailed among reactor experts throughout most of the day about the condition of the TMI-2 reactor

had declined. At the same time, the collaboration between the state government and the NRC was showing signs of mistrust and alienation. In
addition, the citizens of the area, though remarkably composed, demonstrated symptoms of growing anxiety. The brief flurry of panic that followed Sternglass's statements to the press revealed an increasing level of
stress within the population.

An NRC staff member who was a part of Vollmer's team that traveled to Three Mile Island on Thursday morning experienced another vivid,
if impressionistic, display of public apprehension. Elinor G. Adensam, a
nuclear engineer and a section leader in the Office of Nuclear Reactor
Regulation, returned to her motel after a long day at the site and went
to its coffee shop for dinner. When the young man who waited on her
found out that she worked for the NRC, he told her that he had planned
a trip to Paris in the near future and asked her if she thought he "would
make it." She was surprised by the question and started to respond that
he would be fine unless his airplane crashed. But she suddenly realized
he was so worried about the accident at TMI-2 that he was afraid he
might die before he had a chance to go to France. When she told him
that she knew of nothing that would cause him to miss the trip, he sank
into a chair with vast relief. The waiter's anxieties did not reflect a majority view within the vicinity of Three Mile Island. A public opinion sampling taken by the Associated Press and NBC on Thursday night showed
that 42 percent of area residents surveyed were "not concerned about
their safety" and another 7 percent said that they were "not very concerned." But the same poll also found that 26 percent of those questioned
were "very concerned" and another 22 percent were "somewhat concerned" about their safety. The percentage of the population that was
"very concerned" or "somewhat concerned" increased substantially the
next day, when the accident at Three Mile Island turned into a full-blown
crisis.[20]

Chapter 6

Friday, March 30

"Going to Hell in a Handbasket"

The gradual recognition by Met Ed and NRC officials that cooling the TMI-2 reactor and bringing it to a safe shutdown would be more difficult than they originally conceived set the stage for the events and decisions of Friday, March 30. A series of developments created an escalating sense of crisis among government officials, media representatives, and the public. The emergency was triggered when the NRC misinterpreted information about a release of radioactive gases from the plant. Before the day ended, the NRC and the state of Pennsylvania agreed amid considerable testiness on an evacuation of pregnant women and small children from the area, the White House became deeply involved in the response to the accident for the first time, President Carter designated an NRC staff member as his personal representative to take command at the site, new concerns arose over the presence of a hydrogen bubble in the reactor and the possibility of a core meltdown, public anxieties increased, press accounts showed increasing alarm, and a general atmosphere of insecurity and danger became more pervasive. By any standard, it was a momentous and stressful day for the growing number of people whose lives were touched, or potentially touched, by the Three Mile Island accident.

For at least one top NRC official, the morning began calmly enough. Harold R. Denton, director of the NRC's Office of Nuclear Reactor Regulation, arrived at the incident response center "rather sanguine about the whole accident" and expecting "to find conditions steadily improving." After putting in long hours at the response center on Wednesday night and the following day, he had gone home to get some sleep on Thursday evening without learning about the troubling new indications from the plant. Denton had been appointed in July 1978 to his position as head of the office that evaluated reactor safety issues and reviewed li-

Figure 11. Harold R. Denton at the NRC's Incident Response Center, March 29, 1979 (NRC).

cense applications for plants, after working for fifteen years in various posts with the AEC's regulatory staff and the NRC. He was a native of Rocky Mount, North Carolina, where he grew up in a family of modest means. He attended North Carolina State College, which in 1953 had opened the first research and training reactor operated by a college or university in the United States. Denton, who chose the college largely because it was affordable, first majored in civil engineering but switched to nuclear engineering when he found out about the campus reactor. He graduated with a bachelor's degree in 1958 and took a job at the Savannah River nuclear weapons complex in South Carolina.

Five years later Denton joined the AEC's regulatory staff as a reactor inspector. Despite his lack of advanced degrees, he won the respect of his peers and superiors for his technical abilities. But that was only a part of the reason he was appointed director of the Office of Nuclear Reactor Regulation, perhaps the most visible and demanding technical position in the NRC. The commissioners to whom he was ultimately responsible were also impressed that he demonstrated a broader perspective on nuclear safety issues than many engineers, and that he could express his ideas in terms nonexperts could understand. Denton had little experience in talking to members of Congress or the press, however, and he expressed qualms about this deficiency to Chairman Hendrie. Hendrie replied that Denton should not be greatly concerned, because in his own capacity as chairman he would be the principal NRC spokesman in dealing with Congress and the media.[1]

Despite Hendrie's assurances, when NBC's *Today Show* requested an appearance by "a senior reactor safety official" to discuss the Three Mile Island accident, Denton was given the task. He made his national television debut on Friday morning. Among other things, the interviewer, Bob Abernethy, asked how the accident could have happened if the licensing process was sound. Denton replied that "we're still on a learning curve," but that "my hindsight is getting better as a result of these types of events." In response to a question about his opinion of the film *The China Syndrome,* Denton commented that the "movie took some liberties with the response of the [safety] system." Even so, he added, "as drama, I thought it was a very good movie" and "I really enjoyed Jane Fonda's acting."[2]

The China Syndrome attracted a new wave of customers as a result of the Three Mile Island accident. The makers of the movie generally refrained from linking their fictional account with the problems at the plant. Michael Douglas, the producer and one of the stars, declared, "We're all very wary of capitalizing in any sense on a tragedy." Nevertheless, the events at Three Mile Island clearly increased attendance at the film in theaters across the nation and seemed to help boost stock prices for Columbia Pictures. "Sometimes a little ghoulishness can be profitable," remarked one stockbroker. In the Harrisburg area, theaters showing the film, which had opened two weeks earlier, announced in the Friday newspapers that "due to popular demand" they were running late shows over the weekend.[3]

By Friday morning, Met Ed and GPU executives, drawing on the disquieting analysis provided by Richard Wilson at the site, were well aware that the accident at TMI-2 had been more serious than they had believed for most of the previous two days. The high radiation readings in the reactor coolant, the elevated temperatures in sections of the core, and the slowness of the reactor to cool suggested that they faced a complex situation with no easy or obvious solutions. When Wilson talked with Robert Arnold, vice president of the GPU Service Corporation, and Herman Dieckamp, president of GPU, they agreed that the core had probably been uncovered and suffered major damage in the first hours of the accident. They also concluded for the first time that Met Ed and GPU lacked sufficient expertise to deal with the conditions at the plant, and that they needed to reach out aggressively for technical assistance. Dieckamp recalled recognizing that "we were going to need more help, more smarts, the best smarts we could get." As a result, GPU officials consulted on various aspects of reactor behavior with an expanding number of authorities from nuclear vendors, utilities, government agencies, research organizations, and academic institutions.[4]

RADIATION RELEASE AND MURPHY'S LAW

While the utility sought to improve its ability to respond to the accident, some problems required immediate attention. The major source of concern was the growing presence of radioactive gas in the plant's auxiliary building, produced by damage to the reactor core. As the gas accumulated, it increased pressure in the makeup system, which in turn threatened to reduce the amount of water available for cooling the core. Throughout Thursday, plant operators had periodically reduced the pressure in the makeup system by briefly opening a vent to "burp" the gas. The burps discharged puffs of radioactive gas out of the auxiliary building's exhaust stack into the atmosphere, and the plant operators sought to keep the releases to a minimum. In the early morning hours on Friday, however, the pressure from the gas rose to a level that forced open a relief valve and dumped coolant into a storage tank, decreasing the amount that could be used to cool the core. As a result, the four operators in the control room decided they should relieve the pressure on the makeup system by opening a vent valve on the makeup tank, where much of the gas had accumulated. Eventually, they also agreed to keep the vent open for an extended period, even though they realized that this procedure could release more radiation to the environment than the short burps. It seemed to be a reasonable trade-off for the benefits of gaining better command of the pressure in the makeup system and reducing the possibility of a large uncontrolled release if the pressure got too high.

At 7:10 A.M., the operators began the venting process. They acted without consulting high-level managers of Met Ed or GPU and without making their plans clear to the state or the NRC. They did not anticipate that this procedure would significantly raise levels of radiation beyond the boundaries of the site, but in the event that releases exceeded expectations, they had the option of shutting the valve. James R. Floyd, supervisor of TMI-2 operations, requested that the company's helicopter monitor the releases. At about 8:00 A.M., the helicopter recorded a maximum reading of 1,200 millirems per hour 130 feet above the stack through which radiation was leaving the auxiliary building. Floyd later testified that he "wasn't pleased" to learn about that number and was relieved when the measurements from the helicopter promptly declined. He and his colleagues did not regard the peak value as alarming; the burping process on Thursday had produced some transitory readings above the stack that were at least as high without generating worrisome levels off-site. Nevertheless, as a result of poor communications and enormous misunderstandings, the 1,200-millirem reading set off a crisis.[5]

Within a short time after the venting process began, Floyd grew concerned about what might happen if for some reason the valve failed to close when the operators decided to terminate the release. He worried that if, in accordance with Murphy's law—which held that anything that could go wrong, would go wrong—the valve stuck open, "then I'm going to need to move people." With this remote but plausible contingency in mind, he decided to ask state government officials if they were prepared to evacuate the population living downwind from the plant. When he was unable to reach the Pennsylvania Emergency Management Agency (PEMA), he called the Dauphin County civil defense office and asked that it have PEMA contact him at the plant. At 8:40 A.M., Carl Kuehn of PEMA returned Floyd's call. The two men later provided sharply divergent accounts of their conversation. Floyd insisted that he informed Kuehn that he had carried out an "intentional, controlled release" that had produced a reading of 1,200 millirems above the stack before quickly dissipating. Kuehn, however, wrote in PEMA's log that Floyd advised him of an "uncontrolled release" and suggested that an evacuation might be necessary. He told his colleagues that Floyd seemed so upset that he was "going ape." Whatever the truth of the matter, the confusion created by the telephone conversation offered ample support for Murphy's law, though not in the way that Floyd had contemplated.

At about the same time that Floyd and Kuehn talked, PEMA received a call from another Met Ed employee, who reported the 1,200 millirem reading. He made clear that this was a peak level directly above the stack; the measurement at the site boundary was 14 millirems and was expected to fall much lower. PEMA officials relayed information about both calls to Oran Henderson, the director of the agency, who in turn notified Lieutenant Governor Scranton that there had been a 1,200-millirem release from, he said mistakenly, "the cooling tower." Scranton could not reach Thornburgh, who was on his way to his office, but he told Paul Critchlow, the governor's press secretary, about the report. Critchlow asked the

NRC's Karl Abraham what he knew about it, and at about 9:00 A.M., Abraham placed a call to Bethesda to check on the situation.[6]

THE NRC AND EVACUATION

NRC staff members at the incident response center knew nothing about the release from the plant until Abraham called. They had, however, heard from Region I that the utility planned to vent unfiltered radioactive gas directly to the environment in a way that would require a continuous long-term release. This was an inaccurate report based on erroneous information about the status of the makeup system and Met Ed's strategy for reducing pressure. Lake H. Barrett, a section leader in the Office of Nuclear Reactor Regulation, made a quick back-of-the-envelope calculation of the level of radiation that the putative venting procedure might produce on the ground at the site's north gate. The figure he came up with was 1,200 millirems per hour, a value that his colleagues in the incident response center found disturbing because it exceeded federal guidelines for taking protective action. At virtually the same moment that Barrett announced his estimate, the incident response center received Abraham's telephone request from Harrisburg for information about a 1,200-millirem reading at the plant. The coincidence in timing and the number was uncanny, and it forced NRC officials to seriously consider recommending that the state of Pennsylvania order an evacuation of citizens living in the vicinity of Three Mile Island.[7]

The question of emergency planning in the event of a serious nuclear power accident had received some consideration from the AEC and the NRC but had never been a focus of regulatory attention. In the early years of nuclear development, the AEC had required applicants to provide only sketchy procedures for dealing with radiological emergencies, largely because it believed that even the most severe accidents were unlikely to release large amounts of radiation into the environment. In the mid- and late 1960s, when safety experts began to worry that containment might be breached in a worst-case accident, the AEC reexamined its approach to emergency planning. In 1970, the agency issued a strengthened set of requirements listing the items that applications for licenses should contain, including details about who would exercise authority and perform assigned duties during an emergency, arrangements for working with local, state, and federal agencies to notify the public and carry out an evacuation if necessary, and procedures for training employees and conducting drills. The regulations that the AEC published were general guidelines encouraging prospective licensees to tailor emergency plans to specific facilities and locations. The responsibility for carrying out the plans if an accident occurred rested in the hands of state and local governments.[8]

The AEC's rule did not resolve many outstanding questions about emergency preparedness. In 1974 it issued guidance to state and local governments, including a checklist of 154 items they should consider in their planning. Three years later, the NRC, in response to comments from government agencies at all levels, identified 70 of those items as "essential for an acceptable plan." But the effectiveness of emergency planning, as the fire at the Browns Ferry plants in 1975 made abundantly clear, was at best uncertain. Nuclear critics complained that the NRC's requirements were inadequate or, in the words of one antinuclear group, a "grand failure." State and local radiation protection officials expressed confusion about the nature and severity of nuclear accidents for which they needed to prepare. As a result, the U.S. Environmental Protection Agency, which was responsible for setting standards for radiation exposure beyond the boundaries of nuclear plants, and the NRC formed a task force to address those issues. In a report submitted in December 1978, the task force made several recommendations about the kinds of threats that state and local authorities should consider and the size of the areas they should include in their preparations.[9]

A short time after the task force completed its study, the U.S. General Accounting Office published its own evaluation of emergency planning for areas surrounding nuclear power stations. It found that, although nuclear plant owners seemed well equipped to handle radiological emergencies on-site, the ability of state and local governments to respond beyond the boundaries of a plant was less certain. The report called for improved measures to inform the public about how to cope with a nuclear emergency and urged that the NRC issue operating licenses to facilities only when state and local emergency plans met its guidelines. Coincidentally, the General Accounting Office published its findings on March 30, 1979, the same day that emergency planning and evacuation became the preeminent concern for decision makers dealing with the Three Mile Island accident. At that time, 11 states out of 41 with nuclear emergency plans had received formal NRC concurrence, not including Pennsylvania. The state Bureau of Radiation Protection had submitted a plan in 1975, and the NRC had provided comments on it. The bureau sent a revised version to the NRC in 1977 but did not request agency concurrence, which was not legally required and, in the minds of state experts, not necessary. The three counties closest to Three Mile Island had developed plans for an evacuation within a five-mile radius of the plant. State officials were quite certain they were well prepared for a five-mile evacuation; PEMA director Henderson estimated that with sufficient lead time it could be accomplished in three hours. They were considerably less confident, however, about their readiness to evacuate a larger area.[10]

The feasibility of evacuating the region surrounding Three Mile Island received little if any attention in the deliberations of senior NRC staff members at the incident response center on the morning of March 30. Their growing concern about the condition of the plant and the misleading information about releases of radiation convinced them to move quickly on the suddenly urgent question of evacuation. When Harold Denton arrived at the response center after recording his interview for the *Today Show*, he learned that "things were not as sanguine" as they appeared when he had left the previous day. The troubling signs from the plant, he recalled, "kind of destroyed my confidence that we really knew what was going on up there." The news about the 1,200-millirem reading was the "last straw." Denton promptly conferred with other top officials, including Lee Gossick, executive director of operations; John Davis, acting director of the Office of Inspection and Enforcement; Edson Case, deputy director of the Office of Nuclear Reactor Regulation; and Joe Fouchard, director of the Office of Public Affairs. They agreed without dissent to advise the state to order an evacuation of the Three Mile Island vicinity, though they did not clearly specify the size of the radius they wanted to include.

NRC staff officials, without checking with the site for confirmation or further information, acted on the assumption that the 1,200-millirem reading was taken off-site and that the release was either continuous or likely to recur later in the day. Their attitude on recommending evacuation was summed up in their statements "it's time to bite the bullet," "better safe than sorry," and "if we are going to err, let it be on the side of public safety." They gave no thought to the practical problems involved in carrying out an evacuation. Denton later testified that his "sole objective was to minimize the radiation exposure to the public," and for that reason, acting expeditiously was vital. "I did not give any weight to whatever hardship evacuation might cause," he commented. "I saw the key issue as being one of timeliness, to move rapidly." Denton tried to contact the commissioners to inform them of the staff's decision and to ask for their concurrence, but he was unable to reach them. In order to avoid delay, he immediately told Harold E. (Doc) Collins, the assistant director of emergency preparedness in the Office of State Programs and a veteran staff member who worked with state government officials on emergency planning issues, to call the state of Pennsylvania to report the NRC's position.[11]

Collins, unlike Denton and his colleagues who recommended the evacuation, knew that the 1,200-millirem reading was taken above the stack. But he still thought that plant conditions indicated that "things are going to hell in a handbasket." Around 9:15 A.M., about fifteen minutes after Abraham's call from Harrisburg, Collins attempted to reach the state Bureau of Radiation Protection but failed to get through. He then called PEMA and spoke to Henderson. He told Henderson that the NRC recommended that the state "evacuate people out to 10 miles . . . in the direction of the plume." Henderson, with the boundaries of existing emergency plans in mind, suggested that "we'll start with five maybe." Collins replied, "I would certainly start with at least that and you'd better start thinking about moving from 5 to 10." He did not provide Henderson with any details about who in the NRC had decided to advise the state to order an evacuation or the bases for the recommendation.[12]

THE EVACUATION ISSUE IN PENNSYLVANIA

Henderson immediately called Scranton and the Bureau of Radiation Protection to report on his conversation with Collins. He also contacted civil defense authorities in Dauphin, Lancaster, and York Counties and advised them, "We have about a 90 percent chance of conducting this evacuation." The director of the Dauphin County unit, Kevin J. Molloy, quickly decided to announce on a local radio station that "some type of protective evacuation" might become necessary. This message made a strong impression; phone lines were soon flooded with about six times the normal amount of traffic in the Harrisburg area.[13]

The NRC staff at the Three Mile Island site and state officials in the Bureau of Radiation Protection reacted to the news about a possible evacuation with surprise and anger. The NRC's Richard Vollmer was incredulous that no one from headquarters had checked with him before calling the state; one of his colleagues described him as "livid." Charles Gallina, who was working in the TMI-1 control room, first learned about a pending evacuation when a Met Ed employee confronted him with the question "What the hell are you guys doing?" The man disclosed that his wife had heard on the radio that the NRC was "ordering an evacuation downwind," and that she had gone to school to "get our kids out of here." Gallina was astonished because the conditions at the plant and the levels of radiation at the site boundaries did not seem to warrant an evacuation. "I was mad," he later commented. "I was mad at . . . NRC headquarters, which has no business recommending evacuation of anyone."[14]

Staff members of the Bureau of Radiation Protection felt the same way. They were distressed that Collins had talked to Henderson rather than consulting them about the radiation measurements and the advisability of evacuating a segment of the local population. Thomas Gerusky, the bureau director, later commented that Collins's approach was not only "dumb" but also "obscene." As soon as Henderson notified the bureau of Collins's recommendation, Gerusky called Three Mile Island to check on the condition of the plant. He knew about the release and believed that he "had enough information from our people, from DOE people, from the helicopter from NRC, that there wasn't anything significant off site." Gerusky reached Gallina, who agreed with his assessment. At the same time, William Dornsife, the state's nuclear engineer, and Margaret Reilly, the chief of the bureau's division of environmental radiation, carried on a stormy telephone discussion with Collins in Bethesda. Reilly knew Collins from previous contacts on emergency preparedness, and on this occasion, she recalled, "we really unloaded on him." When Collins protested that the decision had been made by "a lot of big wheels sitting here around tables," Dornsife asked him to tell them that they "screwed up our situation . . . incredibly." He and Reilly demanded to know the names of the NRC officials who had determined that an evacuation was necessary. Collins fueled their fury by suggesting that "you don't really need to know names at this point in time." The phone conversations with Gallina and Collins confirmed the conviction of Bureau of Radiation Protection officials that their judgment on the evacuation issue was sound. After an unsuccessful attempt to reach the governor's office by telephone, Gerusky walked to the capitol to deliver his views in person.[15]

The final authority for ordering an evacuation belonged to the governor, and Thornburgh, in his customary manner, attempted to collect and evaluate as much information as possible before acting. As soon as he arrived at his office, he talked to Scranton, who told him of an "uncontrolled release" of 1,200 millirems per hour. A short time later, the lieutenant governor advised him of Henderson's report that Harold Collins of the NRC had recommended an evacuation. The events of the morning placed Thornburgh in an exceedingly difficult position. In contrast to NRC officials in Bethesda, he was acutely mindful of the practical problems and the risks to the population that an evacuation presented. "I had to weigh the potential risks of Three Mile Island against the proven hazards of moving people under panic conditions," he later observed. "No matter how well they are planned, massive evacuations can kill and injure people." The dangers of a large-scale evacuation were apparent for the elderly and infirm, for babies in incubators and other patients in hospitals, and for other members of the population who were not readily mobile. Even healthy citizens faced an increased peril of injury or death in traffic accidents, especially if a sense of panic prevailed among evacuees. The inherent trials of any evacuation were compounded by the uncertainty of how the population would react to a radiological emergency. Intense fear of radiation could undermine efforts to conduct a calm and orderly evacuation. In addition to the serious risks to public health, Thornburgh was aware that an evacuation would assess major economic costs by forcing businesses to close up and lay off employees. "If you really sat down and started to list the numbers of people who would be unavoidably and certainly affected by an evacuation," he remarked, "you [would] see that there are enormous unavoidable risks involved to a wide swath of the population of the area."

For those reasons, Thornburgh declined to order an evacuation unless he determined that conditions at Three Mile Island made it imperative. The limited information he received on Friday morning made him uneasy but did not convince him that "moving people" was the proper course of action. For one thing, he suspected that Henderson was overzealous in his support for evacuation. "PEMA mentality," he commented, "was akin to being all dressed up with no place to go. . . . We had to be careful about that attitude." But the governor was skeptical primarily because he realized that the source of the evacuation recommendation was Harold Collins, who was completely unknown to him. "When some guy who I have never heard of informs my top emergency management guy that we should carry out an evacuation, I want to find out who he is," Thornburgh recalled. "I think anybody would agree that to act upon an evacuation recommendation from somebody we never heard of before was really not a prudent thing to do." With his exasperation growing over the lack of solid information needed to make a decision, Thornburgh decided to call NRC chairman Hendrie directly. In that way he hoped to obtain a clear expression of the NRC's position and find out whether Collins spoke for the commission.[16]

NRC AND STATE DISCUSSIONS OF EVACUATION

As the NRC's commissioners deliberated over the same questions that Thornburgh was addressing, they faced similar uncertainties. Each commissioner learned of the problems at the plant when he arrived at his office on Friday morning. Gossick told the chairman's staff that an "uncontrolled release" measuring about 1,200 millirems per hour had occurred, and reported to Gilinsky that "all hell has broken loose." At about 9:30 A.M., the commission met in a conference room in their downtown Washington offices and talked by speakerphone with staff members in Bethesda. The information available was sketchy, and communications with Three Mile Island remained abysmal. The incident response center had not been able to reach Vollmer or other NRC personnel at the site. "People who go up there fall into a morass," Denton remarked. "It seems like they are never heard from." He revealed that the staff in Bethesda had advised the state to evacuate "out to five miles," though he did not provide any details about Collins's call. For some time, at least two of the commissioners thought Collins was working at the site or in Region I, rather than in the incident response center.

Denton emphasized that Thornburgh wanted a definite recommendation from the NRC on whether to order an evacuation, and Fouchard urged Hendrie to "talk to him immediately." The problem was that the commissioners still lacked the data they needed to make an informed judgment, including the causes and duration of the release, the levels of radiation it produced off-site, the weather conditions that prevailed in the area, and the likelihood that further venting would occur. Therefore, they did not reach firm conclusions to offer the governor. "We are operating almost totally in the blind," Hendrie lamented. "His information is ambiguous, mine is non-existent and—I don't know, it's like a couple of blind men staggering around making decisions."[17]

A short time later, after his own efforts to make connections with Harrisburg failed, Hendrie received a call from a plainly disgruntled Thornburgh. He told the governor, "The state of our information is not much better than I understand yours to be." He suggested that until more data became available to make a decision about evacuation, Thornburgh should advise those who lived northeast of the plant within five miles to stay indoors. As Hendrie and Thornburgh were talking, each received new and encouraging reports about radiation levels. The NRC learned that aerial off-site readings were in the range of 20–25 millirems per hour and dropping; Gerusky informed Thornburgh that off-site measurements were 1.5 millirems per hour and decreasing. The governor believed that the state's readings were probably more current and more accurate than those of the NRC, but Hendrie still thought that asking people who lived downwind to stay inside for a half hour or so was prudent. He was particularly concerned that additional releases might raise radiation levels again.

Thornburgh wanted to know if Hendrie supported the NRC's earlier recommendation to evacuate. "Was your person, Mr. Collins, in your operations center," he asked, "justified in . . . recommending that we evacuate at 9:15 A.M. or was that based on misinformation?" He insisted, "If we get any further such recommendations, we really need to know what the basis of those are." Hendrie replied that he had to check on the reasons behind Collins's advisory. "I can't tell you at the moment," he said. "I just don't know." He promised to contact the governor soon, after he found out more about the circumstances surrounding Collins's call and after the NRC considered the question of evacuation further. Hendrie's suggestion that downwind residents remain indoors for a time did not reflect a formal vote of the commission, though it was consistent with ideas the commissioners expressed before Thornburgh's call and with the information that arrived during the telephone conversation. It effectively overruled the staff recommendation for a five-mile downwind evacuation that Collins had conveyed to the state about an hour earlier. But the question of evacuation remained prominently on the table.[18]

The NRC's response to the crisis of Friday morning vividly demonstrated its lack of command structure and its weakness as an operational agency. The roles and authority of the commission and the staff were ill defined. One result was that senior staff members in the incident response center recommended an evacuation to the state based on erroneous information, without consulting the agency's personnel at the site or the commission. Given what they knew, it was a judicious action. But as Denton later commented, "I learned very embarrassingly, within the hour, that the State and some of our NRC people knew more than we did at the time." It also placed Hendrie in an awkward position because he did not have enough information to answer Thornburgh's questions about Collins's recommendation. Hendrie's uncertainty raised doubts in the minds of the governor and his advisers about the NRC's credibility and effectiveness. "My level of confidence was not 100 percent in what the Commission people were telling us," Thornburgh recalled. "They seemed to be somewhat at a loss to know what to do, and that is really what troubled us." The NRC staff had not exceeded its authority in advising an evacuation, and the commissioners did not believe that its action was an inappropriate exercise of its prerogatives. But the ambiguity in lines of authority confused and frustrated outsiders, especially in the state government. "There was a very real urgent feeling in the Governor's Office," Scranton observed, "that there was something out of control down there."[19]

WHITE HOUSE INVOLVEMENT IN THE CRISIS

As NRC and state officials struggled to deal with the emergency, concerns about the situation soon arose with equal intensity at the White House, which became deeply involved in the crisis for the first time on Friday morning. During the previous two days, Jessica Mathews had kept abreast of developments in her informal role as the contact point for the White House, but conditions had not seemed to require presidential intervention. At about 9:00 A.M. on Friday, she learned of the 1,200-millirem reading from a news wire story and a telephone call from Gilinsky. Realizing that this was "a substantial amount of radioactivity," she immediately informed her boss, Zbigniew Brzezinski, who in turn reported to President Carter. The president, who had served as an officer in the U.S. Navy's nuclear submarine program for about one year in 1952–1953, knew enough about radiation hazards to recognize that a release of that magnitude could be a major threat to public health.

Carter had acquired memorable firsthand acquaintance with radiation exposure during his tour of duty in the nuclear navy. He was a member of a team sent to help disassemble the core in an experimental reactor in Chalk River, Canada, that had suffered a serious accident in 1952. Carter and his colleagues, dressed in protective suits, entered the reactor building and "worked frantically for our allotted time." They received their annual maximum permissible exposure in one minute and twenty-nine seconds. "There were no apparent aftereffects from this exposure," Carter later wrote. "Just a lot of doubtful jokes among ourselves about death versus sterility."[20]

Carter's military experience with nuclear reactors did not steer him to a clear position on nuclear power as president. During his election campaign in 1976, he emphasized the need for energy conservation and the development of solar power and clean-burning coal; he described the use of nuclear power as "a last resort only." Shortly after assuming office, he incensed the already uneasy nuclear power industry by announcing that the reprocessing of spent fuel to extract plutonium would be "indefinitely" deferred. While nuclear proponents viewed reprocessing as a vital step to assure an adequate supply of fuel for reactors in the future, Carter opposed it because it increased the risk that more countries would build nuclear weapons. Nevertheless, the president regarded nuclear power as an essential component of his energy policies. "When I say 'last resort,'" he explained to news editors in January 1978, "it doesn't mean that it's a necessary evil. . . . There's a legitimate role for atomic power to play." Carter's statements in support of nuclear power did not placate the technology's proponents; Jon Payne, editor of *Nuclear News,* complained in early 1979 that the administration was a two-faced "Janus" that set forth a "blurred image" of its position. The president's energy programs did, however, disturb nuclear critics. Thomas Cochran of the Natural Resources Defense Council grumbled that Carter had "shifted his nuclear policy" in a way that was "not consistent with his campaign pledges."[21]

Carter's ambivalence toward nuclear power did not inhibit him from acting promptly when he learned of the Three Mile Island crisis on Friday morning, presumably because the potentially severe effect on public health and safety far outweighed the more nebulous long-term consequences for his energy policies. A short time after Brzezinski told him of the 1,200-millirem reading, the president called Hendrie, who outlined what he knew about the causes of the accident and the reasons for venting earlier that morning. Hendrie expressed his concern about further releases from the plant, but acknowledged that he could not be certain about plant conditions because "communications with [the] site aren't good enough to be on top of." Carter offered to install an effective communications system so the NRC would have ready access to the site, and so he could "pick up the phone and talk directly with the site" himself. When he asked that the NRC send an expert who was "the best in the country" to Three Mile Island, Hendrie replied that either Harold Denton or senior members of his staff would go to the site. Carter, with growing impatience, requested that Denton himself "go directly." He also suggested that if the NRC was doubtful about evacuation, "I think it would be good to err on the side of safety." The president did not know that the NRC staff had acted precisely on that premise in recommending an evacuation a short time before.[22]

As soon as his conversation with Hendrie ended, the president called Thornburgh. The governor complained that the NRC had "overreacted" to the news of the release from the plant, and Carter agreed that the state had done the "right thing" by not ordering an evacuation. Thornburgh said that he needed "one good man" who could evaluate the situation at the plant and "advise us as to the crucial problems." Carter replied that he was sending "the best man available" as his "personal representative"— Harold Denton. The president had not used the term "personal representative" when he talked to Hendrie, nor did Hendrie use it when he told Denton of his assignment. But that was the title that Denton soon acquired and the role that he played from the moment he arrived at the site. Perhaps fortunately, neither Thornburgh nor Carter knew at that time that Denton had strongly supported the NRC's ill-starred evacuation recommendation just two hours earlier and had instructed Collins to inform the state.[23]

In addition to arranging for Denton to go to the site and ordering the installation of a communications system that would link the White House and the NRC's incident response center with Three Mile Island, Carter requested that Jack H. Watson, secretary to the cabinet and assistant to the president for intergovernmental affairs, be briefed on the situation. Watson was an Atlanta attorney who had originally earned the president's respect for his service as chairman of the Georgia Human Resources Board when Carter was governor. He had excelled, Carter later wrote, "in explaining complex and sometimes unpopular issues to the public." In his job at the White House, Watson worked frequently with federal agencies and with high officials in state and local governments on domestic issues that required consultation and cooperation, including natural disasters.

Until the morning of March 30, Watson knew nothing about Three Mile Island beyond what he read in the newspapers, and he was not well acquainted with nuclear power technology or radiation hazards. In accordance with the president's instructions, Mathews and Colonel William E. Odom, Brzezinski's military aide, briefed Watson and his deputy, Eugene Eidenberg, on the "very, very limited" information then available about the situation at the plant. Although he had received no specific assignment from Carter, Watson assumed he was likely to be responsible for marshaling and coordinating the activities of federal agencies in response to the accident. The role that federal agencies should play in dealing with the crisis was unclear, but he was aware of two important considerations. One was that the state of Pennsylvania retained the final authority for ordering an evacuation if it became necessary. The other was that the NRC was an independent regulatory agency rather than a cabinet department, which meant that it was not obligated to carry out the wishes of the White House. Nevertheless, Watson was also mindful of the resources and influence that the White House commanded, and he was prepared to mobilize them to provide whatever assistance might be beneficial to those on the front lines.[24]

THE ADVISORY EVACUATION

While the White House staff was swinging into action, the NRC commissioners were weighing the question of evacuation. By that time, they had learned that off-site levels of radiation were low and diminishing; therefore, the problem they faced was not as acute as the staff had believed when it recommended an evacuation to the state. But the commissioners remained concerned that further releases from the plant might be necessary to relieve pressure in the makeup system. With that contingency in mind, they deliberated over what advice they should offer Thornburgh, but their discussion, largely because of the scarcity of good information, was inconclusive. Commissioner Peter A. Bradford sought to focus on the crucial issue when he asked his colleagues to consider what they would do if they "had a good friend and his pregnant wife and small children" in the area of Three Mile Island. Bradford's sensitivity to this issue had just been heightened in a conversation with his staff legal assistant, Thomas R. Gibbon, whose wife was expecting a child in the near future.[25]

Bradford had joined the NRC in 1977, within days after Hendrie became chairman. His appointment, reflecting the Carter administration's ambivalence toward nuclear power, was an effort to balance Hendrie's pronuclear views with a nominee acceptable to nuclear critics. Bradford had graduated from Yale University in 1964, taught English and American history in Greece for a year, and then returned to Yale to attend law school. After receiving his law degree in 1968, he worked briefly on a study of the Federal Trade Commission performed by Ralph Nader's organization. Bradford then served as an adviser to the governor of Maine, Kenneth Curtis, specializing in questions relating to oil, power, and the environment. In 1971, Curtis appointed him to the state public utilities commission. His experiences provided the basis for a book that Bradford published in 1975 on oil refinery development on the coast of Maine that was sharply critical of the oil industry and sympathetic to environmental concerns. Bradford was not a participant in the nuclear power debate before his appointment to the NRC, and he did not take a doc-

trinaire position on the subject. Nuclear proponents cited his work for
Nader as an ominous sign, but he pointed out that Nader had not been
involved in nuclear power issues at the time.[26]

After becoming a member of the commission, Bradford tended to align
with Gilinsky in raising questions about the safety of nuclear power,
which frequently caused clashes with Hendrie and Kennedy. As one observer pointed out in 1978, Hendrie and Kennedy were inclined to accept the judgment of the NRC staff on safety matters and to "protect
nuclear power from adverse publicity that might be misinterpreted by
the public." Bradford and Gilinsky, in contrast, were "more inclined to
call attention to possible problems and hazards and to allow full public
airings of such matters." The other member of the commission, John
Ahearne, often provided the swing vote on closely contested issues. The
lines of division were not firm or inviolable, but they were sufficiently
pronounced to generate sharp dissension. Collegiality among the commissioners was a rare commodity. On one occasion, for example,
Kennedy instructed his personal staff not to talk to members of Gilinsky's personal staff, an order that the female members of both staffs by-
passed by meeting in the women's restroom.

On the morning of March 30, however, the urgency of the crisis took
precedence over the differences among the commissioners. Taking their
cue from Bradford, they reached an informal agreement that the NRC
should recommend that pregnant women and small children "who could
reasonably leave the area might be well-advised to do so." In this way,
the most sensitive members of the population could avoid even small exposures that might result from further releases from the plant. The commission did not intend that pregnant women and children should evacuate "at all costs" but believed it would be prudent if they could leave
"without totally disrupting their lives."[27]

While the commissioners discussed the question of evacuation, Thornburgh waited with growing impatience for them to advise him of their
position. The events that followed the 1,200-millirem reading, he later
recalled, made Friday morning the most trying time of the entire crisis
for him, and he was frustrated that the NRC failed to supply more prompt
and helpful guidance. After his first conversation with Hendrie, the governor had made an appeal on local radio for the population to remain
calm, and Paul Critchlow, the governor's press secretary, had announced
at a briefing that residents who lived within ten miles of the plant should
stay indoors and keep their windows shut. The tensions of the moment
were heightened around 11:20 A.M., when a civil defense siren in Har-

risburg began to sound. The signal, apparently activated inadvertently, continued to blare for several minutes before Scranton managed to get it turned off.[28]

A short time later, Hendrie's call came in. He told the governor, "We really don't know what is going on. . . . The plant is not under control and it is not performing the way it should." In light of the continuing uncertainties, Hendrie and Thornburgh agreed on recommending that pregnant women and small children evacuate the area. This was consistent with the collective judgment of the NRC commissioners and with advice that the governor had received from the state secretary of health, Gordon K. MacLeod. Hendrie told Thornburgh, "If my wife were pregnant and I had small children in the area, I would get them out because we don't know what is going to happen." In reaching accord on this issue, they adopted the same position that nuclear critic Ernest Sternglass had advanced the previous day. Conditions at Three Mile Island appeared much more worrisome than they had seemed on Thursday, which convinced Hendrie and Thornburgh of the need to take precautionary measures. They did not accept Sternglass's suggestion that the radiation that had already escaped from the plant posed a serious threat to public health, but they were concerned about the risk of larger and more hazardous releases.[29]

After his conversation with Hendrie, Thornburgh and his staff agreed to advise pregnant women and pre-school-age children within a five-mile radius of the plant to evacuate until further notice. They settled on a distance of five miles because existing emergency plans covered an area of that size and it seemed to offer an adequate margin of safety if further releases of radiation occurred. In order to ease the pain for parents with both pre-school- and school-age children, they also decided to close all twenty-three schools within the five-mile radius. At 12:30 P.M., Thornburgh announced his advisory at a crowded press conference. He explained that although radiation measurements were "no higher" than the previous day, the possibility of further releases from the plant led him "to exercise the utmost of caution." He also reported that President Carter's "personal representative," Harold Denton, would soon arrive "to assist me and work with our experts."[30]

The citizens of the Harrisburg area took Thornburgh's advice seriously. As thousands of people made hasty preparations to leave their homes, phone lines jammed, lines formed at gasoline stations, and traffic backed up. Parents went to pick up their school-age children or waited anxiously for them to arrive home. There was palpable concern, confusion, and

Figure 12. Thornburgh announcing an advisory evacuation, March 30, 1979. On his right are Paul Critchlow, press secretary (seated), Craig Williamson, deputy director of the Pennsylvania Emergency Management Agency, and Thomas Gerusky, director of the Bureau of Radiation Protection of the Department of Environmental Resources. Scranton stands to Thornburgh's left (The Historical Society of Dauphin County).

anger. One mother later wrote about the anguish she felt when her children told her not to breathe outside and asked why "the electric company put all of that radiation in our air." An estimated 83 percent of pregnant women and preschool children within a five-mile radius, or about 3,500 individuals, evacuated. They were joined by many of their neighbors. Approximately 144,000 people within a fifteen-mile radius of the plant evacuated at some point during the crisis, and 51 percent of them did so on Friday. The streets of Goldsboro were deserted, except, reported the *New York Times,* for "a brown-and-white dog, wandering aimlessly, oblivious to the radiation that was leaking from the crippled nuclear power plant just across the muddy Susquehanna."

Most of the people who evacuated found refuge with friends or family members outside the immediate area. Anita Tighe of Mechanicsburg, about fifteen miles from the plant, fled to Ohio with her family because, she said, "you feel like you're sitting in the middle of a disaster movie." The evacuation centers established by civil defense authorities attracted

Figure 13. A family arriving at the evacuation center in Hershey, Pennsylvania (The Historical Society of Dauphin County).

only a small percentage of those who left their homes. The Hershey sports arena, normally the site of hockey games, basketball tournaments, and ice shows, was rapidly transformed into an evacuation center after its managers were told that they might need to accommodate as many as 14,000 people. But the number of evacuees housed and fed at the arena at one time during the crisis never exceeded 180.[31]

In the face of uncertainty, stress, and potentially grave danger, the public generally remained composed. The chief of police of Middletown, where about 20 percent of the population evacuated, noted that "at no time was there any sign of panic." The citizens of central Pennsylvania demonstrated their stolid poise even as the situation at Three Mile Island appeared to deteriorate. "Calm Harrisburg Strides through Alert," headlined the *Harrisburg Patriot*. They also displayed their traditional confidence in their leaders by apparently accepting Thornburgh's assurances that there was "no reason for panic or implementation of emergency measures." The stoicism that prevailed in the population presented some difficulties for the news media. One camera crew arrived in Middletown to film evacuating citizens, but found only empty streets. When a pickup truck carrying a family and its possessions suddenly appeared, the crew members, according to a later account, "swarmed" around it. To their disappointment, they discovered that the family was not fleeing in terror but rather was moving into the community.[32]

THE HYDROGEN BUBBLE

While state and NRC policy makers were considering the need for an evacuation, Met Ed, GPU, and NRC experts weighed the newly recognized complexities of lowering the temperature of the crippled reactor's core. By Thursday evening, it had become clear to both utility and NRC officials that the core had suffered major damage on the first day of the accident; the best approach for cooling the core and safely shutting the plant down was much less clear. Although the core seemed to be reasonably stable and was not increasing in temperature, it was not cooling as rapidly or as certainly as the experts had initially anticipated. Their concern was that the damaged sections were hot enough to cause extensive melting of fuel, and in the worst case, a meltdown of the entire core. It was essential to find a way to provide additional cooling. To make matters more precarious, the condition and dependability of the one reactor cooling pump circulating water through the core were questionable, and if it stopped working, the risks of a meltdown substantially increased.

The problem of cooling the core was greatly complicated by the presence of a large gas bubble in the top of the pressure vessel, the container that housed the core. By Thursday evening, it was apparent that the bubble was not condensable, because various attempts over the previous two days to shrink it had failed. The only explanation logical to experts at Babcock and Wilcox, Met Ed, GPU, and the NRC was that the bubble was composed mostly of hydrogen produced by severe damage to the fuel rods. This conclusion was confirmed when the utility discovered that hydrogen in the containment building had generated a sizable burn or explosion on Wednesday that had gone unnoticed in the confusion during the early hours of the accident. The hydrogen bubble, which measured about a thousand cubic feet and occupied most of the pressure ves-

sel's dome, represented a major obstacle to reducing the temperature of
the core. In order to inject coolant from the emergency core cooling system into the core, the pressure in the vessel had to be lowered; but if the
pressure were lowered, the bubble was likely to expand, uncover the core,
and reduce the existing flow of coolant to the core. It was also possible
that conditions in the pressure vessel were enough in themselves to increase the volume of the bubble. The situation was both unprecedented
and unforeseen, which was unsettling to the experts trying to devise an
appropriate solution.[33]

At 12:40 P.M., less than an hour after Hendrie and Thornburgh agreed
on the advisory evacuation, Roger J. Mattson, a division director in the
Office of Nuclear Reactor Regulation, offered the commissioners a disturbing assessment of the plant's status. Mattson's analysis commanded
the respect and attention of his colleagues on the NRC staff and the commissioners because of their high regard for his abilities. He had joined
the regulatory staff of the AEC in 1967 and was immediately assigned
to evaluate issues relating to the performance of emergency core cooling
systems, which was just becoming a major source of concern for reactor
experts. He focused on emergency cooling at the Oyster Creek facility
in New Jersey, then under construction, and worked closely and com-
patibly with the AEC's project manager for the plant, Victor Stello. In
1969, Mattson took a leave of absence to earn a Ph.D. in mechanical engineering at the University of Michigan. When he returned to the AEC
in 1972, he attended every installment of the ECCS hearings. He watched
with, as he later put it, "joy in my heart," when Daniel Ford grilled Milton Shaw, director of the AEC's Office of Reactor Technology and Development, about ECCS reliability. Mattson had strongly resented Shaw's
efforts to prevent the regulatory staff from obtaining information about
research on emergency core cooling. In his job with the regulatory staff,
Mattson frequently discussed a wide range of safety matters with Hendrie, then the AEC's deputy director of licensing, as they sat with their
feet propped up on Hendrie's desk. Mattson was well known within the
NRC not only for his wide-ranging technical prowess but also for his direct manner and willingness to voice sometimes unvarnished opinions.

Speaking from the incident response center, Mattson communicated
his views on the situation at Three Mile Island to Hendrie and the other
commissioners. He told them that his "best guess" was that the core had
been uncovered for "a long period of time" on the first day of the accident, which caused "failure modes, the likes of which have never been
analyzed." He outlined the problems that the hydrogen bubble presented

and revealed that reactor experts had not found a sure method of eliminating it. Mattson was angry that the staff's earlier recommendation for
an evacuation had not been carried out. He argued that the condition of
the reactor, the 1,200-millirem reading and the possibility of further venting, and the difficulties created by the bubble made an evacuation necessary. "I'm not sure why you are not moving people," he declared. "I
don't know what we are protecting at this point. I think we ought to be
moving people." The commissioners carefully considered Mattson's position, but they did not take any steps to follow his advice. They had just
gone through strained and more than slightly embarrassing deliberations
with Thornburgh on the evacuation issue, and they were disinclined to
make a decision without more complete and reliable information. Denton was already on his way to the site, and they wanted a report from
him before reaching a conclusion on whether to recommend an evacuation. Although they recognized that the situation was serious, they had
no reason to believe it was urgent enough to require immediate action.
Hendrie's feeling was, he later recalled, "Let's not panic ourselves into
unfortunate and precipitous actions."[34]

Nevertheless, the bubble problem clearly demanded a solution, and
NRC staff members performed calculations and considered ways to remove it without impairing core cooling. They also contacted experts
around the nation to seek guidance on how to deal with the bubble. One
possible approach was to open the relief valve on the pressurizer and vent
the hydrogen bubble out of the pressure vessel into the containment building, but this was not certain to achieve the desired results. Further, specialists working on the problem worried that expulsion of the hydrogen
into containment could cause an explosion exceeding the design capabilities of the building—which could occur if sufficient oxygen was
present to combine with the hydrogen from the bubble to form a combustible mix. Although there was little oxygen in the pressure vessel, there
was a great deal in the containment structure. Indeed, the presence of
hydrogen and oxygen in containment had produced in the first hours of
the accident the combustion or explosion that went unnoticed for two
days.[35]

While the NRC staff collected and analyzed information about the
bubble, Hendrie went to the White House to discuss the accident with
federal officials. At 1:30 P.M., an ad hoc group of White House and
agency representatives gathered at the request of the National Security
Council to learn about conditions at Three Mile Island and make decisions about organizing federal assistance and coordinating public infor-

mation. Hendrie reported that the plant was "stable at present." He disclosed, however, that the hydrogen bubble could prevent adequate cooling of the core, and that, if this occurred, a serious release of radiation to the environment was possible. Hendrie estimated that emergency planning officials would have advance warning of six to twelve hours if a major release seemed imminent. He suggested that, under those conditions, an evacuation of an area stretching twenty miles downwind from the plant, one that could include as many as one hundred thousand people, would be necessary.

Having heard Hendrie's not altogether reassuring testimony, the officials at the meeting quickly agreed that Jack Watson should chair an interagency task force to coordinate federal activities and serve as the federal contact with state and local authorities. In addition to the NRC, there were at least six federal agencies that could play a role in responding to the accident, including some that were already involved: the Department of Energy; the Department of Health, Education, and Welfare; the Environmental Protection Agency; the Federal Disaster Assistance Administration; the Federal Preparedness Agency; and the Defense Civil Preparedness Agency. Those in attendance at the meeting also decided that, to "prevent confusing and contradictory reporting," the White House press secretary, Jody Powell, would coordinate press releases and briefings with Watson, Thornburgh's office, and Denton, who would be the "single source of information about conditions at the plant." Based on previous experience during times of crisis, the White House regarded "the need for accurate information" as one of its "highest priorities." President Carter promptly endorsed the actions taken at the meeting and officially designated Watson as coordinator "of the efforts of Federal agencies to limit any physical damage and to prevent any personal injury from the Three Mile Island nuclear power plant."[36]

After the White House meeting ended, Watson called Thornburgh to advise him of the arrangements for coordinating federal activities and working in concert with the state, especially if evacuation became necessary. By that time, the governor had already contacted Jessica Mathews, who was the first person to tell him about the hydrogen bubble. At 3:45 P.M., shortly after talking with Mathews and Watson, Thornburgh received a call from Hendrie. Hendrie offered much the same information he had provided at the White House meeting. He suggested that the hydrogen bubble was not an immediate threat and reported that industry and government experts were "working hard" to find a solution to the problem. When Thornburgh asked about the chances that the bubble could explode and "rupture the vessel," Hendrie responded, "There isn't any oxygen in there to combine with that hydrogen, so the answer as far as I know is pretty close to zero." But he cautioned that, in the event of a "major release" of radiation considerably larger than the levels measured to date, an evacuation as far out as twenty miles might be required. He estimated that the probability of such a release was about 5 percent and that the likelihood of a core meltdown was perhaps 1 percent.[37]

THE MELTDOWN THREAT

During the afternoon of March 30, the NRC set up a pressroom for briefing reporters in the building that housed the incident response center. It took this action at the suggestion of Jody Powell, who told Gilinsky that speaking to the news media all at once was preferable to talking to reporters individually by telephone. At about the same time that Hendrie called Thornburgh, Frank Ingram of the NRC's Office of Public Affairs enlisted two senior staff members working in the incident response center—Brian Grimes of the Office of Nuclear Reactor Regulation and Dudley Thompson of the Office of Inspection and Enforcement—to meet with the press. At one point during their briefing, a reporter asked whether a meltdown of the plant was possible, and Grimes replied that yes, a meltdown, while not likely, was possible. A little later, Thompson affirmed that the presence of the bubble made a meltdown possible, though he qualified his statement by explaining that the chances of the China syndrome as presented in the movie of that name were "essentially zero."

Despite the caveats that Grimes and Thompson offered, the press seized on their acknowledgment that a meltdown could happen. This was the first time that the press had received this information from official sources. Within minutes, United Press International ran a story on its wire quoting Thompson as saying, "We are faced with a decision within a few days . . . on how to cool down the core. We face the ultimate risk of a meltdown, depending on the manner we cope with the problem." The UPI story made a strong and immediate impact. The NRC's Office of Public Affairs was inundated with phone calls and a staff member reported from Pennsylvania that people were "pulling their hair" at the news. When reporters quizzed Jody Powell at a White House press conference, he complained that the report had caused "unwarranted and disproportionate amounts of speculation." He also suggested to Hendrie that the NRC issue a press release to mitigate the effect of Thompson's statement (Grimes was not quoted in the UPI story).[38]

In response to Powell's request and their own frustration with the tone of the UPI story, Hendrie, Ahearne, and Kennedy undertook the painful task of writing a press release. Gilinsky and Bradford did not participate, because they had gone to report on the accident at a meeting with officials of the Department of Health, Education, and Welfare. The three commissioners readily agreed that the press release should begin by countering the UPI story with a statement from Hendrie that there was "no imminent danger" of a meltdown at TMI-2. As they drafted information about the plant's condition, however, Ahearne became concerned that the "whole flavor is very optimistic." Kennedy denied that the tone was overly sanguine and cautioned against including statements that would be "hyped by a factor of a hundred" by the media. Eventually, the commissioners concurred on a version that cited the "severe damage" to the fuel and the possibility that the bubble could lead to "further damage" of "some of the fuel." They also offered assurances that "the reactor is being maintained in a stable condition." The press release attempted to undercut the UPI story without denying that the plant had suffered serious damage, and it sought to explain the problems at the plant without causing exaggerated alarm—a formidable if not hopeless challenge. The NRC's press release understated the uncertainties of gaining control of the plant and achieving a "final safe state for the fuel."[39]

DENTON IN PENNSYLVANIA

While the commissioners in Washington and the NRC staff in Bethesda were weighing the bubble problem and responding to the tempest generated by the meltdown story, Harold Denton flew to Three Mile Island in an Air Force helicopter provided by the White House. He was accompanied by Fouchard, Stello, and several other NRC staff members. The helicopter landed in a cornfield directly behind the observation center across the highway from the plant at about 2:00 in the afternoon. Denton talked briefly with Vollmer and then conferred with Met Ed and GPU officials in the observation center. He asked them if space was available where he could meet with the NRC contingent at the site and make phone calls to the NRC. Met Ed offered Denton and his colleagues the use of a house next door that belonged to one of its employees, Edward J. (Dewey)

Schneider. It furnished a haven for them from the noisy, crowded bedlam of the observation center.[40]

After his discussions with utility officials and NRC staff members, Denton felt confident that the reactor was stable, and that it posed far less of an immediate threat than he had believed earlier in the day. His presence at the site enabled him to receive more current and more reliable information and alleviated his worst fears about the condition of the plant. "I just felt much more comfortable with my understanding of the status of the plant than I did back in Bethesda," he later commented. Denton was also relieved that Met Ed appeared to fully understand the problems it faced and had taken preliminary steps to deal with them. "This takes a little bit of the pressure off the immediacy of my concern this morning," he remarked. Nevertheless, he was troubled by his perception that the utility was "a little shy . . . of technical talent."[41]

Denton's understanding when he went to Three Mile Island was that he would take charge of the NRC staff at the site and maintain contact with state officials; he did not realize that his duties also included talking to the news media as the "president's representative" or personally reporting to the president. Shortly after arriving at the site, he learned that Carter wished to talk to him. Denton instructed his secretary, Doris F. Mossburg, to make connections with the White House. When Mossburg, who had never called the president of the United States, asked how to do that, Denton, in the stress of the moment, snapped, "I don't know. That's *your* problem!" Mossburg dialed the White House switchboard, and the operator who answered promptly put Denton in touch with Carter. He informed the president that the core was "badly damaged," and outlined what he knew about the condition of the plant. Carter offered to "make the full resources of the Federal government available" and asked Denton to call again once he "had a better understanding of the situation."[42]

After his conversation with the president, whom he found "very well informed," Denton reported on his evaluation of the plant and his discussion with Carter to the commissioners. He complained that communications at the site were still "frightfully inadequate." Indeed, the incident response center had encountered considerable difficulty in contacting Denton to tell him to call the president. But the communications problem was soon eased. The first improvement occurred when Stello called a friend in the Pennsylvania state police and persuaded him to place a mobile communications trailer at the site. This increased the number of telephone lines available for making calls. At about the same time, as

Carter had promised Hendrie, the White House arranged for the installation of dedicated lines between the site, the White House, the NRC,
and the governor's office. Denton was given a red phone that connected
him directly to the White House switchboard.[43]

Denton spoke to Governor Thornburgh for the first time at 4:05 P.M.
and reiterated much of what Hendrie had told the governor a few minutes earlier about the status of the plant. He agreed to brief the governor later in the evening and to join him in a press conference. At virtually the same time, the UPI story quoting Dudley Thompson on the
possibility of a meltdown at the plant hit the wires and set off a new
surge of alarm. Denton did not know about the report until he talked
briefly with a group of reporters on Dewey Schneider's lawn. Denton
met informally with the press because, as Fouchard explained, "there was
no way we could hide him." Denton was caught off guard when a reporter inquired about the NRC's "concern about [a] meltdown." He responded that "there was no imminent hazard" and declined to answer
most of the other questions he was asked on the grounds that he and
Thornburgh would hold a press conference later. "It was just a small
group of people but they were pretty persistent," Denton told Hendrie.
"I'm sure that tonight in Harrisburg it's going to be a mob scene."[44]

Denton and several of his colleagues arrived at the governor's office
at about 8:30 P.M. to meet with Thornburgh, Scranton, Gerusky, Dornsife, Henderson, and other state leaders. By that time, the confidence of
state officials in the NRC had been badly shaken. Although Thornburgh
later remembered that he immediately saw Denton as a man whose judgment he could trust, Denton and Vollmer, who was a part of the NRC
contingent, recalled that the initial attitude of the governor and his advisers was reserve and suspicion. Thornburgh remained in the unenvi-
able position of having to evaluate the accident and the dangers it posed
to the citizens of central Pennsylvania. He was responsible for ordering
an evacuation if it were necessary, but obtaining the information necessary to make an informed decision was exceedingly difficult. He had dismissed Met Ed as a reliable source of counsel on the first day. He drew
on the expertise of the state's own radiation protection professionals, but
their numbers were small and their resources limited. He was not favorably impressed with the NRC's efforts to deal with the accident or
provide assistance to the state. The reservations that Gallina's overly optimistic statement to the press and the wastewater issue created on Thursday had been reinforced by the uncertainties and indecision that had surrounded the NRC's evacuation recommendation on Friday morning.

Thornburgh's annoyance with and distrust of the NRC, perhaps amplified when Denton and his staff arrived at his office an hour and a half late, was apparent when the meeting began.

Within a short time, however, Denton overcame Thornburgh's misgivings, and the tone of the meeting became much more positive. Denton affirmed that he did not believe an immediate evacuation was necessary or that a meltdown was likely. He saw the principal problem as one of finding a way to reduce the size of the bubble, and he disclosed that the NRC was sending more staff to the site because he thought Met Ed's technical capabilities were "thin." He suggested that the plant would not reach a cold shutdown, in which the temperature of the water in the core was lowered below the boiling point, for several days. Denton's command of the technical and safety issues raised by existing conditions at the plant impressed Thornburgh and other state officials, but his frankness and unassuming confidence seemed to be at least as instrumental in winning their respect. From that point on, Thornburgh placed his faith in Denton as his chief adviser in dealing with the effects and possible hazards of the accident at Three Mile Island.[45]

Thornburgh described the practical problems of carrying out an evacuation and told Denton and his colleagues about pitfalls they had not previously appreciated. He explained that evacuating only an area downwind from the plant, as the NRC had suggested, was difficult because the state's emergency plans were based on moving everyone within a specified radius and could not be "rapidly readjusted." Even the best evacuation plans were hardly foolproof. "I learned that the farmers wouldn't leave their animals and the Amish refused to leave under any conditions," Denton later recalled. "There were hospital problems and nursing home problems, and tremendous social problems involved in local community disruption." He commented at the meeting that, in light of those risks and costs, the decision not to order a general evacuation under the existing conditions could not "be faulted." But he cautioned that procedures to reduce the size of the hydrogen bubble might still require an evacuation.[46]

As soon as the meeting ended, Thornburgh and Denton met with a large group of reporters who jammed the media center at the capitol. The governor introduced Denton as the president's "personal representative" and announced that a general evacuation was not necessary "at this time." He then turned the podium over to Denton, who had participated in only one press briefing in his entire career and had not anticipated assuming the leading role this time. In response to questions posed by persistent and skeptical reporters, he told them what he knew, or thought he knew, about the condition of the plant without discounting the severity of the accident or the uncertainties of reaching a safe shutdown. It was, he said, the "most serious accident in the life of the reactor program." Asked by a reporter if he knew what he was doing, Denton replied, "Well I think we know what we are doing, yes, but we have never had such extensive fuel damage before in the life of a reactor." He declared, however, that the chances of a meltdown were "very remote." He carefully explained that he viewed a meltdown as "molten fuel and a complete loss of coolant" and acknowledged that some fuel melting might have occurred. In his discussion of the complications created by the bubble, he asserted that there was no risk of an explosion in the pressure vessel.[47]

Denton's evaluation of the status of the plant and the potential hazards to public health was quite similar to the NRC's press release on the meltdown story, though he was more candid about the complexities of eliminating the bubble. His statements were more cautious than the assessments offered by Met Ed and NRC officials at the site on the first two days of the accident; Denton avoided the wide-ranging assurances and unduly optimistic predictions that had undermined their credibility. Reporters at the press conference, like state officials earlier in the evening, seemed to be impressed not only with the substance of Denton's remarks but also with the unflappable and unrehearsed manner of his presentation. Although some reporters grumbled that he used too much jargon, most judged his performance more favorably. Curtis Wilkie of the *Boston Globe,* for example, found Denton's responses to be unusually credible and commented, "It's rare that I'm inclined to believe a government official." One reporter asked Fouchard, a former newsman, if he had coached Denton on how to address the media. Fouchard laughed and replied that Denton's demeanor in the press conference was definitely not the product of training or instruction but simply the result of acting naturally in the face of acute pressure.[48]

Despite Denton's calming influence, the events of the day substantially amplified public concern. Media accounts of the dangers of the accident, which by Friday was covered by about four hundred reporters at the scene, showed increasing alarm. The evening news programs of the three major television networks, drawing on the comments of Brian Grimes and Dudley Thompson at their press briefing in Bethesda, offered disturbing reports. John Chancellor of NBC told his audience that "there was serious trouble today" at Three Mile Island, and that the reactor would be "very dangerous" until it was cooled. Frank Reynolds of ABC warned about the "possibility" of a meltdown "that would be, in plain language, a catastrophe." Walter Cronkite of CBS informed the 16 million viewers of his top-ranked news program, "The world has never known a day quite like today. It faced the considerable uncertainties and dangers of the worst nuclear power plant accident of the atomic age." He underscored the tone of his message by adding, "And the horror tonight is that it could get much worse." One journalist who remembered Cronkite's "calming voice" during previous national crises found his comments on Three Mile Island to be more unnerving than the series of other reports she had heard about the accident throughout the day.

Newspaper headlines and articles were not as uniformly disquieting as the television coverage: they ranged from low-key to inflammatory. Reporters for local newspapers who lived in the community were more inclined than their out-of-town counterparts to weigh the impact of their stories on the population of the area. They tried to avoid exaggerating the dangers of the accident and were sometimes troubled when, as one local newsman put it, "the national and international media blew it all out of proportion." Nevertheless, by any standard, the news about the plant was more ominous on Friday than on the first two days of the accident, and press accounts reflected that reality.[49]

The source of much of the unsettling news of the day was the NRC, especially its reports that a meltdown was possible. As agency experts tried to evaluate the condition of the plant, they were most concerned that the hydrogen bubble in the pressure vessel would inhibit cooling of the core and cause a massive melting of fuel. By the end of the day on Friday, another potentially grave problem began to trouble them—the risk of a hydrogen burn or explosion that could rupture the pressure vessel and perhaps lead to a breach of containment. This emerged as the focus of attention and anxiety for the NRC on Saturday, and it led to another day of growing apprehension for the people of central Pennsylvania and for the federal, state, and local government officials trying to protect them from the consequences of the accident.

Chapter 7

Saturday, March 31

"You're Causing a Panic!"

O n Saturday, March 31, 1979, the fourth day of the Three Mile Island emergency, there were some encouraging indications that conditions in the plant were improving. Thermocouple readings showed that temperatures in the core continued to decline. Although small amounts of radioactive gases escaped from the auxiliary building into the atmosphere, radiation measured at ground level was consistently low (.2 to .5 millirems per hour in the direction of the plume around Middletown). By the middle of the afternoon, three of the four reactor coolant pumps were operable, which alleviated concerns about losing the single pump that had circulated water through the core since Wednesday evening. Nevertheless, the crisis had not ended. "Let me say, as frankly as I know how, bringing this plant down is risky," Roger Mattson told the NRC commissioners. "No plant has ever been in this condition, no plant has ever been tested in this condition, no plant has ever been analyzed in this condition." The major source of uncertainty and anxiety, at least for NRC officials in Washington and Bethesda, was the possibility that the hydrogen bubble in the pressure vessel might burn or explode and set off a train of events that could breach containment.[1]

GROWING CONCERN OVER HYDROGEN

When NRC chairman Hendrie had talked to Governor Thornburgh on Friday afternoon, he told him the chances of a hydrogen explosion in the pressure vessel were "pretty close to zero" because of the lack of "any oxygen in there." Soon afterward, however, Hendrie became troubled about the amount of oxygen that would be generated in the vessel through the process of radiolysis, in which radiation caused the disassociation of water molecules into hydrogen and oxygen. If sufficient oxygen were

Figure 14. Helicopter taking radiation readings at Three Mile Island. This view of the plant is looking northwest (National Archives 220-TMI-DE9040070-3).

present in the vessel, it could migrate into the bubble and create a volatile mixture that could burn or even explode. The consequences of a hydrogen burn were uncertain, but it had the potential to generate a pressure pulse that might fracture the walls of the vessel. An explosion would be even more destructive. "If there's anything I don't particularly think I need at the moment," Hendrie told his fellow commissioners on Friday evening, "it's . . . for the bubble to be in a flammable configuration." If the pressure vessel, which held the core in place, failed, the likelihood of a catastrophic accident that breached containment increased by indeterminate but uncomfortable proportions.[2]

Hendrie's concern grew as the evening wore on. The fundamental problem was to estimate the quantity of free oxygen needed for combustion or an explosion and the amount being produced in the vessel from radiolysis. Although some of the free oxygen would recombine with hydrogen to form water, the question of how much might remain to form a combustible mix was difficult to ascertain. When Hendrie performed his own rough calculations, he found that they were not "coming out very good." He called staff members at the incident response center and requested that they promptly analyze the potential hazards of oxygen evolution in the vessel. He remained worried enough that at 2:00 A.M. on Saturday he telephoned Mattson for confirmation that NRC experts were working on the issue. Hendrie's anxiety about the dangers of the hydrogen bubble made a strong impression on staff members both because of his generally unruffled demeanor and his technical acumen. "If Joe is worried," an NRC official commented later, "we had better take it seriously—not because we are scared of him, but because he is that good."[3]

In response to Hendrie's concerns, Mattson asked two groups of NRC staff members to investigate the possible threat that free oxygen in the pressure vessel would present. Mattson was not an expert on the subject, but he took on, along with his other responsibilities, the job of coordinator of the NRC's effort to address what had quickly emerged as an urgent question. Beginning in the early hours of Saturday morning, NRC staff members made calculations to estimate the rate of oxygen evolution in the vessel and the potential for combustion or an explosion in the bubble. They also placed calls to experts at Babcock and Wilcox, Westinghouse, national laboratories, research institutions, and government contractors. The answers they received did not provide clear or uniform conclusions. Nevertheless, by about 2:00 on Saturday afternoon, Mattson had collected reports "from four independent sources, all with known credentials in this field," indicating that free oxygen was present in the vessel.

The most influential of the early estimates came from a conversation between Saul Levine, director of the NRC's Office of Nuclear Regulatory Research, and Robert Ritzman, a physical chemist with a company called Science Applications Incorporated. Ritzman, whom Levine considered the leading authority on the subject, calculated that the generation of free oxygen could be as much as 1 percent of the volume of the hydrogen bubble per day, though he believed it was probably only about one-tenth of that rate and could be zero. He also estimated that the bubble could ignite if the mixture contained 8 to 9 percent oxygen. Other experts provided similar, though far from definitive, analyses, and some suggested that the bubble could become flammable, in a worst-case calculation, at 4 or 5 percent. The concentration of oxygen required for a hydrogen explosion was much higher, in the range of 11 percent or more.

Those figures were generally but not entirely reassuring for NRC officials trying to judge the magnitude of the danger. Although the experts agreed that the bubble did not pose an immediate threat, it could conceivably become flammable in two or three days, depending on the rate of generation and how much free oxygen was already present in the vessel. The chances of hydrogen combustion in two or three days seemed remote, but none of the experts with whom the NRC consulted could be sure about the accuracy of their estimates.[4]

Despite the prevailing uncertainty about the extent of the threat and the amount of time available to deal with it, the NRC staff did not regard the danger as urgent enough to require an immediate evacuation of the population around Three Mile Island. The consensus among the experts projected that the bubble would not reach a flammable condition for several days, especially since there was no ignition source to start the mixture burning. Therefore, they believed they had time to find a solution to the problem. Mattson was certainly willing to recommend an evacuation if he deemed it necessary; indeed, the previous day he had strenuously urged the commissioners to advise the state to evacuate. He had changed his opinion after learning that large radiation releases from the plant were not continuous, but he remained concerned that an evacuation might still be essential if the bubble problem could not be resolved. Hendrie, who had sounded the alarm over the bubble, took the same position and told his fellow commissioners that an evacuation was not needed immediately. His colleagues were worried, however, by the uncertainties in the calculations and the possible outcome if, as Bradford remarked, "you assume the worst case in each of the uncertainties." When Kennedy asked Mattson whether such worst-case assumptions would indicate a more urgent hazard, he responded, "I can't answer the question." But he was confident that "we're not grossly underestimating" the severity of the threat.[5]

Although the commissioners were uneasy about the bubble, they accepted Hendrie and Mattson's view that they should not recommend an immediate evacuation. They continued to deliberate over the possible need to evacuate in the near future. Even if the bubble were eliminated, the general state of the TMI-2 reactor remained a troubling question. The signs of improvement were encouraging, but the reactor could not be counted on to remain stable after the heavy damage it had suffered. Kennedy commented, "You have to assume that at some point you have a . . . system which is working in a mode for which it was never designed

and in a mode which nobody understands or knows much about." Therefore, an evacuation remained a genuine possibility.

UNEASY CALM IN PENNSYLVANIA

While the NRC considered the need for a general evacuation, state and
local agencies considered how it could be carried out. Hendrie reiterated
his earlier estimate that there would be six to twelve hours' advance warning to conduct an evacuation if the condition of the plant deteriorated.
Denton told Thornburgh, and later the commissioners, that "if everything
failed" in the plant, the lead time could be as little as thirty minutes,
though he thought "several hours" was much more likely. State officials
claimed that they could evacuate the city of Harrisburg within two hours,
and a twenty-mile radius in about five hours. No estimate, of course, was
verifiable, and the unavoidable uncertainties about evacuation contributed to the pressures under which policy makers labored.[6]

Extending the preexisting plans for a five-mile evacuation to a radius of ten or twenty miles was a formidable task. The twenty-mile radius, for example, included not only more than six hundred thousand
people but also thirteen hospitals and a prison. In preparing new plans,
the staff of the Pennsylvania Emergency Management Agency and
county civil defense agencies were further encumbered by a lack of current information about the status of the plant and guidance from the
governor's office, and by increasing fatigue and frustration among emergency workers.[7]

The population of the area remained calm but anxious. "Most people
I know did what I did," said Delbert Hipple, who lived a few miles from
the plant. "They packed their bags, filled the car with gas, and waited."
Two longtime residents of Middletown, Anne and Edward Trunk, later
recalled that "most residents went about their routine of Saturday shopping and tending to household chores while trying to keep abreast of the
news." The citizens of the region continued to rely heavily on radio bul-
letins for up-to-date information and kept alert for sirens or other signals that something was amiss at the plant. They also spent a lot of time
on the telephone, sometimes with distant friends and relatives who heard
false reports about the situation in central Pennsylvania. There was one
rumor, for example, that Middletown had been completely obliterated
and another that the entire population of the town had been evacuated
by helicopter. Local residents viewed with suspicion and consternation

the deluge of reporters who descended on them in search of news stories. "The news media had invaded the area and made their presence
known to the people," the Trunks commented. "The emphasis was to
focus in on anyone who displayed emotion or fear."[8]

The same pattern of media behavior was evident when Thornburgh
and Scranton, accompanied by their wives, visited evacuees at the Hershey sports arena early Saturday afternoon. The news media had arrived
in large numbers to report on the shelter shortly after it was set up the
previous day. Early on Saturday morning, more than three hundred reporters rushed the evacuees, whom they outnumbered by about two to
one. One pregnant woman became dizzy from the barrage of flashbulbs,
which sparked fears that she was going into labor. Edward Koast, the
local director of the Red Cross, observed that reporters gave more attention to "people who looked distraught" than to "those who seemed
to be relaxed." To provide relief for both parents and children, Herco,
the corporation that owned the Hershey Chocolate Company and the
town's entertainment complex, conducted tours of its zoo, amusement
park (which was not yet open for the season), and Chocolate World mu-
seum and confectionery. When the governor and his party arrived, about
115 evacuees remained in the arena. Thornburgh's plans to circulate
among them to shake hands and answer questions were inhibited by the
crush of reporters who followed him. He spoke to the evacuees on the
public address system at the arena and thanked them for their "calm and
patience." But he could not answer their most pressing questions about
how soon the emergency would end. His visit was, he later remarked,
"a stark reminder of the responsibility of governing." He vividly recalled
"young children, mothers carrying babies, and their bewilderment and
confusion over a technology they clearly didn't understand, seeking reassurance that the situation was being handled."[9]

The governor and his constituents in central Pennsylvania increasingly
looked to Harold Denton for affirmation that the "situation was being
handled." Denton talked to Thornburgh and Scranton at 9:35 on Saturday morning and told them that, although the condition of the plant
was "slightly better," achieving a cold shutdown would take several more
days. When he conferred with the commissioners later in the morning,
he learned of Hendrie's fears about the flammability of the hydrogen bubble in the pressure vessel. Denton responded that a hydrogen burn was
not "high on my scale of concerns," and he was inclined to believe it was
not a major threat because of the "lack of an ignition mechanism." But,
like his colleagues on the NRC staff, he could not dismiss the problem,

Figure 15. Denton speaking to reporters at a crowded press conference in Middletown, Pennsylvania, March 31, 1979. At his left, a partly visible Karl Abraham holds a telephone receiver to transmit proceedings to NRC headquarters (Defense Civil Preparedness Agency).

especially since Hendrie was so worried about it. He promised Hendrie that he would alert the governor to the new bubble issue.[10]

A short time later, Denton briefed a throng of reporters at a press conference held in the Middletown Borough Hall, where he sat under a basketball hoop and talked into a bank of microphones, tape recorders, and cameras. In a largely futile attempt to transmit the proceedings to NRC headquarters, Karl Abraham, the Region I public affairs officer, sat next to Denton and held up a telephone receiver. Denton declared that he saw "things moving in a positive direction" and maintained that the chances of the entire core melting appeared even lower than they had the previous day. Reporters' questions focused on differences between what Denton was telling them and what Met Ed officials had said in a press conference an hour or so earlier. The most glaring discrepancy was that Met Ed's vice president, Jack Herbein, had suggested that "the crisis is over," while Denton was insisting that the "crisis won't be over" until the plant reached a cold shutdown.[11]

Herbein's optimistic assessment was based on the progress that Met Ed had made in removing the hydrogen bubble from the pressure vessel. The company used two approaches to the degassing process, which it began Friday night. The first involved using the letdown and makeup systems that circulated through the auxiliary building and that, during normal plant operations, filtered impurities from the water that cooled the core. The problem with this approach to degassing was that it increased the amount of radioactivity in the auxiliary building and contributed to the releases escaping out the stack.

The second method for degassing the pressure vessel was to cautiously force hydrogen through the pressurizer into containment. This was not an open-and-shut process; there was no valve that could be opened remotely to vent the hydrogen from the pressure vessel. The utility employed an indirect method in which it sprayed water into the pressurizer, where a "significant fraction" of the hydrogen gas separated from the liquid coolant. The gas was then vented out of the pressurizer into the containment building. The major risk of this procedure was that it would deliver enough hydrogen to combine with the oxygen already present in the containment atmosphere to cause combustion or an explosion. In contrast to the problem of increasing the amount of oxygen in the pressure vessel, the concern about the process of venting through the pressurizer was to avoid raising the concentration of hydrogen in containment to hazardous levels. The amount of hydrogen required to become flammable or explosive, according to conservative estimates, was 4 to 6 percent of the volume of the air in the building. Met Ed's measurements of the hydrogen concentration in containment at 7:00 A.M. on Saturday, after the degassing had gone on for some time, were 1.7 percent, and they remained at a level of 2 percent or less as the process continued.[12]

To further reduce the concentration of hydrogen in containment, on Friday evening the utility began to install two hydrogen recombiners. Their purpose was to remove hydrogen from the containment atmosphere and combine it with oxygen to form water. The disadvantage of running the recombiners was that they would draw highly radioactive gas from containment. Therefore, to provide shielding, Met Ed needed a large supply of lead bricks to surround the recombiners as they operated in the auxiliary building. While the company waited for a sufficient supply of lead bricks to arrive from laboratories and industrial sites in Pennsylvania, New York, and Maryland, the recombiners remained out of service. Still, Herbein announced at Met Ed's press conference that he believed the venting process had reduced the size of the hydrogen bubble in the pressure vessel to two-thirds of its original size without raising the amount of hydrogen in containment to hazardous levels.

NRC officials were skeptical about Herbein's claim. Estimating the size of the bubble was unavoidably imprecise, and Edson Case, Denton's deputy, remarked that Met Ed had "always been more optimistic than we are." The NRC was not convinced that the bubble had diminished dramatically and agency experts remained concerned that venting hydrogen into containment would create dangerous conditions. Although some staff members argued that the containment building was so large that the amount of hydrogen added to it from the vessel was "trivial," others thought it prudent to suspend the venting until the containment atmosphere could be further sampled and the recombiners were operating. At 3:00 in the afternoon, Victor Stello, who served as Denton's right-hand man at the site, told the utility to stop the process, at least temporarily. Herbein had advised reporters that he thought the chances of a hydrogen explosion were "exceptionally minimal," but nobody, including his own colleagues, could be certain about the accuracy of his assessment. Robert Arnold, vice president of GPU's Service Corporation, remembered driving in stormy weather to his motel after leaving the plant on Saturday evening. As he crossed the Susquehanna River a few miles from Three Mile Island, he heard what he "thought were thunderclaps." But the sounds made him nervous enough that when he got to his room, he promptly contacted the plant to make sure "there had not been any kind of explosion."[13]

THE WHITE HOUSE AND EVACUATION

While NRC and state officials were evaluating the status of the TMI-2 reactor and the need for evacuation, the White House staff was collecting information and marshaling federal resources. President Carter received updates from Denton at 8:00 A.M. and again at 12:25 P.M. on Saturday. Jack Watson and his deputy, Eugene Eidenberg, spent long hours on the telephone with federal and state authorities. They provided critical support to the NRC in speeding supplies of lead bricks to Three Mile Island for shielding the hydrogen recombiners. The NRC, with the timely cooperation of the Department of Energy, managed to locate several sources for bricks, but it encountered difficulties in moving them expeditiously to the plant. Although Defense Department agencies were willing to help, they requested "a lot of paperwork and funding citations" that delayed the process. Eidenberg had a late-night conversation with a high-ranking Army officer who wanted to know who would pay the costs before he authorized shipment of a supply of bricks. Eidenberg overcame the officer's reservations only by threatening to ask Secretary of Defense Harold Brown to call him personally. Once the White House intervened, military agencies acted promptly to load stockpiles of bricks into C-131 transport planes and ship them to the site. By Sunday morning, more than two hundred tons of bricks, enough to meet the anticipated needs at the plant, had arrived.[14]

The central concern at the White House, as at the NRC and the governor's office, was the advisability and feasibility of evacuation. William Odom of the National Security Council staff informed Zbigniew Brzezinski on Saturday morning that "a major population crisis relocation" would probably occur "sometime today." Other federal officials urged that the White House seriously consider recommending that Thornburgh order an immediate evacuation. The most prominent advocate of this position was Joseph A. Califano Jr., the secretary of Health, Education, and Welfare. His department included several agencies that played a role in protecting the public from the effects of radiation, especially the Public Health Service, the Centers for Disease Control, the National Institutes of Health, and the Food and Drug Administration. After consulting with scientists and administrators from those agencies, Califano advised Watson in a memorandum on Saturday afternoon that "public health requires—at a minimum—that full scale preparations for an evacuation of the population within ten miles of the plant be undertaken on an urgent basis." He argued that, unless the NRC could "provide firm assurances" that the TMI-2 reactor was "cooling safely" and that "extensive destruction of the core" could be "ruled out," the White House should "consider recommending to the Governor immediate evacuation."[15]

To review the question of evacuation and the measures undertaken by federal agencies to prepare for an emergency, Watson held a meeting late Saturday afternoon with representatives from the White House staff, NRC, the Environmental Protection Agency, the Federal Disaster Assistance Administration, and the Department of Health, Education, and Welfare. Watson reminded them that the role of the federal government was to offer support and assistance to the state and "emphasized [that] the federal profile must remain low." He solicited the views of those in attendance about evacuation and called first on Jessica Mathews, who later commented that, after working for Congressman Udall and the National Security Council for several years, this was the first time she felt that something she said could have a "direct effect on people's lives." In weighing the need for evacuation throughout the day, she had wavered between her concern about the uncertain condition of a badly damaged reactor and the unavoidable risks of an evacuation. She eventually concluded "in a very close, anguished call" that an evacuation was not advisable, at least at that time. Mathews based her judgment primarily on the pitfalls and costs of conducting a large-scale evacuation, and secondarily, on the harmful effect it would have on the nuclear industry. Although she was not a strong supporter of nuclear power, she believed it was an important component in the nation's mix of energy resources.[16]

The consensus among the other officials at the meeting apparently was the same. When Watson reported to the president, he did not pass along or express support for Califano's thinly veiled appeal for a White House recommendation for an immediate evacuation. In some ways, advising Thornburgh to evacuate would have been the easier and, politically at least, less chancy course of action for the White House. If Thornburgh rejected the advice and the plant failed, the White House could take credit for offering sound guidance. If Thornburgh accepted the advice and the plant remained intact, the state rather than the White House seemed likely to receive the brunt of blame for ordering an unnecessary evacuation. By refraining from recommending an evacuation, the White House opened itself to severe criticism if a breach of containment released high levels of radiation to the environment.

Watson decided against advising the president to recommend an immediate evacuation to Thornburgh because he was mindful of the risk of deaths, injuries, and economic losses it would impose on the population. Although he and his colleagues took Califano's views seriously, they were even more impressed with the warnings they received from other federal experts about the daunting hardships and dangers of a full-scale evacuation. In light of the disquieting unknowns about the status of the plant, arriving at a position was still painfully difficult. In a rare moment of respite from telephone calls, meetings, and memoranda, when he had a chance to consider what was at stake, Watson murmured to himself, "God, let me do the right thing." In the end, he placed his confidence in Harold Denton's judgment that the hydrogen bubble did not present an immediate threat. Watson accepted Denton's assessment in part because he believed that experts on the front lines in Pennsylvania had a better grasp of the situation than policy makers in Washington. But he did so largely because he was impressed with Denton after talking to him on the telephone and watching him on television. Watson was especially struck by Denton's willingness to voice his opinions without masking his own uncertainties about the condition of the plant or glossing over the problems that had to be resolved.[17]

Although Watson did not support a recommendation to the state for an immediate evacuation, he recognized that a "precautionary evacuation" might become necessary within a few days. Commissioners Gilinsky and Bradford, who represented the NRC at the White House meeting, had told those who attended that there was "no low-risk answer to the hydrogen bubble problem." Therefore, decisions were still pending about what measures offered the best approach to eliminating the bubble and about whether the population should be moved before acting on any of these measures. "It is clear that the major discretionary decision the Governor and we will face in the next 2–3 days is whether to evacuate, as a precaution, before intervening at the reactor site to dissipate the hydrogen bubble," Watson told the president. "Current estimates indicate that every intervention option under consideration carries risks to the public health and safety." Watson strongly urged Gilinsky and Bradford to improve the NRC's emergency planning guidelines by preparing "criteria to be used in determining whether a precautionary evacuation is indicated" and evaluating "the nature and extent of such an evacuation in light of likely radiation dispersal patterns."[18]

THE HYDROGEN EXPLOSION PANIC

At 2:45 P.M. on Saturday, Hendrie met with reporters in the briefing room in Bethesda that the NRC had set up the previous day. He realized that the White House wanted Denton to be the sole source of information for the media about conditions at the plant, and had expressed his support for that arrangement in conversations with Jody Powell. But reporters covering the Three Mile Island story in the Washington area clamored for a press conference with NRC policy makers, and, at the urging of Frank Ingram of the Office of Public Affairs, Hendrie reluctantly took on the assignment on behalf of the commission. As he remembered it, Ingram told him that "somebody's got to say something, . . . or they will tear the building down."[19]

The reporters whom Hendrie addressed were not hostile but they were persistent, and he soon regretted his decision to hold the press conference. He later described it as a "disaster," largely because statements that "wouldn't have excited undue unrest" in context created a "hell of

Figure 16. NRC chairman Hendrie at his press conference in Bethesda, Maryland, March 31, 1979 (photo by Ellsworth Davis. © 1979, *The Washington Post.* Reprinted with permission).

a flap" when aired in an incomplete form. Asked whether an evacuation would be necessary before dealing with the hydrogen bubble, Hendrie replied that it might prove to be a "prudent precautionary measure." He estimated that an evacuation would extend to a distance of between ten and twenty miles in a downwind quadrant. When a reporter wondered about the chances of a hydrogen explosion, Hendrie commented that it was "a problem which is of concern and which we are working on very intensively at the moment." His own uneasiness about the bubble had somewhat diminished during the day, and he expressed the view that prevailed among the experts whom the NRC consulted, that "we are some time from any possibility of a flammable condition." Hendrie sought to be candid without causing excessive alarm, but his remarks, especially the first official acknowledgment that a hydrogen explosion was a matter of concern, soon led to an eruption of panic in central Pennsylvania.[20]

Hendrie's discomfort with the outcome of his press briefing was apparent immediately. After exchanging banter about press exaggerations and distortions with his fellow commissioners and NRC staff members, he said in jest, "Which amendment guarantees freedom of the press? I'm against it." He was serious, however, in worrying about how his statements to the press would be interpreted, and within a short time his concerns proved to be well founded. At 4:25 P.M. he heard from an angry Thornburgh, who had received a "flood of inquiries" about Hendrie's supposed statement that an evacuation was inevitable. Hendrie denied those reports and told the governor that the press was "trying to . . . work us at cross purposes." He also suggested that although the hydrogen bubble did not seem as threatening as he had feared earlier in the day, a precautionary evacuation might still be necessary. His explanations did not entirely placate Thornburgh, who regarded Hendrie's comments to the press as evidence of his "unreliability."[21]

Meanwhile, Stan Benjamin, a respected veteran reporter for the Associated Press (AP), followed up on Hendrie's press conference by making inquiries about the hydrogen explosion issue. He collected information from a briefing that Case conducted after Hendrie spoke to reporters and from calls to NRC staff members in Bethesda. The story he wrote led with disturbing news: "Federal officials said tonight that the gas bubble inside the crippled reactor at Three Mile Island is showing signs of becoming potentially explosive." Moreover, Benjamin cited an anonymous NRC source who suggested that the "critical point could be reached within two days."

The article drew on Hendrie's comments about the possibility of a hydrogen explosion and included caveats indicating that a crisis was not inevitable. Nevertheless, it was an unsettling report that was made more distressing by the testimony that an explosion could occur so soon. Mattson had told the commissioners early in the afternoon that in a worst case the bubble could become flammable in two or three days; most of the experts whom the NRC staff contacted thought it would take several days. The meaning of "critical point" in Benjamin's article was unclear, but it appeared to refer to a hydrogen explosion, which by all authoritative estimates would require even more time. The article, and subsequent public discussions of the hydrogen bubble, clouded the distinction, at least in terms of timing, between flammable and explosive conditions in the bubble. The unnamed NRC source of the estimate that an explosion was possible in two days apparently was present when Mattson talked with the commissioners, but neither Benjamin nor later investigations revealed the person's identity.[22]

At 8:23 P.M., AP issued an "urgent" advisory of the upcoming story that Benjamin had prepared, which included little more than a summary of the opening sentence. A short time later, another bulletin announced that an anonymous NRC source had disclosed that an explosion could occur within two days. By the time the full story went out on the AP wire at 9:02, the news it contained had already set off a furor. Radio stations in the Harrisburg region aired the AP advisory, and television channels ran streamers across the bottom of the screens that residents were watching. Once again, state agencies and the NRC were swamped with telephone inquiries from anxious citizens. Victor Stello called the NRC's incident response center and reported that "all hell has broken loose up here." Many people who had not evacuated the previous day did so on Saturday evening and Sunday in response to the hydrogen bubble scare. Approximately 29 percent of the total number of people who evacuated during the crisis, or roughly 42,000 people, departed from their homes at this time. Later surveys showed that among the reasons that citizens gave for leaving the area at some point during the crisis, the bubble was cited as decisive more often than any other single consideration.[23]

The possibility of an explosion in the TMI-2 reactor was dismaying in itself, but public fears were almost certainly magnified by the association that people made between a hydrogen explosion in the plant and a hydrogen bomb. Opinion polls continued to show that the popular misconception that a reactor could blow up like an atomic bomb was deeply rooted. A Harris survey in April 1979 found that 66 percent of those questioned believed that a nuclear power plant that failed could cause a "massive nuclear explosion," a number that had increased from 39 percent four years earlier. Anne and Edward Trunk of Middletown remembered that among the ominous "speculative reports" that circulated locally on Saturday were the risks of a "nuclear bomb situation." Press accounts sometimes fed those apprehensions, at least among their own readership. The *Philadelphia Inquirer* ran a front-page subheadline on Saturday morning suggesting that, in the case of a meltdown at Three Mile Island, the "worst scenario" was "explosion, fallout." Only on an inside page did it explain that the "explosion would not be an atomic explosion." The *New York News* published a headline in its Sunday edition that read, "Hydrogen Blast Threat Looms," and the *Atlanta Journal and Constitution* informed its readers the same day that "a meltdown is literally a runaway bomb." The extent to which the people of central Pennsylvania believed that a hydrogen explosion at Three Mile Island would have the effect of a hydrogen bomb is impossible to measure. But

THE UNTHINKABLE

Figure 17. A Paul Conrad cartoon that appeared in the *Los Angeles Times* on April 3, 1979. The image graphically articulated the public's fear of a nuclear explosion at Three Mile Island (© 1979, *Los Angeles Times*. Reprinted by permission).

it seems axiomatic that fear of a nuclear explosion contributed substantially to the intensity of the public's reaction to the Associated Press story, especially the truncated version that hit the airways on Saturday evening.[24]

The AP bulletin came as an exceedingly unpleasant surprise to NRC staff members at the plant site. The trailer that housed agency operations at Three Mile Island did not have a television or radio, and they were not aware of the storm brewing over Hendrie's remarks at his press conference or Benjamin's report that a hydrogen explosion could occur in two days. Further, they had failed to appreciate the depth of concern in Bethesda over the bubble. Stello recalled that the "story caught me cold" when the White House called to ask about it. Fouchard, the NRC's director of public affairs, first learned about the AP advisory from Richard D. Lyons, a reporter for the *New York Times*. Fouchard immediately called Ingram and asked him to check with Stan Benjamin about the text of the full story. Benjamin read his story to both Ingram and Case, who agreed that it was an accurate account of comments made by NRC officials in Bethesda, though Case later said that he did not hear the information it included about the bubble reaching a "critical point" in two days. Fouchard and Stello were incredulous that their colleagues had found the story to be unobjectionable; Stello expressed his astonishment that Case did not consider it "unfactual."[25]

The White House was equally exasperated. As soon as he learned about the AP story, Jody Powell called Fouchard and reiterated that Denton should be the sole source of information about the condition of the plant. Eugene Eidenberg made the same point in a conversation with Case; he emphasized that "it was a serious mistake . . . to have information coming from multiple sources." This was precisely the problem that the White House had sought to avoid, because, as Jessica Mathews recalled, it was concerned about "confusing everybody and raising anxiety levels by having conflicting stories come out." Jack Watson talked with both Hendrie and Gilinsky and "asked that they tighten and improve control of the NRC public information process out of Washington."[26]

Watson also called Thornburgh, who was "*very* concerned" about the impact of the story "on an already anxious population in the vicinity of the site." The governor had not been greatly worried about the bubble because Denton did not regard it as an urgent matter. He was blindsided by the AP report, and he was furious that statements from NRC headquarters had created pandemonium in central Pennsylvania. A sputtering Paul Critchlow, Thornburgh's press secretary, burst into Karl Abraham's temporary quarters at the state capitol and shouted that NRC officials in Washington should "keep their . . . mouths shut because the Governor is getting pretty sick of it. You're causing a panic!" Critchlow immediately called Denton, who told him that a hydrogen explosion was a "postulation," and that the situation at the plant had not changed. Critchlow issued a press release at once in which he quoted Denton as saying "there is no cause for alarm."[27]

Denton, accompanied by Fouchard, promptly traveled from the NRC trailer at the site to the capitol to brief Thornburgh. They arrived at about

9:30 P.M., and with the governor's approval, first met informally with about forty reporters. It was clear that media representatives were worried not only about the consequences of a hydrogen explosion at the plant for the population of the area but also for their own safety. After first hearing of the AP advisory, a group of about twenty of them charged into Critchlow's office and asked "if we should get out of here." The reporters "weren't after a story," he recalled. "They wanted to know if they were in danger." Robert Hager, who covered the Three Mile Island crisis for NBC television, later compared his own apprehension to what he experienced in reporting stories from Vietnam, Northern Ireland, and the Iranian revolution. When Denton arrived at the capitol, he assured reporters assembled in the newsroom that the bubble was not an immediate threat.[28]

After alleviating the fears of reporters, Denton met with Thornburgh, Scranton, and several other top state officials. He told them there was a possibility of a hydrogen explosion, but that it would not be a problem in the "near future." Speaking in what Thornburgh described as a "very cool, reassuring, 'business-as-usual' tone," he also estimated that the size of the bubble in the pressure vessel was about 90 percent of what it had been the previous day. On the spur of the moment, the governor decided that Denton should address the media in a formal setting. At 11:00 P.M., Thornburgh opened a press conference attended by about two hundred reporters by announcing that, in Denton's view, "there is no eminent catastrophic event forseeable [sic]." He urged "those who may have reacted or overreacted to reports to the contrary . . . to listen carefully to [Denton's] characterization of the current status of the situation."

After that introduction, Denton repeated his earlier assurances and fielded a variety of questions. He said that "there is no danger of even flammability of the hydrogen in the near term," and that he wished "to dispel any fear that anyone has regarding detonations in either the containment or the reactor vessel." He denied any fundamental discrepancy between his position and that of Hendrie, because they agreed that "there is no near term danger at all." Denton asserted that Hendrie's statement about a twenty-mile evacuation was "speculation from the chairman as to what he would consider precautionary measures" and suggested that such steps might prove necessary only if efforts to reduce the bubble and adequately cool the core were unsuccessful. In that event, he explained, "if all systems eventually fail and you lose all the water in the core," the result could still be "a core melt-down." But he considered a worst-case occurrence to be highly improbable. Denton's remarks, from all indications, went a long way toward curbing the panic that had gripped central Pennsylvania in the wake of the AP advisory. After the press conference, AP sent out a revised story that toned down the original version by including Denton's far less alarming evaluation of the dangers of a hydrogen explosion.[29]

The Saturday night briefing confirmed Denton's status as the "man of [the] hour": as the *New York Times* reported, he had "catapulted out of the nameless obscurity of the Federal bureaucracy into the national limelight." During and shortly after the Three Mile Island crisis, he was the subject of feature stories in newspapers and magazines that provided details about his background, education, family, and even the value of his home in Maryland and the models of cars he drove. Some reporters collected personal information about Denton by talking to his wife, Lucinda, and to his teenage children, who disregarded their mother's instructions not to speak to the press. When a reporter for the *Chicago Sun-Times* asked eighteen-year-old Elizabeth Denton about the pressures her father was facing, she replied that he handled "stress situations very well," and added, "but then you'd have to if you raised three teen-agers."

The people of central Pennsylvania showed a remarkable measure of trust in and respect for Denton, which greatly enhanced his credibility and enabled him to ease their worst fears about the possible effects of the accident. They generally accepted his judgments despite their tendency to be wary of outsiders, especially from the federal government. The local population warmed to Denton so readily in no small part because, except for a trace of a Southern accent, he seemed like one of them. A resident of Middletown commented after watching one of Denton's press conferences on Saturday, "Now here's someone who looks like an ordinary guy. Not like those goddamn know-it-all snobs they got down there at Met Ed." Denton's down-to-earth manner and unaffected response to his sudden celebrity earned the admiration of the people of the Susquehanna Valley. They felt kinship with a man who was confident and unflappable when talking to clamorous reporters, but who became visibly flustered when local citizens requested his autograph in restaurants or on the streets of Middletown. "He has become a father-figure to thousands of traumatized people in this region who look to him as the last word, the only word, on the peril at Three Mile Island," the *Harrisburg Patriot* editorialized on April 5, 1979. "Denton is already an honorary citizen of this grateful state in the hearts and minds of all the people of Pennsylvania."[30]

A PRESIDENTIAL VISIT

President Carter spent most of Saturday, March 31, on a one-day political trip to Wisconsin. While he was in transit aboard Air Force One, he
received a memorandum from Stuart Eizenstat, special assistant to the
president for domestic affairs, strongly recommending that, "unless it is
unsafe," he visit Three Mile Island. "This would show leadership and
personal concern," Eizenstat argued. "Our current posture appears to
be one of indifference." Jody Powell supported Eizenstat's proposal by
expressing his own "concern about our current posture" and his view
that a trip to the plant might be "worthwhile." Carter agreed, and apparently somebody from the White House staff called the NRC trailer,
where Stello voiced confidence that the president would not be endan-
gered by coming to the site. Carter announced during a speech on Saturday evening in Milwaukee that he would visit Three Mile Island in the
"near future."

Following the president's announcement, Jack Watson promptly
notified Thornburgh, who was "most gracious," and Jody Powell reached
Denton in Harrisburg while he was meeting with state officials. The White
House also informed Hendrie, though it did not solicit his opinion about
the possible risks of the visit or invite him to accompany the presidential party. Thornburgh told reporters at his 11:00 P.M. press conference
that Carter's plans were a "further refutation of the kind of alarmist reaction that has set in in some quarters." Later that night, after Carter returned from Wisconsin, White House officials decided that the trip would
take place the following afternoon.[31]

THE NRC'S EVACUATION GUIDELINES

While the White House was making arrangements for Carter's trip, a
group of NRC staff members worked through the night on evacuation
guidelines. At the meeting he held on Saturday afternoon, Watson had
urged Commissioners Gilinsky and Bradford to develop criteria for deciding on a precautionary evacuation. Gilinsky took the lead in carrying
out this assignment. He directed Case and Mattson to form a task force
to prepare a document that outlined triggering events and NRC procedures for recommending an evacuation, and he requested that it be drafted
by 6:00 the following morning. They agreed the guidelines would be useful, but they were uncertain that agency experts who had endured four
days of stress and growing fatigue could complete such a complex task

overnight. One staff member protested, "It just doesn't make any sense. Gilinsky wants it done, tell him to do it. . . . It's crazy at this point." Mattson met with the task force, "listened to their moans and groans," and told them, "It's possible to do it by 6:00 A.M. if you put your minds to it. It can be done, and don't tell me how tired you are."[32]

Despite their discontent and weariness, the members of the task force produced a document shortly after their deadline. Gilinsky was generally satisfied with it but substantially reduced its length. He believed that "for decisionmaking purposes if it were more than two or three pages, we wouldn't be able to use it." The guidelines addressed the issue of "who decides" to recommend an evacuation by considering different situations. If an evacuation was required immediately, the senior NRC official at the site would make a recommendation to the governor. If an "unplanned event" occurred that allowed some time for deliberation, the chairman of the NRC, "after consulting with Commissioners if possible," would make a recommendation. In a "planned event involving significant additional risk," the entire commission would act.

The evacuation guidelines included tables that specified suitable responses to a series of "unplanned events" and differing warning times. In a "sequence leading to a core melt" for which a four-hour lead time was available, for example, a precautionary evacuation of an entire two-mile radius and a five-mile, ninety-degree downwind sector seemed advisable if containment was likely to hold. If containment was expected to be breached, with an estimated twenty-four-hour advance warning for the failure to occur, a full five-mile radius and a ten-mile, ninety-degree downwind sector seemed appropriate. In the case of a hydrogen bubble inside the pressure vessel in the "flammable range," the document recommended the same precautionary evacuation of a two-mile radius as for a core melt in which containment would not be breached. The guidelines that the NRC prepared were obviously not definitive, but Gilinsky hoped they would provide a reasonable basis for the commissioners' deliberations over a precautionary evacuation at Three Mile Island, which remained the most pressing question they would face on Sunday, April 1.[33]

Saturday was a harrowing day for federal and state policy makers trying to decipher the critical unknowns about the condition of the TMI-2 reactor and to make the correct call on whether to evacuate the area around the plant. The process of reaching a sound decision was clouded with uncertainties and fraught with tension. The potential hazards of the hydrogen bubble in the pressure vessel were the primary source of concern and the subject of alarming news stories. The governor and his advisers were angry with NRC headquarters, frustrated by the lack of conclusive information about the plant, and anxious about the effects of the continuing crisis on the local population. They were not amused, and immediately lodged a complaint with NBC television, when its late night comedy program *Saturday Night Live* announced a contest to name a new capital of Pennsylvania to replace Harrisburg.[34]

Chapter 8

Sunday, April 1

"Look What We Have Done to These Fine People"

The crisis phase of the Three Mile Island accident ended on Sunday, April 1, 1979, but it did not reach its conclusion easily, painlessly, or unambiguously. While Harold Denton and his colleagues at the site in Pennsylvania continued to regard the hydrogen bubble as, at worst, a distant threat, experts at NRC headquarters learned that it might be a greater danger than they had previously believed. As a result, a majority of the commissioners agreed to recommend to Governor Thornburgh a general advisory evacuation of the area around Three Mile Island. Meanwhile, President Carter, who had accepted Denton's judgment about the condition of the plant, visited the site and held a press conference in Middletown. The discrepancy between the views of the NRC staff in Pennsylvania and agency officials in Bethesda was finally resolved when they agreed that there was no oxygen in the bubble to imperil the integrity of the TMI-2 reactor or the safety of the citizens of the region. After creating a great deal of agonizing uncertainty, the possibility of a hydrogen explosion turned out to be a false alarm. And by the end of the day on Sunday, Metropolitan Edison had succeeded in drastically reducing the size of the much debated and much feared hydrogen bubble.

THE BUBBLE ISSUE IN PENNSYLVANIA

After the fears caused by the Associated Press's hydrogen explosion story on Saturday subsided, the residents of central Pennsylvania who had not evacuated maintained a posture of watchful, uneasy composure. "The citizens of the area have thus far behaved extremely well," Jack Watson and Jessica Mathews told President Carter in a memorandum they drafted early Sunday morning. "Despite the disturbing, confusing, and often contradictory information they have had to digest in the last several days, there has been no panic, and no misbehavior." The *New York Times* ran a story under the headline "A Calm Returns to Middletown, but Some Continue to Lie Low." It quoted Ed Drayer, who lived close to the plant and whose niece's wedding reception had been postponed on Saturday: "I'm not worried about the plant. Maybe I should be but I'm not. One of my neighbors pulled out so fast that she took her kid without even any diapers on." Another local resident noted that "big shots" at the plant had not evacuated their own families. "They must know something," she remarked, "for I know the plant manager and he loves his sons as much as anybody."[1]

Nevertheless, the dangers posed by the damaged plant clearly remained a source of anxiety for citizens of the area. Articles in local newspapers and statements from state and federal authorities reminded residents that a large-scale evacuation, perhaps out to twenty miles, might still be necessary. A substantial minority did not wait for official action. By Sunday, about 135,000 people, more than 20 percent of those who lived within a twenty-mile radius, had evacuated. The ambivalence of the population about leaving their homes sometimes was evident within individual families. One woman awoke on Saturday morning and "vomited from nerves." Her husband went to play golf, and when he returned home he found that she had gone with their two children to Philadelphia.[2]

While the size of the population in the general vicinity of Three Mile Island diminished from voluntary evacuations, the number of people in the area adjacent to the plant grew dramatically. By the end of the day on Friday, the NRC had sent seventy-four staff members to the site, and in response to the requests of GPU for technical assistance, an expanding force of industry experts began to arrive on Saturday. The convocation was further swelled by staff members from government agencies other than the NRC, support personnel, construction workers, curiosity seekers, and media representatives. By noon on Sunday, "Trailer City," which surrounded the observation center across the highway from the plant, was cluttered with twenty-two trailers, parked vehicles, and telephone and electric cables strung in a sea of mud. Living conditions ranged from uncomfortable to primitive. Trailer City had its own daily newsletter, the *Trailer City News,* written by Met Ed employees. Its first issue on Sunday evening offered, among other items, instructions for finding portable toilets. It also announced that food and beverages, which were served in Dewey Schneider's garage, had run short on Sunday, but promised improvements for the following day. On Monday, however, it reported, "We had some problems with the breakfast sandwiches" because

Figure 18. An early stage of Trailer City, looking west. The TMI-2 plant is at top center. The observation center is the white building with the slanted roof. Dewey Schneider's home stands to the right of the observation center among the trees. The cornfield at the bottom of the photo served as a helicopter landing area (National Archives 220-TMI-DE9040025–29).

"the rain got to them." The hardships of living in motels and working in Trailer City were dwarfed by the increasing fatigue that resulted from four days of tension and lack of sleep, at least for many NRC staff members at the site. Victor Stello recalled that he slept little, if at all, on Friday and Saturday nights, and Denton and other agency officials carried on with a similar shortage of rest.[3]

The principal concern of Denton and his colleagues late Saturday and early Sunday was the hydrogen bubble. Although they did not regard it as an immediate or major threat, Denton began to ask himself after the AP story hit the wires, "Does somebody know something I don't?" He told Stello to take another look at the issue. Stello, in turn, assigned Merrill A. (Mat) Taylor, an NRC staff member at the site, to investigate "whether or not [a] hydrogen explosion in [the] vessel should be of worrying concern." Stello was convinced that his colleagues in Bethesda had greatly overestimated the risk of a burn or explosion, but he sought confirmation for his view.

Taylor worked on the problem throughout the night and consulted with NRC experts in Bethesda and at the site. By about 8:00 on Sunday morning, he had concluded that his colleagues in Bethesda "didn't know what the hell they were talking about," and that a hydrogen explosion in the pressure vessel was "an exceedingly remote possibility." He based his judgment largely on experiments conducted at Oak Ridge National Laboratory a decade or so earlier. They suggested that, under the conditions existing in the TMI-2 reactor, "no net evolution of oxygen should be anticipated" in the vessel. This was consistent with Stello's belief—based on his own knowledge and discussions with others at the site—that the process of radiolysis would not produce free oxygen in the hydrogen-rich environment in the pressure vessel. The oxygen that evolved would simply recombine with hydrogen to form water. In a worst case, if some free oxygen remained, the rate of generation would be so low that "many weeks" would be required to create a flammable mixture. Therefore, Stello was confident that the hydrogen bubble did not present a "worrying concern."[4]

Having resolved the bubble issue to his own satisfaction, Stello, who was a "good Catholic," decided to attend Sunday mass in Middletown. The service was sparsely attended, and Stello was surprised when the priest offered general absolution to the congregation. This rite was given in rare cases where individuals, such as soldiers preparing to fight a battle, could not make confessions to a priest, and where large-scale loss of life seemed imminent. It was an emotional moment for the parishioners. "Everybody started crying, and I started crying," Stello recalled. His empathy with the plight of the local population sprang at least in part from growing up in sections of central Pennsylvania where accidents and other hardships took a heavy toll. Stello's father had worked as a coal miner before black lung disease and serious injuries forced him to change occupations. He established a pizza parlor, and the family of thirteen, including three sons and eight daughters, struggled to make ends meet. Stello once remembered that they sometimes depended on the largess of local charities for basic needs. He earned an academic scholarship and played football at Bucknell University in Lewisburg, Pennsylvania, but left in his sophomore year to join the army. After suffering an accident in which he lost an eye, he returned to Bucknell and graduated in 1958.

Two years later he received a master's degree in mechanical engineering from his alma mater.

Stello began his professional career with the Pratt and Whitney Aircraft Company of Middletown, Connecticut, where, among other projects, he worked on safety issues connected with the development of a nuclear-powered airplane. At the same time, he completed forty-two hours of graduate work toward a Ph.D. in engineering at Rensselaer Polytechnic Institute. Stello joined the regulatory staff of the AEC in 1966. His burly build and sometimes gruff manner obscured a softer, more sentimental side of his personality. Colleagues captured the two aspects by, on the one hand, using football imagery to describe him as "one of our front-four," and by, on the other hand, calling him a "teddy bear." At Three Mile Island on the morning of April 1, he clearly was moved by his experience at mass. "When the priest offered general absolution, you could really see that people were shaken," he later commented. Stello thought that the hydrogen bubble problem had unnecessarily alarmed the local population, and he regarded the NRC's contributions to the scare as "outrageous." He returned from the church service in a highly emotional frame of mind and remarked unhappily to Joe Fouchard, "Look what we have done to these fine people!"[5]

THE BUBBLE ISSUE IN BETHESDA

At about the same time that Stello reconfirmed his view that the hydrogen bubble was not a serious threat, his colleagues in Bethesda arrived at a more troubling position. Chairman Hendrie, Roger Mattson, and others at headquarters were aware that oxygen produced in the pressure vessel from radiolysis would recombine with hydrogen. But they were uncertain about the extent to which this "back reaction" would occur, especially since the size of the bubble and the temperature, pressure, and humidity conditions in the vessel could not be measured with precision. Therefore, NRC staff members continued to consult with experts around the nation for their estimates of the rate of recombination, the amount of free oxygen that might remain, and the level that could create a flammable or explosive mixture. Specialists affiliated with national laboratories, universities, government laboratories, and private companies performed complex calculations to try to resolve those questions and, not surprisingly, came up with differing results. At about 9:00 on Sunday morning, Mattson arrived at the incident response center after getting a few hours of sleep. He met with three top officials in the NRC's Office of Nuclear Regulatory Research—Saul Levine, director; Robert J. Budnitz, deputy director; and Thomas E. Murley, head of the division of reactor safety research. They had discussed the bubble problem with a number of leading authorities, and, as Mattson recalled, he said to them, "It's time to stop this wishy-washy all over the place. What do we think?" Having had some sleep, he recalled, "maybe I was feeling my oats." In view of the continuing uncertainties, the tension at the meeting, Budnitz recalled, was "so thick you could cut it with a knife."[6]

Mattson needed a clear statement of the collective judgment of his colleagues because he was preparing to leave with Hendrie for Three Mile Island momentarily. Around 2:00 A.M. on Sunday, Denton had awakened Hendrie at home and "strongly urged" him to come to the site for Carter's visit. He thought it was "entirely appropriate" for Hendrie "to accompany the President" and "show the flag." In order to be "up to speed" when he briefed Carter, Denton requested that Mattson report on the latest findings of the bubble investigation. Mattson, therefore, pressed his colleagues to reach an agreement on the hazards that the bubble posed that he could deliver to Denton.[7]

The values on which Mattson, Levine, Budnitz, and Murley concurred, based on a "distillation" of the information they had received, were "a little more negative" than the estimates of the previous day. "For some reason," Mattson later commented, "my six hours off changed [the projections] from 2 or 3 days until it was flammable to it was flammable now." He and his colleagues quickly decided on numbers that seemed appropriate in light of existing data: the bubble would be flammable if it contained 5 percent oxygen; it would be explosive if it contained 11–12 percent oxygen; free oxygen was being created at a rate of 1 percent per day; and the concentration of oxygen in the bubble was then 5 percent. If those values were correct, they indicated that the bubble was already in a flammable condition. Nevertheless, the danger did not seem immediate because there did not appear to be an ignition source or a likelihood of spontaneous combustion. Budnitz expressed concern about the possibility of spontaneous ignition, but, in Mattson's words, "it was the collegial judgment that there was no danger of spontaneous ignition at that level of oxygen." It was less clear whether the numbers that the group adopted were worst-case estimates or "realistic" limits. In either event, Mattson was confident that the bubble did not present a short-term threat; he concluded, "We have still got a problem, but it is not immediate." A short time after his meeting with his colleagues, he and Hendrie departed by automobile for Three Mile Island.[8]

CARTER'S TRIP TO THREE MILE ISLAND

While NRC officials at the site and in Bethesda were collecting information about the bubble and evaluating its risks, the White House was preparing for Carter's visit to the crippled plant. Jessica Mathews received a call at home at 2:00 A.M. instructing her to work on a briefing paper for the president, who was scheduled to fly to Three Mile Island after he attended church services on Sunday. When she arrived at her office later in the morning, she talked with Zbigniew Brzezinski, Jody Powell, and Vice President Walter F. Mondale by telephone about the objectives of the president's visit to the site. She also had a lengthy conversation with Denton or one of his colleagues at the NRC trailer. Mathews was told that "there was nothing in the condition of the reactor at that time to cause immediate concern." She also was informed that the bubble could still be a long-term hazard and that a precautionary evacuation might be necessary if potentially risky actions had to be taken to eliminate it.[9]

Mathews and Jack Watson collaborated on a memorandum for the president that they prepared Sunday morning. They reminded him that the purposes of the visit were to show his "personal concern" for the safety of the population of the area and to express his confidence that federal, state, and local government officials were "doing everything that can and should be done to deal with the situation." They also warned Carter that his trip was "fraught with potential pitfalls," and cautioned him against "sending any false messages that the danger is over, or making any predictions as to what will happen." Mathews and Watson advised the president that the TMI-2 reactor was a "tired and scarred system" that was still dangerous and unpredictable. "In the opinion of all those working on the problem," they wrote, "a precautionary evacuation sometime in the next few days is *at least* a distinct possibility, if not a probability." With those admonitions in mind, Carter, accompanied by his wife, Rosalynn, Watson, Powell, and the White House science adviser, Frank Press, departed by helicopter at 12:16 P.M. for a fifty-two-minute flight to the Harrisburg airport, three miles north of Three Mile Island in Middletown.[10]

As the White House prepared for the trip, Hendrie and Mattson were motoring to Middletown at such excessive speed that they were pulled over by a police officer. Once they explained that they were NRC officials on their way to Three Mile Island, he gave them clearance "to go on down the interstate highway at high speed." They wanted to reach Middletown before the White House helicopter landed, in part to brief Denton on the

Figure 19. President Carter arriving at the Harrisburg airport for a tour of Three Mile Island, April 1, 1979. Left to right: Thornburgh, White House Press Secretary Jody Powell, Secretary to the Cabinet Jack Watson, Carter, Science Adviser Frank Press, and in the gray vested suit, Congressman Robert S. Walker. The man behind Walker's right shoulder is unidentified (Jimmy Carter Library).

bubble investigation and in part to provide Hendrie the opportunity to greet the president. Neither Hendrie nor anyone else from the NRC had been invited to fly with Carter to the site. Hendrie and Mattson arrived at Three Mile Island well in advance of the presidential party. They stopped first at the NRC trailer but drove immediately to the airport after learning that Denton and Stello had already gone there.[11]

As soon as they arrived at the airport, Mattson reported to Denton and Stello on the consensus of opinion about the bubble in Bethesda—that it did not present an immediate problem but could pose serious long-term difficulties. Stello, who was still in an emotional state of mind from his experience at mass and who was convinced that the NRC had frightened the people of central Pennsylvania without cause, promptly and vocally responded that the judgment of those in Bethesda was wrong. He insisted that there was no free oxygen in the pressure vessel and that there was no threat of either combustion or explosion of the hydrogen bubble. Mattson and Stello were longtime colleagues who regarded each other with a great deal of respect and affection, but they were also strong-minded professionals who did not back away from forcefully express-ing their views. At the airport, they engaged in an animated discussion that vented but did not resolve their differences.

The sharp disagreement between Stello and Mattson placed Denton in a decidedly awkward position. "Poor Harold is there, he's got to meet with the President in five minutes and tell it like it is," Mattson later com-mented. "His two experts are not together. One comes armed to the teeth with [information from] all these national laboratories and naval reac-tors people and highfalutin Ph.D.'s around the country, saying . . . this is his best summary. And his other [expert] is saying, "I don't believe it. I can't prove it yet, but I don't believe it." Denton realized that he could not settle the issue on the spot and, as the White House helicopter ap-proached the airport, quickly concluded that he would inform the pres-ident about both of the competing arguments. Even the more pessimistic view that Mattson brought from Bethesda did not require immediate action.[12]

While Mattson, Stello, and Denton were considering the risks of the bubble in a hallway of the building where the president's briefing would soon take place, Hendrie left the airport. He had gone there "to see if I ought to stand by for the President or not" and was told that he should not, even though he was chairman of the NRC. The White House had made hasty preparations for the trip and had not included Hendrie's name on the lists of those authorized to meet the president. White House officials were not happy with Hendrie for holding his ill-fated press con-ference the previous day, but they did not deliberately snub him in Mid-dletown. They did not know he had decided to travel to the site, and ap-parently a lower-level staff member, acting on standing procedures, informed him that he should leave the airport before the president ar-rived. Hendrie returned immediately to the NRC trailer. Mattson's name was not on the advance lists either, but he was allowed to attend the briefing for the president and other invited officials, perhaps because he accompanied Denton and Stello.[13]

Shortly after Carter's helicopter landed, Denton, with Stello's assis-tance, conducted a forty-minute briefing for the White House contingent, Governor Thornburgh, Lieutenant Governor Scranton, and members of Congress from the local area. Denton reiterated much of what he and other NRC officials at the site had been saying since the previous evening about the condition of the plant and the dangers of the bubble. Although he did not regard flammability of the bubble as an immediate problem, he did not suggest that its potential dangers could be dismissed. Denton summarized the opposing views of Stello and Mattson without endorsing either one and made clear that their differences had not been resolved. Carter demonstrated his knowledge of nuclear reactors by asking a series of informed questions about the accident and the bubble.

When the briefing ended, a small group that included President and Mrs. Carter, Thornburgh, and Denton toured the plant site and the TMI-2 control room. They wore bright yellow booties over their shoes to protect them from traces of radiation on the ground. When the tour ended, Denton was distressed to discover that the personal dosimeters that President and Mrs. Carter wore indicated that they had received an exposure of about 100 millirems, which was too low to present a serious danger but too high to dismiss casually. After a few bad moments, during which Denton worried that he might be responsible for having irradiated the president and the first lady, it turned out that their instruments, which had been provided by Met Ed, were not cleared after each usage. By subtracting the value of the previous readings from the measurements on their badges, it was determined that the president and Mrs. Carter had received no exposure. This was consistent with the readings on Denton's dosimeter, provided by the NRC, and Thornburgh's dosimeter, provided by the state, which were both zero.[14]

After touring the plant, Carter held a joint press conference with Thornburgh and Denton at the Middletown Borough Hall. He closely followed the advice that Watson and Mathews had offered in the memorandum prepared a few hours earlier. The president expressed his "admiration for the citizens of the area who have behaved in a calm and responsible manner." But, without mentioning the word *evacuation,* he also cautioned them that the crisis had not ended, and that the governor might ask them "to take appropriate action" during the following few days. Carter's visit won acclaim from local leaders and many citizens for showing his concern about the effects of the accident and for calming the jitters of the population. Thornburgh thanked him for "the courage and concern he had demonstrated at a time when such a personal gesture is most helpful." Congressman Robert S. Walker, a Republican who represented Lancaster County and who was a frequent critic of the Carter administration, hailed the president's appearance as a "move of courage and a move of compassion." Mayor Robert G. Reid of Middletown, who had been working under stressful conditions for four days to promote the safety of his community and to plan for a full-scale evacuation in

Figure 20. President and Mrs. Carter, Denton, and Thornburgh (barely visible behind Denton) touring the TMI-2 control room while wearing protective booties. To Mrs. Carter's left is James R. Floyd, supervisor of TMI-2 operations (Jimmy Carter Library).

case it became necessary, echoed those sentiments. He thought Carter's visit "was really a shot in the arm," because "people felt that . . . he wouldn't come here if things were really that bad."[15]

THE RESOLUTION OF THE BUBBLE ISSUE

While Denton went with Carter to the plant and the press conference, Mattson and Stello returned to the NRC trailer. Their "number one priority," Mattson recalled, "was to straighten the situation out on hydrogen and fast." Although neither had prevailed during their argument at the airport, they had convinced one another that the issue of whether free oxygen was present in the pressure vessel must be reexamined. "I had shaken him that there were people who believed there could be oxygen," Mattson commented, "and he had shaken me that there was a very strong opinion that there couldn't be any oxygen." The resolution of their differences was delayed when the driver of the car in which Mattson was riding got lost. It took him nearly an hour to reach the trailer from the airport.

While Mattson was taking an involuntary tour of Middletown, Stello explained the bases for his position to Hendrie and suggested that the assumptions used by the authorities that Mattson cited were "far too conservative by a factor of 50 or 60." He also placed calls to experts in whom he had confidence at the General Electric Company in San Jose, California, and at the Bettis Atomic Power Laboratory in Pittsburgh, a facility operated by Westinghouse under a Department of Energy contract. Within a short time, both General Electric and Bettis provided information that confirmed Stello's judgment. Their conclusions were influential if not decisive in persuading both Hendrie and Mattson that the abundance of hydrogen in the pressure vessel suppressed the generation of free oxygen that could form a combustible or explosive mixture in the bubble. "By latish afternoon," Hendrie later remarked, "it was clear that we had been chasing a myth. . . . You weren't getting any net oxygen and never had."[16]

At about the same time that Hendrie became convinced the bubble did not present a serious threat, his fellow commissioners decided that the NRC should recommend a general evacuation of the area around the plant. They had drifted in and out of the meeting in Bethesda that Mattson had held before he drove to the site with Hendrie, so they were well aware of the new concerns about the bubble at that time. They met at 11:35 A.M. in Bethesda to discuss the evacuation guidelines that the staff, at Gilinsky's behest, had worked through the night to prepare. The four commissioners scrutinized the complexities, uncertainties, and terminology of the staff document to try to finalize policies and procedures on recommending an evacuation. After deliberating over a variety of issues for some time, their efforts took on greater urgency when Robert Budnitz of the Office of Nuclear Regulatory Research briefed them about the possible dangers that the bubble posed. Budnitz, who held a Ph.D. in physics from Harvard University, had first become involved in nuclear power issues in 1974 as a member of an American Physical Society committee that evaluated a major AEC study on reactor safety. He had joined the NRC as deputy director of research in 1978 after heading the energy and environment division of Lawrence Berkeley Laboratory, a research facility in California funded by the Department of Energy.[17]

The consensus of the NRC staff and its consultants on Sunday morning was that, even if the oxygen in the bubble had reached flammable proportions, combustion was unlikely because there was no ignition source. Drawing on preliminary calculations performed by several experts, including Bernard Lewis of Combustion and Explosives Research in Pittsburgh, who was the author of a textbook on hydrogen and oxygen combustibility, Budnitz provided a more disquieting analysis. He told the commissioners that spontaneous ignition of the hydrogen bubble was conceivable if temperatures in the vessel rose significantly. Budnitz warned that a hydrogen burn could create a powerful pressure pulse that might cause the pressure vessel to fail. He also reported that, if the bubble did not burn, it could eventually accumulate enough oxygen to generate a spontaneous explosion as a result of sufficiently high temperatures, or perhaps even from contact with sharp surfaces at existing temperatures. Budnitz acknowledged that his information was based on rough estimates with great uncertainties, and he did not suggest that the projected threat was immediate. Nevertheless, his statements were unsettling because, if combustion or detonation of the bubble fractured the pressure vessel, it would substantially increase the chances that, in a matter of hours, a breach of containment could occur.[18]

Budnitz's briefing convinced the commissioners in Bethesda to support an advisory evacuation for the entire population within a two-mile radius of Three Mile Island. They adopted this approach because of the continuing uncertainties about the condition of the reactor and the risks it imposed on the population. In the view of Commissioner Bradford, the lack of solid data and unambiguous expert opinions provided ample reason to recommend an extended evacuation to Thornburgh. Given the paucity of reliable information, Bradford commented, the only consideration that counterbalanced the need for a wider advisory evacuation was that "no one as yet has been able to come up with an ignition mechanism" for the bubble. He had favored a more inclusive evacuation since Friday and regarded Budnitz's report as an affirmation of his judgment. The briefing played a major role in persuading Ahearne and Kennedy, who were less inclined to expand the evacuation advisory, to back his position. The two-mile distance was consistent with the evacuation guidelines that the NRC staff had prepared on Saturday night. Gilinsky did not participate in the discussion with his colleagues because he had gone to confer with Jessica Mathews at the White House, but he agreed with them when they called him there. In contrast to their frequent and sometimes bitter disputes over regulatory issues, in this situation the commissioners in Bethesda achieved rare and prompt unanimity.[19]

The commissioners' agreement was informal. Although they had enough votes to reach a policy decision, they did not want to take official action without consulting Hendrie at the site. At about 4:20 P.M., Kennedy informed Hendrie of the conclusion his colleagues had reached. Hendrie explained that he was now confident the bubble would not burn or explode, because of the lack of free oxygen. He told Kennedy that recommending an evacuation "would not be a warranted step," and "would probably be unwise in view of the uneasy feeling of the general population." At about the same time, Mattson learned that NRC staff members in Bethesda had received new information supporting the view that oxygen evolution was not a problem, in some cases from the same experts who had given more alarming estimates earlier. Therefore, the proposed recommendation for an immediate evacuation of a two-mile radius became moot. The new consensus among authorities both in Bethesda and at Three Mile Island ended the concern over the bubble that had commanded so much attention in the NRC, and generated so much fear in central Pennsylvania, before turning out to be a stunning miscalculation.[20]

The NRC soon received a great deal of criticism and suffered considerable embarrassment for its performance on the hydrogen bubble issue. Experts from both outside and inside the agency wondered how it had blundered so badly. The NRC had begun its investigation of the bubble issue after Hendrie became concerned by his own back-of-the-envelope calculations. This in itself gave a certain credibility to the possibility of a flammable bubble, because Hendrie's experience and technical ability were so highly regarded by the other commissioners and the NRC staff. The problem was, he later said jokingly, "I didn't know as much as they thought I did." Once the NRC undertook a full-fledged evaluation of the bubble, it was hampered by uncertainties about conditions in the reactor and the difficulty of the calculations its staff and consultants carried out. Although the agency's experts were aware that recombination of oxygen and hydrogen would take place in the pressure vessel, they were much less certain about the rate of recombination. Answering the critical question of whether the rate of recombination exceeded the rate of the generation of free oxygen from radiolysis required complex calculations that produced problematic results. The NRC would have benefited if its staff had included specialists in reactor water chemistry, who might have recognized more quickly that free oxygen would not be present in the hydrogen-rich atmosphere of the pressure vessel. At one point during his briefing of the commission, Budnitz had remarked, "One thing I've found out, this agency needs chemists."

When the NRC contacted experts around the country about the dangers of the bubble, it received a series of troubling, though tentative, assessments. One reason was that the staff in Bethesda generally had not raised the key question of whether the generation of free oxygen was possible. Following its customary practice of estimating worst-case effects, it assumed that oxygen could be present in the vessel and inquired about the rate of evolution, the level of flammability, the effects of combustion, and other matters that turned out to be irrelevant to conditions in the reactor. The information that Budnitz provided to the commission, for example, was based on the staff's efforts to find out what the consequences of hydrogen combustion might be, not on whether the bubble contained enough oxygen to burn. Stello, by contrast, began his review of the bubble threat, which was far less elaborate than that of his colleagues in Bethesda, by asking whether free oxygen could even be produced in the vessel. He received the right answers promptly, first from Mat Taylor and later from Bettis and General Electric. On Sunday afternoon, when Mattson asked the same question of the experts that Bethesda had contacted earlier, it made them "step back and scratch their heads and think again."

The NRC also erred in the bubble investigation because of the urgency of the Three Mile Island crisis. It had to make tentative judgments about conditions and their possible effects before it received definitive answers from experts. By the time experts agreed that the bubble was not flammable or explosive, the issue had become a major concern for both government officials and the public. During his press conference on Saturday, for example, Hendrie cited genuine, though provisional, discomfort about the bubble that soon triggered a burst of panic in Pennsylvania. In addition to a lack of time to weigh the problem fully, the NRC once again suffered from a breakdown of communications. Some agency staff members and industry experts were convinced at the outset that free oxygen would not evolve in the vessel, but their opinions never reached Mattson and other responsible officials. Although the ad hoc process that the NRC followed in its assessment of the bubble was flawed, its decision to study the issue in the first place was sound. The favorable outcome of the investigation on Sunday afternoon produced a vast sense of relief among those who had worried about the potential consequences of a flammable or explosive bubble.[21]

Criticism of the NRC's examination of the bubble issue began immediately. At 7:00 on Sunday evening, Hendrie, Mattson, and other NRC officials met with members of the Industry Advisory Group that GPU had established to assist with the accident. By that time, about

Figure 21. Roger J. Mattson and Denton in the NRC trailer at the TMI site (NRC).

thirty experts from utilities, nuclear vendors, universities, research institutions, and national laboratories had arrived at the site to provide technical support. They upbraided the NRC for its evaluation of the dangers of the bubble. Edwin Zebroski, director of the nuclear systems and materials department of the Electric Power Research Institute, for example, voiced "strong dismay" that the NRC had not recognized immediately that the "explosion issue was a non-problem because the existence of oxygen as postulated was physically impossible." He complained that the agency had failed to meet the standards of "sophomore-level nuclear engineering."[22]

After the meeting with the Industry Advisory Group, Hendrie received criticism of the NRC's performance from a different perspective when he went with Denton to meet Thornburgh and other state officials in Harrisburg. The governor was still angry about the evacuation recommendation made by the NRC staff on Friday morning and Hendrie's comments at his press briefing the following day. Hendrie's apology for the remark that evacuation within a twenty-mile radius might be necessary did not appease Thornburgh. When Hendrie complained in a private conversation about the "thinness" of Met Ed's technical capabilities, the governor asked what that indicated about the validity of the NRC's licensing procedures. The continuing tensions over the accident were presumably reduced by a report from Denton on the bubble. He disclosed that the size of the bubble had diminished to an estimated three hundred cubic feet (from its original size of about a thousand cubic feet). Even without threatening to burn or explode, the bubble could remain an obstacle to cooling the core and reaching cold shutdown, but the welcome news of its deflated dimensions meant that the level of danger had decreased.[23]

Met Ed technicians had continued to vent the bubble through the pressurizer and the letdown system during Saturday and Sunday. Stello had instructed them to stop the process of degassing through the pressurizer on Saturday afternoon to make certain it was not adding an excessive amount of hydrogen to the containment atmosphere. Once Met Ed determined that the level of hydrogen remained below the estimated 4 percent flammability limit, it resumed this procedure and periodically took samples to measure concentrations of hydrogen. By Sunday afternoon, even after two days of venting, the concentration of hydrogen was about 2.5 percent of the air in the containment building, which was higher than the 1.7 percent on Saturday morning but well short of the conservative estimates for flammability. The recombiners were not yet operating to remove hydrogen from containment; the company hoped to have them running the next day. By late Sunday, Met Ed was convinced that the bubble in the pressure vessel had virtually disappeared. Although Denton was not that optimistic, even imprecise methods of measurement made clear that it had been sharply reduced.[24]

The resolution of the bubble issue closed the acute phase of the Three Mile Island crisis. After five days of harrowing uncertainty and unrelenting stress, tensions at the site and in Bethesda eased. On Saturday and Sunday, the potential risks of the bubble had taken center stage as the most alarming threat to the population of the area surrounding the plant. But even when fears about the effects of a hydrogen burn or explosion turned out to be groundless, serious problems persisted at the plant. Denton and his colleagues were concerned that what was left of the bubble would inhibit cooling of the core. The plant had still not reached a cold shutdown, and a precautionary evacuation might still be necessary. Although the worst of the crisis had passed, the sense of relief was tempered by uncertainties that endured and problems that remained to be solved.

Chapter 9

The Immediate Aftermath of the Accident

Although the concern about a flammable or explosive bubble in the pressure vessel of the TMI-2 reactor proved to be unfounded, reactor experts still faced other potential problems. NRC chairman Joseph Hendrie told White House staff members on Monday, April 2, 1979, that, although the "acute" phase of the accident seemed to have ended, a "chronic phase of reduced—*but still serious*—risk" loomed.[1] Over the next several days, as conditions at the plant continued to improve and confidence increased that it would not release large amounts of radiation to the environment, everyday life in central Pennsylvania gradually returned to normal. At the same time that fear of massive radioactive fallout from the accident diminished, the political fallout intensified. Questions about the long-term consequences of the accident and the performance of responsible officials incited sharp criticism of the utility, the NRC, and to a lesser extent, other federal and state agencies. Those issues inflamed the already bitter controversy over the future of nuclear power.

GUARDED OPTIMISM ABOUT PLANT CONDITIONS

Even when the NRC determined that the hydrogen bubble would not burn or explode, it remained concerned that the bubble's presence would inhibit cooling of the core. Early on Monday morning, Met Ed circulated an internal memorandum suggesting that this problem had been solved. "We think," it said, "the bubble has gotten so small that it may have disintegrated." The company instructed its staff not to share its judgment with the press, but one of its employees, to the dismay of his superiors, told a reporter. The news spread rapidly and was a focus of attention when Harold Denton held a press conference in Middletown at

11:15 A.M. He announced that the bubble had "shown a dramatic decrease" in size and was perhaps as small as 50 cubic feet. But he added
that the measurements were imprecise and that he did not "want to be
stampeded into concurring that the bubble is actually this small." He
had told Hendrie privately a short time earlier that the size of the bubble was "25 cubic feet plus or minus 200."

Denton's caution reflected the NRC's position during the previous two
days as well as advice from the White House. Early on Monday morning, Roger Mattson, who was manning the NRC trailer at the site while
Denton and Victor Stello went off to get some sleep, took a call from the
White House on the red phone. The person with whom he talked suggested that telling the press that the bubble had disappeared could
backfire if the report turned out to be false. Throughout his press conference, Denton was upbeat but guarded in his evaluation of the plant's
condition. He said that his concern about an explosion of the bubble was
"diminishing," but he did not disclose that NRC experts and their consultants had agreed that the lack of free oxygen in the bubble made combustion or detonation inconceivable. He addressed the outcome of the
issue only indirectly by explaining that the projected rate of oxygen evolution in the pressure vessel that he had reported the previous day had
been "very, very conservative, and that the actual rate is much lower."
Denton's reticence on the resolution of the hydrogen explosion issue was
consistent with his reluctance to sound overly sanguine about the plant's
status. He was also disinclined to volunteer details about the NRC's internal debates and errors in calculating the risks of a hydrogen burn or
explosion.[2]

Shortly after Denton spoke to reporters in Middletown, Hendrie met
with his fellow commissioners in Washington. He told them that the bubble had been eliminated or at least greatly reduced "by mechanisms which
are a good deal less traumatic than we thought might have to be the case."
Nevertheless, Hendrie emphasized that many uncertainties and potential dangers remained to be addressed. Once the bubble had completely
disappeared, the plant's residual heat removal system could be activated.
This system was largely made up of heat exchangers and pumps used in
shutting down a plant under normal operating conditions, and activating it would be a major step toward bringing the TMI-2 reactor to a cold
shutdown. The concern about running the residual heat removal system
was that its pumps, which were not designed to move highly radioactive
water, had a relatively high leak rate. Since they would be transferring
water that Hendrie described as "murderously hot" from containment

into the auxiliary building, the leakage would have to be controlled so that the radiation was "not just free to wander around the auxiliary building." Hendrie cited several other problems that could still cause serious risks and perhaps require a precautionary evacuation, including the loss of a reactor coolant pump, a breakdown in steam condensate equipment, or a disruption of electrical power. He pointed out that the favorable aspect of such malfunctions, should they occur, was that they would provide "a number of hours" of warning time to conduct an evacuation. The NRC staff arrived at the even more comforting conclusion that, because the core had cooled substantially in the four days since the accident, and because the "concrete basemat" of the TMI-2 reactor was "unusually thick," the core would "not melt its way through containment" in the event of a major failure.[3]

After meeting with his colleagues, Hendrie delivered the same information about the status of the plant to Jack Watson, Eugene Eidenberg, and Jessica Mathews at the White House on Monday afternoon. Although the signs were promising, they were still ambiguous enough that responsible officials did not want to declare an end to the emergency or dismiss the possibility of a precautionary evacuation. Watson told President Carter that, in changing from "acute" to "chronic" readiness, "we need to define and recommend a maintenance mode of emergency preparedness that will meet the conditions we anticipate to last over the next weeks and perhaps months."[4]

In Harrisburg, state officials proceeded with contingency planning for an evacuation, though at a considerably reduced level of immediacy and tension. On Monday afternoon, one of the hydrogen recombiners at the plant was placed into operation. This alleviated lingering concerns about the chances of a hydrogen explosion in the containment building. Measurements of hydrogen concentration in the containment atmosphere were still only about 2 percent, well below a dangerous level. As the crisis eased, state efforts focused on the possible need for a limited evacuation to avoid excessive radiation exposures for some segment of the population, rather than for a full-scale emergency evacuation. To guard against the effects of releases of any magnitude, Governor Thornburgh announced that the advisory evacuation for pregnant women and pre-school-age children would remain in effect, and that schools within a five-mile radius of the plant would stay closed until further notice. The population of the area was encouraged by the cautious optimism that federal and state officials expressed, but continued to be wary. Local citizens jammed banks to withdraw money, and often to vacate accounts and clear out safety deposit boxes, in case they had to evacuate their homes.[5]

Although government leaders and area residents were concerned about the possibility that high levels of radiation would escape from the plant, the actual amounts measured off-site from the intermittent releases remained well below annual population exposure limits. The highest reading recorded by NRC instruments on Sunday, April 1, taken one-half mile east-northeast of the plant, was 1.1 millirems per hour at ground level. The next highest reading, taken four-tenths of a mile east of the site, was .4 millirem per hour. The other samples, measured at thirty-seven locations out to twelve miles from the plant, were .1 millirem per hour or less. An interagency group of federal government experts from the NRC, the Environmental Protection Agency, and the U.S. Department of Health, Education, and Welfare made a preliminary estimate of the radiation exposure that the population of the area surrounding the plant had received between the day of the accident and the afternoon of April 2. It calculated that a person who stayed at a point one-half mile northeast of the plant for the entire period would have received a maximum total dose of about 80 millirems, far short of the annual nonoccupational permissible dose of 500 millirems for an individual. The federal experts also projected that releases from the plant as a result of the accident would produce "less than one" fatal case of cancer over the "total lifetime of the population" who lived within a fifty-mile radius. Hendrie told a Senate hearing that the radiation readings were, "for accident conditions, quite low," though "obviously much larger than normal operation would permit."[6]

The most disturbing discovery about radiation releases was that, for the first time, traces of iodine-131 were detected, on Monday, April 2. Previous measurements had found only noble gases, which do not bond chemically with body tissues. Iodine-131, however, concentrates in the milk of cows that graze in contaminated pastures. If the milk is consumed, iodine-131 tends to lodge in the thyroid gland, where it can cause cancer or other serious conditions. Analysis of several milk samples collected around the plant on Saturday and Sunday following the accident showed amounts of iodine-131 that were slightly higher than normal levels. They were far below the level at which the U.S. Department of Health, Education, and Welfare recommended that dairy cows be kept from grazing in pasture land, and local herds were already on stored feed. Nevertheless, the measurements were a source of discomfort for citizens of the region. Thornburgh immediately took steps to assess the severity of the problem and, once he was satisfied that the iodine-131 readings were inconsequential, to reassure the public. He announced that there was "no present danger to consumers from milk produced in this area," and discounted the "sensational reports and unfounded rumors that inevitably occur." He pledged to continue monitoring for iodine and to report information about the effects of the accident "accurately, responsibly, and in the proper perspective."[7]

The *CBS News* reporter Diane Sawyer captured the mood of NRC and state officials in light of the reduced size of the bubble and the remaining problems to be addressed. She told her television audience that authorities believed "that we may be beyond the worst crisis, but it's still too soon for a celebration."[8]

SAFE SHUTDOWN

At a press conference on Tuesday afternoon, April 3, 1979, Denton was much less equivocal in his assessment of plant conditions than he had been the previous day. New measurements with more sophisticated procedures had convinced him that the bubble was, in fact, gone from the pressure vessel. He told reporters that "the bubble has been eliminated, for all practical purposes," and that "we no longer consider hydrogen explosion as a significant problem." One recombiner was working (the other was held in reserve), and the hydrogen concentration in the containment atmosphere was 2.1 percent. The temperature in the primary system was 281 degrees Fahrenheit, which was well above a cold shutdown level but low enough to keep the reactor in a stable condition. Denton estimated that radiation readings in the containment dome were still at the exceedingly dangerous level of about 30,000 rads an hour.

The "preferred plan" for reaching a cold shutdown was to carry out long-term cooling of the reactor by "natural circulation." This procedure would remove heat from the core through the plant's secondary system by taking advantage of the difference in density of the heated water in the reactor and the water cooled by the steam generators. It would take longer to establish than other cooling options, but offered the benefits of providing greater reliability than power-driven cooling pumps and of replacing residual heat removal system pumps that would circulate highly contaminated water outside the containment building.[9]

Progress toward a complete shutdown of the plant was slow, but as temperatures in the core fell and radiation emissions remained small, lingering concerns about the chances of a meltdown or a major release of radiation diminished. On April 9, Denton told reporters he was convinced that the "likelihood for an event or a release requiring special precautionary measures is very remote." Although technically the plant had not yet reached a state of cold shutdown, he declared, "I consider the crisis over today with . . . regard to the status of the core." At the same press conference, Thornburgh called off the advisory evacuation for pregnant women and pre-school-age children and announced that public schools within a five-mile radius of the plant would reopen the next day. By that time, most citizens who had left their homes during the emergency had already returned, and the state had closed the evacuation center at the Hershey sports arena. The burdens of evacuation were perhaps eased by a decision of the Internal Revenue Service that permitted evacuees an extra month to file their federal tax forms, though it cautioned taxpayers who took advantage of this extension that they would have to pay interest on any amounts owed the government at the time of the original filing deadline.

Denton remained a much admired figure in central Pennsylvania. Some area residents wore T-shirts that said, "Thank you Harold Denton." The day that schools reopened, S. Beth Wolf, a first-grade teacher in Middletown, wanted to find a way to encourage her students to express their feelings about the frightening and perhaps traumatic experiences of evacuating their school and hearing about the possible effects of the accident. After they decided to send a letter to Denton, whom they knew as the "man who let the air out of the bubble," Wolf wrote her students' statements on a poster-size sheet of paper. The first graders thanked Denton for "saying we could come back and for saving hundreds of lives." They revealed that they were "very scared and frightened" by the accident. "We were afraid the bubble would pop," they explained. "We wanted to go far away because our houses are too close and we would have been very sick and maybe our houses would have exploded." The letter received a great deal of attention from area media. A crew from a local television station took Wolf to meet Denton at his home in Maryland and filmed an interview that was shown to the students the following day.[10]

Denton returned home on April 17 and left Stello in charge at the site. Although the core continued to cool steadily, enough problems arose along the way to extend the period for reaching a cold shutdown beyond the ten days that Denton had projected two weeks earlier. On April 27, Stello informed reporters that the process of cooling the plant by natural circulation had begun. He refrained from using the term *cold shutdown*, a term which meant that all temperature indicators were less than

Figure 22. First-grade students in Middletown, Pennsylvania. The children pose with a letter they wrote to Denton (The Historical Society of Dauphin County).

water's boiling point of 212 degrees Fahrenheit. One thermocouple reading remained as high as 340 degrees. Nevertheless, even the hottest parts of the core were clearly cooling, and the few locations that showed elevated temperatures were not a matter of concern. In light of the achievement of natural circulation, Stello announced, "I have no question about the safety of the reactor now. It is safely shut down."[11]

POLITICAL FALLOUT

The Three Mile Island accident, not surprisingly, incited widespread criticism of nuclear power technology, the nuclear industry, and the NRC. The crisis and the international attention it commanded redoubled the determination and enhanced the credibility of the antinuclear movement. Nuclear critics were quick to air their judgments about the causes, consequences, and lessons of the accident. Ralph Nader commented, "This is the beginning of the end of nuclear power in this country." Daniel Ford of the Union of Concerned Scientists charged that the "nation's nuclear power program has been grossly mismanaged," and called for Hendrie's removal because he was "unfit as the principal regulator of the U.S. nuclear power program." At two meetings in Harrisburg on April 22, 1979, Helen Caldicott, an outspoken opponent of nuclear power and president of the five-hundred-member Physicians for Social Responsibility, urged her listeners to "stop nuclear power and save the world."[12]

The Three Mile Island accident triggered a series of antinuclear rallies. Over the weekend of April 7–8, 1979, ten demonstrations were held across the nation to protest against nuclear power. A spokesman for the antinuclear Clamshell Alliance regarded the rallies as confirmation that "last week's accident really touched the hearts and nerves of a lot of people." Several hundred people who attended a rally in Harrisburg on April 8 heard William Vastine, coordinator of a group called Three Mile Island Alert, declare, "We have not come to praise TMI but to bury it." They carried signs with slogans such as "I Survived TMI—But What about My Baby?," "Every Dose Is an Overdose," and "TMI—Rotten to the Core." A rally in Washington, D.C., on May 6, 1979, attracted a crowd estimated at sixty-five to seventy-five thousand—more than any previous anti–nuclear power demonstration in the United States. It featured well-known performers such as Joni Mitchell, Graham Nash, and Jackson Browne and speakers such as Nader, Jane Fonda, and California governor Jerry Brown. "What a fantastic day," exclaimed Tom Hayden, one of the most prominent protesters of the Vietnam War era. "It reminds me of the best days of the 1960s." The turnout for the rally indicated, Luther J. Carter observed in *Science* magazine, "that since Three Mile Island there is enough opposition to nuclear power to support protests on the grand scale of the civil rights and antiwar demonstrations."[13]

Public opinion polls conducted shortly after the accident gave credence to that view by showing a decline in popular support for nuclear power. They suggested even more clearly, however, that the public as a whole remained deeply ambivalent about expanding the use of the technology. A *New York Times*–CBS poll taken on April 5, 1979, compared responses with those from a survey in July 1977. In each case, respondents were asked, "Would you approve or disapprove of building more nuclear power plants?" In 1977, 69 percent of those surveyed approved, while 21 percent disapproved. After Three Mile Island, 46 percent approved and 41 percent disapproved. The same pattern was evident in another question: "Would you approve or disapprove of building a nuclear power

Figure 23. Demonstrators at an antinuclear rally in Washington, D.C., May 6, 1979 (AP/Wide World Photos).

plant in your community?" In 1977, 55 percent approved while 33 percent disapproved. In 1979, only 38 percent approved and 56 percent disapproved. A Harris poll taken on April 4–5, 1979, showed similar results. In October 1978, 57 percent of those who participated in a sampling had supported the construction of more nuclear power plants in the United States. After TMI, the number slipped to 52 percent, versus 42 percent who opposed the construction of new plants. A Gallup survey of April 6–9, 1979, also showed softening support for nuclear power. Yet it indicated that 63 percent of those questioned thought it was "somewhat" or "extremely" important to build more nuclear plants. In addition, 65 percent opposed the closing of all operating power reactors. The results of the various polls suggested that the Three Mile Island accident had substantially increased the public's misgivings about nuclear power but had not persuaded it to abandon the technology.

Much of the criticism that followed the Three Mile Island crisis centered on the NRC's performance, both before and during the accident.

Nader accused the NRC of regulatory laxness in allowing Met Ed to receive tax breaks by placing the TMI-2 plant into commercial operation before the end of 1978. Agency representatives took sharp issue with this allegation by explaining that the key date from the perspective of safety was the NRC's approval of an operating license. In the case of TMI-2, it had issued the license in February 1978. The date of commercial operation was "an administrative thing" between the state Public Utility Commission and Met Ed that was completely separate from the NRC's safety review.

On April 4, 1979, during the first congressional hearing after the accident, Hendrie was grilled by members of the Subcommittee on Health and Scientific Research of the Senate's Committee on Labor and Human Resources. Richard S. Schweiker, a Republican from Pennsylvania, declared that he was "appalled by the confusion, contradictions, and misinformation which characterized the response to the accident." Democrat Edward M. Kennedy of Massachusetts, chairman of the subcommittee, complained that at a time of an "extraordinary" threat to the public, the NRC's regulatory system "really broke down." Hendrie readily acknowledged that the situation at the plant was still not "hunky-dorie" but strongly denied charges that the NRC had deliberately covered up information or acquiesced in major releases of radiation from the plant.[14]

The attacks on the NRC escalated after transcripts of commission meetings held during the Three Mile Island crisis were made public. The formal, closed meetings of the commission had been recorded on portable tape machines. The commissioners had been aware that their deliberations were being taped but did not anticipate that transcripts of the meetings would become public within a short time. The presence of a cassette recorder did not inhibit their comments on the crisis; the tapes captured in unflinching detail their concerns, uncertainties, frustrations, disagreements, and jokes about the problems they were facing. Hendrie remarked at one point that he "shudder[ed] to think of what" would be recorded, but he later suggested that the tape machine should not curb discussion, because "it gets awkward if we're going to have to think about everything we say." The NRC turned over transcripts of the commission meetings in response to demands from congressional committees, and Congressman Udall's staff immediately made them available to reporters.[15]

The release of the meeting transcripts spawned a series of unflattering news stories about the NRC's performance. They highlighted the com-

mission's uncertainties about the causes of the accident, the need for evacuation, and the best approach to cooling the core. The accounts suggested
that the NRC was not only perplexed about how to deal with the accident but also committed to playing down its potential effects. Senator
Patrick J. Leahy, a Democrat from Vermont, wrote privately that he was
outraged that the transcripts revealed "an almost total lack of information or control by the commission and at the same time an insidious attempt to withhold some information from the people." His colleague
Gary Hart, a Democrat from Colorado and chairman of the Subcommittee on Nuclear Regulation of the Senate Committee on Environment
and Public Works, described the transcripts as "both distressing and
alarming" because the commission was "totally unprepared for the kind
of crisis which occurred." The *Harrisburg Patriot* angrily concluded that
the transcripts demonstrated a "callous, unacceptable attitude" on the
part of the commissioners.

News reports of the transcripts were necessarily abridged versions that
featured highlights and sometimes ignored the context of the discussions
among the commissioners. They generally portrayed the process of
drafting press releases as an effort by the commission, with the collaboration of the White House, to deceive the public by understating the potential dangers of the accident. The allegation that NRC and Carter administration officials issued misleading assurances about plant conditions
received a great deal of attention, but it caricatured their attempts to be
forthright about what they knew without fueling rumors, distortions, and
exaggerations. On the other hand, the *Washington Post* editorialized that
the White House and the NRC acted properly in weighing the content
and potential impact of the information they released about the accident.
"This is not an invitation to lying, but rather an invitation to being responsible," it argued. "Pell-mell, premature, panic-inducing information
could have led to terrible consequences."[16]

The segments of the transcripts that probably drew the most notice
were two statements made by Hendrie during tense moments of the crisis. The first occurred on Friday morning, March 30, as the commission
deliberated over whether to recommend that Thornburgh order an evacuation. Hendrie remarked that, in the absence of reliable information
from the plant, he and the governor were "like a couple of blind men
staggering around making decisions." When this comment received
prominent coverage in news stories about the meeting transcripts, it generated a barrage of criticism. The National Federation of the Blind, for
example, castigated Hendrie for "personal ignorance" and "gross in-

sensitivity" in reinforcing "false stereotypes" about the blind. A contrite Hendrie offered a public apology for his "unfortunate reference to blind persons" in a moment of "intense frustration." He regretted his use of "the old cliche about being blind" and affirmed that he "intended no disparagement of anyone with a sight impairment."[17]

Hendrie did not apologize, however, for his other widely quoted statement. On Saturday afternoon, March 31, after suffering through a difficult press conference in which he discussed the hydrogen bubble and the possibility of evacuation, Hendrie commented to his colleagues: "Which amendment guarantees freedom of the press? I'm against it." In the context of the discussion among the commissioners, he clearly was making a joke. Nevertheless, some news reports ignored the context and treated Hendrie's quip as an assault on the first amendment to the Constitution. Jerry W. Friedheim, executive vice president of the American Newspaper Publishers Association, immediately sent Hendrie a copy of the First Amendment and demanded an explanation of "how being opposed to the rights of American citizens . . . could square with public service." Hendrie responded that the "comment was a wry joke, one of those bits of gallows humor that some of us use to vent feelings in a high-stress situation." He complained about media coverage of the accident but, with more than a hint of sarcasm, assured Friedheim of his "continued devotion to the Constitution and all of its Amendments." Hendrie's efforts to clarify his comment on freedom of the press were not entirely successful. More than a year after the accident, he learned to his annoyance that the *Nation* had recently used the quotation and "its incorrect implications" in a direct mail advertisement to attract new subscribers.[18]

Although the release of the commission meeting transcripts focused attention on the NRC's uncertainties, confusion, and indecision, Thornburgh and his advisers were also criticized for their performance during the emergency. Some observers charged that the state refused to provide accurate and timely information in order to maintain public calm and minimize damage to the image of the state of Pennsylvania as a desirable place to live and visit. Edward Jensen, the Harrisburg correspondent for the *Pittsburgh Post-Gazette*, faulted the governor for his efforts to reassure the population. "Instead of meeting regularly with reporters," he wrote, "Thornburgh . . . made ceremonial appearances on local and national television shows, always urging calm and praising Pennsylvanians as 'being made of stern stuff.'" The decision not to undertake a general evacuation stirred questions about the judgment of both the NRC and the state. Anthony Z. Roisman of the Natural Resources Defense

Council asserted that "it was a mistake to not order an immediate evacuation of the people in close proximity to the plant." Nader was more blunt. He contended that "for political reasons the mass evacuation that should have been carried out was not," and he ridiculed the argument that a full evacuation would have been dangerous "because of traffic accidents." While nuclear critics claimed that an evacuation should have been ordered, civil defense authorities complained about poor communications and lack of planning on the part of the state government that could have made a large-scale evacuation "chaotic."[19]

The state's actions on the question of distributing potassium iodide to counter the effects of radioactive iodine-131 also produced considerable second-guessing. Potassium iodide, if taken in suitable amounts at the proper time, blocks the thyroid gland's uptake of iodine-131. At the time of the Three Mile Island accident, it was well recognized as a prophylactic agent against the hazards, including thyroid cancer, of exposure to high levels of iodine-131. On Friday evening, March 30, apparently after consulting with Watson and Eidenberg at the White House, Joseph A. Califano Jr., the secretary of the U.S. Department of Health, Education, and Welfare (HEW), instructed the Food and Drug Administration (FDA), a part of HEW, to procure supplies of potassium iodide as quickly as possible. He wanted to make certain it was available to the population surrounding the plant in the event of a major release of iodine-131. When FDA officials determined that adequate stocks of the drug could not be obtained in the Harrisburg area they promptly made arrangements with the Mallinckrodt Chemical Company of St. Louis to manufacture it on an emergency basis. Without the formality of a written contract with the government, Mallinckrodt called in workers at its plant in Decatur, Illinois, at about 1:00 A.M. on Saturday, March 31, to produce a potassium iodide solution. By 8:00 that evening, the first batch of about 11,000 one-ounce bottles of the drug was shipped in an Air Force cargo jet. Over the next five days, another 225,000 bottles arrived in Harrisburg, where they were stored in a warehouse.[20]

The detection of traces of iodine-131 in milk samples on Monday, April 2, gave increased urgency to the question of whether potassium iodide should be distributed. Eidenberg, presumably as a result of the discovery of iodine-131 off-site, requested that HEW provide guidance on the federal position concerning use of the drug. Although federal agencies had taken the lead to provide supplies of potassium iodide, their role in its administration was limited to advising state officials. Califano, drawing on the counsel of the surgeon general of the United States, the director of the National Institutes of Health, the director of the National Cancer Institute, and the administrator of the FDA, submitted his proposals to the White House on April 3. Based at least in part on outmoded information about the dangers of the hydrogen bubble, Califano's memorandum urged prompt action to make potassium iodide widely available. It called for distribution of the vials to all those who might be exposed to releases of iodine-131 with less than thirty minutes' warning time, which, it said, might include an area as far as ten miles from Three Mile Island. It also recommended that workers at the plant "begin taking blocking doses now."

Eidenberg immediately contacted Jay Waldman in the governor's office to pass along Califano's views. When the state received the memorandum by telecopier a short time later, it produced "considerable concern" on the part of Gordon K. MacLeod, the state secretary of health, and his consultant, Niel Wald, chairman of the Department of Radiation Health at the University of Pittsburgh. They had previously concluded that the immediate distribution of potassium iodide that Califano recommended was unnecessary, or at least premature, and perhaps even hazardous. Their primary reason for taking issue with Califano was that they regarded the measurements of iodine-131 as too low to require protective action. Radiation experts and existing federal guidelines cited a threshold level of 10,000 millirems (or 10 rems) of iodine-131 for administration of potassium iodide, and the greatest estimated exposure of a hypothetical individual to the total release of radiation from the accident was only about 80 millirems. State officials worried that the distribution of potassium iodide would be confusing to already anxious citizens in central Pennsylvania, and that it could lead to panic. Thornburgh later commented that the "psychological effect" of passing out vials of the drug before it clearly was needed "could be devastating." The concern of the governor and his advisers about the public state of mind was compounded by a threat from a local radio station to reveal the location of the warehouse where the potassium iodide was stored, which they believed underscored the "problem of security and danger of a 'run' on the location."[21]

MacLeod and other state officials also objected to Califano's proposals because by then a major release of radiation seemed unlikely. Further, the effectiveness of potassium iodide could be diminished if it were taken prematurely and then found to be needed at a later time, which was a possible, if unlikely, contingency, especially for plant workers. Finally, the ingestion of potassium iodide posed a small danger of undesirable side effects that were a reasonable risk in an emergency but seemed a poor trade-off under the existing circumstances. After extensive discussions with his staff, state and federal health experts, and Denton, Thornburgh rejected Califano's recommendations. The potassium iodide issue provoked obvious irritation toward HEW on the part of state officials, particularly MacLeod, who regarded Califano's advisory as a challenge to his own professional judgment. The ill will increased on April 6 when the *Washington Star* and the *Washington Post* ran stories that drew on Califano's April 3 memorandum to the White House and questioned the state's position. The headline of the *Post* article, referring to both the utility and the state, captured its message: "Power Firm, Pennsylvania Reject Anti-Cancer Medicine." MacLeod responded with a strong defense of the state's decision that barely concealed his resentment. The handling of the potassium iodide question stirred some criticism of state actions but never flared into a major controversy. Eventually, the FDA reclaimed the bottles of the drug it had ordered and shipped them to storage in Little Rock, Arkansas.[22]

Despite the sometimes harsh criticism of federal and state authorities, local opinion polls demonstrated remarkable support for their performance during the Three Mile Island crisis. A telephone survey conducted by the Social Research Center of Elizabethtown College in Lancaster County showed that 69 percent approved of government management of the emergency while 21 percent disapproved. The opinion sampling was taken between April 2 and April 8, 1979, from 375 persons who lived within a fifteen-mile radius of the plant. Faculty members and students who made the calls found that area residents were favorably impressed with Denton and Thornburgh's handling of the accident and with Carter's visit to the plant. Another poll provided similar results. A telephone survey of fifteen hundred households in late July and early August 1979 revealed that Thornburgh and the NRC, which presumably meant Denton, were the most important sources of information during the crisis. In each case, 57 percent of the respondents cited their information as "useful" or "extremely useful." By contrast, only 11 percent placed the information that Met Ed provided in those categories, while 60 percent judged its public statements to have been "totally useless."[23]

CONTINUING FEARS ABOUT RADIATION

Although the Three Mile Island accident released lethal amounts of radiation within the containment structure, extensive monitoring conducted by Met Ed, the NRC, the U.S. Department of Energy, the Environmental Protection Agency, the Food and Drug Administration, and the state of Pennsylvania during and after the emergency disclosed no evidence of large releases to the environment. The preliminary conclusion of a broad consensus of experts was that the effects of radiation from the plant, if any, would be slight. But many of the citizens of central Pennsylvania remained uneasy about the long-term consequences of the accident, and there was no definitive information available to eliminate their anxieties. One problem was the limited availability of instruments to measure releases of radiation, especially early in the accident. Some observers claimed that the readings taken did not provide complete or reliable information about the levels of radiation that might have escaped the plant, and that the effects of the accident might be greater than government estimates indicated. The nagging concern that this issue raised was aggravated by the unresolved scientific questions about, and the continuing controversy over, the risks of exposure to low-level radiation.

In the weeks following the accident, both state and federal officials offered a series of favorable assessments about the probable effects of radiation releases from the accident. While acknowledging that the findings were not definitive, they expressed confidence that a number of different indicators clearly testified to the absence of serious contamination. Investigators continued to search carefully for iodine-131 in milk and, by April 5, had found only a few samples with slightly elevated levels. This was an encouraging sign. John Nikoloff of the state Department of Agriculture pointed out that, in searching for radiation, "milk is one of the first places you are going to see it. If you don't find it in milk you're not going to find it anywhere." Samples of water and foodstuffs such as fish, cheese, vegetables, pretzels, and pancake mix detected, at worst, only trace amounts of radiation. The White House issued a statement on April 6 affirming that there was "absolutely no danger" from food produced in the region surrounding Three Mile Island. The following day, as a "vote of continuing confidence" in the safety of area milk supplies, Thornburgh and Denton, accompanied by their families, took a well-publicized tour of the Hershey chocolate factory.[24]

In a joint program sponsored by the NRC and the Pennsylvania Departments of Health and Environmental Resources, 721 citizens who lived close to Three Mile Island received whole-body counts of radiation levels to check for internal contamination. None of them showed above-normal levels of radiation that could be attributed to the accident. In addition, the state agriculture department investigated widely reported stories that radiation from the accident had caused the deaths of twelve stillborn calves and seven cows on a farm near the plant. After a series of tests, the agency determined that the cause of the deaths was not radiation but severe infection. In a survey of one hundred farms within a five-mile radius of the plant, the department found no evidence of animal disease that was above average in incidence or that could have resulted from radiation poisoning. Other later reports of "unusual animal health problems" as a result of emissions from Three Mile Island also proved to be groundless.[25]

On May 10, 1979, the team of experts from the NRC, EPA, and HEW that had prepared a preliminary estimate of the health effects of the accident five weeks earlier published a report based on more complete data. Although it raised its earlier estimate of the collective dose to the population within a fifty-mile radius of Three Mile Island and increased its worst-case maximum individual dose from 80 millirems to "less than 100" millirems, it reaffirmed its original judgment that off-site radiation measurements from the accident were too low to produce major consequences for public health in the region. The task force concluded that the amount of radiation released beyond the boundaries of the plant presented "minimal risks (that is, a very small number) of additional health effects to the offsite population." It projected that the number of "fatal excess cancers" among those within fifty miles of the plant who were exposed to radiation from the accident was "approximately one," and that the number of "excess health effects," including all cases of fatal and nonfatal cancer and genetic damage to future generations, was "approximately two."

The members of the interagency team recognized that their report was not the final word on the health effects of the accident, but they insisted that their findings were drawn from conservative assumptions to ensure that they "erred on the high side." They went to some lengths to defend the soundness of their data and to counter allegations that available instruments failed to provide sufficient information about radiation releases. Their study was based largely on readings from three sources: twenty ground-level dosimeters that Met Ed, in accordance with NRC regulations, had placed on-site and out to fifteen miles off-site before the accident to measure environmental radiation; thirty-seven ground-level NRC dosimeters installed at off-site locations on Saturday, March 31; and aerial measurements that Department of Energy helicopters had begun making on the afternoon of the first day of the accident. The task force argued that environmental monitoring and food sampling programs were "sufficient to characterize the magnitude of the collective dose and therefore the long-term health effects." It was confident that, if large releases that severely jeopardized public health had occurred, they would have provided enough identifying evidence to be detected by the various measuring and sampling procedures that Met Ed and several federal and state agencies employed.[26]

Others cited greater reservations about the reliability of radiation readings and expressed fears about the long-term ramifications of the accident. On April 7, several environmental and antinuclear organizations called official assessments of the effects of the accident a "nuclear whitewash." Paul Milvey, a professor at the Mount Sinai School of Medicine in New York, suggested a few days later that, in contrast to government calculations, radiation from the accident would cause as many as fifty deaths from cancer over a period of twenty-five years. Chauncey Kepford, who held a Ph.D. in chemistry and represented the Environmental Coalition on Nuclear Power, a Pennsylvania-based group that had long opposed the Three Mile Island plants, offered an even more alarming estimate. He told a subcommittee of the Committee on Science and Technology of the U.S. House of Representatives that the number of people who would die "as a direct result" of the TMI-2 accident seemed likely to range "in the hundreds, maybe in the thousands." He denounced the conclusions of the interagency report on the health effects of the accident as "nothing more than fabrications designed to conceal both the real magnitude of the exposure dose" and the "incredible incompetence of the NRC."

Kepford claimed that the "stagnant air mass" that prevailed at the time of the accident had prevented much radiation from descending to the ground close to the plant and that exposures did "not decrease rapidly with increasing distance from the reactor." Therefore, he asserted that the largest and most serious population exposures occurred beyond the fifteen-mile perimeter in which NRC and Met Ed dosimeters had been placed. NRC officials responded that aerial surveys conducted by the Department of Energy had tracked radiation plumes until they reached a background level and had shown clearly that levels had dropped proportionately as distance from the plant increased. One member of the committee, Robert S. Walker of Lancaster County, agreed with Kepford that the monitoring system was too limited to provide unambiguous measurements of radiation releases. But he revealed that he had seen no evidence to support Kepford's theory when he personally accompanied scientists taking measurements with portable monitors at locations in his district that were well beyond the range of the stationary dosimeters.[27]

Reports of increased risks of cancer and scientific uncertainties about the effects of low-level radiation fueled the high level of anxiety among the population around Three Mile Island. "Even with accurate radiation data—and we cannot be sure the government figures qualify for that description—there remain substantial concerns in regard to what it all means in terms of public health," the *Harrisburg Patriot* observed in an editorial on May 4. "The layman will find little clarification or comfort in the scientific community, which is bitterly divided over the degree of danger posed by low-level radiation." Even as patterns of life returned to normal in the area, indications of public uneasiness, without deteriorating into symptoms of panic, were abundant. Many pregnant women called their physicians or abortion clinics for advice on whether they should consider an abortion because of the accident. Psychiatrists were flooded with patients seeking relief from stress. People who called the Dauphin County Crisis Intervention Center to talk about the accident were "looking for reassurance," one of its supervisors commented. "They need somebody to say things are okay." The uncertainties and apprehensions that citizens of central Pennsylvania experienced in the aftermath of the crisis were perhaps best summarized in a slogan on a T-shirt widely distributed in the area: "I Survived Three Mile Island . . . I Think."[28]

Chapter 10

The Long-Term Effects of Three Mile Island

In the immediate aftermath of the Three Mile Island accident, many observers appealed for thorough, candid, and sober assessments of its causes and long-term consequences. "The crisis of Three Mile Island has not ended. It has just begun," the *Philadelphia Inquirer* editorialized on April 11, 1979. "Even minimal concern for humanity cries out for responsible, exhaustive examination of the circumstances and implications of the accident." Only after the many outstanding questions about the accident were addressed, the *Washington Star* suggested, could "the real debate over the future of nuclear power . . . begin." The crisis heightened the passions of the already intense controversy over nuclear power, enhancing the credibility of nuclear critics while undermining the position of supporters of the technology. Jon Payne, editor of *Nuclear News,* told his readers that the "nuclear industry must face the fact that . . . the TMI accident has put nuclear energy on probation."[1]

As a number of wide-ranging reviews of the accident proceeded, efforts got under way to clean up the highly contaminated plant without endangering public health. The local population responded to the continuing uncertainties it faced with growing anger and bitter expressions of dissatisfaction, particularly with Met Ed and the NRC. At the same time, the nuclear industry and the NRC drew on lessons from Three Mile Island to make a series of improvements designed to prevent the occurrence of another serious accident. Those measures generated further controversy, and long after the accident occurred, Three Mile Island remained a centerpiece—and often *the* centerpiece—of the nuclear power debate.

THE KEMENY COMMISSION INVESTIGATION

The Three Mile Island crisis was quickly followed by several extensive investigations. The NRC, the state of Pennsylvania, congressional committees, and nuclear industry groups sponsored important studies, but the most prominent of the inquiries was conducted by the President's Commission on the Accident at Three Mile Island. In a speech to the nation about energy policies on April 5, 1979, President Carter announced that he would create an independent commission "to investigate the causes" of Three Mile Island and "to make recommendations on how we can improve the safety of nuclear power plants." Six days later he formally established the commission and identified eleven persons he had appointed to it (a twelfth was added a short time later). The projected cost of the study was about $1 million. The White House deliberately avoided placing anyone on the panel who was associated with strong pro- or antinuclear views. Instead, it sought members, as Jack Watson told reporters, "with an open mind and objective frame of reference." Carter named John G. Kemeny, president of Dartmouth College, as chairman of the commission. Kemeny, whom one White House official described as a "brilliant mathematician and computer science expert" and "a superb administrator," had joined the faculty at Dartmouth in 1954 and served as its president since 1970.[2]

The Kemeny Commission operated under stringent time constraints. The president instructed it to submit a final report on Three Mile Island within six months after its first meeting. The commission conducted its investigation by assigning staff members and consultants to task forces that examined technical issues, the roles of the NRC and Met Ed, emergency preparedness, public information, and health effects. After holding a series of public hearings, taking more than 150 depositions, and collecting about three hundred cubic feet of documents, it presented its findings to Carter on October 30, 1979, and released them to the public the following day. The completed study consisted of a 179-page overview and nine volumes of task force reports that totaled more than 2,200 pages.[3]

The commission offered a harsh indictment of Babcock and Wilcox, Met Ed, GPU, and the NRC. It explained that it had no mandate to draw conclusions about the future of the nuclear industry or to make comparisons of nuclear power with other sources of energy. It did not intend to show either that "nuclear power is inherently too dangerous to permit it to continue and expand" or that "the nation should move forward aggressively to develop additional commercial nuclear power." Rather, the commission suggested "that if the country wishes, for larger reasons, to confront the risks that are inherently associated with nuclear power, fundamental changes are necessary if those risks are to be kept within tolerable limits." It maintained that critical improvements in reactor safety required major revisions, if not a revolution, in organization, practices, procedures, and above all, the "mindset" of the nuclear industry and the NRC.

According to the Kemeny Commission's report, a number of equipment failures contributed significantly to the Three Mile Island emergency, including problems with the condensate polishers, indicator lights in the control room, and the pilot-operated relief valve (PORV) on the pressurizer. It faulted both the utility and the NRC for lapses in quality assurance and maintenance. Nevertheless, the commission emphasized that the "basic problems are people-related." It expressed confidence that the "equipment was sufficiently good that, except for human failures, the major accident at Three Mile Island would have been a minor incident." Therefore, the key to reducing the likelihood of nuclear accidents was to correct prevalent attitudes that led to operator errors, management deficiencies, and regulatory complacency. The Kemeny report concluded that the "most serious 'mindset'" that had to be overcome was "the preoccupation of everyone with the safety of equipment, resulting in the down-playing of the importance of the human element in nuclear power generation."[4]

The Kemeny Commission found many ways in which insufficient consideration of the "human element" had converted minor equipment malfunctions into a severe accident at TMI-2. The most obvious and perhaps most serious problem was that training requirements for reactor operators and supervisors were "inadequate" and "shallow." Existing programs had left plant operators ill prepared for the situation that confronted them on the morning of the accident and played a major role in producing the errors that uncovered the core. The commission concluded that Met Ed, GPU, Babcock and Wilcox, and the NRC shared responsibility for the shortcomings in operator training. Those inadequacies were compounded by design flaws that undermined the efforts of the plant staff to deal with the accident. They included the cacophony of undifferentiated alarms, the inconvenient arrangement of instruments and controls, and the absence of clear indicators either of levels of water in the pressure vessel or of the position of the stuck-open PORV.

In addition to the deficiencies in the control room, the Kemeny Commission identified other human factors that substantially contributed to the accident. It complained that the management of GPU, Met Ed, and Babcock and Wilcox "failed to acquire enough information about safety problems, failed to analyze adequately what information they did acquire,

or failed to act on that information." As a result, the companies that designed and operated the Three Mile Island plants suffered from a "serious lack of communication about several critical safety matters." The
Kemeny Commission found the NRC to be equally delinquent in this regard. It pointed out, for example, that Babcock and Wilcox and the NRC
had not assimilated or communicated important safety information after the incident at the Davis-Besse reactor in Ohio in 1977. The chain of
events at Davis-Besse was similar to what later occurred at Three Mile
Island, but in that case an accident had been averted when an operator
stopped the escape of coolant through the pressurizer by closing a block
valve. Neither Babcock and Wilcox nor the NRC had taken effective action to draw lessons from Davis-Besse or provide warnings to other plant
owners that "could have prevented the accident" at TMI-2.

Babcock and Wilcox and the NRC, according to the report, had been
similarly remiss in their response to information that anticipated that
plant operators could misinterpret signs of a loss-of-coolant accident
resulting from a minor malfunction. In 1977, Carlyle Michelson, an engineer with the Tennessee Valley Authority and a consultant to the NRC's
Advisory Committee on Reactor Safeguards, had drafted a report that
analyzed how, under certain accident conditions, the level of water in
the pressurizer could mislead operators about the amount of coolant in
the core. This situation had led to serious errors during the TMI-2 accident when operators worried more about the pressurizer going solid
than about a loss of coolant from the core. Although both Babcock and
Wilcox and the NRC had received drafts of Michelson's report, they
had not found it urgent enough or convincing enough to pursue. It remained buried in bureaucratic channels until after the Three Mile Island crisis.

The Kemeny Commission criticized the NRC not only for ineffective
communications but also for poor management, misplaced priorities, and
complacent attitudes. It contended that, in keeping with the "old promotional philosophy" of the AEC, the NRC "sometimes erred on the
side of the industry's convenience rather than carrying out its primary
mission of assuring safety." The Kemeny Commission charged that the
NRC's performance in dealing with vital regulatory questions raised serious doubts about the agency's ability to provide adequate safety from
nuclear power hazards. Among the problems it enumerated were the
NRC's failure to resolve many generic safety issues, lack of systematic
evaluation of safety information from operating plants, use of a flawed

licensing process that overlooked some potentially serious safety matters, undue reliance on licensee information for its inspection and enforcement activities, inattention to emergency planning, and ill-defined lines of authority. "With its present organization, staff, and attitudes," the Kemeny Commission concluded, "the NRC is unable to fulfill its responsibility for providing an acceptable level of safety for nuclear power plants."[5]

Although the Kemeny Commission strongly rebuked the NRC and the companies that designed, owned, and operated TMI-2, it also offered some favorable judgments about the effects of the accident. It supported the estimates of the NRC and other agencies that releases of radiation from the plant would not produce significant public health consequences. "Based on our investigation of the health effects of the accident," the Kemeny Commission reported, "we conclude that in spite of serious damage to the plant, most of the radiation was contained and the actual release will have a negligible effect on the physical health of individuals." It also suggested, somewhat more equivocally, that even if the accident had melted the core, containment would not have been breached. At this time, no one knew that large portions of the core had, in fact, melted during the early stages of the accident. The Kemeny Commission stated that, although it could not be certain, it believed that "even if a meltdown occurred, there is a high probability that the containment building and the hard rock on which the TMI-2 containment building is built would have been able to prevent the escape of a large amount of radioactivity."[6]

The Kemeny Commission submitted a list of forty-four recommendations that it believed were of "vital importance" for reducing and managing the risks of nuclear power. Not surprisingly, it emphasized the need for changes to overcome the "mindset" that had severely underestimated human factors. It called on both the NRC and the nuclear industry to upgrade training requirements and programs for reactor operators and to devote far greater attention to the functionality of control rooms and instruments. It urged a series of other steps to provide more effective management, better communications, clearer procedures, and systematic assessment of industry-wide operating experience. In addition, the commission pressed for improvements in equipment design and availability, on-site and off-site radiation monitoring, emergency planning, and the delivery of timely and intelligible information to the public and the news media. Probably its most controversial recommendation was that the

NRC's commission-style form of governance be replaced with a single administrator in order to remedy management deficiencies, internal communication problems, and vague lines of authority.[7]

The report elicited a mixed response. Some observers hailed the quality of its investigation and thoughtfulness of its recommendations. Senator Alan K. Simpson, a Republican from Wyoming and ranking minority member of the Subcommittee on Nuclear Regulation of the Senate Committee on Environment and Public Works, called it "a fair and balanced appraisal of the accident and its implications." NRC and nuclear industry representatives expressed agreement with many, though not all, of the study's conclusions. They had begun implementing at least some of the reforms that the Kemeny Commission recommended even before it completed its work. Others, by contrast, announced keen disappointment with the results of the investigation. The *Harrisburg Patriot* commented that, although in some ways the report was "an excellent piece of work," it had "little new to tell the people who lived through the nightmarish days" of the crisis. Nuclear critics complained that the Kemeny Commission did not urge a moratorium on the construction of nuclear power plants. The panel had seriously considered calling for a moratorium on the issuance of new construction permits, but the proposal narrowly failed to win the support of a majority. The commission's refusal to recommend a moratorium prompted Ralph Nader, for example, to suggest that its contents had "no teeth."[8]

The Carter administration carefully weighed its response to the findings of the Kemeny Commission. The White House staff and executive agencies directly involved in nuclear power issues "firmly and completely" endorsed thirty-eight of the forty-four recommendations in the report. Three central issues related to the Kemeny Commission's conclusions— the future of nuclear power, the structure of the NRC, and the status of nuclear licensing—created more internal division. Although the Kemeny Commission had no mandate to address the role of nuclear power in the nation's energy policies, the White House staff maintained that it was "both appropriate and politically essential" for Carter to state his position. Most of the president's advisers were convinced that nuclear power was an indispensable component of the administration's energy program, but they also were acutely aware that Three Mile Island strengthened the political appeal of nuclear critics. They were particularly concerned that Senator Edward Kennedy or Governor Jerry Brown could capitalize on antinuclear sentiment to challenge Carter's bid for reelection in 1980.

The White House staff and other advisers strongly opposed the Kemeny Commission's recommendation to replace the NRC with a new agency headed by a single administrator. They did not believe the panel had shown that a new agency would be more effective in addressing the problems it identified. They argued that shifting to a single administrator would not only politicize regulatory decisions but also undermine the advantages of "a diversity of perspectives in an open and deliberative process." Further, they pointed out that even if the White House backed the Kemeny Commission's view, the recommendation to alter the structure of the NRC "enjoys no support with key members of Congress." On the question of issuing new licenses, administration officials advised against adopting a position on politically charged proposals for a moratorium on construction permits. But they suggested that taking a stand on the review of operating licenses for the thirty-eight new plants that would be completed by the end of 1982 was advisable. They sought to allow time for essential reforms to be placed in effect without causing "adverse energy impacts." Their sensitivity to energy sufficiency had been heightened by rising oil prices and escalating public anxieties over gasoline supplies in the summer of 1979.[9]

Carter followed the guidance of his advisers when he issued his response to the Kemeny Commission's recommendations on December 7, 1979. He attempted to find a middle ground on the prospects for nuclear power that neither dismissed its importance to the nation's energy supplies nor discounted the arguments of nuclear critics. He declared, as he had done in earlier statements, that "nuclear power is an energy source of last resort." But he added, "We do not have the luxury of abandoning nuclear power or imposing a lengthy moratorium on its further use." The president supported the NRC's recent decision to suspend the issuance of construction permits and operating licenses until it explored the lessons of the Three Mile Island accident and developed plans to carry out reforms. However, he urged the NRC to move quickly to make safety improvements and end what it called a licensing "pause" within six months. Carter also revealed that he would submit a plan to Congress to reorganize the NRC, not by abolishing the commission but by strengthening the executive powers exercised by the chairman, especially during an emergency. He announced that he would select a new chairman from outside the agency, and that, in the interim, he had appointed Commissioner John Ahearne to replace Joseph Hendrie in that position. Although Hendrie was removed as chairman, he remained a member of the commission.[10]

THE NRC'S RESPONSE TO THREE MILE ISLAND

While the Kemeny Commission and the White House were considering measures to improve nuclear safety, the NRC was conducting its own review of the ways in which its assumptions, procedures, policies, and priorities had contributed to the accident. An NRC staff member remarked a few days after the crisis ended, "This accident has been a real shock because it has shown there are an awful lot of things we just don't know about reactors." Commissioner Peter Bradford called it "a searing experience for the technical experts" in the agency. On April 20, 1979, the NRC began its first formal study of the accident. The Office of Inspection and Enforcement set out to compile a full account of the facts and to determine whether the licensee had violated agency regulations. The investigation was completed in July 1979, and although it made no claim to being definitive, it attributed the accident largely to operator errors. It cited Met Ed for 148 violations of NRC operating, procedural, and reporting requirements. In October 1979, Victor Stello, who had recently been appointed director of the Office of Inspection and Enforcement, notified the utility that the NRC was levying fines of $155,000, a record penalty, for the violations. The assessments would have totaled $725,000 had it not been for statutory limitations on the amounts the NRC could collect from licensees.[11]

The second NRC investigation took a broader perspective. In May 1979, the Office of Nuclear Reactor Regulation organized a task force, directed by Roger Mattson, to examine the lessons that the NRC should learn from the Three Mile Island accident and apply to the regulation of the nuclear industry. Less than three months later, the task force issued its first report, which presented a series of "short-term recommendations" that were "narrow, specific, and urgent." Among other items, it urged the placement of instruments in control rooms that directly showed the level of coolant in the core and—in pressurized water reactors—the position of the PORV on the pressurizer. It also called for prompt action to improve the control of hydrogen production in an accident and to clearly define the roles and authority of control room operators and supervisors.

In October 1979, the task force released a final report that offered proposals on "safety questions of a more fundamental policy nature." It reached the same conclusion as the Kemeny Commission about the need to focus on human factors in improving reactor safety. "The primary deficiency in reactor safety technology identified by the accident," the task force declared, "was the inadequate attention that had been paid by all levels and all segments of the technology to the human element and its fundamental role in both the prevention of accidents and the response to accidents." It recommended a number of steps that the nuclear industry should take to address this problem. It insisted that corporate managers must become committed to and involved in operational safety. It also appealed for a series of measures to strengthen plant operators' training, qualifications, and ability to respond to "unusual situations." In addition to urging the industry to correct weaknesses that Three Mile Island had exposed, the task force called for important changes in the NRC's regulatory approach, including the development of "safety goals" to use as a benchmark for evaluating regulatory requirements, better coordination of safety and licensing reviews within the NRC, and creation of an "emergency response team" to deal immediately with accidents.[12]

The most elaborate of the NRC's studies of Three Mile Island was carried out by its "special inquiry group." The commissioners decided within a short time after the accident that they wanted a wide-ranging and candid evaluation of its causes and its implications for NRC programs, even at the risk of overlapping the activities of the Kemeny Commission. The internal review, however, proceeded slowly at first. On May 14, 1979, Commissioner Gilinsky complained to his colleagues that six weeks after the accident they still had not appointed a director of the project. "This situation," he said, "is little short of scandalous." The following month, the commission selected Mitchell Rogovin, a founding partner in the Washington, D.C., law firm of Rogovin, Stern and Huge, to head the investigation. Rogovin had served as chief counsel of the Internal Revenue Service and as an assistant U.S. attorney general during the 1960s. After entering private practice, he had won wide attention for suing President Nixon's Committee to Reelect the President as the counsel of the public interest lobbying group Common Cause, for defending the *New York Times* reporter Neil Sheehan for his role in publication of the Pentagon Papers, and for representing the Central Intelligence Agency in congressional investigations of intelligence activities.

The staff of the NRC's special inquiry group that Rogovin directed included more than fifty professionals from the NRC and twenty-five outside attorneys and consultants. The group took about 270 formal depositions and conducted "hundreds of additional interviews." The cost of the project, originally estimated at $450,000, eventually grew to $3 million. On January 24, 1980, Rogovin submitted the results of the inquiry in a 183-page summary, which was followed a few days later by a 1,272-page, three-volume account of the accident.[13]

In keeping with the special inquiry group's mandate, the Rogovin Report focused mainly, though not exclusively, on the NRC's performance. The fact that the agency paid for the investigation and that many staff members worked on it did not preclude a sharply critical assessment of the NRC's organization, management, regulatory judgment, or response to the TMI-2 accident. Although the Rogovin investigation operated independently of the Kemeny Commission, it covered much of the same ground and reached many of the same conclusions. It echoed the presidential commission in suggesting that the "principal deficiencies in commercial reactor safety today are not hardware problems, they are management problems." It faulted both the nuclear industry and the NRC for inattention to the human element in nuclear safety and charged that the NRC had "virtually ignored the critical areas of operator training, human factors engineering, utility management, and technical qualifications." It asserted that the NRC's organizational structure and management weaknesses made it "incapable" of protecting public health and safety from the risks of nuclear power. "We have found in the Nuclear Regulatory Commission," the report declared, "an organization that is not so much badly managed as it is not managed at all." The Rogovin study not only concurred with many of the criticisms advanced by the Kemeny Commission but also agreed with its favorable assessment of the public health consequences of the accident. The special inquiry group determined that the "effects on the population in the vicinity of Three Mile Island from radioactive releases measured during the accident, if any, will certainly be nonmeasurable and nondetectable."

The recommendations of the Rogovin Report, like its major conclusions, were similar to those of the Kemeny Commission. It urged that the NRC's commission format be abolished and replaced with a single administrator. It called for essential improvements in management oversight, operator training, control room designs, and other aspects of "human factors engineering." It cited the need to upgrade, among other things, emergency planning, radiation monitoring, and the NRC's ability to respond to accidents. The directors of the Rogovin project were sensitive to suggestions that their investigation failed to contribute much of importance beyond the findings and proposals of the Kemeny Commission. George T. Frampton Jr., Rogovin's deputy and law firm colleague, strongly protested when the *Washington Post* called the study a "$3 million disappointment" that contained "little new" and "left much to be desired." He pointed out that the Rogovin Report provided detailed information about the accident that was not available in the Kemeny volumes, and that it offered several new recommendations on such matters as funding emergency preparedness, conducting inspections of operating reactors, and regulating on-site management of plants. Nevertheless, as Gilinsky noted, the recommendations that the report made were, for the most part, "familiar and widely supported."[14]

The NRC commissioners took divergent positions on the value of the Rogovin Report. Ahearne praised it as a "reasoned and sound document" and added that the money the agency paid for it was "well spent." Gilinsky and Bradford, by contrast, expressed reservations. They were especially skeptical of Rogovin's judgment on questions about whether plant operators had deliberately withheld vital information from the NRC on the first day of the accident. The source of the questions on this matter was Henry Myers, science adviser to the House Committee on Interior and Insular Affairs, which was chaired by Morris K. Udall. Drawing on evidence collected by various investigations, Myers concluded that Met Ed officials had withheld from the NRC and the state of Pennsylvania "significant information" about the serious nature of the accident. On January 21, 1980, Udall asked the NRC for its response to Myers's findings. Udall's request came too late to be considered specifically by the NRC's special inquiry group; Rogovin submitted his summary report just three days later. It addressed the issue in general terms, however, by concluding that "the evidence failed to establish that Med Ed management or other personnel willfully withheld information from the NRC." It attributed the delay in recognizing the severity of the accident to confusion, inadequate communications, and preoccupation with stabilizing the plant, rather than calculated action by the utility to conceal crucial data.[15]

In response to questions from Gilinsky and Bradford and another letter from Udall to the NRC, Rogovin and Frampton attempted to "clarify . . . the state of the evidence" on the issue. They conceded that some testimony could be read as support for Myers's allegations, but they insisted that the burden of existing evidence did not demonstrate a deliberate effort by Met Ed to mislead the NRC on the day of the accident. "We found no *direct* evidence of willful withholding of critical information," they reiterated in a memorandum to Ahearne on March 4, 1980. Their conclusion was persuasive to three of the commissioners but still did not convince Gilinsky and Bradford. Neither did it satisfy Udall, who commented that it was "inadequate."[16]

Despite the differences of opinion over those charges, there was wide agreement within the agency on the need for corrective action on a number of fronts. The Kemeny Commission, the special inquiry group, the NRC's other internal investigations, and the experiences of the commissioners and staff during the Three Mile Island crisis made clear that prompt and extensive regulatory reform was essential. In some cases, changes were urgent and straightforward enough to be made within a short time. They included the installation of dedicated telephone lines from each operating nuclear plant to NRC headquarters to alleviate the problem of dreadful communications that had plagued the agency during the early stages of the accident. The NRC created a new Office for Analysis and Evaluation of Operational Data to collect, coordinate, and assess information from operating plants and provide feedback to the agency and licensees. It was intended to strengthen the NRC's ability to recognize and rectify problems, such as those that occurred at Davis-Besse in 1977, before they turned into precursors of major accidents. The NRC expanded and accelerated its resident inspector program, which it had established in 1977, to provide full-time, on-site staff presence at all operating plants. Further, the agency imposed a series of requirements on licensees to address shortcomings that Three Mile Island made obvious, including instrument intelligibility, hydrogen control, radiation monitoring, and plant supervision.[17]

Other regulatory improvements were too complex, and in some cases too controversial, to be imposed without more study and deliberation. The NRC sponsored long-term research on important issues that could not be immediately resolved, such as the causes and results of small-break loss-of-coolant accidents, hydrogen evolution after serious fuel damage, the effect of a severe accident on plant equipment and materials, and human factors in reactor safety. The need to enhance operator training was apparent, and the NRC quickly took initial steps to accomplish this goal. The commission promptly approved more stringent licensing requirements for senior reactor operators, more extensive use of reactor simulators in training programs, and greater agency involvement in monitoring qualification and periodic requalification examinations for operators. Other matters, such as the proper role of the NRC in imposing specific training rules and minimum educational requirements for operators and control room supervisors, were not so easily settled. Similarly, the design and administration of programs to evaluate nuclear plant management, which were unavoidably subjective and inherently controversial, stirred considerable debate. And the NRC provoked a great deal of internal contention and external criticism when it undertook a large-scale effort to develop quantitative safety goals to help determine what constituted an adequate level of safety from nuclear power hazards.[18]

Another complicated, and probably the most controversial, issue that the Three Mile Island accident brought to the forefront of regulatory policy making was emergency planning. It was clear that the industry, the NRC, and the state of Pennsylvania were not well prepared to respond to the possible consequences of the accident, and that corrective measures were required. Congressman Toby Moffett, a Connecticut Democrat and chairman of the Subcommittee on Environment, Energy, and Natural Resources of the House Committee on Government Operations, blasted the NRC for its "policy of malign neglect." Hendrie told Moffett's subcommittee in May 1979, "I don't think that any one needs to be persuaded that thorough emergency preparedness is an essential component in the regulatory structure." Prodded by vocal complaints from Congress and by their own recognition of the need to improve emergency planning, the commissioners adopted a series of measures soon after the crisis ended at TMI. They approved increasing staff resources for emergency planning, upgrading the capabilities of the agency's emergency response center, expanding programs to provide information to the public, and evaluating licensees' emergency preparedness.

Other emergency planning issues required policy decisions that seemed appropriate to consider in the NRC's formal rule making process. In July 1979, the commission decided to conduct expedited rule-making proceedings to strengthen existing regulations. Without a great deal of discussion, it agreed on an "emergency planning zone" with about a fifty-mile radius surrounding a plant as the area for which state and local governments should make preparations. The emergency planning zone was divided into a "plume exposure pathway" out to about ten miles from a plant, in which direct exposure to radiation from an accident was a threat, and an "ingestion exposure pathway" out to fifty miles, in which food could become contaminated. The distances could differ somewhat to allow for local variances in demography, topography, access routes, and jurisdictional boundaries, but they set the basic standards for state and local emergency planning officials to apply to their own locations.[19]

The second question was more difficult to resolve: whether the commission should impose a rule that would make continued operation of, and granting licenses for, nuclear power plants contingent upon an NRC-approved state emergency plan. The nuclear industry and many members of Congress worried that if the NRC adopted such a regulation it would give state or local governments an effective veto over the licensing of nuclear facilities. If state or local authorities declined to submit an emergency plan, extend the emergency planning zone to acceptable distances, or cooperate with federal agencies, they could prevent the licensing of new plants or the operation of existing ones. Several members of Congress urged the NRC not to approve regulations that would offer state or local governments "the authority to defeat the nuclear option simply by refusing to submit an adequate response plan."

Despite this concern, Congress defeated proposals to expand the NRC's statutory authority to provide emergency plans for states that refused to cooperate. Legislation to that effect failed by a narrow margin three times in the Senate in July 1979 on the grounds that it was an unwarranted intrusion by the federal government on activities traditionally performed by the states. The NRC, therefore, had little choice but to frame its regulations on the assumption that state and local governments would work with federal agencies to improve emergency planning. It was committed, as a result of both the lessons of Three Mile Island and political realities, to strengthening existing requirements, but it had no authority to force state or local governments to prepare emergency plans or follow NRC guidelines. Eventually, in August 1980, the agency issued a rule stipulating that it would not approve a new operating license without a satisfactory emergency plan and instructing owners of operating plants to develop adequate procedures. Although it recognized that state and local jurisdictions could use the new rule to thwart the operation of power reactors, it suggested optimistically that "state and local officials as partners in this undertaking will endeavor to provide fully for public protection."[20]

THE NUCLEAR INDUSTRY'S RESPONSE

Like the NRC, the nuclear industry was shocked and humbled by the Three Mile Island accident. Carl Walske, president of the Atomic Industrial Forum, a prominent trade group, said of the industry, "I thought we were better than that before the accident happened." William J. Lanouette, a journalist who had reported on nuclear power for many years, found that although some industry representatives regarded Three Mile Island as a "blessing in disguise," others were "stunned and dispirited." The industry as a whole took prompt action to deal with errors and weaknesses that the crisis revealed. Within two weeks after the accident occurred, the chief executive officers of nuclear utilities established a committee to coordinate their activities and advance their common goals. The TMI-2 emergency made vividly clear to them that their shared interests demanded safe operation of all nuclear plants. A serious accident at one plant could adversely affect, if not destroy, the entire industry. A poorly run nuclear plant threatened to tar the reputation and undermine the financial stability of every other plant, even those with strong performance records.[21]

The committee of nuclear utility executives soon set up two organizations to draw on the lessons of Three Mile Island to upgrade industry-wide performance and enhance safety. They created the Nuclear Safety Analysis Center within the Electric Power Research Institute to investigate the technical aspects of the accident, make judgments about the need for and priority of technical changes, and disseminate findings throughout the industry. The center published its first report on the causes of the accident in July 1979. The other organization that industry executives established was the Institute of Nuclear Power Operations (INPO). Its purpose was to foster improvements in the management of nuclear power plants and to monitor their performance closely. It began operations in January 1980 with an annual budget of $11 million, provided by nuclear utilities, and plans to recruit a staff of two hundred professionals.[22]

It was apparent in the wake of Three Mile Island that senior utility executives had to become more deeply involved in and aware of the day-to-day operations of their nuclear facilities. After conducting inspections of operating nuclear power plants in the United States, INPO found that inadequate management control ranked high among the "foremost safety and reliability issues," because safety problems often "were not known by top management." Industry leaders sought to improve the management of nuclear plants not only to enhance safety but also to reduce the role that the NRC might assume. They were concerned about the agency's new focus on management issues, and they wanted to reduce the "intrusion of government and prescriptive regulation into our management." INPO carried out its mandate by establishing standards for plant performance, rating plants in accordance with those standards, and generally exerting a great deal of peer pressure on utility executives to strive for excellence. One scholar described its approach as "communitarian social control" and "management by embarrassment" of poor performers.[23]

Despite the reforms that the nuclear industry adopted, Three Mile Island remained a major embarrassment and a severe setback to its fortunes. The accident intensified the doldrums that the industry had suffered after the mid-1970s, and it ushered in new trials for beleaguered nuclear proponents. "The nuclear industry is not well," *Time* magazine reported in 1984. "It has been suffering seriously . . . ever since a 1979 accident turned the nuclear plant at Three Mile Island, Pa., into a focal point for public fears and protests." The NRC's post-TMI regulations added significantly to the costs of plants under construction and in operation. The requirements also raised industry concerns that a "big shopping list" of hastily imposed regulations could result in "killing nuclear power." Falling demand for electricity, high interest rates, massive cost overruns, lengthy construction delays, public protests, and, in some cases, outrageously shoddy construction combined to force the cancellation of many plants—twenty-eight by early 1985, some of which were nearly completed. Orders for new nuclear plants after Three Mile Island were inconceivable. As one industry leader commented, "No utility executive in the country would consider ordering one today—unless he wanted to be certified or committed." In a cover story in February 1985, *Forbes* magazine declared that "the failure of the U.S. nuclear power program ranks as the largest managerial disaster in business history, a disaster on a monumental scale."[24]

Over a period of years, the nuclear industry's economic and safety performance benefited from the technical, operational, and managerial reforms undertaken after the Three Mile Island accident. The capacity factor for nuclear plants, which indicated the percentage of time during which they produced power, increased from the 50–60 percent range in the 1970s to 70 percent a decade later. The cost of generating electricity from nuclear power fell substantially during the same period. INPO established the National Academy for Nuclear Training to upgrade, evaluate, and accredit the operator training programs of nuclear utilities. A series of safety indicators, including the number of automatic scrams, safety system actuations, safety system failures, and collective radiation exposure for plant workers, showed consistent and significant industrywide improvement after the mid-1980s.

The performance indicators did not mean that problems at individual plants had been fully resolved or that lapses in safety performance had been eliminated. Perhaps the most serious, or at least the most visible, failure in the decade after Three Mile Island was the discovery in 1987 that plant operators and shift supervisors routinely slept while on duty at the Philadelphia Electric Company's Peach Bottom-2 reactor in Pennsylvania. The NRC shut down the plant for two years, and INPO successfully pressured the utility's board of directors to replace its chief executive and operating officials. This was a sign, wrote Matthew L. Wald in the *New York Times,* "of a basic shift in safety concerns since the accident at Three Mile Island. . . . Now the message seems to be that faulty operators will not be tolerated any more than faulty equipment, and that top management will be held more accountable when there is a human problem."[25]

THE CLEANUP OF TMI-2

While the investigations of the Three Mile Island accident were proceeding and reforms were introduced, the monumental task of cleaning up the plant got under way. Although no one could be certain of the extent of damage to the reactor core, containment structure, or auxiliary building, it was apparent that ridding the plant of radioactive gas, highly irradiated plant components, and an estimated six hundred thousand gallons of contaminated water was an essential and daunting project. The ultimate fate of the reactor remained an open question. Harold Denton suggested at a press conference on April 3, 1979, that TMI-2 would not be back on-line for "as long as four years," and some of his NRC colleagues speculated that the plant might never return to operation. Utility executives took a more optimistic position. Herman M. Dieckamp, president of GPU, told a stockholders' meeting on May 9, 1979, "We think the plant will be out of service for approximately three years."[26]

The prospects for reopening the plant depended in large part on gaining more complete information about its condition, which soon proved to be a demanding and painstaking process. The containment structure was too heavily contaminated for entry immediately after the accident; therefore, major cleanup activities began in the auxiliary building. The level of radioactive gas in the building was reduced to acceptable proportions by repairing leaks in the waste gas system, releasing gas into containment, and other measures. The contaminated water in the auxiliary building was treated by an ion-exchange system that removed virtually all the radioactivity. The water was then stored in holding tanks. Technicians laboriously wiped down exposed surfaces in the building from floor to ceiling and sprayed many areas with high-pressure hoses or other equipment. The city of Lancaster, which drew its water supply from the Susquehanna River, sued the NRC in 1979 to prevent any discharge of water from the plant. In February 1980 an out-of-court settlement effectively prohibited the release of "accident-generated water" to the river, an agreement that the NRC confirmed in subsequent regulatory orders.[27]

The decontamination of the auxiliary building was difficult and at times exasperating, but it was merely a prelude to the more challenging tasks of appraising the damage in the containment building and cleaning it up. The first obstacle to sustained access inside containment was the large volume of radioactive krypton-85, a noble gas, in the building's atmosphere. In order to enhance worker safety and to prevent unplanned releases to the environment, the krypton had to be eliminated. After weighing several options, the NRC staff concluded that the best method was to vent the gas into the atmosphere gradually, producing levels of radiation much lower than the amounts a nuclear plant emitted annually during normal operations. Although purging the gas from containment was not a complicated technical problem, it soon turned out to be a formidable political issue. The citizens of central Pennsylvania, who had demonstrated such remarkable poise during the Three Mile Island crisis, showed less patience and calmness as the cleanup proceeded. The primary source of stress was the recognition that one goal of the cleanup was to reopen the TMI-2 plant, and that Met Ed intended to restart TMI-1. By order of the NRC, the undamaged unit 1, which was shut down at the time of the accident for routine refueling, remained idle. The population of the area, or at least a substantial part of it, objected to the resumption of nuclear power production at Three Mile Island because of fears that the accident had spawned. The question of venting krypton-85 to the environment emerged as the focus of their apprehensions. One year after the accident, the *Washington Post* reported that "some citizens now become almost hysterical over the idea that Three Mile Island will release more radioactivity, no matter how little, in venting the krypton gas."[28]

By early 1980, confidence in the NRC among the population around Three Mile Island had declined sharply, apparently as a result of the well-publicized transcripts of commission meetings during the crisis, criticisms of the NRC in the Kemeny and Rogovin reports, continuing uncertainties over the future of the plant, and fears of the effects of radiation at any level of exposure. In contrast to a poll in April 1979 showing that 69 percent of local residents approved of government management of the accident, a survey taken the following March found that only 32 percent approved.

The anger and mistrust of area citizens was vividly apparent when the NRC conducted public meetings to discuss the venting of krypton-85.

At a raucous meeting in Middletown on March 19, 1980, about five hundred persons packed a fire hall and many others were turned away when the crowd exceeded the building's capacity. Some of those who were denied entry banged loudly and continuously on windows and doors to signal their resentment. The atmosphere inside was no friendlier. Members of the audience cursed stunned NRC staff members with the crudest of epithets or shouted somewhat milder denunciations, such as "liar," "murderer," and "we hate your guts." One woman told NRC officials, "You are no more worthy than a hunk of cow manure." The same pattern occurred at a gathering the following evening in Elizabethtown, Pennsylvania, which featured an irate schoolteacher who attempted to rush the stage before he was restrained by police officers. The vocal expressions of opinion by "people to whom protesting does not come naturally or easily," commented the *Philadelphia Inquirer,* "spilled out a year of pent-up bitterness, fear and frustration." Although most citizens of central Pennsylvania did not condone the abusive behavior of a small number of their neighbors, many shared the same concerns. Nancy Prelesnik, a resident of Hershey, told the NRC commissioners at a public meeting in Washington, D.C., on March 21, 1980, that "the people of the state of Pennsylvania feel we've been sold down the tubes by everyone."[29]

The outcry over venting krypton placed Governor Thornburgh in an awkward position between the anxieties of his constituents and the judgment of technical experts. In hopes of alleviating popular apprehensions and building a broad consensus on removing krypton, and in keeping with his usual approach to difficult issues, he set out to collect and "fully develop all the facts." He invited Harold Denton to confer with him about the options for purging the plant of krypton-85. On March 27, 1980, the eve of the first anniversary of the accident, Thornburgh and Denton held a press conference in Harrisburg. The governor introduced Denton as a person "who has served Pennsylvania well and served me personally well in the past as a source of reliable information." Denton told reporters that he believed venting the krypton was the best alternative in terms of feasibility and radiation safety for both plant workers and off-site residents. He emphasized that the health risks of the procedure were "trivial."

Thornburgh also asked the Union of Concerned Scientists (UCS) for its advice. Within a month, a team of UCS experts, which included a veritable "who's who" of nuclear critics, submitted a report to him. It agreed that removing the krypton was essential and discussed four possible approaches, including venting it to the atmosphere. It concluded that none of the options would present any serious radiation hazards to the public. The UCS study also suggested that, although venting would not cause adverse health effects, it would generate additional stress among the population. After reviewing the UCS report, the NRC reiterated its position that venting was the most attractive alternative and authorized Met Ed to proceed. Thornburgh, satisfied that the process would not threaten public health, supported the NRC's decision. The governor's actions seemed to take the edge off the concerns of his constituents. When the krypton-85 was purged over a period of fifteen days in late June and early July 1980, local residents responded, as the trade journal *Nucleonics Week* observed, with "stoical resolve, tinged with some anxiety and some irritation."[30]

Shortly after the venting was completed, on July 23, 1980, two Met Ed engineers, wearing heavy protective clothing and using respirators to breathe, became the first persons to enter the TMI-2 containment building since the morning the accident took place. Working for twenty minutes in temperatures of about ninety degrees Fahrenheit, they took photographs and measured levels of radiation. Even after technicians explored the inside of the containment structure in hundreds of subsequent entries, the condition of the core remained a towering unknown. It was apparent that the accident had caused considerable damage to the fuel rods and other elements of the core, but the extent of the destruction could not be determined until the interior of the pressure vessel, which held the core, could be examined. A few days after the accident, the NRC had estimated from analyses of reactor coolant samples that only about 2 to 15 percent of the core had been damaged, and that, at worst, melting of the uranium dioxide fuel pellets appeared to be "insignificant." Later analyses indicated that the damage had been more severe, but for more than three years it remained impossible to observe the core directly and draw reliable conclusions.[31]

In July and August 1982, three camera probes into the core provided the first direct evidence of its condition. Standing on a platform above the pressure vessel, teams of engineers dropped a small underwater camera (1.25 inches in diameter and 1 foot long) through a channel in a control rod to the center of the core thirty-six feet below. This procedure, called Quick Look, furnished limited information but still was an important step toward understanding the status of the core and planning for removal of its damaged contents. The results surprised many of the experts who observed the operation. The camera revealed that the surveyed area of the core once occupied by the top sections of fuel assemblies had been reduced to a large void and a pile of rubble from crushed reactor components. This finding carried ominous implications for the costs and burdens of the cleanup, but officials for GPU Nuclear, a GPU subsidiary formed to manage the utility's nuclear operations, remained optimistic. They declared that they had expected to see rubble and were "encouraged" that the probes seemed to indicate the fuel had not melted. "Broken, shattered pellets are not the same as melted pellets," a company spokesman commented, "and when we're talking about a meltdown, we're talking about melted fuel."[32]

Continuing investigations of the core established, however, that a large portion of the core had melted. In February 1985, inspections of larger portions of the core and analysis of debris provided strong evidence that at least some fuel had melted. This discovery greatly complicated plans for defueling the reactor by removing the remains of the core. Two years later, evaluation of more core samples suggested that about 70 percent of the core had been damaged and that 35–45 percent of it had melted. By the following year, the estimate for core melting had increased to approximately 50 percent. During the accident, the molten fuel "flowed like hot olive oil," commented Edward E. Kintner, executive vice president of GPU Nuclear. By the time the signs of extensive meltdown became clear, the company had abandoned any thoughts of reopening TMI-2.[33]

The defueling process took place in several stages. The first step in cleaning up the containment building was to treat the several hundred thousand gallons of contaminated water in the basement and the reactor coolant system, which was done between 1981 and 1985. This procedure applied the same basic principles of ion exchange used on the water in the auxiliary building but was more complex because of much higher levels of radioactivity in the containment water. The processing of the water from containment removed all but traces of its radioactivity; the water was then transferred to storage. Eventually, more than 2 million gallons of slightly contaminated water from the accident and cleanup were released to the atmosphere through evaporation.

In 1985, after the water from the accident was removed from the containment building basement and the reactor coolant system, technicians began defueling the pressure vessel by removing tons of rubble and fragments of the core. The defueling operation was slow and difficult: to guard against excessive radiation exposure, they were forced to dress in two layers of protective gear, wear heavy gloves that they changed every fifteen minutes, breathe through respirators, and talk through internal micro-

Figure 24. Cleanup operations at TMI-2. Workers in radiation suits stand on a platform above the pressure vessel (courtesy of the Pennsylvania State University Engineering Library).

phones. Guided by television monitors, they used long-handled tools that extended forty feet into the vessel and technologically advanced equipment to cut, chop, drill, dig, and scoop tons of radioactive debris submerged in water. After the material was lifted to the surface, it was placed in canisters and eventually shipped to the Idaho National Engineering Laboratory, a facility funded by the U.S. Department of Energy, for analysis and storage. By the time the defueling was completed in 1990, the total cost of the cleanup had reached about $1 billion. GPU shareholders and customers and the utility's insurance underwriters paid about two-thirds of the amount; the remainder was supplied by the Department of Energy, the electric power industry, the states of Pennsylvania and New Jersey, and the Japanese government and nuclear industry. The Japanese contributed about $18 million for the costs of cleanup in order to acquire information and provide training for their nuclear engineers.[34]

The cleanup operations at TMI-2 yielded a great deal of new and often surprising information about the accident, the most important of which was the revelation that a major core meltdown had occurred. This finding raised critical questions about why the effects of the accident beyond the pressure vessel were so limited. Despite the fact that temperatures rose high enough to melt about half the core, the TMI-2 plant did not release large amounts of radiation to the environment or come close to triggering the China syndrome. It suffered a severe loss-of-coolant accident but did not produce the consequences that reactor experts had projected as possible in such conditions. One vital issue that analysts weighed was why the pressure vessel did not fail. It was not designed to withstand the heat that the accident generated, but it did not burst, split, or melt in a way that would have allowed the core to fall into the containment structure. The question was, as one engineer phrased it, "Why wasn't the core on the floor?"

After extensive investigations, researchers concluded that the first portions of the melted core that flowed toward the bottom of the pressure vessel were cooled by the relatively small volume of water in the lower section. They solidified into a ceramic crust, which helped to preserve the vessel from the heat of the rest of the molten core that relocated from above. Experts had not anticipated this process in projections of the effects of a loss-of-coolant accident, and it suggested to some that the "unexpected enhanced cooling that occurred at TMI-2 may represent an additional safety margin." After the completion of a five-year, $9 million international project in 1993, researchers concluded that "the TMI-2 reactor vessel was more robust than experts believed," but they could not determine how close it had come to failing. The extent to which the findings about the pressure vessel applied to other plants under different conditions was unclear.[35]

Another significant question that the cleanup of the containment building raised was why more radioactive iodine had not escaped from the plant. Although the accident discharged up to 13 million curies of radioactive noble gases to the environment, it released very little of the much more hazardous iodine-131. A curie is a unit of measurement formerly used to indicate the decay rate (or level of activity) of radioactive substances. Of the estimated 64 million curies of iodine-131 in the core at the time of the accident, less than 20 curies leaked to the atmosphere. This was a far smaller release of iodine-131 than reactor experts had postulated in projecting the consequences of a severe reactor accident before Three Mile Island. Researchers found that most of the iodine-131 in the core had combined with other elements to form compounds that dissolved in water or had attached to metal surfaces in the containment building. Under the conditions in the core and the reactor building, the iodine did not remain in a gaseous state long enough to escape from the plant into the environment.

The findings about the disposition of iodine-131 at TMI-2 were welcome, but their broader applicability was debatable. Some authorities
claimed that they demonstrated that existing regulations greatly overestimated the release of iodine and other fission products. This argument
was undermined by a series of experiments conducted at the Idaho National Engineering Laboratory and elsewhere in the mid-1980s that suggested iodine-131 releases in another severe accident might be greater
than those at Three Mile Island. The information that the accident provided on both pressure vessel integrity and iodine-131 leakage was encouraging but ambiguous. On the one hand, it indicated that the worst-
case predictions about the effects of an accident, which formed the basis
of reactor safety programs and regulations, might be overly conservative. On the other hand, it did not prove this conclusively. Despite those
uncertainties, the outcome of the accident definitely disproved the assertions of some nuclear critics that the inevitable result of a core meltdown would be a breach of containment and a major release of hazardous
forms of radiation to the environment.[36]

THE RESTART OF TMI-1

As the early phases of the TMI-2 cleanup proceeded, the reopening of
TMI-1 proved to be equally problematic. The operation of the undamaged TMI-1 plant was vital to the financial stability of GPU and its subsidiaries, which had been severely impaired by the loss of TMI-2's production and the growing costs of the cleanup. Within weeks after the
accident, utility executives appealed to the NRC for prompt consideration of the restart of unit 1 once required equipment, training, and operational changes were made. But it soon became obvious that return-
ing TMI-1 to service would take much longer than the company hoped.
The delay arose in part from strong opposition in Pennsylvania to reopening the plant and from complex regulatory and legal issues. One
key question that commanded attention was whether the NRC should
consider the psychological effects on the citizens of central Pennsylvania. When an antinuclear group, People Against Nuclear Energy, took
the NRC to federal court to force it to weigh the psychological stress
that allowing TMI-1 to operate would impose on the population of the
area, it won a surprising victory. The NRC argued that it had no statutory basis for evaluating the psychological consequences of its technical
decisions, and that such considerations should be left to mental health
experts. The U.S. Court of Appeals for the District of Columbia disagreed.

In January 1982, it ordered the agency to "prepare an environmental assessment regarding the effects of the proposed restart . . . on the psychological health of neighboring residents and on the well-being of the surrounding communities." The ruling was overturned by the U.S. Supreme Court on April 19, 1983, but it contributed significantly to retarding an NRC decision on TMI-1.[37]

The restart of unit 1 was also delayed by the utility's own blunders, which raised questions and stirred controversy within the NRC over management issues. In August 1981, the NRC's Office of Inspection and Enforcement reported that two TMI-1 shift supervisors had cheated on senior reactor operator examinations earlier in the year. Later investigations by Met Ed uncovered further evidence of cheating on other examinations dating back as far as August 1979. The NRC praised the company for its cooperation in addressing the problem but fined it for a "lack of established procedures to assure that exams and quizzes were administered properly." In 1983, Met Ed was indicted for providing false information about tests on coolant leaks from the pressurizer of the TMI-2 plant before the accident. It pleaded guilty to one count and no contest to six other counts of criminal misconduct for willfully misrepresenting the results of the tests. In addition, an emergency drill that was conducted in November 1983 revealed "major deficiencies" that cast doubts on the ability of GPU Nuclear (which had replaced Met Ed) to operate TMI-1 in accordance with regulatory requirements.[38]

Those and other developments that reflected poorly on the management of the Three Mile Island plants fueled the acrimony of the debate over reopening TMI-1. Indeed, GPU's managerial competence was the central issue in the deliberations over restart. Opponents charged that GPU had failed to take responsibility for its errors or make meaningful changes in its management approach or attitudes. The utility, said one petition to the NRC, "lacks the requisite character to safely operate a nuclear reactor." Governor Thornburgh appealed to the NRC in 1984 to postpone a decision until funding of the TMI-2 cleanup was secure and misgivings about the management of the utility were fully investigated. "There should be no choice at all between resolving safety questions before cranking up a nuclear reactor," he commented, "or simply putting off those questions and crossing our fingers." The NRC commissioners disagreed sharply among themselves about the integrity of GPU management and instructed the agency staff to review the issue. The staff reported in August 1984 that GPU had replaced the executives who were primarily responsible for the company's management failures and had improved its performance in key areas. Therefore, it found "no significant adverse implications for key TMI-1 management or personnel." William G. Kuhns, chairman of the board and chief executive officer of GPU, supported the staff's position in a statement to the commission. "We have made mistakes. We have been humbled. We have been humiliated," he declared. "But we do respectfully suggest . . . that we have learned from these mistakes and have brought into being a strong nuclear organization that has benefited from that learning."[39]

More than six years after the TMI-2 accident, the commission officially endorsed Kuhns's argument. On May 29, 1985, despite appeals from Thornburgh for further delay and objections from interveners, it authorized the restart of TMI-1 by a vote of four to one. The majority contended that GPU had demonstrated "the necessary competence and integrity to provide reasonable assurance of safe operation of TMI-1" and had presented convincing evidence that the "past failings at TMI will not be repeated." The dissenting commissioner, James K. Asselstine, took strong exception. He announced that he was dubious that GPU Nuclear had the "requisite corporate integrity and competence" to operate TMI-1 safely. Federal court injunctions postponed the operation of the plant, but on October 2, 1985, the Supreme Court declined to extend stays imposed by a lower court. One week later, TMI-1 returned to service. Thornburgh urged the people of central Pennsylvania to accept the court's decision, and a protest against the restart attracted only about fifty demonstrators.[40]

STUDIES OF HEALTH EFFECTS

While cleanup procedures at the TMI-2 plant were performed and the battle over restarting TMI-1 was waged, public health professionals conducted epidemiological studies to assess health effects of the accident on the local population. A series of investigations strongly supported the early projections of federal and state officials, the Kemeny Commission, the Rogovin Report, and the Governor's Commission on Three Mile Island (chaired by Lieutenant Governor Scranton) that the accident would have little, if any, adverse impact on the health of area residents. The first study, conducted by the Pennsylvania Department of Health and the federal Centers for Disease Control, found in April 1980 that, contrary to some reports, neither fetal nor infant mortality had risen in the six months following the accident within a ten-mile radius of Three Mile Island.

Four years later, in response to allegations that radiation from Three

Mile Island had sharply increased cancer mortality, the state health department undertook a preliminary evaluation of cancer deaths within a twenty-mile radius of the plant between 1974 and 1983. The survey, published in 1985, showed that cancer deaths were no higher than normal after the accident (indeed, the total number was slightly lower than expected). The department cautioned that its findings were not a final assessment because of the latent period of most cancers. It later conducted another study of cancer rates between 1982 and 1989 among people who lived within five miles of the plant and again detected no increase in cancer.[41]

The Department of Health's conclusions were corroborated in a 1990 study sponsored by the Three Mile Island Public Health Fund, created by a federal court order in 1981 to supply financial support for analyses of radiation effects in the area. Maureen C. Hatch, Jeri W. Nieves, and Mervyn Susser, all of whom were epidemiologists at Columbia University, and Jan Beyea, senior energy scientist at the National Audubon Society and a prominent critic of nuclear power, carried out the investigation. Six years earlier, Beyea had headed a study, also sponsored by the TMI Public Health Fund, that described weaknesses in the data on radiation releases during the accident and uncertainties about the estimates of the doses received by the population of the area. The new investigation in which he participated suggested that emissions from the accident had been too low to increase the incidence of cancer within a ten-mile radius of the plant. Based on an examination of hospital records, Hatch (the lead investigator) and her collaborators determined that cancer rates between 1975 and 1985 did "not provide convincing evidence that radiation releases from the Three Mile Island nuclear facility influenced cancer risk." They found that a "small wave" of excess cancers had occurred among some residents in 1982, but they observed no correlation between the incidence of cancer and radiation exposure. The researchers submitted that the slightly higher cancer rates might be attributable to stress caused by the accident. They acknowledged that insufficient time had elapsed to make definitive judgments, but they discerned no signs of an elevated incidence of cancer from radiation in the records of nineteen hospitals in the Three Mile Island vicinity.[42]

The findings of the Hatch investigation were contested by a team of researchers from the University of North Carolina: Steve Wing, David Richardson, Donna Armstrong, and Douglas Crawford-Brown. They published an article in 1997 that not only directly challenged the Hatch study but also questioned the consensus among experts that the health effects of radiation from Three Mile Island ranged from imperceptible to nonexistent. Wing and his associates contended that Hatch's investigation was flawed by limitations imposed by the TMI Public Health Fund and by a preconceived bias against showing a correlation between plant releases and cancer rates. Using the same data as Hatch and colleagues, the North Carolina researchers concluded that radiation from the accident had increased the incidence of leukemia and lung cancer. They also suggested that their findings indicated that radiation releases during the accident were greater than previously reported. The arguments of Wing and his collaborators elicited a strong rebuttal from Hatch, Susser, and Beyea. They denied that their study had been impaired by the funding agency or by their own preconceptions. Calling the Wing article "tendentious and unbalanced," they reaffirmed their judgment that radiation releases during the accident "were in fact within the range of official dose estimates."[43]

A study published in 2000 offered strong, though not definitive, support for the position of Hatch and her coauthors. Evelyn O. Talbott and a team of colleagues from the Graduate School of Public Health at the University of Pittsburgh found no increase in "radiosensitive" cancer attributable to radiation from the Three Mile Island accident among a cohort of 32,135 people who lived within a five-mile radius of the plant between 1979 and 1992. They used data originally collected by the Pennsylvania Department of Health in 1979 that included information about individuals' medical histories, previous radiation exposures, and whereabouts during the ten days after the accident. "The mortality surveillance of this cohort to date," Talbott and her coauthors wrote, "does not provide consistent evidence that low-dose radiation releases during the TMI accident had any measurable impact on the mortality experience."

Two years later, Talbott and her associates published an updated report that surveyed the same cohort of people through 1998. It provided substantial confirmation of the conclusions of the earlier study, especially since it covered a period long enough for slow-developing forms of cancer to show up. Talbott summarized the new findings by commenting, "When you compare observed with expected cancer, there is virtually no difference." The study found a slight increase in cancers among those who might have been exposed to higher (but still "very tiny") levels of radiation from the accident, but it was unclear if this was a statistical "blip" or a positive correlation. "You would expect, really by chance, when you do 20 or more analyses [of cancer incidence], you're going to have a couple that by random chance come up," Talbott explained. In any event, she added, "you still need to report it when you see it."[44]

THE CHERNOBYL DISASTER

For several years, Three Mile Island held the dubious distinction of being the site of the world's worst nuclear power plant accident. In April 1986 it surrendered that status after a monumental accident at the Chernobyl nuclear power station in the Soviet Union that released vast quantities of radiation into the atmosphere. Three Mile Island and Chernobyl became widely linked as nuclear disasters that graphically illustrated the dangers of nuclear technology.

During a test on the safety system at unit 4 of the Chernobyl nuclear complex, the operating crew took a series of actions that led to the destruction of the reactor. As part of their experiment, technicians turned off the emergency core cooling system and withdrew nearly all the control rods. As a result, they lost control of the reactor. This caused powerful explosions that blew off the roof of the reactor building and quickly released a huge inventory of radioactive elements to the atmosphere. The explosions also ignited graphite blocks in the core and set off raging fires inside the reactor building, which spewed even more radiation to the outside. Over a few days, an estimated 100 million to 200 million curies of radioactivity escaped from the ruins of the plant.

There were some similarities in the accidents at Three Mile Island and Chernobyl. Both accidents were due largely to operator errors that exacerbated design flaws or mechanical malfunctions. In both cases, technicians overrode safety systems that could have prevented or mitigated the damage. But there were also major differences between Three Mile Island and Chernobyl. The design of commercial power reactors in the United States incorporated physical principles that precluded the loss of control that led to the runaway reaction at Chernobyl. Further, the Soviet reactor had no containment building that could withstand the forces of a severe accident and prevent or at least slow the escape of fission products to the environment.

In addition to critical distinctions in design, the scale and consequences of the Chernobyl accident contrasted sharply with those at Three Mile Island. Although precise measurements were unattainable, Chernobyl released enormous quantities of both noble gases and more volatile and more hazardous radioactive elements, including iodine-131, strontium-

90, cesium-137, and plutonium. About 20 percent of the inventory of io-dine-131 in the plant, an estimated 7 million curies, escaped to the at-mosphere (compared to less than 20 curies during the Three Mile Island accident). Detectable levels of radiation from the Chernobyl disaster spread far beyond the immediate area of the plant to more distant parts of the Soviet Union, to many other parts of Europe, and even to the United States and Japan. In Sweden, Poland, Germany, Austria, and Hungary, government officials were worried enough about radiation levels to or-der the destruction of some milk, meat, and crops. An estimated 50,000 people who lived near the Chernobyl plant received radiation exposures of 50 rads or more. About 130,000 residents were permanently resettled because of contamination of their homes, fields, forests, and water sup-plies. Thirty-one plant employees and emergency workers died within a short time from radiation poisoning; another 238 suffered from acute radiation syndrome.[45]

The long-term consequences of Chernobyl for the health of those who received lower exposures were less clear, though they were unquestion-ably much more harmful than the effects of Three Mile Island. In the im-mediate aftermath of the accident, scientists offered widely divergent es-timates of how many cancer deaths from Chernobyl would occur over a few decades, ranging from a few thousand to more than 100,000. Epi-demiological data collected over an extended period after the accident did not provide clear testimony on its likely long-term health effects. By 1992, there was unmistakable evidence that cases of thyroid cancer sharply increased among children in areas that had received the heavi-est doses. In the Gomel region of Belarus, located just north of Cher-nobyl, where the norm had been 1 or 2 cases of thyroid cancer among children per year, 38 cases were diagnosed in 1991 alone. About 1,800 cases of childhood thyroid cancer were detected in Belarus, Ukraine, and Russia between 1990 and 1999. The rate of childhood thyroid cancer declined after 1995, but incidence of the disease among adolescents more than doubled between 1996 and 2001.[46]

Although the trends in thyroid cancer were distressing, other evidence of radiation effects from Chernobyl was more favorable. The World Health Organization found no increase in leukemia by 1993 among the populations hit hardest by fallout from the accident. This was surpris-ing, because a growth in the incidence of leukemia was the earliest sign of long-term radiation effects among the survivors of the atomic bombs dropped on the Japanese cities of Hiroshima and Nagasaki in 1945. Based on that experience, experts had expected that excess cases would appear

among victims of Chernobyl between 1991 and 1993. But the anticipated rise in the incidence of leukemia did not materialize. In 2000, the
United Nations Scientific Committee on the Effects of Atomic Radiation, while acknowledging the preliminary status of its conclusions, reported after studying available data that, "apart from the significant increase in thyroid cancer after childhood exposure, there is no evidence
of other radiation-related health effects," including leukemia, other
forms of cancer, or "non-malignant disorders." Within a short time after the publication of those findings, however, new studies produced more
disquieting results. They suggested that children of parents exposed to
radiation from Chernobyl, especially those who cleaned up the reactor
after the accident, showed an excess of genetic mutations.[47]

Despite the ambiguities in the data from the Chernobyl accident, it
clearly caused more death, illness, dislocation, and property damage than
Three Mile Island. Nevertheless, the dramatic differences in their consequences did not prevent wide identification of Chernobyl and Three Mile
Island as twin emblems of nuclear calamity. The *Baltimore Sun* remarked
on this association, for example, when it commented in 1989, "For many,
the two accidents have come to symbolize the impossibility of safely using nuclear power." Public opinion polls taken after Chernobyl indicated
another steep decline in support for nuclear power in the United States.
An *ABC News–Washington Post* survey in May 1986, for example, found
that 78 percent of respondents opposed the construction of more nuclear
plants in the United States. A *CBS News* poll showed that 55 percent of
those questioned believed that an accident as severe as Chernobyl was
likely in the United States. Still, the prevailing public attitude toward nuclear power even after Chernobyl was ambivalence. The *ABC News–
Washington Post* poll found that a majority of respondents opposed shutting down operating plants by 54 percent to 41 percent. The TMI and
Chernobyl accidents provided a new level of urgency to the nuclear power
controversy and focused unprecedented public attention on it, but they
did not settle the issues that had animated the debate since the early
1970s.[48]

THREE MILE ISLAND IN HISTORICAL PERSPECTIVE

Before the Three Mile Island accident, as the controversy over nuclear
power became increasingly bitter and divisive, nuclear critics warned that
a technological system as complex as a nuclear plant could never be made
foolproof. They claimed that a major accident that seriously threatened

public health and safety was possible and perhaps inevitable. Nuclear proponents countered those claims by insisting that nuclear plants had so many redundant safety features that an accident that released large amounts of radiation to the environment was highly unlikely and probably impossible.

Despite the apparent incompatibility of those positions, Three Mile Island offered substantial support for both. The events at TMI-2 on the morning of March 28, 1979, demonstrated vividly that operating deficiencies could defeat the efforts of designers, owners, and regulators to prevent a serious nuclear accident. Although the safety systems in the plant worked as designed, they could not save it from the combined forces of management weaknesses, limited operator training, inattention to human factors, confusing instrumentation, and other problems. The result was a meltdown that converted the core of the reactor into a pile of radioactive rubble.

Yet even though the core of the TMI-2 plant was destroyed, the accident did not release large amounts of hazardous radiation into the surrounding countryside. It did not cause a failure of the reactor's pressure vessel or approach a breach of containment. The concept of defense-in-depth, the basic philosophy that guided the regulatory decisions of the AEC and the NRC, was tested as never before. In the face of a massive core meltdown, it worked. Although the serial equipment malfunctions and operator errors that occurred at Three Mile Island had never been anticipated, they did not trigger the China syndrome. The consequences of the accident could conceivably have been worse if more of the core had melted and the pressure vessel had failed, but reactor experts concluded that, even in that event, there was "little chance" that containment would have been breached in a way that allowed an uncontrolled release of radiation.[49] The applicability of the Three Mile Island accident to other plants under different conditions was uncertain. But the results suggested that nuclear proponents had underestimated the risks of a major accident at a nuclear plant in the United States, and that nuclear critics had overstated the likely consequences.

The Three Mile Island accident, despite its favorable outcome in terms of releasing only small quantities of the most dangerous forms of radiation to the environment, was a harrowing experience. During five days of crisis, experts struggled to figure out what was happening inside the reactor building while federal and state government officials deliberated over whether the population of the area should be evacuated. Those officials were forced to weigh the risks of conducting a general evacuation against the chances of a massive release of radiation from the plant. The dilemma was made excruciating by the lack of reliable data about the condition of the plant and by the absence of experience in carrying out a full-scale evacuation under the threat of serious public exposure to radiation. Operating in extraordinarily trying circumstances, NRC officials and authorities in other agencies made mistakes. But they kept their goals and priorities in proper order. They made decisions in light of the sometimes confusing and usually insufficient information available to them, with the protection of public health and safety foremost in their minds. From the time the accident occurred, responsible officials in the state government, the NRC, the White House, and other agencies treated the welfare of the people of central Pennsylvania as their highest concern.

In retrospect, the irony of the agonizing deliberations over how to respond to the accident is that nobody knew that the core of the plant had melted. NRC experts and other reactor authorities made reasonable judgments about the condition of the reactor but failed to diagnose the extent of the damage it suffered. Had they recognized the true status of the plant, they would have recommended, and Thornburgh would have ordered, a full-scale evacuation. This would have been an easy and obvious, though unwelcome, decision. However, the process of evacuating the population, perhaps out to a twenty-mile radius, would have been difficult and costly. The nuclear industry, the NRC, and the state were ill prepared for an evacuation on such a massive scale, the inherent hardships of which were likely to be compounded by intense public fears of radiation.

Several years after the accident, NRC commissioner Gilinsky commented, "What shook the public the most was seeing the men in white coats standing around and scratching their heads because they didn't know what to do. The result was that accidents were taken seriously in a way they never had been before."[50] Three Mile Island exposed a multitude of weaknesses that had to be addressed, as several comprehensive postaccident reports made clear. The blame for the oversights, lapses, and failures that led to the crisis fell on both the U.S. nuclear industry and the NRC. The accident drove them out of a prevailing and dangerously complacent consensus that they had resolved the most critical reactor safety issues. Although they had never claimed that a major accident that released dangerous quantities of radiation was impossible, they regarded it as virtually inconceivable. Three Mile Island made the possibility disturbingly credible. As a result, both the industry and the NRC adopted wide-ranging reforms intended to focus ample attention on human factors in reactor safety, improve equipment and instrumentation, strengthen communications, upgrade emergency planning, and monitor the effectiveness of plant management. In that way they sought to avoid another Three Mile Island. Engineers often learn more from technological failure than they do from success, and the accident provided a succession of failures from which to draw lessons.[51]

The extensive reforms that the nuclear industry and the NRC introduced within a short time after Three Mile Island did not resolve all nuclear safety issues. Charles Perrow, a Yale University sociologist who had served as a consultant to the Kemeny Commission, asserted in a widely noticed book published in 1984 that, "unless we are very lucky," one or more severe nuclear accidents "will appear in the next decade and breach containment."[52] Perrow's prediction did not come true, and the safety improvements that followed the Three Mile Island crisis, along with a fundamentally conservative regulatory and design approach, deserved more credit than he allowed. Nevertheless, the accident graphically revealed that serious consequences could arise from unanticipated developments in a nuclear power plant and fueled the already intense controversy over nuclear power.

Opponents of nuclear technology cited the experience of Three Mile Island in objecting to the start-up of some plants in the years following the accident. Pointing to the confusion and uncertainty about evacuating the vicinity of the plant, antinuclear forces raised the issue of emergency planning to a new level of concern and sustained debate. Other long-standing issues, including operational safety, radiation standards, risk assessment, waste disposal, and licensing procedures, continued to stir animated and sometimes bitter disputes between nuclear critics and nuclear proponents. The controversy lost some of its immediacy as a national issue in the 1990s as the last plants ordered during the pre-TMI era received operating licenses. But it flared again when the terrorist attacks on the World Trade Center towers and the Pentagon building on September 11, 2001, spawned greatly enhanced apprehensions about nuclear plant security. Nuclear power facilities were not specifically designed to guard against airplanes flown by terrorists into containment structures or spent-fuel storage buildings. In such cases, as in many other aspects of nuclear safety, no definitive answers were available for the questions that arose. Government authorities, nuclear industry experts, nuclear critics, and the general public had to make judgments about nuclear power based on extensive but incomplete evidence, informed but contestable projections, and increasing but still limited operating experience. Evaluating the risks and the advantages of the technology remained an uncertain and inherently controversial process.

With the exception of the fears of a terrorist attack by means of a hijacked commercial airliner, the nuclear power debate of the 1970s had framed the basic issues that caused so much continuing conflict. Three Mile Island transformed mostly theoretical projections about a severe nuclear power accident into a starkly and alarmingly real emergency. It heavily influenced public attitudes toward nuclear power. As the single most familiar and memorable event in the history of commercial nuclear power in the United States, it played a major, and in many ways, decisive role in spurring controversy, increasing uncertainty, and elevating public fears of the technology. The apprehension and distrust that citizens expressed so vividly in the Harrisburg area after the emergency reflected in an acute form the widespread misgivings about nuclear technology throughout the United States. After the accident, a significant percentage of Americans moved from ambivalence to opposition in their views on building more nuclear plants.

The public anxieties that the TMI-2 accident created or heightened often obscured the fact that it fell far short of a catastrophe. It did not reach or even come close to producing the disastrous consequences that antinuclear activists had predicted in their campaigns against nuclear power during the 1970s, and that reactor experts had envisioned in their worst-case projections. Three Mile Island did not cause any immediate loss of life. According to a consensus of authorities, the effect on public health in the area was at worst slight and more probably negligible. At least for the periods covered in extensive epidemiological studies, the accident did not increase rates of cancer or other diseases among the neighboring population. Except for the plant itself, it did not destroy or damage property in the region.

Nevertheless, the memories of the tension, uncertainty, and confusion so prominent during the Three Mile Island emergency made a much stronger impression on popular perceptions than the generally favorable outcome or subsequent efforts to improve reactor safety. For that reason, the accident was widely recalled as a major catastrophe. Two books published in 2002 about Three Mile Island for children aged nine to twelve, for example, were each a part of a series on disasters that included volumes on the sinking of the *Titanic* in 1912, the explosion of the *Challenger* space shuttle in 1986, the oil spill in Alaska from the Exxon tanker *Valdez* in 1989, the bombing of the Alfred P. Murrah federal building in

Oklahoma City in 1995, and the terrorist attack on the World Trade Center in New York.[53] Three Mile Island clearly demonstrated and considerably strengthened the potent and probably unique capacity of nuclear power among modern civilian technologies to inspire public fear.[54] The dual legacy of the crisis was, on the one hand, to galvanize regulatory and operational improvements that reduced the risks of another severe accident and, on the other hand, to increase opposition to the expansion of nuclear power. In those regards, Three Mile Island remained a "big deal," as the Rogovin Report described it in 1980, for decades after the accident that riveted the attention of the world on a scenic, peaceful, and previously obscure corner of the Susquehanna River valley.

Notes

CHAPTER 1. THE NUCLEAR POWER DEBATE

1. *The China Syndrome,* written by Mike Gray, T. S. Cook, and James Bridges, Columbia Pictures, 1979.

2. *New York Times,* March 16, April 4, 1979; *Baltimore Sun,* March 26, 1979; *Washington Post,* March 29, 1979; David Ansen, "Nuclear Politics," *Newsweek* (March 19, 1979): 103; Stanley Kauffmann, "What Price Thrills?" *New Republic* (April 7, 1979): 24–25; Mike Gray and Ira Rosen, *The Warning: Accident at Three Mile Island* (New York: W. W. Norton, 1982), p. 142.

3. *New York Times,* March 11, 1979; Kenneth Turan, "Anchored to Reality," *The Progressive* 43 (May 1979): 52–53; Mike Gray to Henry Kendall, February 16, 1979, Box 60 (no folder), Papers of the Union of Concerned Scientists, Massachusetts Institute of Technology Archives, Cambridge, Massachusetts.

4. *New York Times,* March 18, 1979; *Boston Globe,* March 29, 1979; *Washington Post,* March 30, 1979.

5. Nuclear Regulatory Commission Special Inquiry Group, *Three Mile Island: A Report to the Commissioners and to the Public* (Washington, D.C.: Government Printing Office, 1980), 1:1.

6. George T. Mazuzan and J. Samuel Walker, *Controlling the Atom: The Beginnings of Nuclear Regulation, 1946–1962* (Berkeley: University of California Press, 1984), pp. 22–23, 77–82, 92–96, 203–8.

7. Hazel Gaudet Erskine, "The Polls: Atomic Weapons and Nuclear Energy," *Public Opinion Quarterly* 27 (summer 1963): 164; "Big Hurdle for A-Power: Gaining Public Acceptance," *Nucleonics* 21 (October 1963): 17–24; Stanley M. Nealey, Barbara D. Melber, and William L. Rankin, *Public Opinion and Nuclear Energy* (Lexington, Mass.: D. C. Heath and Company, 1983), p. 4; Mazuzan and Walker, *Controlling the Atom,* p. 418.

8. U.S. Congress, Joint Committee on Atomic Energy, *Nuclear Power Economics: 1962 through 1967,* 90th Cong., 2d sess., 1968, p. 15; J. Samuel Walker,

Containing the Atom: Nuclear Regulation in a Changing Environment, 1963–1971 (Berkeley: University of California Press, 1992), pp. 392–98.

9. "When the Music Stops," *Forbes* (February 1, 1969): 3; Walker, *Containing the Atom*, pp. 30–31.

10. *Nucleonics Week*, February 25, 1965; Jeremy Main, "A Peak Load of Trouble for the Utilities," *Fortune* 80 (November 1969): 116–19, 205; Walker, *Containing the Atom*, pp. 32–36, 267–70.

11. "Fossil Competition Fades in U.S.," *Nuclear Industry* 19 (January 1972): 6–9; "'72 Sets Sales Record," pt. 2, *Nuclear Industry* 19 (November–December 1972): 7–10; "AEC Capacity Forecast to 2000," *Nuclear Industry* 20 (March 1973): 20–21; *Nucleonics Week*, December 14, 1972, January 10, 1974.

12. White House Press Release, "Statement by the President," June 29, 1973, Staff Member Office Files, Energy Policy Office, Richard M. Nixon Papers, Nixon Presidential Materials Project, National Archives, College Park, Maryland; Glenn Schleede to Jim Cannon, November 18, 1975, Domestic Council— Glenn R. Schleede Files, Box 25 (Nuclear Energy 1975, General), Gerald R. Ford Papers, Gerald R. Ford Library, Ann Arbor, Michigan; "The Energy Emergency," November 7, 1973, *Presidential Documents: Richard Nixon, 1973,* Vol. 9, No. 45, pp. 1312–18; *President's Report on the State of the Union,* 94th Cong., 1st sess., 1975, H. Doc. 94–1, pp. 5–6; David E. Nye, *Consuming Power: A Social History of American Energies* (Cambridge: MIT Press, 1998), pp. 217–19.

13. Dick Livingston to Jim Cannon, November 18, 1975, Domestic Council— Glenn R. Schleede Files, Box 25 (Nuclear Energy 1975, Overview Memo), Ford Papers; "Why Atomic Power Dims Today," *Business Week* (November 17, 1975): 98–106; "Nuclear Dilemma," *Business Week* (March 25, 1978): 54–68; "Another Peak Year," *Nuclear Industry* 21 (January 1974): 3–6; "Deferrals of Nuclear Power Plant Construction Continue," *Nuclear Industry* 21 (September 1974): 17; "Industry Groping for Answers to Utility Financing Crisis," *Nuclear Industry* 21 (October 1974): 17–19; *Nucleonics Week*, September 19, 1974; Richard F. Hirsh and Adam H. Serchuk, "Momentum Shifts in the American Electric Utility System: Catastrophic Change—or No Change at All?" *Technology and Culture* 37 (April 1996): 280–311; Richard F. Hirsh, *Technology and Transformation in the American Electric Utility Industry* (Cambridge: Cambridge University Press, 1989), pp. 110–13; John Robert Greene, *The Presidency of Gerald R. Ford* (Lawrence: University Press of Kansas, 1995), pp. 67–81.

14. Ken Pedersen to Commissioner Ahearne, January 31, 1979, Subject File, Box 630 (Energy—Nuclear, 1977–78), Victor Gilinsky Papers, Hoover Institution on War, Revolution, and Peace Archives, Stanford University, Palo Alto, California; "A Call to Arms," *Nuclear Industry* 22 (August 1975): 7–10; "Record Turnout, Marked Concern," *Nuclear Industry* 25 (January 1978): 3–4; *Nucleonics Week*, January 16, 1975, July 10, 1975, November 24, 1977; Peter Stoler, "The Irrational Fight against Nuclear Power," *Time* (September 25, 1978): 71–72; "Nuclear Dilemma," *Business Week*, p. 54.

15. "Is Nuclear's Defense Worth the Effort?" *Nuclear Industry* 25 (January 1978): 26–27; J. Samuel Walker, *Permissible Dose: A History of Radiation Protection in the Twentieth Century* (Berkeley: University of California Press, 2000), pp. 18–22.

16. *Nucleonics Week,* June 20, 1963; Walker, *Containing the Atom,* pp. 387–93.

17. The issues of thermal pollution, radiation emissions, and reactor safety in the late 1960s and early 1970s are discussed in detail in Walker, *Containing the Atom,* pp. 139–202, 267–362, 388–407.

18. "Don't Confuse Us with Facts," *Forbes* (September 1, 1975): 20.

19. Roger Smith, "The Nuclear Critic: What Lies Ahead?" attachment to *Nucleonics Week,* April 25, 1974; Frank Graham Jr., "The Outrageous Mr. Cherry and the Underachieving Nukes," *Audubon* 79 (September 1977): 50–66; President's Commission on the Accident at Three Mile Island, *Report of the Public's Right to Information Task Force* (Washington, D.C.: Government Printing Office, 1979), p. 1. For excellent studies of the antinuclear movement, see Brian Balogh, *Chain Reaction: Expert Debate and Public Participation in American Commercial Nuclear Power, 1945–1975* (Cambridge: Cambridge University Press, 1991); and Thomas Raymond Wellock, *Critical Masses: Opposition to Nuclear Power in California, 1958–1978* (Madison: University of Wisconsin Press, 1998).

20. Victor Gilinsky, Memorandum to the Files, December 16, 1976, Personal NRC File, Box 13 (F.13.9), Gilinsky Papers; Graham, "The Outrageous Mr. Cherry," pp. 56–57.

21. "David Comey Combines Dedication with a Thirst for Knowledge," *Nuclear Industry* 20 (April 1973): 27–28; McKinley C. Olson, "Nuclear Energy: It Costs Too Much," *Nation* 219 (October 12, 1974): 331–33; Dorothy Nelkin, *Nuclear Power and Its Critics: The Cayuga Lake Controversy* (Ithaca: Cornell University Press, 1971), pp. 58–64; Walker, *Containing the Atom,* pp. 378–86.

22. *San Francisco Sunday Examiner and Chronicle,* March 24, 1974; "Squeaky Wheel," *New Yorker* 48 (December 16, 1972): 27–28; John H. Adams, "Responsible Militancy: The Anatomy of a Public Interest Law Firm," *Record of the Association of the Bar of the City of New York* 29 (1974): 631–46; *Five-Year Report, 1970–1975* (New York: Natural Resources Defense Council, 1976), pp. 5, 15; Wellock, *Critical Masses,* pp. 101–13.

23. Robert Gillette, "Nuclear Power: Hard Times and a Questioning Congress," *Science* 187 (March 21, 1975): 1058–62; Dorothy Nelkin, *The University and Military Research: Moral Politics at M.I.T.* (Ithaca: Cornell University Press, 1972), pp. 56–65; Smith, "The Nuclear Critic," p. 2.

24. Daniel F. Ford and Henry W. Kendall to Richard Sandler, November 4, 1972, Box 37 (Nader/Lippmann Correspondence), "Transcript of Ralph Nader's Remarks on Nuclear Reactor Safety on the ABC-TV 'Dick Cavett Show,'" December 13, 1972, Box 37 (Nader Transcript, Cavett Show), Union of Concerned Scientists Papers; "Nader's Conglomerate," *Time* (June 11, 1973): 82; *Nucleonics Week,* December 21, 1972.

25. Pat Fogarty to Hal Stroube, January 15, 1973, Box 32 (Atomic Industrial Forum), Union of Concerned Scientists Papers; John A. Harris to the Commissioners, January 3, 1973, Records of the Atomic Energy Commission, History Division, Department of Energy, Germantown, Maryland; "Effort to Put ACRS on the Spot Highlights New AEC Opposition," *Nuclear Industry* 20 (January 1973): 15–17; *Nucleonics Week,* November 21, 1974.

26. "Some Scientists Question Nuclear Power Safety," *National Wildlife* 10 (August–September 1972): 19; "Fuel Cycle Rulemaking," *Nuclear Industry* 20 (February 1973): 15–20; "Effort to Put ACRS on the Spot," ibid., p. 16; "Nuclear Licensing Detente?" *Nuclear News* 17 (September 1974): 42–44; *Nucleonics Week,* October 3, November 21, 1974; *Christian Science Monitor,* May 24, 1977; *New York Times,* October 5, 1977; Frank von Hippel to Morris K. Udall, February 6, 1975, Box 338 (Interior, E&E Subcommittee—Nuclear Correspondence), Morris K. Udall Papers, University of Arizona, Tucson; Frank von Hippel, "A Perspective on the Debate," *Bulletin of the Atomic Scientists* 31 (September 1975): 37–39.

27. *Wall Street Journal,* January 26, 1972; "Just How Safe Is a Nuclear Power Plant?" *Reader's Digest* 100 (June 1972): 95–100; *Nucleonics Week,* April 24, 1975; "Nuclear Energy Alert," *Nation* 222 (March 13, 1976): 302; David Dinsmore Comey, "The Perfect Trojan Horse," *Bulletin of the Atomic Scientists* 32 (June 1976): 33–34; Susan Schiefelbein, "Is Nuclear Power a License to Kill?" *Saturday Review* (June 24, 1977): 10; Donna Warnock, *Nuclear Power and Civil Liberties: Can We Have Both?* (Washington, D.C.: Citizens' Energy Project, 1978), p. 2; John G. Fuller, *We Almost Lost Detroit* (New York: Reader's Digest Press, 1975), pp. 18, 64; J. Samuel Walker, "Regulating against Nuclear Terrorism: The Domestic Safeguards Issue, 1970–1979," *Technology and Culture* 42 (January 2001): 107–32.

28. John Abbotts to Gene L. Woodruff, July 26, 1974, Henry W. Kendall to Woodruff, July 25, 1974, Box 8 (Nuclear Energy Controversy, 1974–1980), Fred M. Schmidt Papers, University of Washington, Seattle; U.S. Congress, Joint Committee on Atomic Energy, *Hearings on Nuclear Reactor Safety,* 93rd Cong., 2d sess., 1974, p. 514; Amory B. Lovins, "Energy Strategy: The Road Not Taken?" *Foreign Affairs* 55 (October 1976): 65–96; Allen L. Hammond, "'Soft Technology' Energy Debate: *Limits to Growth* Revisited?" *Science* 196 (May 27, 1977): 959–61; *New York Times,* July 24, October 16, 1977.

29. Transcript of *CBS News Special,* "Nuclear Power: What Price Salvation?" March 31, 1974, Box 32 (CBS), Union of Concerned Scientists Papers; *Washington Star-News,* April 2, 1974; *New York Times,* March 9, 1975; "Kouts Says Data Inadequate for Thorough Reliability Analysis, Raps Nader on Leaks," *Nuclear Industry* 21 (May 1974): 35; "Proposed NRC Steps to Stimulate Higher Plant Reliability," *Nuclear Industry* 22 (March 1975): 32–33; Deborah Shapley, "Nuclear Power Plants: Why Do Some Work Better Than Others?" *Science* 195 (March 25, 1977): 1311–13; Gladwin Hill, "Power Play," *National Wildlife* 14 (October–November 1976): 39; SECY-75-33 (February 7, 1975), SECY-75-377 (July 21, 1975), SECY-75-178 (April 21, 1975), Nuclear Regulatory Commission (NRC) Records, NRC Public Document Room, Rockville, Maryland. "SECY" papers were papers prepared by the staff of the AEC, and later the NRC, to provide information or outline policy options for the commissioners, who used them as a basis for making decisions.

30. Alvin M. Weinberg, "Social Institutions and Nuclear Energy," *Science* 177 (July 7, 1972): 27–34; "As I See It," *Forbes* (July 15, 1972): 30; Ralph E. Lapp, "Nuclear Power Safety: 1973," *New Republic* 168 (April 28, 1973): 17–19;

"Forbes: A Call to Reason," *Nuclear News* 17 (August 1974): 42–43; H. A. Bethe, "The Necessity of Fission Power," *Scientific American* 234 (January 1976): 31; Don G. Meighan [pseud.], "How Safe Is Safe Enough?" *New York Times Magazine* (June 20, 1976): 8–9 ff; Frank von Hippel to Morris K. Udall, February 6, 1975 (note 26 above), Udall Papers; A. David Rossin, "Let's Set the Record Straight," typescript, June 17, 1976, Box 346 (Interior Committee Files: Nuclear Issues, David Rossin Correspondence), Udall Papers.

31. Weinberg, "Social Institutions and Nuclear Energy," pp. 32–33; Bethe, "The Necessity of Fission Power," pp. 27–28; Walker, *Permissible Dose,* pp. 36–66; Walker, "Regulating against Nuclear Terrorism," pp. 108–24.

32. Ralph E. Lapp, *Nader's Nuclear Issues* (Greenwich, Conn.: Fact Systems, 1975), p. 47; Petr Beckmann, *The Health Hazards of Not Going Nuclear* (Boulder, Colo.: Golem Press, 1976), pp. 152–54; Hans A. Bethe, Letter to the Editor, *Foreign Affairs* 55 (April 1977): 636–37; A. D. Rossin and T. A. Rieck, "Economics of Nuclear Power," *Science* 201 (August 18, 1978): 582–89; Dennis J. Chase, "Clouding the Nuclear Reactor Debate," *Bulletin of the Atomic Scientists* 31 (February 1975): 39–40.

33. "Pulling the Plug on A-Power," *Newsweek* (February 24, 1975): 23–24; "How Safe Is Nuclear Power?" *Newsweek* (April 12, 1976): 70; "Hans Bethe Recounts Some Frustrations as a Nuclear Spokesman," *Nuclear Industry* 22 (November 1975): 20–21; "Meeting the Media: Industry Tells Its Side," *Nuclear News* 20 (August 1977): 34–35; "It's Time to End the Holy War over Nuclear Power," *Fortune* (March 12, 1979): 81; *Wall Street Journal,* July 21, 1977; *Washington Post,* March 12, 1978; Commentary by Howard K. Smith, ABC Evening News, September 9, 1975; Statement by Students of Archbishop Carroll High School, n.d., NRC Records.

34. Robert Gillette, "Nuclear Advocates 34, Opponents 8," *Science* 187 (January 31, 1975): 331; Robert Gillette, "Nuclear Critics Escalate the War of Numbers," *Science* 189 (August 22, 1975): 621; Philip M. Boffey, "Nuclear Power Debate," *Science* 192 (April 9, 1976): 120–22; "Scientists Speak Out: 'No Alternative to Nuclear Power,'" *Bulletin of the Atomic Scientists* 31 (March 1975): 4–5; "Nuclear Hazards," *Bulletin of the Atomic Scientists* 31 (April 1975): 3.

35. "Five MIT Nuclear PhD's Wearing Environmental Tags, Blast Nader," *Nuclear Industry* 21 (June 1974): 11–12; "Nader Responds to Forbes Group's 'Call to Reason,'" *Nuclear News* 17 (November 1974): 60; *New York Times,* February 3, 1976; "The San Jose Three," *Time* (February 16, 1976): 78; "The Apostates," *Newsweek* (February 16, 1976): 64; "Forbes: A Call to Reason," pp. 42–43; "Don't Confuse Us with Facts," p. 28; Wellock, *Critical Masses,* pp. 165–66.

36. "The Siege of Seabrook," *Time* (May 16, 1977): 59; "The No-Nuke Movement," *Newsweek* (May 23, 1977): 25–26; "Antinuclear Protests Are Busting Out All Over," *Science* 200 (May 19, 1978): 746; Jon Payne, "Seabrook: A Cause Celebre," *Nuclear News* 21 (September 1978): 45; *Washington Post,* October 8, 1978; "Three Demonstrations Test Non-Violent Tactics," *Nuclear Industry* 25 (November 1978): 26; Henry F. Bedford, *Seabrook Station: Citizen Politics and Nuclear Power* (Amherst: University of Massachusetts Press, 1990), pp. 76–93.

37. "Majority Favors Nuclear—Harris Survey," *Nuclear News* 18 (September 1975): 31–34; "Second Harris Poll Finds Public Still Favors Nuclear," *Nuclear News* 20 (January 1977): 31–35; Gallup Poll Press Release, July 22, 1976, Box 34 (Gallup Poll), Union of Concerned Scientists Papers; Nealy, Melber, and Rankin, *Public Opinion and Nuclear Energy,* pp. 15–60.

38. Wellock, *Critical Masses,* pp. 147–72.

39. "Voters Reject Six Initiatives," *Nuclear Industry* 23 (November 1976): 5; "Nuclear Initiatives: Two Sides Disagree on Meaning of Defeat," *Science* 194 (November 19, 1976): 811–12; "Montana Passes a Nuclear Initiative," *Science* 202 (November 24, 1978): 850; *Christian Science Monitor,* November 5, 1976; *New York Times,* November 9, 1976; *Washington Post,* November 9, 1978; Paul Slovic, Baruch Fischhoff, and Sarah Lichtenstein, "Rating the Risks," *Environment* 21 (April 1979): 14–21, 36–39.

40. John P. Holdren, "The Nuclear Controversy and the Limitations of Decision-Making by Experts," *Bulletin of the Atomic Scientists* 32 (March 1976): 20–22; Wellock, *Critical Masses,* p. 163.

41. Robert Jay Lifton, "Nuclear Energy and the Wisdom of the Body," *Bulletin of the Atomic Scientists* 32 (September 1976): 16–20; Roger M. Williams, "Massing at the Grass Roots," *Saturday Review* 4 (January 22, 1977): 14–18; Christoph Hohenemser, Roger Kasperson, and Robert Kates, "The Distrust of Nuclear Power," *Science* 196 (April 1, 1977): 25–34; "Anti-Atom Alliance," *Newsweek* (June 5, 1978): 27; Nealy, Melber, and Rankin, *Public Opinion and Nuclear Energy,* p. 83.

42. E. F. Schumacher, *Small Is Beautiful: Economics as If People Mattered* (London: Blond and Briggs, 1973; reprint, New York: HarperCollins, 1989), p. 143; Spencer R. Weart, *Nuclear Fear: A History of Images* (Cambridge: Harvard University Press, 1988), p. 54; Walker, *Permissible Dose,* pp. 145–53.

43. Alvin M. Weinberg, "The Moral Imperatives of Nuclear Energy," *Nuclear News* 14 (December 1971): 33–37; "Clerics Soften Nuclear Posture," *Nuclear Industry* 23 (March 1976): 28; Philip M. Boffey, "Plutonium: Its Morality Questioned by National Council of Churches," *Science* 192 (April 23, 1976): 356–59; Margaret N. Maxey, "Nuclear Energy Debates: Liberation or Development?" *Christian Century* 93 (July 21–28, 1976): 656–61; Extracts from General Conference Resolution on Energy, May 6, 1976, Box 25 (Subject File: Nuclear, General), Papers of Carlton Neville, Jimmy Carter Library, Atlanta, Georgia.

44. Richard Rovere, "Letter from Washington," *New Yorker* 53 (January 2, 1978): 54–58; Carroll Pursell, "The Rise and Fall of the Appropriate Technology Movement in the United States," *Technology and Culture* 34 (July 1993): 629–37; Schumacher, *Small Is Beautiful,* p. 313; Wellock, *Critical Masses,* pp. 157–67; Weart, *Nuclear Fear,* pp. 341–43.

45. Hans A. Bethe, "The Controversy about Nuclear Power," typescript, c. January 1977, Box 4 (Bethe, Hans A., and Related Correspondence), Schmidt Papers; C. Hosmer, "The Anatomy of Nuclear Dissent," draft, March 31, 1976, Domestic Council—Glenn R. Schleede Files, Box 26 (Nuclear Energy 1976, General), Ford Papers; Lapp, *Nader's Nuclear Issues,* p. 3; "It's Time to End the Holy War over Nuclear Power," *Fortune,* p. 81.

CHAPTER 2. THE REGULATION OF NUCLEAR POWER

1. The AEC's statutory conflict of interest and its impact on regulatory programs are discussed in George T. Mazuzan and J. Samuel Walker, *Controlling the Atom: The Beginnings of Nuclear Regulation, 1946–1962* (Berkeley: University of California Press, 1984), pp. 68–76, 122–46, 196–99, 373–406, 419–23; and in J. Samuel Walker, *Containing the Atom: Nuclear Regulation in a Changing Environment, 1963–1971* (Berkeley: University of California Press, 1992), pp. 51–56, 407–14, 417–20.

2. *New York Times,* July 22, 1971; *Los Angeles Times,* July 24, 1971; *Washington Post,* October 21, 1971; AEC Press Release, October 20, 1971, Nuclear Regulatory Commission Records, NRC Public Document Room, Rockville, Maryland (hereafter cited as NRC Records, Rockville).

3. *Nucleonics Week,* January 6, June 22, October 26, 1972; "The New AEC Is Listening to the Public," *Business Week* (March 4, 1972): 102–4; Ralph E. Lapp, "Nuclear Power Safety: 1973," *New Republic* 168 (April 28, 1973): 17–19; Margaret Mead, "Our Lives May Be at Stake," *Redbook* 144 (November 1974): 52–56; F. T. Hobbs, Memorandum for the Record: Chairman's Meeting with Regulatory Staff, October 19, 1971, O&M-6 (Meetings and Correspondence), Program Files of the Office of the Secretary, Record Group 431 (Records of the Nuclear Regulatory Commission), National Archives, College Park, Maryland (hereafter cited as NRC Records, College Park).

4. Mazuzan and Walker, *Controlling the Atom,* pp. 194–96, 404–6; Walker, *Containing the Atom,* pp. 51–54; Hobbs, Memorandum for the Record, October 19, 1971, NRC Records, College Park.

5. Roy L. Ash to President Nixon, June 4, 1973, White House Special File, Staff Member Office Files, Staff Secretary, Box 99 (Energy Message IV), "President's Statement on Energy: Summary Outline and Fact Sheet," June 29, 1973, Staff Member Office Files, Energy Policy Office, Box 45 (Energy—June 29, 1973, Statement), Richard M. Nixon to Carl Albert, June 29, 1973, White House Central Files—Subject Files, FG 999, Box 16 (Energy and Natural Resources, Department of), Richard M. Nixon Papers, Nixon Presidential Materials Project, National Archives, College Park, Maryland; *Public Papers of the Presidents of the United States: Richard Nixon, 1973* (Washington: Government Printing Office, 1975), p. 626; *Nucleonics Week,* June 21, July 5, 1973.

6. "Why It's a Good Idea to Break Up the AEC," *Business Week* (June 30, 1973): 40–41; "Dixy Lee Ray Takes Over amid Uncertainty about AEC's Future," *Nuclear Industry* 20 (February 1973): 24–25; *Nucleonics Week,* May 31, 1973, January 17, 1974; *Washington Post,* April 1, 1973; U.S. Congress, House, Committee on Government Operations, *Hearings on Energy Reorganization Act of 1973,* 93rd Cong., 1st sess., 1973, pp. 65–68, 156–58; Transcript of *Panorama,* WTTG-TV, December 12, 1973, AEC Records, Department of Energy; Peter A. Bernard to Edward J. Bauser, July 10, 1973, General Correspondence, Box 198 (JCAE Outgoing Mail), Papers of the Joint Committee on Atomic Energy, Record Group 128 (Records of the Joint Committees of Congress), National Archives, Washington, D.C. (hereafter cited as JCAE Papers).

7. *Nucleonics Week,* July 5, 1973; Claude E. Barfield, "Energy Report: Com-

promise Is Expected on Reorganization Plans," *National Journal Reports* 6 (March 23, 1974): 439–44; U.S. Congress, Senate, Committee on Government Operations, Subcommittee on Reorganization, Research, and International Organizations, *Hearings to Establish an Energy Research and Development Administration and a Nuclear Energy Commission,* 93rd Cong., 1st sess., 1973, p. 229; Robert J. Duffy, *Nuclear Politics in America: A History and Theory of Government Regulation* (Lawrence: University Press of Kansas, 1997), pp. 112–16.

8. *Nucleonics Week,* June 6, August 22, September 5, September 26, October 10, 1974; "Senate's ERDA Bill," *Nuclear Industry* 21 (June 1974): 3–5; "Energy Reorganization Bill," *Nuclear Industry* 21 (October 1974): 3–5; John Reich to John O. Pastore, July 15, 1974, General Correspondence, Box 186 (Pastore, John), JCAE Papers; Duffy, *Nuclear Politics in America,* pp. 116–22.

9. *Nucleonics Week,* October 17, 1974; Jon Payne, "Hoping for the Best," *Nuclear News* 18 (February 1975): 25; Llewellyn King, "The AEC Is Dead; Long Live the AEC," *New Scientist* 64 (October 31, 1974): 328–29.

10. "Nuclear News Briefs," *Nuclear News* 16 (August 1973): 25; *Nucleonics Week,* August 9, 1973, January 9, 1975; Robert Gillette, "William Anders: A New Regulator Enters a Critical Situation," *Science* 187 (March 28, 1975): 1173–75; Glenn Schleede to Ken Cole, April 15, 1974, White House Central Files—Subject File, FG 78, Box 2 (EX FG 78 Atomic Energy Commission), Nixon Papers.

11. Samuel A. Schulhof to Ken Cole, November 16, 1974, White House Central Files—Subject File, FG 384, Box 202 (Nuclear Regulatory Commission); Brent Scowcroft to Don Rumsfeld, November 25, 1974, Staff Secretary James E. Connor Files, Personnel Decisions Files, Box 53 (Nuclear Regulatory Commission), Gerald R. Ford Papers, Gerald R. Ford Library, Ann Arbor, Michigan; "New 'Energy Team' Named," *Nuclear News* 17 (December 1974): 34–36; *Nucleonics Week,* December 19, 1974.

12. President's Commission on the Accident at Three Mile Island (hereafter referred to as the Kemeny Commission), *The Need for Change: The Legacy of TMI* (Washington, D.C.: Government Printing Office, 1979), pp. 21–22; Nuclear Regulatory Commission Special Inquiry Group, *Three Mile Island: A Report to the Commissioners and to the Public* (Washington, D.C.: Government Printing Office, 1980), 1:112–14 (hereafter referred to as the Rogovin Report); "The Nuclear Regulatory Commission: More Aggressive Leadership Needed," General Accounting Office Report EMD-80-17, January 1980, printed in U.S. Congress, Senate, Committee on Governmental Affairs, *Hearings on Reorganization Plan No. 1 of 1980,* 96th Cong., 2d sess., 1980, pp. 300–402; "Ford Signs ERDA Bill, AEC Abolished," *Nuclear News* 17 (November 1974): 40–41; "Enter NRC, ERDA," *Nuclear Industry* 22 (January 1975): 3–6.

13. William A. Anders speech to the National Wildlife Federation, "Regulating Nuclear Power in the Public Interest," March 15, 1975, NRC Records, Rockville; Ken Cole to President Ford, January 18, 1975, White House Central Files—Subject File, FG 384, Box 202 (Nuclear Regulatory Commission), Ford Papers; James G. Phillips, "Energy Report: Anders Rejects Charges of NRC Bias against Industry," *National Journal Reports* 7 (June 28, 1975): 968–72; *Nucleonics Week,* June 19, 1975; Gillette, "William Anders," pp. 1173, 1175.

14. "A Boon for NRC," *Nuclear Industry* 22 (February 1975): 8–9; "Pu Recycle Issue," *Nuclear Industry* 22 (May 1975): 3–4; "A Call to Arms," *Nuclear Industry* 22 (August 1975): 7–9; *Nucleonics Week,* May 22, June 19, August 7, 1975; Phillips, "Anders Rejects Charges," pp. 968–69; "How Safe Is Nuclear Power?" *Newsweek* (April 12, 1976): 71.

15. Gus Speth, Memorandum Re. NRC Decision on Plutonium Recycle, November 13, 1975, Box 37 (Natural Resources Defense Council, Inc.), Union of Concerned Scientists Papers, Massachusetts Institute of Technology Archives, Cambridge, Massachusetts; *Nucleonics Week,* December 4, 1975.

16. NRC Press Release, January 20, 1976, NRC Records, Rockville; U.S. Congress, Joint Committee on Atomic Energy, *Hearings on Investigation of Charges relating to Nuclear Reactor Safety,* 94th Cong., 2d sess., 1976, pp. 97–135, 581–621, 1490–1639; "Pollard Resigns over Safety Concerns," *Nuclear News* 19 (March 1976): 46–47; *Wall Street Journal,* August 5, 1976; *60 Minutes,* February 8, 1976, Video No. VBA1439, Motion Picture, Broadcasting and Sound Division, Library of Congress, Washington, D.C.

17. *New York Times,* January 21, February 10, February 11, February 12, February 20, 1976; "Debate on Safety Stirs Senate," *Nuclear Industry* 23 (February 1976): 2–5; John A. Harris to Commissioner Mason, March 2, 1976, NRC Records, Rockville; *60 Minutes,* February 8, 1976, Library of Congress.

18. Walker, *Containing the Atom,* pp. 37–56.

19. Ibid., p. 54; *Nucleonics Week,* May 4, 1972, May 10, 1973; U.S. Congress, Congressional Budget Office, *Delays in Nuclear Reactor Licensing and Construction: The Possibilities for Reform* (March 1979); Dixy Lee Ray to President Nixon, November 7, 1973, Domestic Council—Glenn R. Schleede Files, Box 24 (Nuclear Energy 1974, Power Plants), Ford Papers.

20. Glenn Schleede to Tom Korologos and Max Friedersdorf, July 26, 1974, Congressional Relations—Patrick O'Donnell and Joseph Jenckes Files, Subject File, Box 4 (Energy—Nuclear Power), Max L. Friedersdorf to James C. Cleveland, July 16, 1975, White House Central File—Subject Files, FG 384 (AT2—Industrial), Ford Papers; Edward J. Bauser to Melvin Price and others, June 5, 1974, General Correspondence, Box 197 (JCAE Outgoing Mail), JCAE Papers; Jim McIntyre and Stu Eizenstat to President Carter, c. March 1978, Staff Offices—Science and Technology Advisor to the President (Press), Subject File, Box 6 (Nuclear Policies), Papers of Jimmy Carter, Jimmy Carter Library, Atlanta, Georgia; "Message from the President," *Nuclear News* 17 (January 1974): 29; "Licensing Legislation," *Nuclear Industry* 22 (May 1975): 9–10; William D. Metz, "Nuclear Licensing: Promised Reform Miffs All Sides of Nuclear Debate," *Science* 198 (November 11, 1977): 590–93.

21. James B. Graham to Edward J. Bauser, October 9, 1972, General Correspondence, Box 14 (Atomic Safety and Licensing Board of Appeals), JCAE Papers; Thomas L. Kimball to Dixy Lee Ray, July 11, 1974, NRC Records, Rockville; Victor Gilinsky to George F. Murphy Jr., November 10, 1975, Domestic Council—Glenn R. Schleede Files, Box 26 (Nuclear Energy 1976, Licensing), Ford Papers; Gus Speth speech, "A Smaller Tomorrow," September 29, 1977, Box 2 (1977 Public Affairs), Intra-Agency Memorandums 1977–1983, Office of the Administrator, Record Group 412 (Records of the Environmental

Protection Agency), National Archives, College Park, Maryland; Jon Payne, "Fortune Telling in the Nuclear Age," *Nuclear News* 17 (June 1974): 53; Leonard J. Koch, "Nuclear Power: Ten More Years?" *Nuclear News* 18 (August 1975): 87–91; John E. Ward, "The Need for Licensing Reform: A Technical Perspective," *Nuclear News* 21 (April 1978): 53–58.

22. Steven Ebbin and Raphael Kasper, *Citizen Groups and the Nuclear Power Controversy: Uses of Scientific and Technological Information* (Cambridge: MIT Press, 1974), p. 31.

23. Kemeny Commission, *Staff Report on the Role of the Managing Utility and Its Suppliers* (Washington, D.C.: Government Printing Office, 1979), pp. 4–5, and *Staff Report of the Public's Right to Information Task Force* (Washington, D.C.: Government Printing Office, 1979), p. 41; Met-Ed–GPU Fact Sheet on Three Mile Island Nuclear Generating Station, n.d., Box 23B (GPU Plant Operation, 1979), Robert S. Walker Papers, Millersville University, Millersville, Pennsylvania.

24. Kemeny Commission, *Staff Report on the Role of the Managing Utility and Its Suppliers,* pp. 7–12, 26–30, 38; Babcock and Wilcox advertisement, *Nuclear News* 18 (November 1975): 28–29; Met-Ed–GPU Fact Sheet, Walker Papers.

25. Daniel F. Ford, *Three Mile Island: Thirty Minutes to Meltdown* (New York: Penguin Books, 1982), pp. 34–35; Susan Q. Stranahan, *Susquehanna: River of Dreams* (Baltimore: Johns Hopkins University Press, 1993), pp. 2–3, 186; Jack Brubaker, *Down the Susquehanna to the Chesapeake* (University Park: Pennsylvania State University Press, 2002), pp. ix–xiii; Rogovin Report, 1:2.

26. Rogovin Report, Vol. 2, Pt. 2, p. 620; Congressional Quarterly, *Congressional Districts in the 1980s* (Washington, D.C.: Congressional Quarterly, 1983), pp. 480–84; David J. Walbert, *Garden Spot: Lancaster County, the Old Order Amish, and the Selling of Rural America* (New York: Oxford University Press, 2002).

27. Kemeny Commission, *Staff Report of the Public's Right to Information Task Force,* p. 45; Mountain West Research, *Three Mile Island Telephone Survey: Preliminary Report on Procedures and Findings (NUREG/CR-1093),* October 1979, NRC Records, Rockville; Paul B. Beers, *Profiles from the Susquehanna Valley* (Harrisburg: Stackpole Books, 1973), pp. 125–31; Edwin D. Eshelman and Robert S. Walker, *Congress: The Pennsylvania Dutch Representatives, 1774–1974* (Lancaster: Concorde Publishing, 1975), pp. 56–63; Robert Del Tredici, *The People of Three Mile Island* (San Francisco: Sierra Club Books, 1980), p. 48; Richard L. Thornburgh, interview by author, Washington, D.C., July 10, 2001.

28. Kemeny Commission, *Staff Report of the Public's Right to Information Task Force,* pp. 34–46; Rogovin Report, 1:2–3.

29. Rogovin Report, Vol. 2, Pt. 1, pp. 66–77.

30. Ibid., pp. 84–111, 287–306; Kemeny Commission, *Staff Reports on Emergency Preparedness, Emergency Response* (Washington, D.C.: Government Printing Office, 1979), pp. 14–16; *Nuclear Regulatory Commission Issuances: July 1, 1978–December 31, 1978* (Washington, D.C.: Government Printing Office, n.d.), 8:9–68, 293–97; *Harrisburg Patriot,* March 29, 1979.

31. Kemeny Commission, *Staff Report of the Public's Right to Information Task Force*, pp. 38–39, *Staff Report on the Role of the Managing Utility and Its Suppliers*, pp. 53–59, *Staff Reports of the Technical Assessment Task Force* (Washington, D.C.: Government Printing Office, 1979), 4:61–62; Rogovin Report, Vol. 2, Pt. 1, pp. 108–16, 203–12.

32. Rogovin Report, 1:2; Ford, *Three Mile Island*, p. 38; Walker, *Containing the Atom*, pp. 272–73; Met-Ed–GPU Fact Sheet, Walker Papers.

33. *York Daily Record*, March 26, 1979.

CHAPTER 3. DEFENSE IN DEPTH

1. U.S. Congress, Joint Committee on Atomic Energy, *Hearings on Licensing and Regulation of Nuclear Reactors*, 90th Cong., 1st sess., 1967, p. 63.

2. For introductions to reactor technology and safety, see Richard Wolfson, *Nuclear Choices: A Citizen's Guide to Nuclear Technology* (Cambridge: MIT Press, 1991), pp. 95–192; and Anthony V. Nero Jr., *A Guidebook to Nuclear Reactors* (Berkeley: University of California Press, 1979), pp. 3–108.

3. For a detailed discussion of the emergency core cooling issue through 1971, see J. Samuel Walker, *Containing the Atom: Nuclear Regulation in a Changing Environment, 1963–1971* (Berkeley: University of California Press, 1992), pp. 169–202.

4. AEC Press Release, January 7, 1972, Nuclear Regulatory Commission Records, NRC Public Document Room, Rockville, Maryland (hereafter cited as NRC Records, Rockville); National Intervenors' Press Release, January 29, 1972, Records of the Atomic Energy Commission, History Division, Department of Energy, Germantown, Maryland; *Nucleonics Week*, January 20, 1972.

5. Docket No. RM 50-1, *Hearings in the Matter of Acceptance Criteria for Emergency Core Cooling Systems for Light Water Cooled Nuclear Power Reactors*, pp. 890–1013, 2397, 7325–7468, NRC Records, Rockville; "A Long Drawn Out Affair," *Nuclear Industry* 19 (February 1972): 11–20; *Nucleonics Week*, February 17, April 13, 1972; Roger J. Mattson, interview by author, Golden, Colorado, September 26, 2001.

6. AEC Regulatory Staff, "Emergency Core Cooling in Water-Cooled Power Reactors: An Interim Technical Report," draft, November 1, 1971 (Exhibit 740B), "Testimony of the AEC Regulatory Staff," December 28, 1971 (Exhibit 1001), Docket RM 50-1, NRC Records, Rockville; Walker, *Containing the Atom*, pp. 190–99.

7. Alvin M. Weinberg to James R. Schlesinger, February 9, 1972, ID&R-6 REG (Hazard Evaluation), Program Files of the Office of Secretary, Record Group 431 (Records of the Nuclear Regulatory Commission) National Archives, College Park, Maryland (hereafter cited as NRC Records, College Park); *Nucleonics Week*, February 17, March 16, 1972; "ECCS Enters New Phase," *Nuclear Industry* 19 (April 1972): 5–10; "ECCS: Exploring Areas of Uncertainty," *Nuclear News* 15 (May 1972): 30–31; Robert Gillette, "Nuclear Reactor Safety: At the AEC, the Way of the Dissenter Is Hard," *Science* 176 (May 5, 1972): 492–98.

8. "Aerojet Nuclear Asks to Clear Up 'Distortions' in ECCS Record," *Nu-*

clear Industry 19 (May 1972): 23–25; "Westinghouse Fuel Redesign to Reduce Cladding Temperature," *Nuclear Industry* 19 (October 1972): 48; "Long, Hot Summer," *Nuclear News* 15 (July 1972): 27; *Nucleonics Week,* March 30, April 27, October 26, 1972; "Memorandum of Daniel Ford Reporting His June 30–July 1, 1972, Discussions with Martin J. O'Boyle of Westinghouse Electric Corporation," n.d., Box 55 (Plasticman *[sic]*), Union of Concerned Scientists Papers, Massachusetts Institute of Technology Archives, Cambridge, Massachusetts.

9. M. J. Domagala to A. W. Jackson, February 18, 1972, AEC Records, Department of Energy; *Nucleonics Week,* April 20, 1972; Robert Gillette, "Reactor Safety: AEC Concedes Some Points to Its Critics," *Science* 178 (November 3, 1972): 482–84; "Final Version Closely Resembles Its Tentative Conclusions," *Nuclear Industry* 20 (April 1973): 17–19; William B. Cottrell, "The ECCS Rule-Making Hearing," *Nuclear Safety* 15 (January–February 1974): 30–55.

10. AEC Press Release, December 28, 1973, NRC Records, Rockville; *Wall Street Journal,* November 6, 1973; "ECCS: A Final Rule," *Nuclear Industry* 20 (December 1973): 3–4; *Nucleonics Week,* January 10, 1974.

11. For articles that discussed the ECCS issue with varying degrees of criticism of the AEC, see, for example, *New York Times,* December 11, 1971, July 17, 1972; *Chicago Tribune,* March 12, 1972; *New Orleans Times-Picayune,* April 2, 1972; *Los Angeles Times,* August 6, 1972, April 29, 1973; *Washington Star,* November 2, 1972; *Idaho Falls Post-Register,* November 5, 1972; Tom Alexander, "The Big Blowup over Nuclear Blowdowns," *Fortune* 87 (May 1973): 216–19, 299–315; Edward Edelson, "Scientific Facts behind the Hassle over Atomic Energy," *Popular Science* 203 (September 1973): 78–81, 112–14; Gillette, "Nuclear Reactor Safety," pp. 492–98 and "Reactor Safety," pp. 482–84 (see notes 7 and 9 above). The quotation is from Ralph E. Lapp, "Nuclear Power Safety: 1973," *New Republic* 168 (April 28, 1973): 17–19.

12. AEC Press Release, November 15, 1972, NRC Records, Rockville; *Nucleonics Week,* June 29, September 7, November 16, 1972; Robert Gillette, "Nuclear Safety: Damaged Fuel Ignites a New Debate in AEC," *Science* 177 (July 28, 1972): 330–31; "Perspective on Fuel 'Crisis,'" *Nuclear Industry* 19 (September 1972): 8–11.

13. Memorandum for the Record, Limited Attendance Session 75–15, September 30, 1974, and October 1, 1974, Memorandum for the Record, Limited Attendance Session 75–17, November 13, 1974, John C. Hoyle, Memorandum for the Record, February 24, 1975, SECY-75–16A (January 28, 1975), SECY-75–657 (November 10, 1975), SECY-78–623 (December 4, 1978), Citizens for a Better Environment Press Release, October 6, 1978, NRC Press Releases, January 29, December 5, 1975, all in NRC Records, Rockville; Mike Duval to President Ford, January 29, 1975, White House Central File—Subject Files, FG 384 (AT2—Industrial), Papers of Gerald R. Ford, Gerald R. Ford Library, Ann Arbor, Michigan; William A. Anders to Dixy Lee Ray, February 4, 1975, Subject File, Box 32 (NRC), Papers of Dixy Lee Ray, Hoover Institution on War, Revolution, and Peace Archives, Stanford University, Palo Alto, California.

14. L. Manning Muntzing to the Commission, May 15, 1972, O&M-7 REG (Reactor Safeguards, Adv. Comm.), Program Files of the Office of the Secretary, NRC Records, College Park; SECY-75–668 (November 18, 1975), John E. Ward

to Joseph Hendrie, May 12, 1978, Hendrie to Ward, August 15, 1978, *Antici- pated Transients without Scram for Light Water Reactors: Staff Report (NUREG- 0460)*, April 1978, NRC Records, Rockville; Muntzing to Harold G. Mangels- dorf, January 22, 1973, AEC Records, Department of Energy; *Nucleonics Week,* September 7, 1972, March 1, 1973; "Upgrading Emergency Shutdown Systems Affects 124 Plants," *Nuclear Industry* 20 (October 1973): 20; David Okrent, *Nuclear Reactor Safety: On the History of the Regulatory Process* (Madison: University of Wisconsin Press, 1981), pp. 236–60.

15. SECY-R-622 (January 11, 1973), Dixy Lee Ray to Harold G. Mangels- dorf, February 5, 1973, ID&R-6 (Hazards Evaluation), Program Files of the Office of the Secretary, NRC Records, College Park; SECY-75–274 (June 13, 1975), SECY-79–78 (January 31, 1979), W. R. Stratton to Ray, February 13, 1974, Harold R. Denton to Roger S. Boyd and others, January 23, 1979, NRC Records, Rockville.

16. SECY-78–342A (August 25, 1978), John Abbotts, "The Steam Line Break Accident: A Case Study of Regulatory Lag," June 1978, NRC Records, Rockville.

17. Joint Committee on Atomic Energy, *Hearings on Browns Ferry Nuclear Plant Fire,* 94th Cong., 1st sess., 1975, pp. 183–457; Special Review Group, *Rec- ommendations Related to Browns Ferry Fire (NUREG-0050),* February 1976, NRC Press Release, May 6, 1976, NRC Records, Rockville; *National Observer,* August 23, 1975; "NRC Faults TVA for Broad Range of Safety Violations in Fire," *Nuclear Industry* 22 (August 1975): 23–25; "Panel Criticizes NRC Pro- cedures," *Nuclear Industry* 23 (March 1976): 25–27.

18. *Wall Street Journal,* March 25, 1975; *New York Times,* March 26, 1975; *National Observer,* August 23, 1975; "Incident at Browns Ferry," *Newsweek* (October 20, 1975): 113; "A Point Was Made," *Nuclear Industry* 22 (September 1975): 6–7.

19. Joint Committee on Atomic Energy, *Browns Ferry Nuclear Plant Fire,* pp. 286–385; Special Review Group, *Recommendations Related to the Browns Ferry Fire,* pp. 7, 26–27, NRC Records, Rockville; *National Observer,* August 23, 1975.

20. SECY-76–545 (November 12, 1976), Ben Huberman to the Commission, December 6, 1976, NRC Records, Rockville.

21. Nuclear Regulatory Commission Special Inquiry Group, *Three Mile Is- land: A Report to the Commissioners and to the Public* (Washington, D.C.: Gov- ernment Printing Office, 1980), Vol. 2, Pt. 1, pp. 149–72.

CHAPTER 4. WEDNESDAY, MARCH 28

1. Anthony V. Nero Jr., *A Guidebook to Nuclear Reactors* (Berkeley: Uni- versity of California Press, 1979), pp. 77–93; Richard Wolfson, *Nuclear Choices: A Citizen's Guide to Nuclear Technology* (Cambridge: MIT Press, 1991), pp. 95– 169; U.S. Congress, Senate, Committee on Environment and Public Works, Sub- committee on Nuclear Regulation, *Nuclear Accident and Recovery at Three Mile Island: A Special Investigation,* 96th Cong., 2d sess., 1980, pp. 25–31.

2. The account of the early moments of the accident is drawn from several

investigations conducted shortly after it occurred: President's Commission on the Accident at Three Mile Island (hereafter referred to as the Kemeny Commission), *The Need for Change: The Legacy of TMI* (Washington, D.C.: Government Printing Office, 1979), pp. 90–96; Kemeny Commission, *Staff Reports of the Technical Assessment Task Force* (Washington: Government Printing Office, 1979), 4:121–259; Nuclear Regulatory Commission Special Inquiry Group, *Three Mile Island: A Report to the Commissioners and to the Public* (Washington: Government Printing Office, 1980), 1:7–15 (hereafter referred to as the Rogovin Report); Nuclear Regulatory Commission, *Investigation into the March 28, 1979, Three Mile Island Accident by Office of Inspection and Enforcement (NUREG-0600),* August 1979, Nuclear Regulatory Commission Records, NRC Public Document Room, Rockville, Maryland; Ellis Rubinstein, "The Accident That Shouldn't Have Happened," *IEEE Spectrum* 16 (November 1979): 33–42; Senate Subcommittee on Nuclear Regulation, *Nuclear Accident and Recovery at Three Mile Island,* pp. 25–35.

3. Kemeny Commission, *The Need for Change,* pp. 90–92, and *Staff Reports of the Technical Assessment Task Force,* 3:189–90; Rogovin Report, 1:9–15; Senate Subcommittee on Nuclear Regulation, *Nuclear Accident and Recovery at Three Mile Island,* pp. 65–66, 99.

4. Kemeny Commission, *Staff Reports of the Technical Assessment Task Force,* 3:4–89; Rogovin Report, Vol. 2, Pt. 2, pp. 597–606; NRC, *NUREG-0600,* pp. I-1-29 to I-1-30.

5. Kemeny Commission, *Staff Report on the Role of the Managing Utility and Its Suppliers* (Washington: Government Printing Office, 1979), pp. 89–105; Rogovin Report, 1:16–17; Depositions of Frederick Joseph Scheimann, July 25, 1979, pp. 174–84, Box 26, and William H. Zewe, July 26, 1979, pp. 92–127, Box 33 (Depositions, 1979), Papers of the President's Commission on the Accident at Three Mile Island, Record Group 220 (Records of Temporary Committees, Commissions, and Boards), National Archives, College Park, Maryland (hereafter referred to as the Kemeny Commission Records).

6. Kemeny Commission, *The Need for Change,* p. 93; Rogovin Report, 1:16–17; Senate Subcommittee on Nuclear Regulation, *Nuclear Accident and Recovery at Three Mile Island,* pp. 96–97; Scheimann Deposition, pp. 178–80, Kemeny Commission Records.

7. Kemeny Commission, *The Need for Change,* p. 99; Rogovin Report, 1:18; Senate Subcommittee on Nuclear Regulation, *Nuclear Accident and Recovery at Three Mile Island,* pp. 104–6; Rubinstein, "Accident That Shouldn't Have Happened," p. 40.

8. Kemeny Commission, *The Need for Change,* p. 100; Rogovin Report, 1:19–23; Senate Subcommittee on Nuclear Regulation, *Nuclear Accident and Recovery at Three Mile Island,* pp. 107–10; *Nucleonics Week,* February 28, 1985; Craig C. Faust, telephone interview by author, November 2, 2001.

9. Kemeny Commission, *The Need for Change,* pp. 100–103, and *Staff Report on the Role of the Managing Utility and Its Suppliers,* pp. 169–71; Rogovin Report, 1:12–25; Senate Subcommittee on Nuclear Regulation, *Nuclear Accident and Recovery at Three Mile Island,* pp. 79, 99–112; NRC, *Annual Report, 1979* (Washington, D.C.: Government Printing Office, 1980), p. 16, and *NUREG-*

0600, pp. 1A-44 to 1A-50; Rubinstein, "Accident That Shouldn't Have Happened," p. 38; Philip L. Cantelon and Robert C. Williams, *Crisis Contained: The Department of Energy at Three Mile Island* (Carbondale: Southern Illinois University Press, 1982), p. 30; NRC TMI Investigation, interview with William Zewe, June 28, 1979, pp. 7–8, NRC Records.

10. Oran K. Henderson to Dick Thornburgh, March 29, 1979, Box 1 (Chron File, Thursday 3–29–79), "Chronology—Three Mile Island, Confidential Draft," n.d., Box 1 (Chronology—Work File and Notes by Governor), Department of Environmental Resources, Bureau of Radiation Protection Actions, n.d., Box 1 (Department of Environmental Resources), William P. Dornsife, "The TMI Crisis: What Really Caused the Crisis?" paper prepared for annual meeting of the American Nuclear Society, June 12, 1980, all in the Papers of Richard L. Thornburgh, Archives Service Center, University of Pittsburgh, Pittsburgh, Pennsylvania; Deposition of Richard L. Thornburgh, August 17, 1979, pp. 4–13, Box 30 (Depositions, 1979), Kemeny Commission Records; Kemeny Commission, *The Need for Change*, p. 101, and *Staff Reports on Emergency Preparedness, Emergency Response* (Washington, D.C.: Government Printing Office, 1979), pp. 78–81.

11. Thornburgh Deposition, pp. 12–13, Kemeny Commission Records; *Philadelphia Bulletin*, May 18, 1978; *The Pennsylvania Manual, 1980–81* (Harrisburg: Department of General Services, 1981), p. 298; Mike Gray and Ira Rosen, *The Warning: Accident at Three Mile Island* (New York: W. W. Norton, 1982), pp. 131–32.

12. Kemeny Commission, *The Need for Change*, p. 103, and *Staff Reports on Emergency Preparedness, Emergency Response*, pp. 85–86; Rogovin Report, 1:28–29.

13. Kemeny Commission, *Staff Report of the Public's Right to Information Task Force* (Washington: Government Printing Office, 1979), pp. 80–96; B. H. Cherry to H. M. Dieckamp, March 29, 1979, Box 398 (TMI-GPU/Met Ed Memos), Papers of Morris K. Udall, University of Arizona, Tucson.

14. "Transcription, Press Conference of Lieutenant Governor William W. Scranton, 3d, Incident at Three Mile Island," March 28, 1979 (10:55 A.M.), Box 1 (Chron File, Wednesday 3–28–79), Department of Environmental Resources, Bureau of Radiation Protection Actions (note 10 above), Thornburgh Papers; Depositions of Margaret Reilly, July 16, 1979, p. 54, Box 24, and William W. Scranton III, July 25, 1979, pp. 15–16, Box 27 (Depositions 1979), Kemeny Commission Records; Kemeny Commission, *Staff Report of the Public's Right to Information Task Force*, p. 84, and *Staff Reports on Emergency Preparedness, Emergency Response*, pp. 90–91.

15. W. W. Anderson to Mark S. Knouse, April 10, 1979, Box 1 (Chronology—Work File and Notes by Governor), Scranton Press Conference, March 28, 1979 (note 14 above), Department of Environmental Resources, Bureau of Radiation Protection Actions (note 10 above), Thornburgh Papers; Kemeny Commission, *The Need for Change*, p. 102, and *Staff Reports of the Public Health and Safety Task Force* (Washington: Government Printing Office, 1979), pp. 28, 146; Rogovin Report, Vol. 2, Pt. 2, pp. 328, 355–60; Cantelon and Williams, *Crisis Contained*, pp. 27–43; J. Samuel Walker, *Permissible Dose: A History of Radiation*

Protection in the Twentieth Century (Berkeley: University of California Press, 2000), pp. 23–28, 31–46, 91–102.

16. U.S. Congress, House, Committee on Interior and Insular Affairs, Subcommittee on Energy and the Environment, *Hearings on Accident at the Three Mile Island Nuclear Powerplant,* 96th Cong., 1st sess., 1979, pp. 6–7; Rogovin Report, 1:44; *New York Times,* March 29, 1979.

17. Anderson to Knouse, April 10, 1979 (note 15 above), "Chronology— Three Mile Island" (note 10 above), Thornburgh Papers; Scranton Deposition, pp. 16–17, Kemeny Commission Records; Depositions of John Giles Herbein, September 19, 1979, pp. 34–37, and William P. Dornsife, September 19, 1979, pp. 11–12, NRC Special Inquiry Group, NRC Records; Kemeny Commission, *Staff Reports on Emergency Preparedness, Emergency Response,* pp. 91–92; Rogovin Report, Vol. 2, Pt. 2, p. 328.

18. "Transcription, Press Conference of Lieutenant Governor William W. Scranton, 3d, Incident at Three Mile Island," March 28, 1979 (4:30 P.M.), Box 1 (Chron File, Wednesday 3–28–79), Thornburgh Papers; Kemeny Commission, *Staff Report of the Public's Right to Information Task Force,* p. 99.

19. Chronology of NRC Response to Three Mile Island Accident, April 6, 1979, NRC Records; Deposition of Boyce H. Grier, August 17, 1979, pp. 28–31, Box 14 (Depositions 1979), Kemeny Commission Records; Rogovin Report, Vol. 2, Pt. 3, pp. 943–44.

20. Rogovin Report, Vol. 2, Pt. 3, pp. 944–45; Senate Subcommittee on Nuclear Regulation, *Nuclear Accident and Recovery at Three Mile Island,* pp. 260– 71; Deposition of Joseph Mallam Hendrie, October 9, 1979, pp. 42–46, Three Mile Island Special Inquiry Group, NRC Records; Joseph M. Hendrie, interview by author, Upton, New York, May 30, 2001.

21. Victor Gilinsky to Chairman Rowden, Commissioner Mason, and Commissioner Kennedy, December 23, 1976, NRC Records; Gilinsky to R. Emmett Tyrrell Jr., September 15, 1981, Personal NRC Files, Box 11 (Tyrrell, R. Emmett Jr.), Papers of Victor Gilinsky, Hoover Institution on War, Revolution, and Peace Archives, Stanford University, Palo Alto, California; Morris K. Udall to President Carter, October 19, 1978, Box 272 (Interior Committee, Environment and Energy Subcommittee—Nuclear Issues), Udall Papers; *Nucleonics Week,* April 14, 1977; U.S. Congress, Senate, Committee on Environment and Public Works, *Hearing on Nomination of Victor Gilinsky,* 96th Cong., 1st sess., 1979, p. 5.

22. Telephone log, March 28, 1979, General TMI Investigations, Box 484 (IRC/Telephone), Gilinsky Papers; Victor Gilinsky, interview by author, Rockville, Maryland, April 24, 2001.

23. Jessica Tuchman Mathews to Zbigniew Brzezinski, March 28, 1979, White House Central File, Subject File—Disasters, Box DI-1, Papers of Jimmy Carter, Jimmy Carter Library, Atlanta, Georgia; Deposition of Jessica Tuchman Mathews, August 23, 1979, pp. 5–14, Box 20 (Depositions 1979), Kemeny Commission Records; Gilinsky telephone log, March 28, 1979, Gilinsky Papers; Jessica T. Mathews, interview by author, Washington, D.C., June 7, 2001.

24. Samuel J. Chilk, Memorandum for the Record, August 6, 1979, Transcript of Incident Response Center TMI Tapes, Day 1, Channel 6/24, pp. 1362– 90, NRC Records; Senate Committee on Environment and Public Works, Sub-

committee on Nuclear Regulation, *Three Mile Island Nuclear Powerplant Accident,* 96th Cong., 1st sess., 1979, pp. 320–23.

25. Frank Press to Jimmy Carter, April 18, 1978, Staff Offices—Office of Staff Secretary Handwriting File, Box 81, Carter Papers; NRC Press Release, July 31, 1978, NRC Records; "NRC Moves to Fill Senior Echelon Positions," *Nuclear Industry* 25 (August 1978): 24–25; Deposition of John F. Ahearne, August 29, 1979, p. 200, Box 1 (Depositions 1979), Kemeny Commission Records; John F. Ahearne, interview by author, Research Triangle Park, North Carolina, March 30, 2001; Peter A. Bradford, interview by author, New York, May 21, 2002.

26. Ahearne Deposition, pp. 200–205, Kemeny Commission Records; Deposition of John F. Ahearne, October 12, 1979, pp. 119–23, NRC Special Inquiry Group, NRC Records; Ahearne, interview by author.

27. House Subcommittee on Energy and the Environment, *Hearings on Accident at Three Mile Island Nuclear Powerplant,* pp. 94–102; Deposition of James C. Higgins, August 17, 1979, pp. 8–14, Box 16 (Depositions 1979), Kemeny Commission Records.

28. Kemeny Commission, *The Need for Change,* p. 107, and *Staff Report on the Role of the Managing Utility and Its Suppliers,* pp. 174–86; Rogovin Report, 1:30–47; Senate Subcommittee on Nuclear Regulation, *Nuclear Accident and Recovery at Three Mile Island,* pp. 124–51.

29. Transcript of TMI Tapes, Day 1, Channel 6/24, pp. 1438–39, 1511–18; Deposition of Victor Stello Jr., July 24, 1979, pp. 73–84, Box 28 (Depositions 1979), Kemeny Commission Records; Gilinsky telephone log, March 28, 1979, Gilinsky Papers; Rogovin Report, Vol. 2, Pt. 3, pp. 948–49.

30. Rogovin Report, 1:40–41; Senate Subcommittee on Nuclear Regulation, *Nuclear Accident and Recovery at Three Mile Island,* pp. 141, 151.

31. Transcript of TMI Tapes, Day 1, Channel 3/21, pp. 582–83, Channel 5/23, pp. 1142–46, Channel 17/203C, pp. 2031–32, 2155, Deposition of Frank L. Ingram, September 28, 1979, pp. 44–45, NRC Special Inquiry Group, NRC Records.

32. Transcript of TMI Tapes, Day 1, Channel 6/24, p. 1459, Channel 7/25, pp. 1650–55, 1668–70.

33. Transcript of TMI Tapes, Day 1, Channel 7/25, pp. 1668–73, Richard T. Kennedy to Lee V. Gossick, March 10, 1977, Kennedy to Chairman Hendrie, June 30, 1978, Kennedy to Chairman Ahearne, May 30, 1980, NRC Records; Dick Kirschten, "The Curious Goings-On at the Nuclear Regulatory Commission," *National Journal* (May 27, 1978): 841.

34. Transcript of TMI Tapes, Day 1, Channel 2/20, pp. 383–89, Channel 3/21, pp. 634–40, Channel 6/24, pp. 1483–89, Channel 19/203D, p. 2363, NRC Press Release, March 28, 1979, NRC Records; *New York News,* March 29, 1979.

35. Kemeny Commission, *Staff Reports on Emergency Preparedness, Emergency Response,* pp. 82–94; Rogovin Report, Vol. 2, Pt. 3, pp. 944, 950; "Chronology—Three Mile Island" (note 10 above), Thornburgh Papers.

36. "Transcription, Press Conference of Lieutenant Governor William W. Scranton, 3d, Incident at Three Mile Island," March 28, 1979 (10 P.M.), Box 1 (Chron File, Wednesday 3-28-79), Thornburgh Papers; Transcript of TMI Tapes, Day 1, Channel 6/24, pp. 1604–5, Deposition of Charles O. Gallina,

pp. 34–40, September 14, 1979, NRC Special Inquiry Group, NRC Records; Kemeny Commission, *Staff Reports on Emergency Preparedness, Emergency Response,* p. 94, and *Staff Report of the Public's Right to Information Task Force,* p. 108.

37. Thornburgh Deposition, pp. 23–24, Kemeny Commission Records; "Chronology—Three Mile Island" (note 10 above), Thornburgh Papers; *Washington Star,* April 4, 1979; *New York Times,* April 4, 1979; Richard L. Thornburgh, interview by author, Washington, D.C., July 10, 2001.

38. Thornburgh Deposition, pp. 24–29, Kemeny Commission Records; John G. Fuller, *We Almost Lost Detroit* (New York: Reader's Digest Press, 1975); Thornburgh, interview by author.

CHAPTER 5. THURSDAY, MARCH 29

1. President's Commission on the Accident at Three Mile Island (hereafter referred to as the Kemeny Commission), *Staff Report of the Public's Right to Information Task Force* (Washington, D.C.: Government Printing Office, 1979), pp. 218–28; Nuclear Regulatory Commission Special Inquiry Group, *Three Mile Island: A Report to the Commissioners and to the Public* (Washington, D.C.: Government Printing Office, 1980), 1:48 (hereafter referred to as Rogovin Report); *Harrisburg Evening News,* March 29, 1979; *Harrisburg Patriot,* March 29, 1979; *New York Times,* March 29, 1979; *Philadelphia Inquirer,* March 29, 1979; *Reading (Pa.) Times,* March 29, 1979; *Wall Street Journal,* March 29, 1979; *Washington Post,* March 29, 1979.

2. Transcripts of *Good Morning America,* March 29, 1979, *The Today Show,* March 29, 1979, and *Thursday Morning,* March 29, 1979, Media Monitor, Nuclear Regulatory Commission Records, NRC Public Document Room, Rockville, Maryland.

3. Kemeny Commission, *Staff Report of the Public's Right to Information Task Force,* pp. 170–71; Rogovin Report, 1:54.

4. Rogovin Report, Vol. 2, Pt. 3, p. 1063; Transcript of Met-Ed Press Conference, March 29, 1979, NRC Records.

5. Deposition of Kevin J. Molloy, September 21, 1979, pp. 57–58, NRC Special Inquiry Group, Transcript, WTTG-TV, *The Ten O'Clock News,* March 29, 1979, Media Monitor, NRC Records; *Harrisburg Patriot,* March 30, 1979; *New York Times,* March 30, 1979; *Lancaster Intelligencer Journal,* March 30, 1979.

6. J. Samuel Walker, *Permissible Dose: A History of Radiation Protection in the Twentieth Century* (Berkeley: University of California Press, 2000), pp. 36–107.

7. Ibid., pp. 101–2; Governor's Fact Finding Commission, *Shippingport Nuclear Power Station: Alleged Health Effects* (Harrisburg: n.p., 1974); *Nucleonics Week,* January 11, April 19, May 3, 1973, July 4, September 5, 1974; *New York Times,* May 31, 1973; J. Samuel Walker, *Containing the Atom: Nuclear Regulation in a Changing Environment, 1963–1971* (Berkeley: University of California Press, 1992), pp. 334–37.

8. Transcript of Incident Response Center TMI Tapes, Day 2, Channel 2/7,

p. 2454, Channel 5/23, p. 1720, Channel 6/24, pp. 2040–42, 2109–13, NRC Records; Kemeny Commission, *Staff Report of the Public's Right to Information Task Force,* pp. 222–23, and *Staff Reports on Emergency Preparedness, Emergency Response* (Washington, D.C.: Government Printing Office, 1979), p. 101; Robert Del Tredici, *The People of Three Mile Island* (San Francisco: Sierra Club Books, 1980), p. 98.

9. Transcript of Proceedings, President's Commission on the Accident at Three Mile Island, April 26, 1979, Papers of Richard L. Thornburgh, Archives Service Center, University of Pittsburgh, Pittsburgh, Pennsylvania; Kemeny Commission, *Staff Reports on Emergency Preparedness, Emergency Response,* p. 96.

10. "Chronology—Three Mile Island, Confidential Draft," n.d., Box 1 (Chronology—Work File and Notes by Governor), Mark Knouse, Handwritten Notes on 3 Mile Island Tour, n.d., Transcript of Governor's Press Conference, March 29, 1979, Box 1 (Chron File, Thursday 3–29–79), Thornburgh Papers; Interview of Lieutenant Governor William W. Scranton III, July 25, 1979, pp. 21–23, Box 27, Deposition of Richard L. Thornburgh, August 17, 1979, pp. 37–39, Box 30 (Depositions, 1979), Papers of the President's Commission on the Accident at Three Mile Island, Record Group 220 (Records of Temporary Committees, Commissions, and Boards), National Archives, College Park, Maryland (hereafter referred to as Kemeny Commission Records).

11. "Chronology—Three Mile Island," Thornburgh Papers; Thornburgh Deposition, pp. 39–41, Kemeny Commission Records; Rogovin Report, Vol. 1, p. 58, Vol. 2, Pt. 3, p. 952.

12. Transcript of Meeting, "Briefing on Three-Mile Island Incident," March 29, 1979, NRC Records.

13. "Statement by Honorable Morris K. Udall, Briefing on the Accident at the Three Mile Island Nuclear Power Plant," March 29, 1979, Box 389 (Three Mile Island Nuclear Plant Statements, Questions), Papers of Morris K. Udall, University of Arizona, Tucson; Transcript, CBS Radio News, March 29, 1979, Media Monitor, Deposition of Dr. Joseph Mallam Hendrie, October 9, 1979, pp. 54–56, NRC Special Inquiry Group, NRC Records; Rogovin Report, Vol. 2, Pt. 3, p. 952; *Harrisburg Patriot,* March 30, 1979; *Lancaster Intelligencer Journal,* March 30, 1979.

14. AEC Press Release, May 12, 1972, Lee V. Gossick to All NRC Employees, Announcement No. 171, November 9, 1977, NRC Records; *Nucleonics Week,* June 27, 1974; *Washington Post,* January 13, January 23, 1978; *New York Times,* March 31, 1979; *Philadelphia Inquirer,* April 9, 1979; *Baltimore Sun,* May 29, 1979; Nancy Zacha Godlewski, "Hendrie: Charting a Steady Course," *Nuclear News* 27 (June 1984): 90–93.

15. Deposition of Dr. Roger Joseph Mattson, September 24, 1979, pp. 32–33, 46, 64–67, 71, NRC Special Inquiry Group, NRC Records; Deposition of Robert L. Tedesco, July 27, 1979, pp. 50–54, Box 29 (Depositions, 1979), Kemeny Commission Records; Rogovin Report, Vol. 2, Pt. 3, p. 952.

16. Deposition of Richard Vollmer, September 21, 1979, pp. 6–32, Mattson Deposition, pp. 29–31, NRC Special Inquiry Group, NRC Records; Richard H. Vollmer, interview by author, Arnold, Maryland, January 3, 2002.

17. NRC TMI Investigation, interview with Dick Wilson, June 1, 1979, p. 10, NRC Records; Rogovin Report, Vol. 1, pp. 57–58, Vol. 2, Pt. 3, pp. 841–42; Vollmer, interview by author.

18. Transcript of TMI Tapes, Day 2, Channel 2/7, p. 2469, Channel 6/24, pp. 2051–55, 2061–64, NRC Records; Kemeny Commission, *Staff Reports on Emergency Preparedness, Emergency Response*, pp. 98–99, and *Staff Report of the Public's Right to Information Task Force*, pp. 111–16.

19. Transcript of TMI Tapes, Day 2, Channel 6/24, pp. 2134–38, 2179–85, NRC Records; Deposition of Karl Abraham, August 16, 1979, Box 1 (Depositions, 1979), pp. 44–54, Thornburgh Deposition, p. 42, Kemeny Commission Records; Kemeny Commission, *Staff Reports on Emergency Preparedness, Emergency Response*, pp. 102–6, and *Staff Report of the Public's Right to Information Task Force*, pp. 116–24.

20. *Harrisburg Evening News*, March 30, 1979; Elinor G. Adensam, interview by author, Rockville, Maryland, January 10, 2002.

CHAPTER 6. FRIDAY, MARCH 30

1. Deposition of Harold Ray Denton, October 4, 1979, p. 91, Nuclear Regulatory Commission Special Inquiry Group, Transcript of Incident Response Center TMI Tapes, Day 2, Channel 6/24, pp. 1995–2004, NRC Records, NRC Public Document Room, Rockville, Maryland; *Harrisburg Patriot*, April 4, April 16, 1979; Joseph M. Hendrie, interview by author, Upton, New York, May 30, 2001; Harold R. Denton, interview by author, Knoxville, Tennessee, September 9, 2001.

2. Transcript of TMI Tapes, Day 2, Channel 6/24, p. 1996, Transcript of *The Today Show*, March 30, 1979, Media Monitor, NRC Records.

3. *Harrisburg Patriot*, March 16, March 30, 1979; *Baltimore Sun*, March 30, 1979; *New York Times*, April 4, 1979.

4. NRC Special Inquiry Group, *Three Mile Island: A Report to the Commissioners and to the Public* (Washington, D.C.: Government Printing Office, 1980), Vol. 2, Pt. 3, pp. 877–79 (hereafter referred to as the Rogovin Report).

5. Deposition of James R. Floyd, September 13, 1979, pp. 72–80, NRC Special Inquiry Group, Transcript of TMI Tapes, Day 2, Channel 2/3, pp. 841–44, NRC Records; Deposition of James C. Higgins, August 17, 1979, pp. 47–56, Box 16 (Depositions, 1979), Papers of the President's Commission on the Accident at Three Mile Island, Record Group 220 (Records of Temporary Committees, Commissions, and Boards), National Archives, College Park, Maryland (hereafter referred to as Kemeny Commission Records); Rogovin Report, Vol. 1, pp. 59–61, Vol. 2, Pt. 3, pp. 841–45; President's Commission on the Accident at Three Mile Island (hereafter referred to as Kemeny Commission), *Staff Reports on Emergency Preparedness, Emergency Response* (Washington, D.C.: Government Printing Office, 1979), pp. 96, 108.

6. "Chronology—Three Mile Island, Confidential Draft," n.d., Box 1 (Chronology—Work File and Notes by Governor), Papers of Richard L. Thornburgh, Archives Service Center, University of Pittsburgh, Pittsburgh, Pennsylvania; Floyd Deposition, pp. 82–86, NRC Records; Interview of Lieutenant Gov-

ernor William W. Scranton III, July 25, 1979, pp. 24–25, Box 27 (Depositions, 1979), Kemeny Commission Records; Rogovin Report, 1:61–62; Kemeny Commission, *Staff Reports on Emergency Preparedness, Emergency Response,* pp. 109–10.

7. Deposition of William P. Dornsife, July 24, 1979, pp. 65–78, Box 7, Deposition of Lake H. Barrett, July 28, 1979, pp. 45–57, Box 2 (Depositions, 1979), Kemeny Commission Records; Rogovin Report, 1:62.

8. J. Samuel Walker, *Containing the Atom: Nuclear Regulation in a Changing Environment, 1963–1971* (Berkeley: University of California Press, 1992), pp. 223–25.

9. Nuclear Regulatory Commission, *Guide and Checklist for Development and Evaluation of State and Local Government Radiological Emergency Response Plans in Support of Fixed Nuclear Facilities (NUREG-75/111),* December 1, 1974, and "Supplement No. 1 to NUREG-75/111," March 15, 1977, NRC Records; U.S. Congress, House, Committee on Government Operations, Subcommittee on Environment, Energy, and Natural Resources, *Hearings on Emergency Planning around U.S. Nuclear Powerplants: Nuclear Regulatory Commission Oversight,* 96th Cong., 1st sess., 1979, pp. 62, 405–526.

10. Oran K. Henderson to Robert S. Walker, April 16, 1979, Box 23A (Shutdown and Restart of TMI, 1979), Papers of Robert S. Walker, Millersville University, Millersville, Pennsylvania; Patty McCormick to Governor Thornburgh and others, April 19, 1979, Paul Critchlow to Roland Page, April 20, 1979, Box 5 (Robert C. Wilburn, April 1979), Thornburgh Papers; House Subcommittee on Environment, Energy, and Natural Resources, *Hearings on Emergency Planning,* pp. 261–71; Kemeny Commission, *Staff Reports on Emergency Preparedness, Emergency Response,* pp. 30–36.

11. Depositions of Harold Collins, July 28, 1979, pp. 52–65, Box 5, Harold R. Denton, August 2, 1979, p. 135, Box 6, and Barrett, pp. 63–65 (Depositions, 1979), "Third Meeting of the President's Commission on the Accident at Three Mile Island," transcript, May 31, 1979, pp. 303–6, Box 5 (Hearings, 1979), Kemeny Commission Records; Interview of Harold E. Collins, September 19, 1979, pp. 30–38, NRC Special Inquiry Group, NRC Records; Rogovin Report, Vol. 2, Pt. 3, p. 956.

12. Interview of Oran K. Henderson, September 20, 1979, pp. 61–63, Collins interview, pp. 37–41, NRC Special Inquiry Group, Transcript of TMI Tapes, Day 3, Channel 2/20, pp. 101–5, NRC Records.

13. Deposition of Kevin J. Molloy, July 26, 1979, pp. 48–51, Box 21 (Depositions, 1979), Kemeny Commission Records; Henderson interview, p. 61, NRC Special Inquiry Group, NRC Records; Kemeny Commission, *Staff Report of the Public's Right to Information Task Force* (Washington, D.C.: Government Printing Office, 1979), p. 137.

14. Deposition of Charles O. Gallina, August 16, 1979, pp. 82–89, Box 13 (Depositions, 1979), Kemeny Commission Records; Richard H. Vollmer, interview by author, Arnold, Maryland, January 3, 2002; Elinor G. Adensam, interview by author, Rockville, Maryland, January 10, 2002.

15. Dornsife Deposition, pp. 61–64, Interview with Margaret Reilly, July 16, 1979, pp. 117–33, Box 24, Deposition of Thomas M. Gerusky, July 24, 1979,

pp. 52–56, Box 13 (Depositions, 1979), Kemeny Commission Records; Deposition of Thomas M. Gerusky, September 19, 1979, p. 53, NRC Special Inquiry Group, Transcript of TMI Tapes, Day 3, Channel 4/22, pp. 995–1005, NRC Records.

16. Deposition of Richard L. Thornburgh, August 17, 1979, pp. 50–66, Box 30, Scranton interview, pp. 25–26, Box 27 (Depositions, 1979), Kemeny Commission Records; "Chronology—Three Mile Island," Thornburgh Papers; U.S. Congress, House, Committee on Science and Technology, Subcommittee on Natural Resources and Environment, *Hearings on Three Mile Island Nuclear Plant Accident,* 96th Cong., 1st sess., 1979, pp. 51–52; Richard L. Thornburgh, interview by author, Washington, D.C., July 10, 2001.

17. Deposition of Victor Gilinsky, September 8, 1979, pp. 155–77, Box 13, Deposition of Peter A. Bradford, September 10, 1979, p. 203, Box 4 (Depositions, 1979), Kemeny Commission Records; Transcript of Commission Meeting, March 30, 1979, pp. 1–16, NRC Records.

18. Transcript of Commission Meeting, March 30, 1979, pp. 17–29, NRC Records; "Chronology—Three Mile Island," Thornburgh Papers; John H. Austin, interview by author, Aiken, South Carolina, September 11, 2001; Thornburgh, interview by author.

19. Deposition of Joseph M. Hendrie, September 7, 1979, pp. 208–9, Box 15 (Depositions, 1979), Denton Deposition, p. 135, Thornburgh Deposition, pp. 57–60, Bradford Deposition, pp. 182–84, 203–4, Scranton interview, p. 26, Kemeny Commission Records; Deposition of John F. Ahearne, October 12, 1979, pp. 35–50, Deposition of Victor Gilinsky, October 5, 1979, pp. 63–66, Deposition of Richard T. Kennedy, October 2, 1979, pp. 114–18, NRC Special Inquiry Group, NRC Records.

20. Deposition of Jessica Tuchman Mathews, August 23, 1979, pp. 20–25, Box 20 (Depositions, 1979), Kemeny Commission Records; Jimmy Carter, *Why Not the Best?* (Nashville: Broadman Press, 1975), p. 56; Nicholas Wade, "Carter as Scientist or Engineer: What Are His Credentials?" *Science* 193 (August 6, 1976): 462–63.

21. Frank Press and John Deutch to the Vice President and others, November 21, 1979, Staff Offices—Counsel (Cutler), Box 100 (Nuclear Regulatory Commission), Papers of Jimmy Carter, Jimmy Carter Library, Atlanta, Georgia; *Wall Street Journal,* October 19, 1977; Jon Payne, "Janus in Washington, D.C.," *Nuclear News* 22 (February 1979): 31; J. Samuel Walker, "Nuclear Power and Nonproliferation: The Controversy over Nuclear Exports, 1974–1980," *Diplomatic History* 25 (spring 2001): 215–49.

22. Transcript of "Telephone Conversation with President Carter and Joseph Hendrie," March 30, 1979, Staff Offices—Office of Staff Secretary Handwriting File, Box 125, Carter Papers.

23. Handwritten notes of "Telephone Conversation re 3-Mile Nuclear Power Plant," March 30, 1979, ibid.; Thornburgh Deposition, pp. 61, 77–78, Kemeny Commission Records; "Chronology—Three Mile Island," Thornburgh Papers; Transcript of TMI Tapes, Day 3, Channel 7/25, pp. 1685–86.

24. Deposition of Jack Watson, September 6, 1979, pp. 4–20, Box 31 (Depositions, 1979), Kemeny Commission Records; Jimmy Carter, *Keeping Faith:*

Memoirs of a President (New York: Bantam Books, 1982), p. 45; Jack Watson, interview by author, Philomont, Virginia, May 17, 2001.

25. Hendrie Deposition, pp. 223–24, Kemeny Commission Records; Deposition of Joseph Mallam Hendrie, October 9, 1979, pp. 96–98; Gilinsky Deposition, p. 62, NRC Special Inquiry Group, NRC Records; Peter A. Bradford, interview by author, New York, May 21, 2002.

26. *Energy Daily,* June 30, 1977; *Nucleonics Week,* July 14, 1977; NRC Press Release, August 15, 1977, NRC Records; Peter Amory Bradford, *Fragile Structures: A Story of Oil Refineries, National Security, and the Coast of Maine* (New York: Harper's Magazine Press, 1975).

27. Notes of Tom Gibbon, n.d., p. 9, attached to Dornsife Deposition, Hendrie Deposition, pp. 223–24, Kemeny Commission Records; Hendrie Deposition, p. 98, Ahearne Deposition, pp. 171–74, NRC Special Inquiry Group, NRC Records; Dick Kirschten, "The Curious Goings-On at the Nuclear Regulatory Commission," *National Journal* (May 27, 1978): 840–42; Sandra M. Joosten, interview by author, Rockville, Maryland, February 19, 2002; Bradford, interview by author.

28. Deposition of Kevin Molloy, September 21, 1979, p. 46, NRC Special Inquiry Group, NRC Records; "Chronology—Three Mile Island," Thornburgh Papers; Kemeny Commission, *Staff Reports on Emergency Preparedness, Emergency Response,* pp. 120–21; Rogovin Report, 1:67; Thornburgh, interview by author.

29. Gerusky Deposition, pp. 62–66, Kemeny Commission Records; Kemeny Commission, *Staff Reports on Emergency Preparedness, Emergency Response,* pp. 121–23.

30. Transcript, "Press Conference of Gov. Dick Thornburgh and Lt. Gov. William Scranton 3d," March 30, 1979, Box 1 (Chron File, 3–30–79), "Chronology—Three Mile Island," Thornburgh Papers; Kemeny Commission, *Staff Reports on Emergency Preparedness, Emergency Response,* pp. 122–23.

31. Linda Young to Dr. Hendrie, n.d., NRC Records; *New York Times,* March 31, 1979; *Philadelphia Inquirer,* March 31, 1979; Rogovin Report, Vol. 2, Pt. 2, pp. 624–27, 638.

32. George M. Miller, Account of Emergency at Three Mile Island Nuclear Generating Station, n.d., NRC Records; AP Wire Story, March 31, 1979, Box 2 (Governor Thornburgh's Set of Wire Stories), Transcript, Press Conference, March 30, 1979, Thornburgh Papers; *Harrisburg Patriot,* March 31, 1979; William Lanouette, "Three Mile Island + 10: Will Press Coverage Be Better Next Time?" Occasional Paper, Media Studies Project Colloquium, Woodrow Wilson International Center for Scholars, March 28, 1989, pp. 69–70.

33. Jessica Tuchman Mathews to President Carter, March 30, 1979, White House Central File, Subject File—Disasters, Box DI-1, Carter Papers; Deposition of Roger Joseph Mattson, September 24, 1979, pp. 70–78, NRC Special Inquiry Group, Transcript of Commission Meeting, March 30, 1979, pp. 57–62, 154, NRC Records; Hendrie Deposition, p. 205, Kemeny Commission Records; Rogovin Report, Vol. 2, Pt. 3, pp. 842–45, 959, 1132–33; Kemeny Commission, *Staff Reports on Emergency Preparedness, Emergency Response,* pp. 123–24; Roger J. Mattson, interview by author, Golden, Colorado, September 26, 2001; Adensam, interview by author.

34. Hendrie Deposition, pp. 205–6, Kemeny Commission Records; Mattson Deposition, pp. 88–95, NRC Special Inquiry, Transcript of Commission Meeting, March 30, 1979, pp. 60–81, NRC Records; Mattson, interview by author.

35. William C. Milstead to D. Crutchfield, May 4, 1979, Thomas E. Murley to the Files, June 13, 1979, NRC Records; Rogovin Report, Vol. 2, Pt. 3, p. 981.

36. William E. Odom to Zbigniew Brzezinski, March 30, 1979, Brzezinski to President Carter, March 30, 1979, White House Central File, Subject File—Disasters, Box DI-1, Jack Watson to President Carter, March 30, 1979, Jimmy Carter to Watson, March 30, 1979, Staff Offices—Office of Staff Secretary Handwriting File, Box 125, Carter Papers; Watson Deposition, pp. 21–30, Kemeny Commission Records.

37. Dick Thornburgh to the File, March 30, 1979, "Chronology—Three Mile Island," Box 1 (Chronology—Work File and Notes by Governor), Thornburgh Papers; Transcript of Commission Meeting, March 30, 1979, pp. 122–33, NRC Records.

38. Deposition of Dudley Thompson, September 21, 1979, pp. 94–102, Deposition of Lee V. Gossick, September 28, 1979, pp. 134–39, NRC Special Inquiry Group, Transcript of TMI Tapes, Day 3, Channel 3/21, pp. 855–58, Channel 6/24, p. 1530, Transcript of Commission Meeting, March 30, 1979, p. 164, NRC Records; UPI Wire Story, March 30, 1979, Central Files, Box 76 (Wire Service Copy and Information), Gilinsky Deposition, pp. 118–20, Kemeny Commission Records; Kemeny Commission, *Staff Report of the Public's Right to Information Task Force*, pp. 61–62, 144–46; *New York Times,* March 31, 1979.

39. Transcript of Commission Meeting, March 30, 1979, pp. 146–49, 167–68, 173–86, NRC Records; NRC Press Release, March 30, 1979, 6:30 P.M., Box 1 (Nuclear Regulatory Commission), Thornburgh Papers.

40. Deposition of Joseph J. Fouchard, September 27, 1979, p. 18, Deposition of Richard Vollmer, September 21, 1979, pp. 42–43, NRC Special Inquiry Group, NRC Records; "Chronology—Three Mile Island," General Public Utilities Corporation, "The TMI-2 Story," booklet, May 25, 1979, no box, Thornburgh Papers; Rogovin Report, Vol. 2, Pt. 3, p. 1207.

41. Deposition of Harold Denton, October 23, 1979, pp. 12–13, 31–32, NRC Special Inquiry Group, Transcript of Commission Meeting, March 30, 1979, pp. 118, 209, NRC Records.

42. Jimmy Carter, handwritten notes of conversation with Denton, 2:45 P.M., March 30, 1979, Staff Offices—Office of the Staff Secretary Handwriting File, Box 125, Carter Papers; Denton Deposition, pp. 23–24, NRC Special Inquiry Group, NRC Records; Denton, interview by author.

43. Transcript of Commission Meeting, March 30, 1979, pp. 106–18, Transcript of TMI Tapes, Day 3, Channel 2/20, p. 253, Channel 3/21, p. 724, Channel 4/22, pp. 1051–52, Vollmer Deposition, pp. 42–45, NRC Special Inquiry Group, NRC Records.

44. Transcript of Commission Meeting, March 30, 1979, pp. 156–60, Fouchard Deposition, NRC Special Inquiry Group, NRC Records; "Chronology—Three Mile Island," Richard Thornburgh, handwritten notes of conversations with Hendrie and Denton, [March 30, 1979], Box 1 (Chronology—Work File and Notes by Governor), Thornburgh Papers.

45. "Chronology—Three Mile Island," Mark Knouse, handwritten notes of meeting in governor's office, March 30, 1979, Box 1 (Chron File, Friday, 3–30–79), Thornburgh Papers; Scranton interview, p. 28, Kemeny Commission Records; Gerusky Deposition, p. 20, NRC Special Inquiry Group, NRC records; Thornburgh, Denton, Vollmer, interviews by author.

46. "Chronology—Three Mile Island," Thornburgh Papers; Denton Deposition, pp. 133–34, Kemeny Commission Records.

47. "Transcript of Press Conference of Governor Dick Thornburgh, Lt. Governor William Scranton 3d, Dr. Harold Denton," March 30, 1979, Box 1 (Chron File, Friday, 3–30–79), Thornburgh Papers; Kemeny Commission, *Staff Report of the Public's Right to Information Task Force,* pp. 59–60; Denton, interview by author.

48. Kemeny Commission, *Staff Report of the Public's Right to Information Task Force,* pp. 60–61; Joseph J. Fouchard, interview by author, Rockville, Maryland, March 8, 2000.

49. Transcript of *NBC Nightly News,* March 30, 1979, Transcript of *ABC World News Tonight,* March 30, 1979, Transcript of *CBS Evening News,* March 30, 1979, Media Monitor, NRC Records; Edwin Diamond and Leigh Passman, "Three Mile Island: How Clear Was TV's Picture?" *TV Guide* (August 4, 1979): 5–12; Kemeny Commission, *Staff Report of the Public's Right to Information Task Force,* pp. 176–77, 222–27; Rogovin Report, 1:4.

CHAPTER 7. SATURDAY, MARCH 31

1. Nuclear Regulatory Commission (NRC) Special Inquiry Group, *Three Mile Island: A Report to the Commissioners and to the Public* (Washington, D.C.: Government Printing Office, 1980), Vol. 2, Pt. 3, pp. 963–65 (hereafter referred to as the Rogovin Report); Transcript of Commission Meeting, March 31, 1979, Commencing at 10:27 A.M., pp. 30–31, Continuation at 12:00 noon, pp. 32, 45–46, 59–61, "Preliminary Notification of Event or Unusual Occurrence" (PNO-79-67E), March 31, 1979, NRC Records, NRC Public Document Room, Rockville, Maryland; Eliot Marshall, "The Crisis at Three Mile Island: Nuclear Risks Are Reconsidered," *Science* 204 (April 13, 1979): 152–53.

2. Transcripts of Commission Meetings, March 30, 1979, p. 217, March 31, 1979, Continuation at 12:00 noon, p. 12, NRC Records; President's Commission on the Accident at Three Mile Island (hereafter referred to as the Kemeny Commission), *The Need for Change: The Legacy of TMI* (Washington, D.C.: Government Printing Office, 1979), p. 126.

3. Transcripts of Incident Response Center TMI Tapes, Day 3, Channel 6/24, pp. 1575–99, 1619–29, Deposition of Roger Mattson, October 17, 1979, pp. 8–10, NRC Special Inquiry Group, NRC Records; Rogovin Report, Vol. 1, p. 79, Vol. 2, Pt. 3, pp. 1133–35. The Rogovin Report printed the NRC's "Bubble Chronology," which was compiled after the accident and which remains the best source for reviewing the NRC's investigation of the hydrogen bubble.

4. Deposition of Roger J. Mattson, August 6, 1979, pp. 180–86, Box 20, Deposition of Robert L. Tedesco, July 27, 1979, pp. 52–56, Box 29 (Depositions,

1979), Papers of the President's Commission on the Accident at Three Mile Island, Record Group 220 (Records of Temporary Committees, Commissions, and Boards), National Archives, College Park, Maryland (hereafter referred to as Kemeny Commission Records); Rogovin Report, Vol. 2, Pt. 3, pp. 964–65, 1135–40; Kemeny Commission, *Staff Reports on Emergency Preparedness, Emergency Response* (Washington, D.C.: Government Printing Office, 1979), pp. 162–65.

5. Transcript of Commission Meeting, March 31, 1979, Continuation at 12:00 noon, pp. 28–50, Deposition of Darrell G. Eisenhut, October 11, 1979, pp. 124–25, Mattson Deposition, pp. 220–27, NRC Special Inquiry Group, NRC Records.

6. Transcript of Commission Meeting, March 31, 1979, Continuation at 12:00 noon, pp. 11–12, 52–58, Deposition of Peter A. Bradford, October 19, 1979, pp. 145–46, NRC Special Inquiry Group, NRC Records; *New York Times,* March 31, 1979; Kemeny Commission, *Staff Reports on Emergency Preparedness, Emergency Response,* pp. 161–64.

7. Kemeny Commission, *The Need for Change,* p. 123, and *Staff Reports on Emergency Preparedness, Emergency Response,* pp. 147, 169–70.

8. UPI Wire Story, 3:39 P.M., March 31, 1979, Box 2 (Governor Thornburgh's Set of Wire Stories), Papers of Richard L. Thornburgh, Archives Service Center, University of Pittsburgh, Pittsburgh, Pennsylvania; Anne D. Trunk and Edward V. Trunk, "Three Mile Island: A Resident's Perspective," in *The Three Mile Island Accident: Lessons and Implications,* ed. Thomas H. Moss and David L. Sills (New York: New York Academy of Sciences, 1981), pp. 175–85; *Washington Star,* April 1, 1979.

9. Schedule for Gov. & Lt. Gov.—Trip to Hershey Arena, March 31, 1979, Box 1 (Chron File, Saturday 3–31–79), Thornburgh Papers; *Harrisburg Patriot-News,* April 1, 1979; *Washington Star,* April 1, 1979; *Lancaster Intelligencer Journal,* March 24, 1989; Kemeny Commission, *Staff Reports on Emergency Preparedness, Emergency Response,* p. 157.

10. William W. Scranton III to the File, March 31, 1979, Box 1 (Chron File, Saturday, 3–31–79), Richard L. Thornburgh, handwritten notes of conversation with Harold Denton, March 31, 1979, Box 1 (Chronology—Work File and Notes by Governor), Thornburgh Papers; Transcript of Commission Meeting, March 31, 1979, Continuation at 12:00 noon, pp. 12–17, Transcripts of TMI Tapes, Day 4, Channel 6/24, pp. 1164–79, NRC Records.

11. Transcripts of TMI Tapes, Day 4, Channel 6/24, pp. 1199–1216, NRC Records; *Washington Star,* April 1, 1979; *New York Times,* April 1, 1979.

12. Metropolitan Edison News Briefing, March 31, 1979, Transcripts of TMI Tapes, Day 4, Channel 6/24, pp. 1097, 1244–50, NRC Records; Rogovin Report, Vol. 2, Pt. 2, pp. 336–38, Vol. 2, Pt. 3, p. 846.

13. Metropolitan Edison News Briefing, March 31, 1979, Transcripts of TMI Tapes, Day 4, Channel 6/24, pp. 1018–55, 1211–28, Deposition of Robert C. Arnold, September 24, 1979, p. 67, NRC Inquiry Group, NRC Records; Kemeny Commission, *Staff Reports of the Technical Assessment Task Force* (Washington, D.C.: Government Printing Office, 1979), 2:21–22; Rogovin Report, Vol. 2, Pt. 2, p. 336, Vol. 2, Pt. 3, pp. 964, 1140–41.

14. Handwritten notes of "Telephone Conversations with Dr. Denton,"

March 31, 1979, Jack Watson to Jimmy Carter, "Status Report—Three Mile Nuclear Facility Report #2," March 31, 1979, Staff Offices—Office of Staff Secretary Handwriting File, Box 125, Papers of Jimmy Carter, Jimmy Carter Library, Atlanta, Georgia; Transcripts of TMI Tapes, Day 4, Channel 6/24, pp. 1030–38, "Preliminary Notification of Event or Unusual Occurrence" (PNO-79–67F), March 31, 1979, NRC Records; Rogovin Report, Vol. 2, Pt. 3, p. 964; Philip L. Cantelon and Robert C. Williams, *Crisis Contained: The Department of Energy at Three Mile Island* (Carbondale: Southern Illinois University Press, 1982), pp. 78–79; Eugene Eidenberg, interview by author, San Francisco, California, September 17, 2002.

15. William E. Odom to Zbigniew Brzezinski, March 31, 1979, Joseph A. Califano Jr. to Jack Watson, March 31, 1979, White House Central File, Subject File—Disasters, Box DI-1, Carter Papers.

16. Summary of White House Meeting on Three Mile Island Nuclear Accident, March 31, 1979, White House Central File, Subject File—Disasters, Box DI-1, Watson to Carter, "Status Report—Three Mile Nuclear Facility Report #2," Carter Papers; Deposition of Jessica Tuchman Mathews, August 23, 1979, pp. 93–97, Box 20 (Depositions, 1979), Kemeny Commission Records; Jessica T. Mathews, interview by author, Washington, D.C., June 7, 2001.

17. Jack Watson to Jimmy Carter, March 31, 1979, "Status Report—Three Mile Nuclear Facility Report #3," Staff Offices—Office of Staff Secretary Handwriting File, Box 125, Carter Papers; Deposition of Jack Watson, September 6, 1979, pp. 56–59, Box 31 (Depositions, 1979), Kemeny Commission Records; Jack Watson, interview by author, Philomont, Virginia, May 17, 2001, and Eidenberg, interview by author.

18. Summary of White House Meeting on Three Mile Island Nuclear Accident, Watson to Carter, "Status Report—Three Mile Nuclear Facility Report #3," Carter Papers; Interview of Peter A. Bradford, September 10, 1979, p. 201, Box 4 (Depositions, 1979), Kemeny Commission Records.

19. Deposition of Joseph Mallam Hendrie, September 7, 1979, pp. 210–11, Box 15 (Depositions, 1979), Kemeny Commission Records; Deposition of Frank L. Ingram, September 28, 1979, pp. 15–17, 28, NRC Special Inquiry Group, NRC Records; Joseph M. Hendrie, interview by author, Upton, New York, May 30, 2001; Kemeny Commission, *Staff Reports on Emergency Preparedness, Emergency Response*, p. 164.

20. Transcript of Press Conference of Chairman Joseph M. Hendrie, March 31, 1979, Box 1 (Chron File, Saturday 3-31-79), Thornburgh Papers; Transcript of Commission Meeting, March 31, 1979, Continuation at 12:00 noon, p. 64, NRC Records; Hendrie Deposition, pp. 211–16, Kemeny Commission Records; Hendrie, interview by author.

21. Transcript of Commission Meeting, March 31, 1979, Continuation at 12:00 noon, pp. 61–64, Beginning at 4:25 P.M., pp. 1–11, NRC Records; "Chronology—Three Mile Island, Confidential Draft," n.d., Box 1 (Chronology—Work File and Notes by Governor), Thornburgh Papers; Watson Deposition, p. 87, Kemeny Commission Records.

22. Deposition of Edson G. Case, October 18, 1979, pp. 140–47, Ingram Deposition, p. 18, NRC Special Inquiry Group, Transcript of Commission Meet-

ing, March 31, 1979, Continuation at 12:00 noon, p. 40, NRC Records; Kemeny Commission, *Staff Report of the Public's Right to Information Task Force* (Washington, D.C.: Government Printing Office, 1979), pp. 153–57.

23. Pennsylvania News Updates, March 31, 1979, Box 1263 (TMI-AP Radio Bulletin, Buildup of Hydrogen), Thornburgh Papers; Deposition of Joseph J. Fouchard, September 27, 1979, p. 52, NRC Special Inquiry Group, Transcripts of TMI Tapes, Day 4, Channel 6/24, p. 1406, Channel 7/25, p. 1641, NRC Records; Rogovin Report, Vol. 2, Pt. 2, pp. 624–28, Vol. 2, Pt. 3, p. 1067; Richard L. Thornburgh, interview by author, Washington, D.C., July 10, 2001.

24. *Philadelphia Inquirer,* March 31, 1979; *New York News,* April 1, 1979; *Atlanta Journal and Constitution,* April 1, 1979; Stanley M. Nealey, Barbara D. Melber, and William L. Rankin, *Public Opinion and Nuclear Energy* (Lexington, Mass.: D.C. Heath and Company, 1983), p. 83; Trunk and Trunk, "Three Mile Island: A Resident's Perspective," p. 182.

25. Deposition of Victor Stello Jr., October 10, 1979, p. 193, Fouchard Deposition, pp. 25, 50, Case Deposition, pp. 147–55, NRC Special Inquiry Group, Transcripts of TMI Tapes, Day 4, Channel 7/25, pp. 1635–38, NRC Records; Kemeny Commission, *Staff Report of the Public's Right to Information Task Force,* pp. 157–59; Merrill A. Taylor, telephone interview by author, November 8, 2002.

26. Watson to Carter, "Status Report—Three Mile Nuclear Facility Report #3," Carter Papers; Deposition of Eugene Eidenberg, August 23, 1979, pp. 83–92, Box 9, Mathews Deposition, pp. 113–17, Watson Deposition, pp. 87–96, Kemeny Commission Records.

27. Watson to Carter, "Status Report—Three Mile Nuclear Facility Report #3," Carter Papers; Governor's Press Office Press Release, March 31, 1979, Box 1 (Chron File, Saturday 3–31–79), "Chronology—Three Mile Island," Thornburgh Papers; TMI Tapes, Day 4, Channel 3/21, pp. 617–21, NRC Records; Kemeny Commission, *Staff Reports on Emergency Preparedness, Emergency Response,* p. 168; Thornburgh, interview by author.

28. "Chronology—Three Mile Island," Thornburgh Papers; Fouchard Deposition, p. 27, Special Inquiry Group, NRC Records; Robert Hager, "A Reporter Recalls Three Mile Island," MSNBC Website, www.msnbc.com/news/253397, accessed on February 2, 2001; Peter M. Sandman and Mary Paden, "At Three Mile Island," *Columbia Journalism Review* 18 (July–August 1979): 43–58; Mike Gray and Ira Rosen, *The Warning: Accident at Three Mile Island* (New York: W. W. Norton, 1982), pp. 242–44.

29. "Chronology—Three Mile Island," Transcript of Press Conference of Governor Dick Thornburgh, Lt. Gov. William Scranton, 3d, Mr. Harold Denton, March 31, 1979, Box 1 (Chron File, Saturday 3–31–79), Thornburgh Papers; Mark S. Knouse to James M. Seif, April 11, 1979, Box 1 (Chronology of Events), Miscellaneous Series, Papers of the Pennsylvania Commission on Three Mile Island, Record Group 25 (Records of Special Commissions), Pennsylvania State Archives, Harrisburg, Pennsylvania; *Reading (Pa.) Eagle,* April 1, 1979; Sandman and Paden, "At Three Mile Island," p. 46.

30. *Chicago Sun-Times,* April 1, 1979; *Los Angeles Times,* April 1, 1979; *New York Times,* April 2, 1979; *Philadelphia Inquirer,* April 2, 1979; *Harrisburg Patriot,* April 4, April 5, April 16, 1979; *Rocky Mount Telegram,* July 22, 1979;

Richard K. Rein, "The Man in the Hot Seat at Three Mile Island Was a Cool Troubleshooter Named Denton," *People* (April 23, 1979): 35; Mike Vargo, "Innocence Lost," *Pennsylvania Illustrated* 4 (August 1979): 23–33 ff; Paul B. Beers, *Profiles from the Susquehanna Valley* (Harrisburg: Stackpole Books, 1973), pp. 13–16; Joseph J. Fouchard, interview by author, Rockville, Maryland, March 8, 2000; Lucinda Denton, interview by author, Knoxville, Tennessee, September 9, 2001.

31. Stuart Eizenstat, Memorandum to President Carter on board Air Force One, March 31, 1979, White House Central File, Subject File—Trips, Box TR-26 (TR 58, Middletown, Pennsylvania), Jody Powell, handwritten notes on Eizenstat memorandum, March 31, 1979, Staff Offices—Office of Staff Secretary Handwriting File, Box 125, Watson to Carter, "Status Report—Three Mile Nuclear Facility Report #3," Carter Papers; "Chronology—Three Mile Island," Transcript of Thornburgh Press Conference, March 31, 1979, Thornburgh Papers; *Baltimore Sun*, April 1, 1979; *Atlanta Journal and Constitution*, April 1, 1979; Rogovin Report, Vol. 2, Pt. 3, p. 1181.

32. Deposition of Roger Joseph Mattson, September 24, 1979, pp. 239–41, NRC Special Inquiry Group, Transcripts of TMI Tapes, Day 4, Channel 4/22, p. 863, Channel 7/25, pp. 629–34; Interview of Victor Gilinsky, September 8, 1979, pp. 121–23, Box 13 (Depositions, 1979), Kemeny Commission Records; U.S. Congress, Senate, Committee on Environment and Public Works, Subcommittee on Nuclear Regulation, *Hearings on Three Mile Island Nuclear Powerplant Accident*, 96th Cong., 1st sess., 1979, pp. 245–48.

33. Gilinsky interview, pp. 123–24, Kemeny Commission Records; Senate Subcommittee on Nuclear Regulation, *Hearings on Three Mile Island*, pp. 181–87.

34. "Chronology—Three Mile Island," Thornburgh Papers.

CHAPTER 8. SUNDAY, APRIL 1

1. Jack Watson and Jessica Mathews to Jimmy Carter, April 1, 1979, White House Central File, Subject File—Disasters, Box DI-1, Papers of Jimmy Carter, Jimmy Carter Library, Atlanta, Georgia; *New York Times*, April 1, 1979; *Philadelphia Inquirer*, April 1, 1979; *Washington Star*, April 3, 1979.

2. Nuclear Regulatory Commission (NRC) Special Inquiry Group, *Three Mile Island: A Report to the Commissioners and to the Public* (Washington, D.C.: Government Printing Office, 1980), Vol. 2, Part 2, p. 624 (hereafter referred to as the Rogovin Report); *Harrisburg Sunday Patriot-News*, April 1, 1979; *Reading (Pa.) Eagle*, April 1, 1979; *New York Times*, April 3, 1979.

3. *Trailer City News*, April 1, April 2, 1979, Central Files, Box 95 (Trailer City News), Papers of the President's Commission on the Accident at Three Mile Island, Record Group 220 (Records of Temporary Committees, Commissions, and Boards), National Archives, College Park, Maryland (hereafter referred to as the Kemeny Commission Records); Deposition of Victor Stello Jr., October 10, 1979, pp. 133–34, NRC Special Inquiry Group, NRC Records, NRC Public Document Room, Rockville, Maryland; General Public Utilities Corporation, "The TMI-2 Story," booklet, May 25, 1979, no box, Papers of Richard L. Thorn-

burgh, Archives Service Center, University of Pittsburgh, Pittsburgh, Pennsylvania; *Philadelphia Inquirer,* April 6, 1979; Rogovin Report, Vol. 2, Part 3, pp. 882, 1117; Roger J. Mattson, interview by author, Golden, Colorado, September 26, 2001.

4. Deposition of Harold R. Denton, August 2, 1979, p. 104, Box 6 (Depositions, 1979), Kemeny Commission Records; Transcripts of TMI Tapes, Day 4, Channel 7/25, pp. 1638–40, NRC Records; Rogovin Report, Vol. 2, Part 3, pp. 1142–45; *Rocky Mount Telegram,* July 22, 1979; Merrill A. Taylor, telephone interview by author, November 8, 2002.

5. Deposition of Joseph J. Fouchard, September 27, 1979, pp. 29–30, NRC Special Inquiry Group, Personal Qualifications of Victor Stello Jr., insert between pp. 474 and 475, Docket No. RM 50–1, *Hearings in the Matter of Acceptance Criteria for Emergency Core Cooling Systems for Light Water Cooled Nuclear Power Reactors,* NRC Records; *Harrisburg Evening News,* April 2, 1979; *Harrisburg Sunday Patriot-News,* April 8, 1979; *Baltimore Sun,* March 27, 1989; Comments of Victor Stello Jr. on Public Broadcasting Service television program, "Meltdown at Three Mile Island" (Steward-Gazit Productions, 1999); Joseph J. Fouchard, interview by author, Rockville, Maryland, March 8, 2000; Richard H. Vollmer, interview by author, Arnold, Maryland, January 3, 2002; Esther Stello, telephone interview by author, May 15, 2002.

6. Transcripts of TMI Tapes, Day 5, Channel 6/24, p. 1069, Deposition of Roger J. Mattson, September 24, 1979, p. 254, October 17, 1979, p. 37, NRC Special Inquiry Group, NRC Records; Deposition of Joseph Mallam Hendrie, September 7, 1979, p. 198, Box 15, Deposition of Robert L. Tedesco, July 27, 1979, p. 55, Box 29, Deposition of Robert Jay Budnitz, August 1, 1979, pp. 21–34, Box 4 (Depositions, 1979), Kemeny Commission Records; Thomas E. Murley, interview by author, Rockville, Maryland, May 31, 2002; Robert J. Budnitz, interview by author, Berkeley, California, September 18, 2002.

7. Transcripts of TMI Tapes, Day 5, Channel 6/24, pp. 1087–92, Mattson Deposition, September 24, 1979, pp. 254–55, NRC Special Inquiry Group, NRC Records.

8. Transcripts of TMI Tapes, Day 5, Channel 6/24, pp. 1069–70, 1099, Mattson Deposition, September 24, 1979, pp. 226–27, 255–58, NRC Special Inquiry Group, NRC Records; Deposition of Roger J. Mattson, August 6, 1979, p. 194, Box 20 (Depositions, 1979), Kemeny Commission Records; Rogovin Report, Vol. 2, Part 3, pp. 1145–46.

9. Deposition of Jessica Tuchman Mathews, August 23, 1979, pp. 117–20, Box 20 (Depositions, 1979), Kemeny Commission Records; "Daily Diary of President Jimmy Carter," April 1, 1979, Carter Papers.

10. Watson and Mathews to Carter, April 1, 1979 (note 1 above), "Daily Diary of President Jimmy Carter," April 1, 1979, Carter Papers.

11. Mattson Deposition, October 17, 1979, p. 74, NRC Special Inquiry Group, NRC Records; Hendrie Deposition, p. 200, Kemeny Commission Records.

12. Stello Deposition, pp. 199–200, Mattson Deposition, September 24, 1979, pp. 261–62, NRC Special Inquiry Group, NRC Records; Mattson Deposition, p. 193, Kemeny Commission Records; Rogovin Report, Vol. 2, Part

3, pp. 1146–47; Kemeny Commission, *Staff Reports on Emergency Prepared-ness, Emergency Response* (Washington, D.C.: Government Printing Office, 1979), p. 175; Harold R. Denton, comments on PBS program "Meltdown at Three Mile Island" (note 5 above); Harold R. Denton, interview by author, Knoxville, Tennessee, September 9, 2001; Mattson, interview by author.

The disagreement between Mattson and Stello at the airport has been the sub-ject of drastic misconstruction in some later accounts of the Three Mile Island accident. Mike Gray and Ira Rosen (*The Warning: Accident at Three Mile Island* [New York: W. W. Norton, 1982]) contended that Mattson and Stello cursed one another in a shouting match over whether or not the bubble would explode. They wrote that, as the president's helicopter approached, Denton's "two top staff ex-perts are shouting about whether or not the place is going to blow up" (p. 253). Gray, who was coauthor of the screenplay for *The China Syndrome,* later em-bellished this version of events in interviews conducted for television programs on Three Mile Island. In the Public Broadcasting System's presentation "Melt-down at Three Mile Island" (1999), he quoted Mattson as supposedly telling Stello at the airport that the "bubble is ready to explode." Gray went even fur-ther in a program titled "Minutes to Meltdown" on NBC's *Dateline,* broadcast on August 14, 2001. He claimed that Mattson "was concerned that literally there could be an explosion at any moment." The interviewer on the show, Dennis Murphy, highlighted the alleged drama of the moment by suggesting that "you have virtually a fist fight going on [between Mattson and Stello] over whether they were going to die in the next 3–4 minutes." Another author, Daniel Mar-tin, advanced a similar story on the PBS program and in a book, *Three Mile Is-land: Prologue or Epilogue?* (Cambridge, Massachusetts: Ballinger Publishing, 1980). He asserted that the experts with whom Mattson and his colleagues con-sulted had concluded on Saturday night that the hydrogen bubble "could ex-plode and rip the entire nuclear system apart at any moment." On Sunday, he added, the president, the first lady, the governor, and others "were all going to walk through a growing time bomb that was destined to go off with the slight-est disturbance" (p. 175).

Even a cursory examination of the abundant available sources makes clear that those accounts are fallacious. They ignore the important distinction between flammable and explosive conditions in the reactor. Neither was desirable, but an explosion seemed more likely to lead to a breach of containment in a worst-case sequence of events. It required a much higher concentration of oxygen in the bub-ble than experts thought might be present on Sunday morning. Mattson did not believe that the bubble was explosive on Saturday or Sunday morning, and nei-ther did any of the experts whom NRC staff members in Bethesda consulted. They were concerned that the bubble was potentially flammable, and that in the worst case, combustion could cause the pressure vessel to rupture. But they did not view the danger as immediate, especially in the absence of any conceivable ignition source. They certainly did not think the bubble could explode at any moment on Sunday and threaten the lives of President Carter or the residents of central Pennsylvania. The problem that worried the NRC staff in Bethesda was not that the plant would suddenly go up in flames, but that the loss of the pressure vessel could lead to the China syndrome. Even in the worst case, this process would take time and would not occur without warning.

The accounts of the argument between Mattson and Stello have been similarly exaggerated. Denton, who was on the scene, did not witness a bitter, cursing showdown between his two colleagues (Denton, interview by author). Mattson agreed that he and Stello participated in a passionate and vociferous discussion but vehemently denied that they cursed one another (Mattson, interview by author). Stello made no mention of such a spectacle before he died in 1999. He and Mattson most assuredly did not argue over whether they might die at any moment from an explosion in the pressure vessel.

13. Stello Deposition, p. 199, Mattson Deposition, September 24, 1979, p. 261, NRC Special Inquiry Group, NRC Records; Hendrie Deposition, p. 200, Kemeny Commission Records; Joseph J. Fouchard, interview by author, Rockville, Maryland, March 8, 2000; Jack H. Watson, interview by author, Philomont, Virginia, May 17, 2001; Jessica Tuchman Mathews, interview by author, Washington, D.C., June 7, 2001; Anne M. Edwards, telephone interview by author, November 14, 2001.

14. Deposition of Harold Denton, October 23, 1979, pp. 85–87, Mattson Depositions, September 24, 1979, pp. 262–64, October 17, 1979, pp. 48–52, NRC Special Inquiry Group, NRC Records; "Daily Diary of President Jimmy Carter," April 1, 1979, Carter Papers; Denton comments on PBS program "Meltdown at Three Mile Island"; *Lancaster New Era,* March 25, 1999; Robert S. Walker, interview by author, East Petersburg, Pennsylvania, June 3, 2002; Denton, interview by author.

15. "Statement of the President to the Press," Middletown, Pennsylvania, April 1, 1979, Staff Offices—Office of Staff Secretary Handwriting File, Box 125, Carter Papers; "Statement by Gov. Dick Thornburgh," April 1, 1979, Box 1 (Chron File, Sunday 4-1-79), Thornburgh Papers; George M. Miller, Account of Emergency at Three Mile Island Nuclear Generating Station, n.d., NRC Records; *Congressional Record,* 96th Cong., 1st sess., 1979, p. 6880; *New York Times,* April 2, 1979; Kemeny Commission, *Staff Reports on Emergency Preparedness, Emergency Response,* p. 176.

16. Mattson Depositions, September 24, 1979, p. 265, October 17, 1979, pp. 66–67, Stello Deposition, 201–3, NRC Special Inquiry Group, NRC Records; Transcript of Third Meeting of the President's Commission on the Accident at Three Mile Island, June 1, 1979, pp. 95–96, Box 6 (Hearings, 1979), Deposition of Victor Stello Jr., July 24, 1979, pp. 109–11, Box 28, Hendrie Deposition, pp. 202–3 (Depositions, 1979), Kemeny Commission Records; Rogovin Report, Vol. 2, Part 3, pp. 1148–50.

17. Transcript of Commission Meeting, April 1, 1979, pp. 1–99, NRC Press Release, November 13, 1979, NRC Records; Rogovin Report, Vol. 2, Part 3, p. 1146; Budnitz, interview by author.

18. Transcript of Commission Meeting, April 1, 1979, pp. 100–116, NRC Records; Budnitz Deposition, pp. 29–33, Kemeny Commission Records; Rogovin Report, Vol. 2, Part 3, pp. 1145, 1147.

19. Transcript of Commission Meeting, April 1, 1979, pp. 131–44, NRC Records; Rogovin Report, Vol. 2, Part 3, p. 1150; Kemeny Commission, *Staff*

Reports on Emergency Preparedness, Emergency Response, p. 179; Peter A. Bradford, interview by author, New York, May 21, 2002.

20. Transcripts of TMI Tapes, Day 5, Channel 6/24, pp. 1368–78, Mattson Deposition, September 24, 1979, p. 266, NRC Special Inquiry Group, NRC Records; Rogovin Report, Vol. 2, Part 3, pp. 1148–50.

21. Transcript of Commission Meeting, April 1, 1979, p. 112, Mattson Depositions, September 24, 1979, pp. 230–34, October 17, 1979, pp. 35–36, 63–67, NRC Special Inquiry Group, NRC Records; Transcript of Third Meeting of the President's Commission on the Accident at Three Mile Island, pp. 96–97, Denton Deposition, p. 114, Kemeny Commission Records; Rogovin Report, Vol. 2, Part 3, pp. 1137–52; Kemeny Commission, *Staff Reports on Emergency Preparedness, Emergency Response,* p. 180; Joseph M. Hendrie, interview by author, Upton, New York, May 30, 2001; Murley, interview by author.

22. Summary of interview with Dr. Edwin Zebroski, conducted September 27, 1979, enclosure in R. C. DeYoung to Zebroski, October 29, 1979, NRC Records; Rogovin Report, Vol. 2, Part 3, pp. 882–83, 1151; Daniel F. Ford, *Three Mile Island: Thirty Minutes to Meltdown* (New York: Penguin Books, 1982), p. 248; Robert A. Szalay, "The Reaction of the Nuclear Industry to the Three Mile Island Accident," in *The Three Mile Island Accident: Lessons and Implications,* ed. Thomas H. Moss and David L. Sills (New York: New York Academy of Sciences, 1981), p. 223.

23. "Chronology—Three Mile Island, Confidential Draft," n.d., Box 1 (Chronology—Work File and Notes by Governor), Mark Knouse to James M. Seif, April 11, 1979, Box 1 (Chron File, Sunday 4–1–79), Thornburgh Papers.

24. Transcripts of TMI Tapes, Day 5, Channel 2/20, pp. 220–23, Channel 10/28, pp. 2158–62, NRC Records; Rogovin Report, Vol. 2, Part 2, pp. 337–39; Kemeny Commission, *The Need for Change: The Legacy of TMI* (Washington, D.C.: Government Printing Office, 1979), p. 135; Michael J. Ross, telephone interview by author, June 11, 2002.

CHAPTER 9. THE IMMEDIATE AFTERMATH OF THE ACCIDENT

1. Jack Watson to Jimmy Carter, April 2, 1979, "Status Report—Three Mile Nuclear Facility Report #4," Staff Offices—Office of Staff Secretary Handwriting File, Box 125, Papers of Jimmy Carter, Jimmy Carter Library, Atlanta, Georgia.

2. Transcript of Press Conference on Three Mile Island, April 2, 1979, Transcript of Commission Meeting, April 2, 1979, p. 3, Nuclear Regulatory Commission (NRC) Records, NRC Public Document Room, Rockville, Maryland; "Chronology—Three Mile Island, Confidential Draft," n.d., Box 1 (Work File and Notes by Governor), Papers of Richard L. Thornburgh, Archives Service Center, University of Pittsburgh, Pittsburgh, Pennsylvania; President's Commission on the Accident at Three Mile Island (hereafter referred to as the Kemeny Commission), *Staff Report of the Public's Right to Information Task Force* (Washington, D.C.: Government Printing Office, 1979), p. 162; Roger J. Mattson, interview by author, Golden, Colorado, September 26, 2001.

3. Transcript of Commission Meeting, April 2, 1979, pp. 3–15, NRC Records; U.S. Congress, Senate, Committee on Environment and Public Works, Subcommittee on Nuclear Regulation, *Hearings on Three Mile Island Nuclear Powerplant Accident,* 96th Cong., 1st sess., 1979, pp. 188–95; Anthony V. Nero Jr., *A Guidebook to Nuclear Reactors* (Berkeley: University of California Press, 1979), p. 86.

4. Jessica Tuchman Mathews, Situation Report on Three Mile Island, April 2, 1979, White House Central File, Subject File—Disasters, Box D1, Watson to Carter, "Three Mile Nuclear Facility Report #4," Carter Papers.

5. Mark Knouse to James M. Seif, April 11, 1979, Governor's Press Office Press Release, April 2, 1979, "Technical Update on Current Situation at Three Mile Island," April 2, 1979, Box 1 (Chron File, Monday 4-2-79), "Chronology—Three Mile Island," Thornburgh Papers; Jimmy Carter, handwritten notes of "telephone conversation with harold denton (3 mile island)," 3:45 P.M., April 2, 1979, Staff Offices, Office of Staff Secretary—Handwriting File, Box 125, Carter Papers; *New York Times,* April 3, 1979; *Washington Post,* April 3, 1979; *Washington Star,* April 3, 1979.

6. "Offsite Population Dose and Risk Assessment from Accident at Three Mile Island Nuclear Station," c. April 2, 1979, Box 86, File 86.5 (TMI—Radiation and Health Effects), Papers of Richard T. Kennedy, Hoover Institution on War, Revolution, and Peace Archives, Stanford University, Palo Alto, California; "Preliminary Notification of Event or Unusual Occurrence" (PNO-79–67H), April 2, 1979, NRC Records; "Technical Update on Current Situation," Thornburgh Papers; U.S. Congress, Senate, Committee on Labor and Human Resources, Subcommittee on Health and Scientific Research, *Hearings on the Three Mile Island Nuclear Accident,* 1979, 96th Cong., 1st sess., 1979, p. 12.

7. "Statement by Governor of Pennsylvania," April 3, 1979, PNO-79–67H, NRC Records; "Chronology—Three Mile Island," Thornburgh Papers; *Washington Star,* April 3, 1979; *Harrisburg Patriot,* April 3, 1979.

8. Transcript of *Tuesday Morning,* April 3, 1979, Media Monitor, NRC Records.

9. Transcript of Commission Meeting, April 3, 1979, pp. 3–4, 9–10, Transcripts of Press Conferences on Three Mile Island, April 3, April 4, April 13, April 24, 1979, NRC Records; *The Cleanup of Three Mile Island Unit 2: A Technical History, 1979 to 1990 (EPRI NP-6931)* (Palo Alto, Calif.: Electric Power Research Institute, 1990), pp. 3–4.

10. "Transcription of Press Conference—Three Mile Island Incident," Governor Dick Thornburgh, April 9, 1979, NRC Records; Internal Revenue Service News Release, April 6, 1979, Box 24B (Testimony before Subcommittee on Nuclear Regulation), Papers of Robert S. Walker, Millersville University, Millersville, Pennsylvania; S. Beth Wolf, telephone interview by author, July 17, 2002; Kemeny Commission, *Staff Reports on Emergency Preparedness, Emergency Response* (Washington, D.C.: Government Printing Office, 1979), pp. 190–92; *Washington Post,* April 10, 1979.

11. Transcripts of Press Conferences on Three Mile Island, April 17, April 27, 1979, NRC Records.

12. "A Nuclear Nightmare," *Time* (April 9, 1979): 8; *Baltimore Sun,* April 4, 1979; *Harrisburg Patriot,* April 23, 1979; *New York Times,* May 25, 1979.

13. *Harrisburg Patriot,* April 9, 1979; *Philadelphia Inquirer,* April 9, 1979; *Washington Star,* April 9, 1979; *Washington Post,* May 7, 1979; Luther J. Carter, "The 'Movement' Moves on to Antinuclear Protest," *Science* 204 (May 18, 1979): 715.

14. *Washington Star,* April 5, 1979; *Washington Post,* April 6, 1979; *Harrisburg Patriot,* April 6, 1979; Nuclear Regulatory Commission Special Inquiry Group, *Three Mile Island: A Report to the Commissioners and to the Public* (Washington, D.C.: Government Printing Office, 1980), Vol. 2, Pt. 1, pp. 203–4 (hereafter referred to as the Rogovin Report); Senate Subcommittee on Nuclear Regulation, *Hearings on Three Mile Island,* pp. 348–55; Senate Subcommittee on Health and Scientific Research, *Hearings on the Three Mile Island Nuclear Accident, 1979,* pp. 1–29.

15. Transcript of Commission Meeting, March 30, 1979, pp. 144, 214, NRC Records; Memorandum for the Record, April 20, 1979, Box 390 (TMI—Udall Notebook), Papers of Morris K. Udall, University of Arizona, Tucson; *Harrisburg Patriot,* April 11, 1979.

16. Patrick J. Leahy to John G. Kemeny, April 13, 1979, Box 3 (Kemeny, 1979), Papers of the President's Commission on the Accident at Three Mile Island, Record Group 220 (Records of Temporary Committees, Commissions, and Boards), National Archives, College Park, Maryland (hereafter referred to as the Kemeny Commission Records); *Washington Post,* April 13, April 14, April 16, 1979; *New York Times,* April 13, 1979; *Washington Star,* April 13, April 14, 1979; *Harrisburg Patriot,* April 16, 1979; *Charlotte News,* April 17, 1979; Peter M. Sandman and Mary Paden, "At Three Mile Island," *Columbia Journalism Review* 18 (July–August 1979): 43–58.

17. National Federation of the Blind, "Resolution—Demand Apology from Joseph M. Hendrie," April 29, 1979, Hendrie to James P. Swed, April 26, 1979, "Statement by NRC Chairman Joseph M. Hendrie," May 10, 1979, NRC Records.

18. Jerry W. Friedheim to Joseph M. Hendrie, April 13, 1979, Hendrie to Friedheim, April 30, 1979, Hendrie to Hamilton Fish, September 15, 1980, NRC Records; *Washington Post,* April 13, 1979; *New York Times,* April 13, 1979; *Des Moines Register,* April 17, 1979.

19. Anthony Z. Roisman to Victor Gilinsky, May 9, 1979, Personal NRC File, Box 10 (Roisman, Anthony), Papers of Victor Gilinsky, Hoover Institution Archives; U.S. Congress, House, Committee on Government Operations, *Hearings on Emergency Planning around U.S. Nuclear Powerplants: Nuclear Regulatory Commission Oversight,* 96th Cong., 1st sess., 1979, p. 21; *Washington Post,* April 14, 1979; *Pittsburgh Post-Gazette,* April 19, 1979; *Philadelphia Bulletin,* April 22, 1979.

20. Joseph A. Califano to Jack Watson, March 31, 1979, White House Central File, Subject File—Disasters, Box DI-1, Carter Papers; Gene Eidenberg to Watson, April 3, 1979, attachment to Eidenberg Deposition, Box 9 (Depositions, 1979), Kemeny Commission Records; Gordon K. MacLeod, "The Decision to Withhold Distribution of Potassium Iodide during the Three Mile Island Event: Internal Working Document," n.d., pp. 2–4, Box 11 (U.S. Nuclear Regulatory Commission: 3-Mile-Island), Papers of Herbert Parker, University of Washing-

ton, Seattle; Kemeny Commission, *Staff Reports on Emergency Preparedness, Emergency Response,* pp. 132–33, 148–49.

21. Neil Wald to Gordon K. MacLeod, April 3, 1979, MacLeod to Dick Thornburgh, April 4, 1979, Box 1 (Chron File, Tuesday 4–3–79), "Chronology— Three Mile Island," Thornburgh Papers; MacLeod, "Decision to Withhold Distribution of Potassium Iodide," pp. 16–17, Parker Papers; Kemeny Commission, *Staff Reports on Emergency Preparedness, Emergency Response,* pp. 187–88.

22. Jay C. Waldman to the File, April 6, 1979, Paul Critchlow to Richard Thornburgh, n.d., Box 1264 (TMI—April 1979), Thornburgh Papers; MacLeod, "Decision to Withhold Distribution of Potassium Iodide," pp. 17–22, Parker Papers; *Washington Star,* April 6, 1979; *Washington Post,* April 6, April 16, 1979; Kemeny Commission, *Staff Reports on Emergency Preparedness, Emergency Response,* pp. 188–90.

23. *Lancaster Intelligencer Journal,* April 11, 1979; Rogovin Report, Vol. 2, Pt. 2, pp. 619–30.

24. *Washington Post,* April 5, 1979; *Baltimore Sun,* April 5, 1979; *Reading (Pa.) Times,* April 6, 1979; *Washington Star,* April 8, 1979; *Wall Street Journal,* April 9, 1979; U.S. Congress, Senate, Committee on Governmental Affairs, Subcommittee on Energy, Nuclear Proliferation and Federal Services, *Hearings on Radiation Protection,* 96th Cong., 1st sess., 1979, pp. 112–17, 134–37; Senate Subcommittee on Health and Scientific Research, *Hearings on the Three Mile Island Nuclear Accident, 1979,* pp. 31–117.

25. NRC Press Release, April 20, 1979, U.S. Nuclear Regulatory Commission and U.S. Environmental Protection Agency, *Investigation of Reported Plant and Animal Effects in the Three Mile Island Area (NUREG-0738),* October 1980, NRC Records; Press Release to All State News Media, May 31, 1979, Box 102A (TMI Press Releases and PR Materials), Walker Papers; *Washington Post,* April 11, 1979; *Harrisburg Patriot,* May 23, 1979.

26. U.S. Congress, House, Committee on Science and Technology, Subcommittee on Natural Resources and Environment, *Hearings on Three Mile Island Nuclear Plant Accident,* 96th Cong., 1st sess., 1979, pp. 123–226; Frank J. Congel, interview by author, Rockville, Maryland, May 8, 2003.

27. *Washington Star,* April 8, 1979; *New York Times,* April 12, April 25, 1979; U.S. Congress, House, Committee on Science and Technology, Subcommittee on Energy Research and Production, *Hearings on Nuclear Powerplant Safety Systems,* 96th Cong., 1st sess., 1979, pp. 30–46, 89–92, 453–81; House Subcommittee on Natural Resources and Environment, *Hearings on Three Mile Island Nuclear Plant Accident,* pp. 14–23.

28. *Philadelphia Inquirer,* April 5, 1979; *Washington Star,* April 5, 1979; *Washington Post,* April 6, April 11, 1979; *Harrisburg Patriot,* April 16, May 4, 1979.

CHAPTER 10. THE LONG-TERM EFFECTS OF THREE MILE ISLAND

1. *Washington Star,* April 3, 1979; *Philadelphia Inquirer,* April 11, 1979; Jon Payne, "Three Mile Island: Many Lessons," *Nuclear News* 22 (May 1979): 31.

2. Michael Cardozo to David Rubenstein, April 7, 1979, Transcript of White

House Press Conference, April 11, 1979, White House Press Release, April 11, 1979, Staff Offices—Counsel (Lipshutz), Box 39 (Nuclear Energy, Presidential Commission on 1979 Three Mile Island Accident), Papers of Jimmy Carter, Jimmy Carter Library, Atlanta, Georgia; *New York Times,* April 6, 1979.

The members of the commission, in addition to Kemeny, were Bruce E. Babbitt, governor of Arizona; Patrick E. Haggerty, former president of Texas Instruments; Carolyn D. Lewis, associate professor of journalism at Columbia University; Paul A. Marks, vice president for health sciences at Columbia University; Cora B. Marrett, associate professor of sociology at the University of Wisconsin, Madison; Lloyd McBride, president of the United Steelworkers of America; Harry C. McPherson, a Washington, D.C., attorney and former special counsel to President Lyndon B. Johnson; Russell W. Peterson, president of the National Audubon Society and former governor of Delaware; Thomas H. Pigford, professor of nuclear engineering at the University of California, Berkeley; Theodore B. Taylor, professor of aerospace and mechanical science at Princeton University and an expert on nuclear safeguards; and Anne D. Trunk, a resident of Middletown and prominent participant in community affairs.

3. President's Commission on the Accident at Three Mile Island (hereafter referred to as the Kemeny Commission), *The Need for Change: The Legacy of TMI* (Washington, D.C.: Government Printing Office, 1979), pp. 1–4, 153.

4. Ibid., pp. 7–25.

5. Ibid., pp. 19–56; Kemeny Commission, *Staff Report on the Role of the Managing Utility and Its Suppliers* (Washington, D.C.: Government Printing Office, 1979), pp. 152–56, and *Staff Report on the Nuclear Regulatory Commission* (Washington, D.C.: Government Printing Office, 1979), pp. 48–51.

6. Kemeny Commission, *The Need for Change,* pp. 12–15.

7. Ibid., pp. 25, 61–79.

8. Floyd W. Lewis to Richard Meserve, November 14, 1979, Roger J. Sherman to Jimmy Carter, November 13, 1979, Staff Offices—Counsel (Cutler), Box 100 (Nuclear Regulatory Commission), Carter Papers; Nuclear Regulatory Commission (NRC), *Views and Analysis of the Recommendations of the President's Commission on the Accident at Three Mile Island (NUREG-0632),* November 1979, NRC Records, NRC Public Document Room, Rockville, Maryland; *Washington Star,* October 31, 1979; Cora Bagley Marrett, "The Accident at Three Mile Island and the Problem of Uncertainty," in *The Three Mile Island Nuclear Accident: Lessons and Implications,* ed. Thomas H. Moss and David L. Sills (New York: New York Academy of Sciences, 1981), pp. 280–91; U.S. Congress, Joint Hearing of Senate Committee on Environment and Public Works, Subcommittee on Nuclear Regulation, and House Committee on Interior and Insular Affairs, Subcommittee on Energy and the Environment, *Report of the President's Commission on the Three Mile Island Accident,* 96th Cong., 1st sess., 1979, pp. 1–14, 58–66.

9. Frank Press and John Deutch to Jimmy Carter, November 26, 1979, Rick Hutcheson to Press, November 30, 1979, Staff Offices—Office of Staff Secretary Handwriting File, Box 157 (11–30–79), Carter Papers; Peter N. Carroll, *It Seemed Like Nothing Happened: America in the 1970s* (New York: Holt, Rinehart, and Winston, 1982; reprint, New Brunswick, N.J.: Rutgers University Press, 1990), pp. 219–20.

10. NRC, *1979 Annual Report* (Washington, D.C.: Government Printing Office, 1980), p. 62.

11. NRC, *1980 Annual Report* (Washington, D.C.: Government Printing Office, 1981), p. 148, *1979 Annual Report*, p. 33, *Investigation into the March 28, 1979, Three Mile Island Accident by Office of Inspection and Enforcement (NUREG-0600)*, August 1979, NRC Records; General Accounting Office, *Three Mile Island: The Most Studied Nuclear Accident in History (EMD-80–109)*, September 9, 1980, pp. 56–57; *New York Times*, April 13, 1979; *Nucleonics Week*, October 29, 1979.

12. *TMI-2 Lessons Learned Task Force Status Report and Short-Term Recommendations (NUREG-0578)*, July 1979, and *TMI-2 Lessons Learned Task Force Final Report (NUREG-0585)*, October 1979, NRC Records.

13. Transcript of Commission Meeting, April 3, 1979, pp. 37–62, Victor Gilinsky to the Commission, May 14, 1979, SECY-79–401 (June 20, 1979), NRC Records; NRC Special Inquiry Group, *Three Mile Island: A Report to the Commissioners and to the Public* (Washington, D.C.: Government Printing Office, 1980), 1:ix–x, 173–78 (hereafter referred to as the Rogovin Report); *Nucleonics Week*, January 31, 1980; *Washington Post*, February 8, 1996.

14. Rogovin Report, 1:89–155; George T. Frampton Jr. to Meg Greenfield, February 1, 1980, with handwritten notations of Victor Gilinsky, General TMI Investigations, Box 514 (NRC/Rogovin), Papers of Victor Gilinsky, Hoover Institution on War, Revolution, and Peace Archives, Stanford University, Palo Alto, California; *Washington Post*, January 30, February 26, 1980.

15. HM [Henry Myers] to MKU [Morris K. Udall], January 21, 1980, Box 389 (Memos to Udall from Henry Myers, Science Adviser, Interior Committee), Papers of Morris K. Udall, University of Arizona, Tucson; Udall to John Ahearne, January 21, 1980, NRC Records; *Nucleonics Week*, January 31, 1980; Rogovin Report, 1:159–60.

16. Morris K. Udall to John Ahearne, February 4, 1980, Mitchell Rogovin and George T. Frampton Jr. to Ahearne, March 4, 1980, NRC Records; *New York Times*, February 18, 1980; *Baltimore Sun*, April 3, 1980; *Nucleonics Week*, March 27, 1980.

17. NRC, *1979 Annual Report*, pp. 2–6, 28–30; *Inside N.R.C*, August 27, 1979; *Washington Post*, July 10, 1979.

18. NRC, *1979 Annual Report*, pp. 6–7, 50, 219, and *An Approach to Quantitative Safety Goals for Nuclear Power Plants (NUREG-0739)*, October 1980, NRC Records; *Inside N.R.C.*, July 27, 1981; Joseph V. Rees, *Hostages of Each Other: The Transformation of Nuclear Safety since Three Mile Island* (Chicago: University of Chicago Press, 1994), pp. 32–40.

19. U.S. Congress, House, Committee on Government Operations, Subcommittee on Environment, Energy, and Natural Resources, *Hearings on Emergency Planning around U.S. Nuclear Powerplants: Nuclear Regulatory Commission Oversight*, 96th Cong., 1st sess., 1979, pp. 25, 89–240, 375, 388, 405–525; SECY-79–499 (August 21, 1979), SECY 79–591 (October 26, 1979), NRC Records.

20. Mike McCormick and John Wydler to John F. Ahearne, December 20, 1979, Clarence J. Brown and others to Ahearne, February 14, 1980, SECY-80–

275 (June 3, 1980), NRC Records; *Congressional Record*, 96th Cong., 1st sess., July 16, 1979, pp. 18663–70; *Nucleonics Week*, July 19, December 6, 1979.

21. William J. Lanouette, "Nuclear Power: An Uncertain Future Grows Dimmer Still," *National Journal*, April 28, 1979, pp. 676–86; Peter Stoler, *Decline and Fail: The Ailing Nuclear Power Industry* (New York: Dodd, Mead, and Company, 1985), p. 115; Rees, *Hostages of Each Other*, p. 1–3, 42–45.

22. Chauncey Starr, "The Three Mile Nuclear Accident: The Other Lesson," in *The Three Mile Island Nuclear Accident: Lessons and Implications*, ed. Thomas H. Moss and David L. Sills (New York: New York Academy of Sciences, 1981), pp. 298–310; Nuclear Safety Analysis Center, *Analysis of Three Mile Island—Unit 2 Accident (NSAC-1)*, July 1979; *Nucleonics Week*, January 3, 1980.

23. Rees, *Hostages of Each Other*, pp. 42–45, 67–110.

24. Peter Stoler, "Pulling the Nuclear Plug," *Time* (February 13, 1984): 34–42; James Cook, "Nuclear Follies," *Forbes* (February 11, 1985): 82–100; *Inside N.R.C.*, March 10, 1980.

25. *Nucleonics Week*, April 2, 1987; *Inside N.R.C.*, April 13, September 28, 1987; *New York Times*, April 6, 1987, March 27, 1988; Stuart F. Brown, "How Do You Feel about Nuclear Power Now?" *Fortune* (March 4, 2002): 130–34; NRC, *Information Digest (NUREG-1350, Vol. 10)*, November 1998, p. 114; Rees, *Hostages of Each Other*, pp. 110–18.

26. Transcript of Press Briefing on Three Mile Island, May 7, 1979, NRC Records; Metropolitan Edison Company, "A Report to the Met-Ed Community," May 30, 1979, Box 102A (Utility Companies, 1979–1981), Papers of Robert S. Walker, Millersville University, Millersville, Pennsylvania; *New York Times*, April 4, 1979; *Wall Street Journal*, April 4, 1979.

27. Electric Power Research Institute, *The Cleanup of Three Mile Island Unit 2: A Technical History, 1979 to 1990 (EPRI NP-6931)* (Palo Alto, Calif.: Electric Power Research Institute, 1990), pp. 3-10 to 3-31, 6-34 to 6-35.

28. *Inside N.R.C.*, December 3, 1979; *Washington Post*, March 28, 1980; Cynthia B. Flynn, "The Local Impacts of the Accident at Three Mile Island," in *Public Reactions to Nuclear Power: Are There Critical Masses?* ed. William R. Freudenburg and Eugene A. Rosa (Boulder: Westview Press, 1984), pp. 205–32; C. P. Wolf, "Public Interest Groups," in *The Three Mile Island Nuclear Accident: Lessons and Implications*, ed. Thomas H. Moss and David L. Sills (New York: New York Academy of Sciences, 1981), pp. 244–56; Electric Power Research Institute, *The Cleanup of Three Mile Island Unit 2*, pp. 3-31 to 3-34.

29. *Philadelphia Bulletin*, March 21, March 23, 1980; *Philadelphia Inquirer*, March 22, March 23, 1980; *Nucleonics Week*, December 6, 1979; Robert Del Tredici, *The People of Three Mile Island* (San Francisco: Sierra Club Books, 1980), pp. 47–48; Wolf, "Public Interest Groups," p. 250; Richard H. Vollmer, interview by author, Arnold, Maryland, January 3, 2002.

30. "Transcription of Press Conference of Gov. Thornburgh and Harold Denton re: TMI," March 27, 1980, no box number (Governor News Releases 1980), Papers of Richard L. Thornburgh, Archives Service Center, University of Pittsburgh, Pittsburgh, Pennsylvania; *Nucleonics Week*, April 10, May 15, May 22, July 3, 1980; *Inside N.R.C.*, May 19, 1980; Electric Power Research Institute, *The Cleanup of Three Mile Island Unit 2*, pp. 3-32 to 3-34, A-5.

31. "Preliminary Notification of Event or Unusual Occurrence" (PNO-79–67S), April 12, 1979, NRC Records; NRC, *1980 Annual Report*, p. 17; "Nuclear News Briefs," *Nuclear News* 22 (May 1979): 21; Malcolm L. Russell and Richard K. McCardell, "Three Mile Island Unit 2 Core Geometry," *Nuclear Technology* 87 (December 1989): 865–74; Electric Power Research Institute, *The Cleanup of Three Mile Island Unit 2*, p. 3-34.

32. "TV at TMI: Hard-Core Rubble," *Science News* (July 31, 1982): 68; *Nucleonics Week*, August 26, 1982; *New York Times*, July 23, 1982; Electric Power Research Institute, *The Cleanup of Three Mile Island Unit 2*, pp. 5-6 to 5-17.

33. *Nucleonics Week*, February 28, 1985; "Studies Show 35 Percent of Unit 2 Core Melted," *Nuclear News* 30 (June 1987): 38; "Roughly Half the Core Melted in 1979 Accident," *Nuclear News* 31 (December 1988): 27; *New York Times*, January 26, 1988; Electric Power Research Institute, *The Cleanup of Three Mile Island Unit 2*, pp. 5-6 to 5-17.

34. William Booth, "Postmortem on Three Mile Island," *Science* 238 (December 4, 1987): 1342–45; Electric Power Research Institute, *The Cleanup of Three Mile Island Unit 2*, pp. 2-20 to 2-21, 6-1 to 6-39, 8-1 to 8-34; *The TMI-2 Chronicle* (Middletown, Penn.: GPU Nuclear, 1995), p. 8.

35. *Nucleonics Week*, October 28, 1993; Klaus Stadie, "The VIP Challenge: What Happened to TMI's Reactor Pressure Vessel?" *Nuclear Engineering International* 39 (March 1994): 38–40; A. M. Rubin and E. Beckjord, "Three Mile Island—New Findings 15 Years after the Accident," *Nuclear Safety* 35 (July–December 1994): 256–69; Booth, "Postmortem on Three Mile Island," pp. 1342–44.

36. F. R. Mynatt, "Nuclear Reactor Safety Research since Three Mile Island," *Science* 216 (April 9, 1982): 131–35; John R. Ireland, James H. Scott, and William R. Stratton, "Good News about Iodine Releases," *Los Alamos Science* 2 (summer–fall 1981): 88–89; E. Michael Blake, "The TMI Decade," *Nuclear News* 32 (April 1989): 45–48; *Inside N.R.C.*, November 11, 1985. The assertion or assumption that a breach of containment would inevitably occur if the core melted was advanced even by informed nuclear critics. See, for example, Joel Primack and Frank von Hippel, *Advice and Dissent: Scientists in the Political Arena* (New York: Basic Books, 1974), p. 212.

37. W. G. Kuhns to Joseph Hendrie, July 11, 1979, NRC Records; W. M. Creitz to Robert S. Walker, July 26, 1979, Box 102B (GPU Clean Up and Safety, 1979–80), Walker Papers; *Nucleonics Week*, September 25, 1980; Eliot Marshall, "Fear as a Form of Pollution," *Science* 215 (January 29, 1982): 481; NRC, *1983 Annual Report* (Washington, D.C.: Government Printing Office, 1984), p. 32; John W. Johnson, *Insuring against Disaster: The Nuclear Industry on Trial* (Macon, Ga.: Mercer University Press, 1986), 250–54.

38. NRC, *Nuclear Regulatory Commission Issuances* 16 (1982): 281–385; *Nucleonics Week*, July 29, 1982; *Inside N.R.C.*, March 5, July 23, 1984; *New York Times*, July 29, 1982; *Philadelphia Inquirer*, November 8, 1983.

39. *Inside N.R.C.*, January 9, January 30, June 11, August 6, August 20, 1984.

40. Ibid., June 10, September 2, October 14, 1985; NRC, *Nuclear Regulatory Commission Issuances* 21 (1985): 1118–81.

41. *Harrisburg Patriot*, April 12, 1980; *New York Times*, April 15, 1980;

Philadelphia Inquirer, June 19, 1991; J. R. Wargo, "State Study of TMI Effects Finds No Evidence of Cancer," *Nuclear Industry* 32 (October 1985): 15–17; Governor's Commission on Three Mile Island, *Report of the Governor's Commission on Three Mile Island* (Harrisburg, Penn.: n.p., 1980), p. 14.

42. Jan Beyea, *A Review of Dose Assessments at Three Mile Island and Recommendations for Future Research* (Philadelphia: Three Mile Island Public Health Fund, 1984); Maureen C. Hatch, Jan Beyea, Jeri W. Nieves, and Mervyn Susser, "Cancer Near the Three Mile Island Nuclear Plant: Radiation Emissions," *American Journal of Epidemiology* 132 (September 1990): 397–412; *New York Times,* July 9, 1982; *Washington Post,* May 27, 1991; *Philadelphia Inquirer,* May 29, 1991.

43. Steve Wing, David Richardson, Donna Armstrong, and Douglas Crawford-Brown, "A Reevaluation of Cancer Incidence near the Three Mile Island Nuclear Plant: The Collision of Evidence and Assumptions," and Maureen Hatch, Mervyn Susser, and Jan Beyea, "Comments on 'A Reevaluation of Cancer Incidence near the Three Mile Island Nuclear Plant,'" *Environmental Health Perspectives* 105 (January 1997): 52–57 ff; *Philadelphia Inquirer,* February 24, 1997; *Nucleonics Week,* February 27, 1997.

44. Evelyn O. Talbott, Ada O. Youk, Kathleen P. McHugh, Jeffrey D. Shire, Aimin Zhang, Brian P. Murphy, and Richard A. Engberg, "Mortality among the Residents of the Three Mile Island Accident Area: 1979–1992," *Environmental Health Perspectives* 108 (June 2000): 545–52; Evelyn O. Talbott, Ada O. Youk, Kathleen P. McHugh-Pemu, and Jeanne V. Zborowski, "Long-Term Follow-Up of the Residents of the Three Mile Island Accident Area," *Environmental Health Perspectives* 111 (March 2003): 341–48; *Washington Post,* November 1, 2002; *New York Times,* November 1, 2002.

45. U.S. Nuclear Regulatory Commission and others, *Report on the Accident at the Chernobyl Nuclear Power Station (NUREG-1250)* (Washington, D.C.: Government Printing Office, 1987), pp. 6-1 to 6-12; Zhores A. Medvedev, *The Legacy of Chernobyl* (New York: W. W. Norton, 1990), pp. 1–225; Grigori Medvedev, *The Truth about Chernobyl* (New York: Basic Books, 1991), pp. 29–136; Yuri M. Shcherbak, "Ten Years of the Chornobyl Era," *Scientific American* 274 (April 1996): 32–37; John F. Ahearne, "Nuclear Power after Chernobyl," *Science* 236 (May 8, 1987): 673–79; Richard Stone, "Living in the Shadow of Chornobyl," *Science* 292 (April 20, 2001): 420–26.

46. Colin Norman and David Dickson, "The Aftermath of Chernobyl," *Science* 233 (September 12, 1986): 1141–43; Lynn R. Anspaugh, Robert J. Catlin, and Marvin Goldman, "The Global Impact of the Chernobyl Reactor Accident," *Science* 242 (December 16, 1988): 1513–19; *New York Times,* September 3, 1992; *Wall Street Journal,* September 3, 1992; *Nucleonics Week,* November 18, 1993, June 8, 2000; Stone, "Living in the Shadow of Chornobyl," p. 425.

47. "Late News in Brief," *Nuclear News* 36 (June 1993): 87; *Nucleonics Week,* April 22, 1993, June 8, December 21, 2000; *BBC News,* May 8, 2001, http://news.bbc.co.uk/hi/english/sci/tech/newsid_1319000/1319386, accessed on May 9, 2001.

48. *New York Times,* July 26, 1986; William Schneider, "Public Ambivalent on Nuclear Power," *National Journal* (June 21, 1986): 1562–63; Office of Tech-

nology Assessment, *Nuclear Power in an Age of Uncertainty (OTA-E-216)* (Washington, D.C.: Government Printing Office, 1984), pp. 211–14; *Baltimore Sun,* March 28, 1989.

49. Kemeny Commission, *Staff Reports of the Technical Assessment Task Force* (Washington, D.C.: Government Printing Office, 1979), 2:118–35.

50. Stoler, "Pulling the Nuclear Plug," p. 36.

51. On the importance of failure for engineers, see, for example, Henry Petroski, "The Success of Failure," *Technology and Culture* 42 (April 2002): 321–28, and Petroski, *To Engineer Is Human: The Role of Failure in Successful Design* (New York: St. Martin's Press, 1985; reprint, New York: Vintage Books, 1992).

52. Charles Perrow, *Normal Accidents: Living with High-Risk Technologies* (New York: Basic Books, 1984), p. 60.

53. Michael Cole, *Three Mile Island: Nuclear Disaster* (Berkeley Heights, N.J.: Enslow Publishers, 2002); Therese DeAngelis, *Three Mile Island* (Philadelphia: Chelsea House Publishers, 2002).

54. The seminal work on this subject is Spencer R. Weart, *Nuclear Fear: A History of Images* (Cambridge, Mass.: Harvard University Press, 1988).

Essay on Sources

This book draws on an abundance of sources that provide information about the Three Mile Island accident. The most important collections of primary documents are the records of the Nuclear Regulatory Commission (NRC), the records of the President's Commission on the Accident at Three Mile Island (the Kemeny Commission), the papers of Richard L. Thornburgh, and the papers of Jimmy Carter.

NRC records relating to TMI are housed in the agency's Public Document Room at its headquarters in Rockville, Maryland. They include thousands of pages of verbatim transcripts of commission meetings and of telephone conversations recorded at the incident response center between March 28 and April 1, 1979. They also include a variety of documents prepared by staff members during and after the accident, communications from outside the agency, and transcripts of depositions conducted by the NRC's special inquiry group, headed by Mitchell Rogovin. NRC documents relating to Three Mile Island were generally made public shortly after the accident. A small number of previously unavailable documents cited in the notes of this book have been added to the Public Document Room's collection.

The records of the Kemeny Commission, a part of Record Group 220 (Records of Temporary Committees, Commissions, and Boards), are available at the National Archives in College Park, Maryland. They contain a large body of documents collected by the commission in the course of its investigation. Among the files are transcripts of depositions of key players in the accident taken under oath. The depositions of both the Kemeny Commission and the Rogovin inquiry are, in effect, oral histories that were done shortly after the event. They offer a wealth of information not available elsewhere. The final reports of the Kemeny and Rogovin investigations and the vast body of evidence and analysis in their supplemental volumes are, in themselves, exceedingly useful sources.

The Thornburgh papers are located in the Archives Service Center at the University of Pittsburgh in Pittsburgh, Pennsylvania. They are essential for understanding the state's response to the TMI accident. Although, for obvious reasons, the governor and his staff did not prepare many documents during the emergency, they did compile an invaluable collection of materials, including an annotated chronology of activities, shortly after the crisis ended.

The Carter papers at the Jimmy Carter Library in Atlanta, Georgia, are the key source for tracing the White House's response to Three Mile Island. They contain documents written by White House staff members, accounts of meetings with federal officials, and best of all, the president's handwritten notes of his conversations with Harold Denton.

In addition, other manuscript collections contain materials of interest on Three Mile Island. The papers of NRC commissioners Victor Gilinsky and Richard T. Kennedy are housed at the Hoover Institution Archives at Stanford University in Palo Alto, California. Gilinsky's collection is an especially rich source on a wide range of regulatory issues he was involved in during his terms as a commissioner between 1975 and 1984. The papers of the Pennsylvania Commission on Three Mile Island at the Pennsylvania State Archives in Harrisburg include copies of many documents that are a part of the Thornburgh collection at the University of Pittsburgh and a few that are unique. The Harold and Lucinda Denton papers at the Pennsylvania State Archives consist mostly of articles and other published materials relating to Denton's role at Three Mile Island. The papers of Morris K. Udall at the University of Arizona in Tucson and Robert S. Walker at Millersville University in Millersville, Pennsylvania, provide useful documentation collected by members of Congress who took a keen interest in the accident. The papers of Herbert M. Parker at the University of Washington in Seattle have a few items of significance on Three Mile Island. (Contrary to the assertion of one report, the Parker papers have not been transferred from the University of Washington to Washington State University, according to archivists at both institutions.)

Several collections of records and manuscripts examined for this book have little or nothing on the Three Mile Island accident but contain valuable materials on the nuclear power debate. Those with an interest in the subject will benefit from consulting the following sources: the records of the Joint Committee on Atomic Energy, a part of Record Group 128

(Records of the Joint Committees of Congress), at the National Archives in Washington, D.C.; regulatory files of the Atomic Energy Commission through June 1974 in the records of the Nuclear Regulatory Commission (Record Group 431), the records of the Environmental Protection Agency (Record Group 412), and the papers of Richard M. Nixon in the Nixon Presidential Materials Project, at the National Archives in College Park, Maryland; records of the Department of Energy in the DOE History Division in Germantown, Maryland; the papers of Gerald R. Ford at the Gerald R. Ford Library in Ann Arbor, Michigan; the papers of the Union of Concerned Scientists at the Massachusetts Institute of Technology Archives in Cambridge, Massachusetts; the papers of Dixy Lee Ray at the Hoover Institution Archives at Stanford University; the papers of Fred M. Schmidt at the University of Washington; and the papers of Carlton Neville at the Carter Library.

To seek information about and clarification of issues that the abundance of documentary evidence does not fully explain, I conducted interviews with many individuals who participated in the response to the accident. I was impressed with the clarity, and even after more than two decades the accuracy, of their memories about events in which they played a role. I was grateful for their willingness to recount their experiences and share their memories in a full, frank, and friendly way. I talked with the following persons either personally or by telephone: Elinor G. Adensam (Rockville, Maryland, January 10, 2002), John F. Ahearne (Research Triangle Park, North Carolina, April 2, 2001), John H. Austin (Aiken, South Carolina, September 11, 2001), Peter A. Bradford (New York, New York, May 21, 2002), Robert J. Budnitz (Berkeley, California, September 18, 2002), Frank J. Congel (Rockville, Maryland, May 8, 2003), Harold R. Denton and Lucinda Denton (Knoxville, Tennessee, September 9–10, 2001), Anne M. Edwards (via telephone, November 14, 2001), Eugene Eidenberg (San Francisco, California, September 17, 2002), Craig C. Faust (via telephone, November 2, 2001), Joseph J. Fouchard (Rockville, Maryland, March 8, 2000), Victor Gilinsky (Rockville, Maryland, April 24, 2001), Joseph M. Hendrie (Upton, New York, May 30, 2001), Sandra M. Joosten (Rockville, Maryland, February 19, 2002), Jessica Tuchman Mathews (Washington, D.C., June 7, 2001), Roger J. Mattson (Golden, Colorado, September 26, 2001), Richard A. Meserve (Rockville, Maryland, April 2, 2002), Thomas E. Murley (Rockville, Maryland, May 31, 2002), Frank Press (via telephone, February 28, 2002), Michael J. Ross (via telephone, June 11, 2002), Esther Stello (via telephone, May 15, 2002), Merrill A. (Mat) Taylor (via telephone, November 8, 2002), Richard L. Thornburgh (Washington, D.C., July 10, 2001), Richard H. Vollmer (Arnold, Maryland, January 3, 2002), Robert S. Walker (East Petersburg, Pennsylvania, June 3, 2002), Jack H. Watson (Philomont, Virginia, May 17, 2001), and S. Beth Wolf (via telephone, July 17, 2002).

This book is the first comprehensive scholarly account of the Three Mile Island accident. Remarkably, in light of the importance of the topic, it has been more than twenty years since any volume has appeared, except for books written for children and young adults. The only previous scholarly study of the accident is Philip L. Cantelon and Robert C. Williams, *Crisis Contained: The Department of Energy at Three Mile Island* (Carbondale, Ill.: Southern Illinois University Press, 1982), which is an excellent discussion of one aspect of the story. Daniel F. Ford, *Three Mile Island: Thirty Minutes to Meltdown* (New York: Penguin Books, 1982), demonstrates both the author's deep knowledge of nuclear power issues and his perspective as a leading critic of the technology. Mike Gray and Ira Rosen, *The Warning: Accident at Three Mile Island* (New York: W. W. Norton, 1982), vividly captures the drama and tension of the crisis but is plagued with factual errors, especially in its account of the hydrogen bubble. The publisher issued a new edition of the book in 2003, but the errors remain. Mark Stephens, *Three Mile Island* (New York: Random House, 1980), and Daniel Martin, *Three Mile Island: Prologue or Epilogue?* (Cambridge, Mass.: Ballinger Publishing, 1980), are factually unreliable and generally undistinguished.

Index

ABC *Evening News* (television program), 20

ABC News–Washington Post survey, 239

Abernethy, Bob, 121

Abraham, Karl (public affairs officer with NRC), 116–17; attempting to transmit press conference to NRC's headquarters, 157; informed of venting of radioactive gas from Three Mile Island, 123; NRC's press release to public, 96

accident, word used in press release, 96

Adensam, Elinor G., 118

Advice and Dissent: Scientists in the Political Arena (Primack and von Hippel), 284n36

Advisory Committee on Reactor Safeguards, 41, 47; investigating core meltdown problems, 54; raising alarms about "anticipated transient without scram" scenarios, 64

AEC. *See* Atomic Energy Commission (AEC)

Ahearne, John F. (NRC commissioner), 69, 90; appointed chairman of NRC, 215; appointment to NRC, 91–92; and divisions among NRC commissioners, 136; drafting press release on crisis, 145; on need to evacuate Three Mile Island vicinity, 185; on the Rogovin Report, 219

airplanes crashing into power plants, 47–48, 242

air pollution, 6

American Electric Power Service Corporation, 4

American Newspaper Publishers Association, 201

American Nuclear Society, 21, 22

Amish, 45, 148

Anders, William A. (NRC chairman), 34, 35; interview with Mike Wallace, 39; on NRC's position, 37; shutting down reactors for pipe cracks, 63

"anticipated transient without scram," 64

antinuclear position, 15–17, 247n19. *See also* demonstrations, antinuclear; nuclear power debate

Armstrong, Donna, 235

Arnold, Robert (vice president, General Public Utilities Corporation), 95, 121, 159

Asselstine, James K., 234

Associated Press, 82, 98; public opinion survey taken by, 118; revision of story on possibility of hydrogen explosion, 169; running story on possibility of hydrogen explosion, 164–65, 166–67, 175

Atlanta Journal and Constitution, 165

atomic bombs, 9, 18; nuclear plant explosion confused with, 165; nuclear power associated with, 25–26

Atomic Energy Act (1954), 3, 29, 41

Atomic Energy Commission (AEC): comparison to NRC, 34, 37; conflict of interest within, 29–31, 251n1; defense-in-depth concept, 52–54; Energy Reorganization Act of 1974, 31–33; estimate of need for nuclear power, 7; evacuation procedures, 124–25; generator capacity factor, 17; Harold R. Denton in, 120; Joseph Hendrie in, 112; low priority of safety issues within, 89

Atomic Industrial Forum, 8, 222

291

Compositor:	Integrated Composition Systems, Inc.
Text:	10/13 Sabon
Display:	Akzidenz Grotesk
Printer and Binder:	Maple-Vail Manufacturing Group